D1612340

חומש קורן מקראות הדורות
THE KOREN MIKRAOT HADOROT

פרשת יתרו

PARASHAT YITRO

קוֹרֵן ירושלים

THE ROHR FAMILY EDITION

חומש קורן מקראות הדורות
THE KOREN MIKRAOT HADOROT

THE ZAHAVA AND MOSHAEL STRAUS EDITION OF SEFER SHEMOT

פרשת יתרו עם רש״י
PARASHAT YITRO WITH RASHI

TORAH TRANSLATION BY
Rabbi Lord Jonathan Sacks שליט״א
FROM THE MAGERMAN EDITION OF THE KOREN TANAKH

RASHI'S COMMENTARY TRANSLATED BY
Rabbi Jonathan Mishkin

•

KOREN PUBLISHERS JERUSALEM

The Koren Mikraot HaDorot, The Rohr Edition
Volume 17: Parashat Yitro
First Edition, 2020

Koren Publishers Jerusalem Ltd.
POB 4044, Jerusalem 9104001, ISRAEL
POB 8531, New Milford, CT 06776, USA

www.korenpub.com

The creation of this work was made possible with the generous support
of the Jewish Book Trust Inc.

Printed in ISRAEL

ISBN 978 965 7760 72 7

KMDYT01

The Rohr Family Edition of
The Koren Mikraot HaDorot
pays tribute to the memory of

Mr. Sami Rohr ז״ל
ר׳ שמואל ב״ר יהושע אליהו ז״ל

who served his Maker with joy
and whose far-reaching vision, warm open hand, love of Torah,
and love for every Jew were catalysts for the revival and growth of
vibrant Jewish life in the former Soviet Union
and in countless communities the world over

and to the memory of his beloved wife

Mrs. Charlotte Rohr (née Kastner) ע״ה
שרה בת ר׳ יקותיאל יהודה ע״ה

who survived the fires of the Shoah to become
the elegant and gracious matriarch,
first in Colombia and later in the United States,
of three generations of a family
nurtured by her love and unstinting devotion.
She found grace in the eyes of all those whose lives she touched.

Together they merited to see all their children
build lives enriched by faithful commitment
to the spreading of Torah and *Ahavat Yisrael*.

Dedicated with love by
The Rohr Family
NEW YORK, USA

עֲטֶרֶת זְקֵנִים בְּנֵי בָנִים
(משלי יז, ו)

Grandchildren
are the crowning glory of the aged
(Proverbs 17:6)

May the learning and traditions of our people
be strengthened by our future generations.
In honor of our wonderful grandchildren

Zahava and Moshael Straus

CONTENTS

FOR PARASHAT YITRO WITH COMMENTARIES AND THE BIBLICAL IMAGINATION
TURN TO THE OTHER END OF THIS VOLUME.

PUBLISHER'S PREFACE

The genius of Jewish commentary on the Torah is one of huge and critical import. Jewish life and law for millennia have been directed by our interpretations of the Torah, and each generation has looked to its rabbinic leadership for a deeper understanding of its teachings, its laws, its stories.

For centuries, *Mikraot Gedolot* have been a core part of understanding the Ḥumash; the words of Rashi, Ibn Ezra, Ramban, Rashbam, Ralbag, and other classic commentators illuminate and help us understand the Torah. But traditional editions of *Mikraot Gedolot* present only a slice in time and a small selection of the corpus of Jewish commentators. Almost every generation has produced rabbinic scholars who speak to their times, from Philo and Onkelos two thousand years ago, to Rabbi Joseph B. Soloveitchik, Rabbi Aharon Kotler, the Lubavitcher Rebbe, and Nehama Leibowitz in ours.

The Koren Mikraot HaDorot – Scriptures or Interpretations for the Generations – brings two millennia of Torah commentary into the hands and homes of Jews around the world. Readers will be able to encounter not only the classic commentators, but to gain a much broader sense of the issues that scholars grappled with in their time and the inspiration they drew from the ancient texts. We see, for example, how Philo speaks to an assimilating Greek Jewish audience in first-century Alexandria, and how similar yet different it is from Rabbi Samson Raphael Hirsch's approach to an equally assimilating nineteenth-century German readership; how the perspectives of Rabbi Soloveitchik and Rabbi Kotler differ in a post-Holocaust world; how Rav Seʾadya Gaon interpreted the Torah for the Jews of Babylonia. It is an exciting journey through Jewish history via the unchanging words of the Torah.

◄

The text of the Torah features the exceptional new translation of Rabbi Lord Jonathan Sacks, together with the celebrated and meticulously accurate Koren Hebrew text. Of course, with the exception of Rashi – for whom we present an entirely new translation in full – the commentaries are selected. We offer this anthology not to limit our reader's exploration but rather as a gateway for further learning of Torah and its commentaries on a broader and deeper level than space here permits. We discuss below how to use this book.

We must thank **Pamela and George Rohr** of New York, who recognized the unique value of the *Koren Mikraot HaDorot* and its ability to communicate historical breadth and context to the reader. For my colleagues here at Koren, we thank you; for the many generations of users who will find this a continuing source of new learning, we are forever in your debt.

We also are indebted to **Zahava and Moshael Straus**, true leaders of this Jewish generation in so many fields, who have invested not only in *Parashat Yitro* but the entire book of Shemot. Together, we were thus able to launch this innovative and unique project.

We are honored to acknowledge and thank **Debra and David Magerman**, whose support for the Koren Ḥumash with Rabbi Sacks's exemplary translation and commentary laid the foundation for the core English text of this work.

Finally, I must personally thank **Rabbi Marvin Hier**, with whom I had a special breakfast some years ago at the King David Hotel. During the meal, he raised the problem that so few people knew the writings of Rabbi Joseph B. Soloveitchik and Rabbi Aharon Kotler on the Torah; and I, who had just read some of Philo's work, had the same reaction. From that conversation came the seed for this project.

HOW TO USE *THE KOREN MIKRAOT HADOROT*

The Koren Mikraot HaDorot will be a fifty-five-volume edition of the Ḥumash (one for each *parasha* plus a companion volume). Each of the fifty-four volumes of the *parashot* can be read from right to left (Hebrew opening side), and left to right (English opening side).

Opening from the Hebrew side offers:

▸ the full Torah text, the translation of Rabbi Sacks, and the full commentary of Rashi in both Hebrew and the new English translation

◀

‣ all *haftarot* associated with the *parasha* of the volume, including Rosh Ḥodesh and special readings, both in Hebrew and English

Opening from the English side presents four sections:

‣ THE TIME OF THE SAGES – includes commentaries from the Second Temple period and the talmudic period

‣ THE CLASSIC COMMENTATORS – quotes selected explanations by Rashi as well as most of the commentators found in traditional *Mikraot Gedolot*

‣ CONFRONTING MODERNITY – selects commentaries from the eighteenth century to the close of the twentieth century

‣ THE BIBLICAL IMAGINATION – features essays surveying some of the broader conceptual ideas as a supplement to the linear, text-based commentary

The first three of these sections each feature the relevant verses, in Hebrew and English, on the page alongside their respective commentaries, in chronological order, providing the reader with a single window onto the text without excessive page turning.

In addition to being a valuable resource in a Jewish home or synagogue library, we conceived of these volumes as a weekly accompaniment in the synagogue. There is scope for the reader to study each *parasha* on a weekly basis in preparation for the reading on Shabbat. One may select a particular group of commentators for study that week, or perhaps alternate between ancient and modern viewpoints. Some readers may choose to delve into the text through verse-by-verse interpretation, while others may prefer a conceptual perspective on the *parasha* as a whole. The broad array of options for learning means this is a series which can be returned to year after year, always presenting new insights and new approaches to understanding the text.

ACKNOWLEDGMENTS

The creation of this book was possible only thanks to the small but exceptional team here at Koren Jerusalem. We are grateful to:

‣ Rabbi Tzvi Hersh Weinreb, שליט״א, who conceptualized the structure of the project and provides both moral and halakhic leadership at Koren

‣ Rabbi Shai Finkelstein, whose encyclopedic knowledge of Torah and its interpreters is equaled only by his community leadership, formerly in Memphis and today in Jerusalem

‣ Rabbi Yedidya Naveh, whose knowledge, organizational skills, and superb leadership brought the disparate elements together

◀

▸ Rabbi Jonathan Mishkin, the principal translator of the commentaries and all of the Rashi, who crafted a fluent, accurate, and eloquent English translation

Our design, editing, typesetting, and proofreading staff, including Tani Bayer, Esther Be'er, Debbie Ismailoff, Estie Dishon, and Carolyn Budow Ben David, enabled an attractive, user-friendly, and accurate edition of these works.

> "One silver basin" (Numbers 7:13) was brought as a symbol of the Torah, which has been likened to wine, as the verse states: "And drink of the wine which I have mingled" (Proverbs 9:5). Because it is customary to drink wine in a basin – as we see in the verse "that drink wine in basins" (Amos 6:6) – he therefore brought a basin. "Of seventy shekels, after the shekel of the sanctuary" (Numbers 7:13). Why? Because just as the numerical value of "wine" [*yayin*] is seventy, so there are seventy modes of expounding the Torah. (Bemidbar Rabba 13:16)

Each generation produces exceptional rabbinic, intellectual leadership. It has been our purpose to enable all Jews to taste the wine of those generations, in the hope of expanding the breadth and depth of their knowledge. Torah is our greatest treasure, and we need the wisdom of those generations to better understand this bountiful gift from God. We hope that we at Koren can deepen that understanding for all who seek it.

Matthew Miller, Publisher
Jerusalem, 5780 (2019)

A NOTE ON THE TRANSLATION OF RASHI

The translation of Rashi's commentary provided here is complete and unabridged, following the meticulously researched Hebrew version of the commentary published by Koren. This version omits some material published in other editions that was found likely to have been added later by Rashi's students and other authors. We have included all of Rashi's numerous grammatical and linguistic discussions, even though these tend to be of less interest to the English-speaking reader, for two reasons: First, we felt it important for the readership to be confident that they are holding a complete version of Rashi's commentary and to know that they are not missing any matter of potential interest it might contain. Second, we wished to impress upon the reader that the elegant Sacks translation of the Torah included in this volume represents only one reading among many possible interpretations. Rashi's inquiries into the meanings of individual words and phrases emphasize the ambiguity of the verses and the potential of any passage to be interpreted in several different ways. This multifaceted nature of the Torah is a central theme of *The Koren Mikraot HaDorot*.

The inclusion of these discussions – often technical and sometimes confusing – bears implications for the translation. Here the translator was often forced to insert himself into the discussion to clearly establish the grammatical difficulty or ambiguity in the Hebrew text that is troubling Rashi. Since these difficulties are not always conveyed in the Sacks verse translation, the reader will find bracketed editorial comments used more aggressively in these discussions. The editor's notes also serve to supply the English-speaking reader with relevant details regarding Hebrew grammar that Rashi assumes to be known to his audience, which are necessary to understanding his point.

◄

Here at the outset, we will provide a very brief overview of the Hebrew system of *binyanim*, or Hebrew verb forms, which is central to so many of Rashi's grammatical arguments.

Hebrew verbs, which are always conjugated by number, person, gender, and tense, are also divided into seven categories of verbs called *binyanim*. Three of these are in the active voice, three passive, and one in a reflexive voice that is neither active nor passive. In theory, any three-letter root (*shoresh*) in Hebrew can be conjugated in any one of these forms, with slightly different meanings in each one, though few roots exist in all forms. Readers who encounter one of Rashi's discourses analyzing to which class a given verb belongs can refer to the following chart to orient themselves.

BINYAN NAME	EXAMPLE (PAST/FUTURE)	VOICE				
Paal (Kal) – פָּעַל (קל)	Katav/Yikhtov – write	Active				
Hifil – הִפְעִיל	Hikdish/Yakdish – consecrate	Active				
Pi'el – פִּעֵל	Giddel/Yegaddel – promote or exalt	Active			Causative	Simple
Hitpael – הִתְפָּעֵל	Hitgaddel/Yitgaddel – become great	Reflexive	Intensive			
Pual – פֻּעַל	Guddal/Yeguddal – be promoted or exalted	Passive				
Hufal – הֻפְעַל	Hukdash/Yukdash – be consecrated	Passive				
Nifal – נִפְעַל	Nikhtav/Yikkatev – be written	Passive				

Each of the three active conjugations pairs with one of the passive ones, as seen in the above chart, such that the seven *binyanim* can be simplified into three more basic forms. The simple form (*paal/nifal*) denotes simple actions. The causative form (*hifil/hufal*) is reserved for actions induced by the subject in the object, e.g., to cause something to become holy (consecrate). The intensive form (*pi'el/pual*) describes a special form of the action, usually more significant or intense. The reflexive form is considered a third subgroup of the intensive form and is used for actions done to oneself.

◄

Rashi's grammatical discussions also focus on the vocalization (*nikkud*, or vowel marks) of the Hebrew text. The reader can review the names of the vowel marks in the following chart, as well as see how these vowels are transliterated in this edition.

VOWEL MARK	NAME	TRANSLITERATION
בְ	*Sheva* (*Ḥataf* when combined with a *segol, pataḥ,* or *kamatz*)	*e* or silent
בֶ	*Segol* (in Rashi's language: *Pataḥ Katan*)	*e*
בַ	*Pataḥ*	*a*
בָ	*Kamatz*	*a* or *o*
בִ	*Ḥirik*	*i*
בֵ	*Tzerei* (in Rashi's language, also: *Kamatz Katan*)	*e* or *ei*
בֹ	*Ḥolam* (in Rashi's language: *Melafum*)	*o*
בֻ	*Kubbutz* (in Rashi's language: *Shuruk*)	*u*
בוּ	*Shuruk*	*u*

For Rashi's terms in Old French, we have been guided by Yisrael Gukovitzky's dictionary *Targum HaLaaz* (1985).

Yedidya Naveh, Managing Editor
Jerusalem, 5780 (2019)

פרשת יתרו
PARASHAT YITRO

חומש עם רש"י
THE HUMASH
WITH RASHI

18 1 Moshe's father-in-law Yitro, priest of Midyan, heard about all
that God had done for Moshe and for His people Israel when
2 the LORD brought Israel out of Egypt. Yitro had received
3 Moshe's wife Tzipora after he had sent her home, together with
her two sons. One was named Gershom, for Moshe had said,
4 "I have been a stranger in a foreign land," and the other, Eliezer,
for he had said, "My father's God has helped me, saving me
5 from Pharaoh's sword." ‣ And now Moshe's father-in-law Yitro

---

יח א| וַיִּשְׁמַע יִתְרוֹ. מַה שְׁמוּעָה
שָׁמַע? קְרִיעַת יַם סוּף וּמִלְחֶמֶת
עֲמָלֵק:

יִתְרוֹ. שִׁבְעָה שֵׁמוֹת נִקְרְאוּ לוֹ:
רְעוּאֵל, יֶתֶר, יִתְרוֹ, חוֹבָב, חֶבֶר,
קֵינִי, פּוּטִיאֵל. יֶתֶר, עַל שֵׁם שֶׁיִּתֵּר
פָּרָשָׁה אַחַת בַּתּוֹרָה: "וְאַתָּה תֶחֱזֶה"
(להלן פסוק כא), יִתְרוֹ, לִכְשֶׁנִּתְגַּיֵּיר
וְקִיֵּים הַמִּצְוֹת הוֹסִיפוּ לוֹ אוֹת;
חוֹבָב, שֶׁחִבֵּב אֶת הַתּוֹרָה, חוֹבָב
הוּא יִתְרוֹ, שֶׁנֶּאֱמַר: "מִבְּנֵי חֹבָב חֹתֵן
מֹשֶׁה" (שופטים ד, יא). וְיֵשׁ אוֹמְרִים:
רְעוּאֵל אָבִיו שֶׁל יִתְרוֹ הָיָה, וּמַהוּ
אוֹמֵר: "וַתָּבֹאנָה אֶל רְעוּאֵל אֲבִיהֶן"
(לעיל ב, יח)? שֶׁהַתִּינוֹקוֹת קוֹרִין לַאֲבִי
אֲבִיהֶן אַבָּא. בְּסִפְרֵי (בהעלותך עח):

חֹתֵן מֹשֶׁה. כָּאן הָיָה יִתְרוֹ מִתְכַּבֵּד
בְּמֹשֶׁה: אֲנִי חוֹתֵן הַמֶּלֶךְ, וּלְשֶׁעָבַר
הָיָה מֹשֶׁה תּוֹלֶה הַגְּדֻלָּה בְּחָמִיו,
שֶׁנֶּאֱמַר: "וַיָּשָׁב אֶל יֶתֶר חֹתְנוֹ"
(לעיל ד, יח):

לְמֹשֶׁה וּלְיִשְׂרָאֵל. שָׁקַל מֹשֶׁה כְּנֶגֶד
כָּל יִשְׂרָאֵל:

אֵת כָּל אֲשֶׁר עָשָׂה. לָהֶם בִּירִידַת
הַמָּן וּבַבְּאֵר וּבַעֲמָלֵק:

---

18 1| וַיִּשְׁמַע יִתְרוֹ – *Yitro heard*: What exactly did Yitro hear? He heard how God had split the Sea of Reeds and how Israel had defeated Amalek.

יִתְרוֹ – *Yitro*: The man Yitro had seven names: Reuel, Yeter, Yitro, Ḥovav, Ḥever, Keini, and Putiel. He was called Yeter because he was responsible for adding [*yitter*] a passage to the Torah, namely, *You, as well, must seek out among the people, capable men etc.* (18:21). A letter [*vav*] was added to the name Yeter to produce the name Yitro after he converted to Judaism and started to observe the commandments. He was called Ḥovav because he loved [*ḥibbev*] the Torah. We know that Ḥovav and Yitro were one and the same, as attested by the verse *The children of Ḥovav the father-in-law of Moshe* (Judges 4:11). Some authorities, however, claim that Reuel was Yitro's father [see Numbers 10:29]. According to that approach, we must explain the verse *When they returned to Reuel their father* [2:18, apparently indicating that Reuel was Moshe's wife's father] by positing that occasionally children refer to their grandfather as "father." Such is the understanding of the Sifrei (Behaalotekha 78).

חֹתֵן מֹשֶׁה – *Moshe's father-in-law*: At this point, Yitro could boast of his connection to Moshe, saying: "I am the king's father-in-law." This contrasted with the past, when Moshe's honor came through his association with his wife's father, as the verse states: *Moshe left and returned to Yeter his father-in-law.* (4:18).

לְמֹשֶׁה וּלְיִשְׂרָאֵל – *For Moshe and for Israel*: Moshe was equal in weight to all the rest of the nation.

אֵת כָּל אֲשֶׁר עָשָׂה – *All that God had done*: Yitro was impressed that God had provided manna for the people, brought water out of the rock, and defeated Amalek.

יח א וַיִּשְׁמַ֞ע יִתְר֨וֹ כֹהֵ֤ן מִדְיָן֙ חֹתֵ֣ן מֹשֶׁ֔ה אֵת֩ כָּל־אֲשֶׁ֨ר יד
עָשָׂ֤ה אֱלֹהִים֙ לְמֹשֶׁ֔ה וּלְיִשְׂרָאֵ֖ל עַמּ֑וֹ כִּֽי־הוֹצִ֧יא יהו֛ה
אֶת־יִשְׂרָאֵ֖ל מִמִּצְרָֽיִם: ב וַיִּקַּ֗ח יִתְרוֹ֙ חֹתֵ֣ן מֹשֶׁ֔ה אֶת־
צִפֹּרָ֖ה אֵ֣שֶׁת מֹשֶׁ֑ה אַחַ֖ר שִׁלּוּחֶֽיהָ: ג וְאֵ֖ת שְׁנֵ֣י בָנֶ֑יהָ
אֲשֶׁ֨ר שֵׁ֤ם הָֽאֶחָד֙ גֵּ֣רְשֹׁ֔ם כִּ֣י אָמַ֔ר גֵּ֣ר הָיִ֔יתִי בְּאֶ֖רֶץ
נָכְרִיָּֽה: ד וְשֵׁ֥ם הָֽאֶחָ֖ד אֱלִיעֶ֑זֶר כִּֽי־אֱלֹהֵ֤י אָבִי֙ בְּעֶזְרִ֔י
וַיַּצִּלֵ֖נִי מֵחֶ֥רֶב פַּרְעֹֽה: ה וַיָּבֹ֞א יִתְר֨וֹ חֹתֵ֥ן מֹשֶׁ֛ה וּבָנָ֥יו

כִּי הוֹצִיא יהוה וְגוֹ'. זוֹ גְדוֹלָה עַל כֻּלָּם:

כִּֽי־הוֹצִיא יהוה – When the Lord brought: This was the greatest achievement of all.

אַחַר שִׁלּוּחֶיהָ. כְּשֶׁאָמַר לוֹ הַקָּדוֹשׁ בָּרוּךְ הוּא בְּמִדְיָן: "לֵךְ שֻׁב מִצְרָיִם", "וַיִּקַּח מֹשֶׁה אֶת אִשְׁתּוֹ וְאֶת בָּנָיו וְגוֹ'" (לעיל ד, יט-כ), וְיָצָא אַהֲרֹן לִקְרָאתוֹ "וַיִּפְגְּשֵׁהוּ בְּהַר הָאֱלֹהִים" (שם פסוק כז), אָמַר לוֹ: מִי הֵם הַלָּלוּ? אָמַר לוֹ: זוֹ אִשְׁתִּי שֶׁנָּשָׂאתִי בְּמִדְיָן וְאֵלּוּ בָּנַי. אָמַר לוֹ: וְהֵיכָן אַתָּה מוֹלִיכָן? אָמַר לוֹ: לְמִצְרָיִם. אָמַר לוֹ: עַל הָרִאשׁוֹנִים אָנוּ מִצְטַעֲרִים וְאַתָּה בָּא לְהוֹסִיף עֲלֵיהֶם? אָמַר לָהּ: לְכִי לְבֵית אָבִיךְ. נָטְלָה שְׁנֵי בָנֶיהָ וְהָלְכָה לָהּ:

2| אַחַר שִׁלּוּחֶיהָ – After he had sent her home: When the Holy One, blessed be He, said to Moshe in Midyan: Go, return to Egypt (4:19), the prophet obeyed, as the verse states: Moshe took his wife and sons and put them on a donkey (4:20). When Aharon came to meet his brother, as the verse states: He went and met him at God's mountain, and kissed him (4:27), he asked of him: "Who are these people with you?" Said Moshe: "This is my wife whom I married in Midyan, and these are our sons." But this distressed Aharon: "Where exactly are you taking them?" Answered Moshe: "I'm bringing them to Egypt with me." Aharon protested: "Here we are anxious about the Hebrews already trapped in Egypt; why would you bring more souls into bondage?" So Moshe turned his wife around and said: "Go back home to your father." So Tzipora took her two sons and left.

וַיַּצִּלֵנִי מֵחֶרֶב פַּרְעֹה. כְּשֶׁגִּלּוּ דָתָן וַאֲבִירָם עַל דְּבַר הַמִּצְרִי וּבִקֵּשׁ לַהֲרֹג אֶת מֹשֶׁה, נַעֲשָׂה צַוָּארוֹ כְּעַמּוּד שֶׁל שַׁיִשׁ:

4| וַיַּצִּלֵנִי מֵחֶרֶב פַּרְעֹה – Saving me from Pharaoh's sword: When Datan and Aviram revealed Moshe's murder of the Egyptian taskmaster to Pharaoh, the king sought to kill Moshe [as reported in 2:15. According to the Midrash, the two quarreling Hebrews in 2:13–14 were Datan and Aviram, who are only introduced by name in Numbers 16]. However, when the executioner attempted to decapitate Moshe, the prophet's neck turned into marble and the sword was rendered useless.

אֶל הַמִּדְבָּר. אַף אָנוּ יוֹדְעִים שֶׁבַּמִּדְבָּר הָיוּ, אֶלָּא בְּשִׁבְחוֹ שֶׁל יִתְרוֹ דִּבֶּר הַכָּתוּב, שֶׁהָיָה יוֹשֵׁב בִּכְבוֹדוֹ

5| אֶל־הַמִּדְבָּר – In the desert: Surely we already know that Moshe and the nation were encamped in the desert. Nevertheless, the text mentions this detail to praise Yitro for meeting

came to Moshe in the desert, bringing his sons and his wife,
6 to where he was encamped by the mountain of God. Yitro
sent word to Moshe, "I am coming to you – your father-in-law
7 Yitro – together with your wife and both of your sons." Moshe
went out to greet his father-in-law and bowed down and kissed
him. Each asked after the other's welfare, and they went inside
8 the tent. And Moshe told his father-in-law all that the LORD
had done to Pharaoh and the Egyptians for Israel's sake, all the
hardship they had encountered along the way, and how the
9 LORD had rescued them. ▸ Yitro delighted in all the good that
the LORD had done for Israel, in His liberating them from the
10 Egyptians – and said, "Blessed be the LORD who has rescued

---

שֶׁל עוֹלָם, וְגָדְלוּ לְבּוֹ לָצֵאת אֶל
הַמִּדְבָּר מְקוֹם תֹּהוּ לִשְׁמֹעַ דִּבְרֵי
תּוֹרָה:

ו| וַיֹּאמֶר אֶל־מֹשֶׁה. עַל יְדֵי שָׁלִיחַ:

אֲנִי חֹתֶנְךָ יִתְרוֹ וְגוֹ׳. אִם אֵין אַתָּה
יוֹצֵא בְּגִינִי צֵא בִּגְּין חֶשְׁתְּךָ, וְאִם אֵין
אַתָּה יוֹצֵא בְּגִין אִשְׁתְּךָ צֵא בִּגְּין שְׁנֵי
בָּנֶיהָ:

ז| וַיֵּצֵא מֹשֶׁה. כָּבוֹד גָּדוֹל נִתְכַּבֵּד
יִתְרוֹ בְּאוֹתָהּ שָׁעָה; כֵּיוָן שֶׁיָּצָא מֹשֶׁה
יָצָא אַהֲרֹן נָדָב וַאֲבִיהוּא, וּמִי הוּא
שֶׁרָאָה אֶת אֵלּוּ יוֹצְאִין וְלֹא יָצָא?

וַיִּשְׁתַּחוּ וַיִּשַּׁק־לוֹ. אֵינִי יוֹדֵעַ מִי
הִשְׁתַּחֲוָה לְמִי, כְּשֶׁהוּא אוֹמֵר:
"אִישׁ לְרֵעֵהוּ", מִי הַקָּרוּי "אִישׁ"?
זֶה מֹשֶׁה (רְאֵה במדבר יב, ג):

ח| וַיְסַפֵּר מֹשֶׁה לְחֹתְנוֹ. לִמְשֹׁךְ אֶת
לְבּוֹ לְקָרְבוֹ לַתּוֹרָה:

---

them there. For Yitro was stirred to leave his comfortable home in Midyan for the desolate wilderness, just to hear the message of the Torah.

6| וַיֹּאמֶר אֶל־מֹשֶׁה – Sent word to Moshe: [Literally, "said to Moshe," although Yitro had not yet arrived. Rashi explains that this was] through an emissary.

אֲנִי חֹתֶנְךָ יִתְרוֹ – I – Your father-in-law Yitro: If you will not come out to honor me, at least set out to greet "your wife." And if she is not worthy of your time, at least come out for the sake of "both of your sons."

7| וַיֵּצֵא מֹשֶׁה – Moshe went out: Yitro was greatly honored at that time, for Moshe, Aharon, Nadav, and Avihu all went out to receive him. And everybody who saw the entourage leaving the camp to greet the approaching dignitary, naturally joined the procession as well.

וַיִּשְׁתַּחוּ וַיִּשַּׁק־לוֹ – Bowed down and kissed him: At first glance, the verse does not reveal who bowed to whom. But it provides a clue when it states that each [ish] asked after the other's welfare, for we know that Moshe is later referred to as an ish [in Numbers 12:3; ish means "man" and carries connotations of importance].

8| וַיְסַפֵּר מֹשֶׁה לְחֹתְנוֹ – Moshe told his father-in-law: Moshe related the entire narrative of the exodus to Yitro, in order to draw him toward the Torah.

◀

וַיָּבֹא אֶל־מֹשֶׁה אֶל־הַמִּדְבָּר אֲשֶׁר־הוּא חֹנֶה שָׁם
הַר הָאֱלֹהִים: וַיֹּאמֶר אֶל־מֹשֶׁה אֲנִי חֹתֶנְךָ יִתְרוֹ
בָּא אֵלֶיךָ וְאִשְׁתְּךָ וּשְׁנֵי בָנֶיהָ עִמָּהּ: וַיֵּצֵא מֹשֶׁה
לִקְרַאת חֹתְנוֹ וַיִּשְׁתַּחוּ וַיִּשַּׁק־לוֹ וַיִּשְׁאֲלוּ אִישׁ־
לְרֵעֵהוּ לְשָׁלוֹם וַיָּבֹאוּ הָאֹהֱלָה: וַיְסַפֵּר מֹשֶׁה לְחֹתְנוֹ
אֵת כָּל־אֲשֶׁר עָשָׂה יהוה לְפַרְעֹה וּלְמִצְרַיִם עַל אוֹדֹת
יִשְׂרָאֵל אֵת כָּל־הַתְּלָאָה אֲשֶׁר מְצָאָתַם בַּדֶּרֶךְ וַיַּצִּלֵם
יהוה: · וַיִּחַדְּ יִתְרוֹ עַל כָּל־הַטּוֹבָה אֲשֶׁר־עָשָׂה יהוה
לְיִשְׂרָאֵל אֲשֶׁר הִצִּילוֹ מִיַּד מִצְרָיִם: וַיֹּאמֶר יִתְרוֹ
בָּרוּךְ יהוה אֲשֶׁר הִצִּיל אֶתְכֶם מִיַּד מִצְרַיִם וּמִיַּד

אֵת כָּל־הַתְּלָאָה – All the hardship: This refers specifically to the crisis at the Sea of Reeds and the battle with Amalek.

הַתְּלָאָה – The hardship: The root of the word telaa is lamed-alef. The prefixed letter tav is an embellishment that sometimes joins the root and is sometimes omitted. We find similar structures in the words teruma ["something raised"], tenufa ["something waved"], tekuma ["rising"], and tenua ["motion"].

9| וַיִּחַדְּ יִתְרוֹ – Yitro delighted: The straightforward meaning of the verb vayihad means that Yitro rejoiced. But the homiletic interpretation is that the man's flesh bristled [naasa ḥiddudin] as he mourned the Egyptian destruction. This illustrates the popular adage: Do not insult gentiles in the presence of a convert or even of his descendant to the tenth generation [see Sanhedrin 94a].

עַל כָּל־הַטּוֹבָה – In all the good: Yitro was pleased with the manna, the [miraculous] well, and the Torah the people had been taught. Above all, he was impressed with how God had liberated Israel from Egypt. For until now not a single slave had succeeded in escaping from the Egyptian prison, yet God had now opened the country's doors to 600,000 men.

10| אֲשֶׁר הִצִּיל אֶתְכֶם מִיַּד מִצְרַיִם – Who has rescued you from Egypt: A harsh nation.

אֵת כָּל־הַתְּלָאָה. שֶׁעַל הַיָּם וְשֶׁל עֲמָלֵק:

הַתְּלָאָה. לָמֶ"ד אָלֶ"ף הִיא מִן הַיְסוֹד שֶׁל תֵּבָה, וְהַתָּי"ו הוּא תִּקּוּן וִיסוֹד הַנּוֹפֵל מִמֶּנּוּ לִפְרָקִים. וְכֵן: תְּרוּמָה, תְּנוּפָה, תְּקוּמָה, תְּנוּעָה:

ט| וַיִּחַדְּ יִתְרוֹ. וַיִּשְׂמַח יִתְרוֹ, זֶהוּ פְשׁוּטוֹ. וּמִדְרָשׁוֹ, נַעֲשָׂה בְּשָׂרוֹ חִדּוּדִין חִדּוּדִין, מֵצֵר עַל אִבּוּד מִצְרַיִם. הַיְנוּ דְּאָמְרֵי אֱנָשֵׁי: גִּיּוֹרָא, עַד עֲשָׂרָה דָּרֵי לָא תְּבַזֵּי אֲרַמָּאָה בְּאַפֵּיהּ (סנהדרין צד ע"א):

עַל כָּל־הַטּוֹבָה. טוֹבַת הַמָּן וְהַבְּאֵר וְהַתּוֹרָה. וְעַל כֻּלָּן "אֲשֶׁר הִצִּילוֹ מִיַּד מִצְרַיִם", עַד עַכְשָׁיו לֹא הָיָה עֶבֶד יָכוֹל לִבְרֹחַ מִמִּצְרַיִם, שֶׁהָיְתָה הָאָרֶץ מְסֻגֶּרֶת, וְאֵלּוּ יָצְאוּ שִׁשִּׁים רִבּוֹא:

י| אֲשֶׁר הִצִּיל אֶתְכֶם מִיַּד מִצְרָיִם. אֻמָּה קָשָׁה:

you from Egypt and Pharaoh and liberated the people from
11 the Egyptians' hands. Now I know that the LORD is greater
than all gods – for He brought upon them what they schemed
12 against others." Then Yitro brought a burnt offering and sacrifices to God. And Aharon and all the elders of Israel came to
13 break bread with Moshe's father-in-law before God. ◄ The next SHENI
day Moshe sat to serve the people as judge. From morning to

וּמִיַּד פַּרְעֹה. מֶלֶךְ קָשֶׁה:

וּמִיַּד פַּרְעֹה – *And from Pharaoh*: A harsh king.

מִתַּחַת יַד־מִצְרָיִם. כְּתַרְגּוּמוֹ, לְשׁוֹן
רִדּוּי וּמָרוּת הַיָּד שֶׁהָיוּ מַכְבִּידִים
עֲלֵיהֶם, הִיא הָעֲבוֹדָה:

מִתַּחַת יַד־מִצְרָיִם – *From the Egyptians' hands*: The term "hand" should be understood as the Targum translates it [*marvat*, meaning "dominion"], referring to the tyranny and domination of the Egyptians. The oppressors held Israel in a tight fist by imposing slavery upon them.

יא| עַתָּה יָדַעְתִּי. מַכִּירוֹ הָיִיתִי
לְשֶׁעָבַר, וְעַכְשָׁיו בְּיוֹתֵר:

11 |**עַתָּה יָדַעְתִּי** – *Now I know*: Although I recognized God in the past, now I am even more convinced of His greatness.

מִכָּל־הָאֱלֹהִים. מְלַמֵּד שֶׁהָיָה מַכִּיר
בְּכָל עֲבוֹדָה זָרָה שֶׁבָּעוֹלָם, שֶׁלֹּא
הִנִּיחַ עֲבוֹדָה זָרָה שֶׁלֹּא עֲבָדָהּ:

מִכָּל־הָאֱלֹהִים – *Than all gods*: Yitro was familiar with all the world's religions, for he had dabbled in all varieties of idolatry.

כִּי בַדָּבָר אֲשֶׁר זָדוּ עֲלֵיהֶם.
כְּתַרְגּוּמוֹ, בַּמַּיִם דְּמוּ לְחַבְּדָם וְהֵם
נֶאֶבְדוּ בַּמַּיִם:

כִּי בַדָּבָר אֲשֶׁר זָדוּ עֲלֵיהֶם – *For He brought upon them what they schemed against others*: [Literally, "for what they schemed against them."] This clause should be understood in light of the Targum [which translates freely: "for the Egyptians were punished with the punishment they plotted for Israel"]. The Egyptians had planned to destroy Israel by drowning them in water, but they themselves were punished that way.

אֲשֶׁר זָדוּ. חֲשֶׁר הִרְשִׁיעוּ. וְרַבּוֹתֵינוּ
דְרָשׁוּהוּ לְשׁוֹן: "וַיָּזֶד יַעֲקֹב נָזִיד"
(בראשית כה, כט), בַּקְדֵרָה שֶׁבִּשְּׁלוּ בָּהּ
נִתְבַּשְּׁלוּ:

אֲשֶׁר זָדוּ – *What they schemed*: The word *zadu* means "acted wickedly." Our Sages associate the verb with the verse *And Yaakov cooked pottage [nazid]* (Genesis 25:29), meaning that the Egyptians cooked up a scheme to murder the Israelites, but in the end they were boiled in their own pot.

יב| עֹלָה. כְּמַשְׁמָעָהּ, שֶׁהִיא כֻּלָּהּ
כָּלִיל:

12 |**עֹלָה** – *A burnt offering*: [The Hebrew ola derives from the root meaning "to rise."] This is an apt name for a type of sacrifice that is burned in totality.

וּזְבָחִים. שְׁלָמִים:

וּזְבָחִים – *Sacrifices*: This term refers to peace offerings. [Unlike burnt offerings, the meat of peace offerings is eaten by the donor.]

פַּרְעֹה אֲשֶׁר הִצִּיל אֶת־הָעָם מִתַּחַת יַד־מִצְרָיִם:
יא עַתָּה יָדַעְתִּי כִּי־גָדוֹל יהוה מִכָּל־הָאֱלֹהִים כִּי בַדָּבָר
יב אֲשֶׁר זָדוּ עֲלֵיהֶם: וַיִּקַּח יִתְרוֹ חֹתֵן מֹשֶׁה עֹלָה וּזְבָחִים
לֵאלֹהִים וַיָּבֹא אַהֲרֹן וְכֹל ׀ זִקְנֵי יִשְׂרָאֵל לֶאֱכָל־לֶחֶם
יג עִם־חֹתֵן מֹשֶׁה לִפְנֵי הָאֱלֹהִים: וַיְהִי מִמָּחֳרָת וַיֵּשֶׁב שני
מֹשֶׁה לִשְׁפֹּט אֶת־הָעָם וַיַּעֲמֹד הָעָם עַל־מֹשֶׁה מִן־

וַיָּבֹא אַהֲרֹן וְגו'. וּמֹשֶׁה הֵיכָן הָלַךְ? וַהֲלֹא הוּא שֶׁיָּצָא לִקְרָאתוֹ וְגָרַם לוֹ אֶת כָּל הַכָּבוֹד? אֶלָּא שֶׁהָיָה עוֹמֵד וּמְשַׁמֵּשׁ לִפְנֵיהֶם:

לִפְנֵי הָאֱלֹהִים. מִכָּאן שֶׁהַנֶּהֱנֶה מִסְּעוּדָה שֶׁתַּלְמִידֵי חֲכָמִים מְסֻבִּין בָּהּ כְּאִלּוּ נֶהֱנֶה מִזִּיו הַשְּׁכִינָה:

יג **וַיְהִי מִמָּחֳרָת.** מוֹצָאֵי יוֹם הַכִּפּוּרִים הָיָה, כָּךְ שָׁנִינוּ בְּסִפְרֵי (ראה מכילתא יתרו, עמלק ח). **וּמַהוּ** "מִמָּחֳרָת"? לְמָחֳרַת רִדְתּוֹ מִן הָהָר. וְעַל כָּרְחֲךָ אִי אֶפְשָׁר לוֹמַר אֶלָּא מִמָּחֳרַת יוֹם הַכִּפּוּרִים, שֶׁהֲרֵי קֹדֶם מַתַּן תּוֹרָה אִי אֶפְשָׁר לוֹמַר "וְהוֹדַעְתִּי אֶת חֻקֵּי וְגו'" (להלן פסוק טז), וּמִשֶּׁנִּתְּנָה תּוֹרָה עַד יוֹם הַכִּפּוּרִים לֹא יָשַׁב מֹשֶׁה לִשְׁפֹּט אֶת הָעָם, שֶׁהֲרֵי בְּשִׁבְעָה עָשָׂר בְּתַמּוּז יָרַד וְשִׁבֵּר אֶת הַלּוּחוֹת, וּלְמָחָר עָלָה בְּהַשְׁכָּמָה וְשָׁהָה שְׁמוֹנִים יוֹם וְיָרַד בְּיוֹם הַכִּפּוּרִים. וְאֵין פָּרָשָׁה זוֹ כְּתוּבָה כַּסֵּדֶר, שֶׁלֹּא נֶאֱמַר "וַיְהִי מִמָּחֳרָת" עַד שָׁנָה אַחֶרֶת. אַף לְדִבְרֵי הָאוֹמֵר יִתְרוֹ קֹדֶם מַתַּן תּוֹרָה בָּא, שִׁלּוּחוֹ אֶל אַרְצוֹ לֹא הָיָה אֶלָּא עַד שָׁנָה שְׁנִיָּה, שֶׁהֲרֵי נֶאֱמַר כָּאן: "וַיְשַׁלַּח מֹשֶׁה אֶת חֹתְנוֹ" (להלן פסוק כז),

---

וַיָּבֹא אַהֲרֹן – *And Aharon came*: Where did Moshe disappear to? Had he not gone out to greet Yitro and to lead the procession honoring him? Actually, instead of eating with the rest of the group, Moshe stood and served Yitro, Aharon, and the elders [in a gesture of respect].

לִפְנֵי הָאֱלֹהִים – *Before God*: We learn from this verse that when one participates in a meal attended by Torah scholars, it is as if he basks in the glory of the Divine Presence.

13 **וַיְהִי מִמָּחֳרָת** – *The next day*: According to the Mekhilta, this was the day following Yom Kippur [and not the day after the celebration reported in the previous verse]. Thus "the next day" means: "the day after Moshe descended from Mount Sinai [with the second tablets, as reported in 34:28–29]." We are forced to posit that Moshe waited until the day after Yom Kippur to judge the nation, because he would not have done so before the Torah had been given to them. Moshe tells Yitro that not only does he *judge between one neighbor and another*, but he *makes God's laws and teachings known* to them (18:16). [Therefore, all this must have transpired after the giving of the Torah.] And is impossible for Moshe to have sat in judgment any time between the time that the Torah was given to Israel [understood to be Shavuot] and Yom Kippur [four months later]. For immediately after revelation, Moshe ascended the mountain and remained in God's presence for forty days until the seventeenth of Tamuz. On that day, Moshe smashed the tablets, and early the next day he went back up the mountain to pray on Israel's behalf. There he stayed for an additional eighty days, finally descending on Yom Kippur. What this means is that the current passage is not written in its proper place, for the phrase "the next day" actually refers to events of

14 evening the people stood before him. When Moshe's father-in-law saw everything Moshe did for the people, he asked, "What is this that you do for the people? Why do you sit alone while all the people stand over you from morning to evening?"

15 "The people come to me to inquire of God," Moshe replied.

16 "When they have a dispute, they come to me and I judge between one neighbor and another, and I make God's laws and teachings known." Moshe's father-in-law said to him, "What you are doing is not good. You will be worn away, and this people along with you. It is too heavy a burden for you. You

---

וְעִנְיָן בְּמַסַּע הַדְּגָלִים שֶׁאָמַר לוֹ
מֹשֶׁה: "נֹסְעִים אֲנַחְנוּ אֶל הַמָּקוֹם
וְגוֹ' חַל נָא תַּעֲזֹב אֹתָנוּ" (כמדבר י,
כט-לא), וְאִם זֶה קֹדֶם מַתַּן תּוֹרָה,
מִשֶּׁשָּׁלְחוֹ וְהָלַךְ הֵיכָן מָצִינוּ שֶׁחָזַר?
וְאִם תֹּאמַר, שָׁם לֹא נֶאֱמַר
יִתְרוֹ אֶלָּא חוֹבָב, וּבְנוֹ שֶׁל יִתְרוֹ
הָיָה – הוּא חוֹבָב הוּא יִתְרוֹ, שֶׁהֲרֵי
כָּתוּב: "מִבְּנֵי חֹבָב חֹתֵן מֹשֶׁה"
(שופטים ד, יא):

וַיֵּשֶׁב מֹשֶׁה... וַיַּעֲמֹד הָעָם. יוֹשֵׁב
כְּמֶלֶךְ וְכֻלָּן עוֹמְדִים, וְהִקְשָׁה הַדָּבָר
לְיִתְרוֹ שֶׁהָיָה מְזַלְזֵל בִּכְבוֹדָן שֶׁל
יִשְׂרָאֵל וְהוֹכִיחוֹ עַל כָּךְ, שֶׁנֶּאֱמַר:
"מַדּוּעַ אַתָּה יוֹשֵׁב לְבַדֶּךָ" וְכֻלָּם
נָצָבִים:

מִן הַבֹּקֶר עַד הָעָרֶב. אֶפְשָׁר
לוֹמַר כֵּן?! אֶלָּא כָּל דַּיָּן שֶׁדָּן דִּין
אֱמֶת לַאֲמִתּוֹ אֲפִלּוּ שָׁעָה אַחַת

---

the following year. Now, there are opinions which claim that Yitro's arrival at Israel's camp did take place before the giving of the Torah. But even those commentators will agree that he did not depart for his homeland Midyan until the second year. True, we read here: *Then Moshe parted from his father-in-law, and the latter went forth, back to his own land* (18:27). But much later, during the march of Israel's banners, we find Moshe attempting to persuade Yitro to accompany the people to the promised land: *We are journeying to the place of which the LORD said, I will give it to you. Come you with us…. Leave us not I pray you* (Numbers 10:29–31). It is therefore difficult to argue that Yitro left Israel before the Torah was given, since then we would have to hypothesize that he returned later if we are to accommodate the discussion in the book of Numbers. But the Torah makes no mention of a second arrival. And lest you argue that in fact Moshe extends his invitation to Ḥovav [the name given in Numbers 10:29] to join Israel on their mission to the land, and that Ḥovav was Yitro's son, I must insist that Ḥovav and Yitro are one and the same. This is made clear by the verse: *The children of Ḥovav the father-in-law of Moshe* (Judges 4:11).

וַיֵּשֶׁב מֹשֶׁה... וַיַּעֲמֹד הָעָם – *Moshe sat …the people stood*: What disturbed Yitro was that Moshe sat like a king on a throne while the people remained standing. This arrangement was disrespectful to the people of Israel, which is why Yitro rebuked his son-in-law, saying: *Why do you sit alone* (18:14), i.e., while everybody else stands?

מִן הַבֹּקֶר עַד הָעָרֶב – *From morning to evening*: Is it really possible that Moshe judged people all day? Rather, what the verse implies is that when a judge rules truthfully and correctly for

◀

יד הַבֹּקֶר עַד־הָעָרֶב: וַיַּרְא חֹתֵן מֹשֶׁה אֵת כָּל־אֲשֶׁר־
הוּא עֹשֶׂה לָעָם וַיֹּאמֶר מָה־הַדָּבָר הַזֶּה אֲשֶׁר אַתָּה
עֹשֶׂה לָעָם מַדּוּעַ אַתָּה יוֹשֵׁב לְבַדֶּךָ וְכָל־הָעָם נִצָּב
עָלֶיךָ מִן־בֹּקֶר עַד־עָרֶב: טו וַיֹּאמֶר מֹשֶׁה לְחֹתְנוֹ כִּי־
טז יָבֹא אֵלַי הָעָם לִדְרֹשׁ אֱלֹהִים: כִּי־יִהְיֶה לָהֶם דָּבָר
בָּא אֵלַי וְשָׁפַטְתִּי בֵּין אִישׁ וּבֵין רֵעֵהוּ וְהוֹדַעְתִּי אֶת־
יז חֻקֵּי הָאֱלֹהִים וְאֶת־תּוֹרֹתָיו: וַיֹּאמֶר חֹתֵן מֹשֶׁה אֵלָיו
יח לֹא־טוֹב הַדָּבָר אֲשֶׁר אַתָּה עֹשֶׂה: נָבֹל תִּבֹּל גַּם־
אַתָּה גַּם־הָעָם הַזֶּה אֲשֶׁר עִמָּךְ כִּי־כָבֵד מִמְּךָ הַדָּבָר

מַעֲלֶה עָלָיו הַכָּתוּב כְּאִלּוּ עוֹסֵק
בַּתּוֹרָה כָּל הַיּוֹם, וּכְאִלּוּ נַעֲשָׂה
שֻׁתָּף לְהַקָּדוֹשׁ בָּרוּךְ הוּא בְּמַעֲשֵׂה
בְּרֵאשִׁית שֶׁנֶּאֱמַר בּוֹ: "וַיְהִי עֶרֶב
וַיְהִי בֹקֶר יוֹם אֶחָד": (בראשית א, ה):

טו| כִּי־יָבֹא. כִּי בָא, לְשׁוֹן הֹוֶה,
"לְמִתְבַּע אֻלְפָן", לְשׁאֹל תַּלְמוּד
מִפִּי הַגְּבוּרָה:

טז| כִּי־יִהְיֶה לָהֶם דָּבָר. מִי שֶׁיִּהְיֶה
לֹו דָּבָר בָּא אֵלַי:

יז| וַיֹּאמֶר חֹתֵן מֹשֶׁה. דֶּרֶךְ כָּבוֹד
קוֹרְאֵהוּ הַכָּתוּב, חוֹתְנוֹ שֶׁל מֶלֶךְ:

יח| נָבֹל תִּבֹּל. כְּתַרְגּוּמוֹ. וּלְשׁוֹנוֹ
לְשׁוֹן כְּמִישָׁה, פלי״שטרי״א בְּלַעַז,
כְּמֹו: "וְהֶעָלֶה נָבֵל" (ירמיה ח, יג),
"כִּנְבֹל עָלֶה מִגֶּפֶן" (ישעיה לד, ד),
שֶׁהוּא כָּמוּשׁ עַל יְדֵי חַמָּה וְעַל
יְדֵי קֶרַח וְכֹחוֹ תָּשׁ וְנִלְאֶה:

even a single hour, the Torah credits him with having sat and studied Torah the entire day. It is as if such an individual has become a partner in creation with the Holy One, blessed be He, as the verse states: *And there was evening and there was morning, one day* (Genesis 1:5).

15| כִּי־יָבֹא – *Come*: The verb is in the present tense [despite the future tense construction]. As the Targum translates, the people would come to "seek learning" [*lemitba ulfan*], to learn the teachings of God.

16| כִּי־יִהְיֶה לָהֶם דָּבָר – *When they have a dispute*: [The Hebrew verse mixes between singular and plural, literally, "When they have a dispute, he comes to me." Rashi explains to whom "he" refers:] Whoever has an issue comes to me.

17| וַיֹּאמֶר חֹתֵן מֹשֶׁה – *Moshe's father-in-law said*: Although the text could have said merely: "his father-in-law said to him," the verse includes Moshe's name as a way of honoring Yitro, identifying him as the father-in-law of the king.

18| נָבֹל תִּבֹּל – *You will be worn away*: The phrase *navol tibbol* should be understood as the Targum translates [*mila tilei* – "you will become worn out"]. The Old French term for this condition is *flestre* [meaning "withered"]. We find a similar term in the verse *The leaf is withered [navel]* (Jeremiah 8:13), and the verse *As leaves wither [kinvol] and fall from the vine* (Isaiah 34:4). Leaves wilt in the sun's heat and die in the frost; they wither and wear out.

◄

19 cannot carry it alone. Now listen to me, let me advise you; and
may God be with you. You speak for the people before God,
20 and bring their concerns to Him. And you must acquaint them
with His precepts and laws, and make known to them the path
21 they are to walk and the way they must act. You, as well, must
seek out among the people, capable men – God-fearing, trustworthy men, who despise corruption; and appoint them over
the people as leaders of thousands, hundreds, fifties, and tens.
22 Have them serve as daily judges for the people; let them bring
the major cases to you, but judge the minor ones themselves.
In this way they will lighten your load, and bear it together

---

גַּם־אַתָּה. לְרַבּוֹת אַהֲרֹן וְחוּר וְשִׁבְעִים זְקֵנִים:

גַּם־אַתָּה – *You*: [Literally, "also you."] The extra word "also" [*gam*] serves to include Aharon, Ḥur, and the seventy elders. [That is, even if they assist you, they will be worn out as well.]

כִּי־כָבֵד מִמְּךָ. כָּבְדּוֹ רַב יוֹתֵר מִכֹּחֲךָ:

כִּי־כָבֵד מִמְּךָ – *It is too heavy a burden*: [Literally, "it is heavier than you." Rashi explains the phrase:] The weight of the burden is heavier than your strength can lift.

יט| אִיעָצְךָ וִיהִי אֱלֹהִים עִמָּךְ. בָּעֵצָה, אָמַר לוֹ: צֵא הִמָּלֵךְ בַּגְּבוּרָה:

19| אִיעָצְךָ וִיהִי אֱלֹהִים עִמָּךְ – *Let me advise you ;and may God be with you*: Do not just take my advice; you ought to consult with God as well.

הֱיֵה אַתָּה לָעָם מוּל הָאֱלֹהִים. שָׁלִיחַ וּמֵלִיץ בֵּינוֹתָם לַמָּקוֹם וְשׁוֹאֵל מִשְׁפָּטִים מֵאִתּוֹ:

הֱיֵה אַתָּה לָעָם מוּל הָאֱלֹהִים – *You speak for the people before God*: Moshe should act as a messenger and as an intermediary between the people and God, seeking His rulings on their behalf.

אֶת־הַדְּבָרִים. דִּבְרֵי רִיבוֹתָם:

אֶת־הַדְּבָרִים – *Their concerns*: [Literally, "the matters." Rashi specifies that this refers to] the people's quarrels.

כא| וְאַתָּה תֶחֱזֶה. בְּרוּחַ הַקֹּדֶשׁ שֶׁעָלֶיךָ:

21| וְאַתָּה תֶחֱזֶה – *You must seek out*: Use your divine inspiration to find these judges.

אַנְשֵׁי־חַיִל. עֲשִׁירִים, שֶׁאֵין צְרִיכִין לְהַחֲנִיף וּלְהַכִּיר פָּנִים:

אַנְשֵׁי־חַיִל – *Capable men*: Rich men. Judges who are wealthy will have no need to flatter others or curry favor.

אַנְשֵׁי אֱמֶת. אֵלּוּ בַּעֲלֵי הַבְטָחָה שֶׁהֵם כְּדַאי לִסְמֹךְ עַל דִּבְרֵיהֶם, שֶׁעַל יְדֵי כָךְ יִהְיוּ דִּבְרֵיהֶם נִשְׁמָעִין:

אַנְשֵׁי אֱמֶת – *Trustworthy men*: Individuals who have faith in God are those whose words can be trusted. As such, disputing parties will have confidence in their judgments.

שֹׂנְאֵי בָצַע. שֶׁשּׂוֹנְאִים אֶת מָמוֹנָם בַּדִּין, כְּהַהִיא דְּאָמְרִינַן: כָּל דַּיָּנָא

שֹׂנְאֵי בָצַע – *Despise corruption*: This refers to a reluctance to let any of their own conflicts reach the stage of litigation [always preferring to reach a negotiated settlement]. As the Sages

◀

יט לֹא־תוּכַל עֲשֹׂהוּ לְבַדֶּךָ: עַתָּה שְׁמַע בְּקֹלִי אִיעָצְךָ וִיהִי אֱלֹהִים עִמָּךְ הֱיֵה אַתָּה לָעָם מוּל הָאֱלֹהִים: כ וְהֵבֵאתָ אַתָּה אֶת־הַדְּבָרִים אֶל־הָאֱלֹהִים: וְהִזְהַרְתָּה אֶתְהֶם אֶת־הַחֻקִּים וְאֶת־הַתּוֹרֹת וְהוֹדַעְתָּ לָהֶם אֶת־ כא הַדֶּרֶךְ יֵלְכוּ בָהּ וְאֶת־הַמַּעֲשֶׂה אֲשֶׁר יַעֲשׂוּן: וְאַתָּה תֶחֱזֶה מִכָּל־הָעָם אַנְשֵׁי־חַיִל יִרְאֵי אֱלֹהִים אַנְשֵׁי אֱמֶת שֹׂנְאֵי בָצַע וְשַׂמְתָּ עֲלֵהֶם שָׂרֵי אֲלָפִים שָׂרֵי כב מֵאוֹת שָׂרֵי חֲמִשִּׁים וְשָׂרֵי עֲשָׂרֹת: וְשָׁפְטוּ אֶת־הָעָם בְּכָל־עֵת וְהָיָה כָּל־הַדָּבָר הַגָּדֹל יָבִיאוּ אֵלֶיךָ וְכָל־ הַדָּבָר הַקָּטֹן יִשְׁפְּטוּ־הֵם וְהָקֵל מֵעָלֶיךָ וְנָשְׂאוּ אִתָּךְ:

---

teach: Any judge who has been compelled to pay money in court is not a real judge.

שָׂרֵי אֲלָפִים – *Leaders of thousands*: Moshe was to appoint six hundred men to have jurisdiction over the 600,000 Israelites who left Egypt.

שָׂרֵי מֵאוֹת – *Leaders of hundreds*: There were six thousand men at this level.

שָׂרֵי חֲמִשִּׁים – *Leaders of fifties*: And twelve thousand men in this group.

וְשָׂרֵי עֲשָׂרֹת – *Leaders of tens*: Sixty thousand.

22 | **וְשָׁפְטוּ** – *Have them serve*: [Although it might appear to be past tense – compare to the same verb in verse 26 – Rashi explains that here the term should be understood as the Targum translates:] "They should serve" [*vidunun*]. The verb is a command.

וְהָקֵל מֵעָלֶיךָ – *They will lighten your load*: [The infinitive absolute form *vehakel* is difficult to understand in this context. Rashi explains the verb as meaning:] This strategy will have the effect of "lightening" your load. We find analogous forms in the verse *Hardening [vehakhbed] his heart* (8:11), and the verse *Smiting [vehakkot] Moav* (II Kings 3:24). In all these cases the verb functions as a present participle.

דְּמַפְּקִין מָמוֹנָא מִנֵּיהּ בְּדִינָא לָאו דַּיָּנָא הוּא:

שָׂרֵי אֲלָפִים. הֵם הָיוּ שֵׁשׁ מֵאוֹת שָׂרִים לְשֵׁשׁ מֵאוֹת אֶלֶף:

שָׂרֵי מֵאוֹת. שֵׁשֶׁת אֲלָפִים הָיוּ:

שָׂרֵי חֲמִשִּׁים. שְׁנֵים עָשָׂר אֶלֶף:

וְשָׂרֵי עֲשָׂרֹת. שִׁשִּׁים אֶלֶף:

כב| וְשָׁפְטוּ. "וִידוּנוּן", לְשׁוֹן צִוּוּי:

וְהָקֵל מֵעָלֶיךָ. דָּבָר זֶה לְהָקֵל מֵעָלֶיךָ. "וְהָקֵל" כְּמוֹ: "וְהַכְבֵּד אֶת לִבּוֹ" (לעיל ח, יח), "וְהַכּוֹת אֶת מוֹאָב" (מלכים ב' ג, כד), לְשׁוֹן הֹוֶה:

23 with you. If you do this, and God so commands, then you
will endure, and all these people will be able to go home in
24 peace." Moshe listened to his father-in-law and did all that he   SHELISHI
25 said. Moshe chose capable men from all Israel and made them
chiefs over the people, leaders of thousands, hundreds, fifties,
26 and tens. They judged the people every day. Any major case
they brought to Moshe, but they decided every minor matter
27 themselves. Then Moshe parted from his father-in-law, and
the latter went forth, back to his own land.

19 1 On the first day of the third month after the Israelites had   REVI'I
2 left Egypt they came to the Sinai Desert. Setting out from
Refidim they had arrived at the Sinai Desert, encamping in

כג | וְצִוְּךָ אֱלֹהִים וְיָכָלְתָּ עֲמֹד.
הַמֶּלֶךְ בַּגְּבוּרָה, אִם מְצַוֶּה אוֹתְךָ
לַעֲשׂוֹת כֵּן – תּוּכַל לַעֲמֹד, וְאִם
יְעַכֵּב עַל יָדְךָ – לֹא תּוּכַל לַעֲמֹד:

וְגַם כָּל־הָעָם הַזֶּה. אַהֲרֹן נָדָב
וַאֲבִיהוּא וְשִׁבְעִים זְקֵנִים הַנִּלְוִים
עַתָּה עִמָּךְ:

כו | וְשָׁפְטוּ. "וְדָיְנִין יָת עַמָּא":

יָבִיאוּן. "מֵיתַן":

יִשְׁפּוּטוּ הֵם. כְּמוֹ יִשְׁפְּטוּ. וְכֵן: "לֹא
תַעֲבוּרִי" (רות ב, ח) כְּמוֹ לֹא תַעֲבֹרִי.
וְתַרְגּוּמוֹ: "דָּיְנִין אִנּוּן". מִקְרָאוֹת
הָעֶלְיוֹנִים (לעיל פסוק כב) הָיוּ לְשׁוֹן
צִוּוּי, לְכָךְ מִתְרַגְּמִין: וִידוּנוּן, יַיְתוֹן,
יְדוּנוּן, וּמִקְרָאוֹת הַלָּלוּ לְשׁוֹן עֲשִׂיָּה:

23| וְצִוְּךָ אֱלֹהִים וְיָכָלְתָּ עֲמֹד – *If God so commands, then you will endure*: Ask God whether He commands you to establish the system I have described. If He does, then you will be able to handle the burden of the nation. If He rejects my approach, you will be unable to withstand the difficulty of judging the people.

וְגַם כָּל־הָעָם הַזֶּה – *And all these people*: The inclusive word *vegam* [literally, "and also"] connotes Aharon, Nadav, Avihu and the seventy elders – the men who have been sitting by you until now.

26| וְשָׁפְטוּ – *They judged*: [As opposed to the use of this verb in verse 22, here it denotes a habitual action, as the Targum translates:] "They would judge the people" [*vedayenin yat amma*].

יָבִיאוּן – *They brought*: [This verb too signifies habitual action, as the Targum translates:] "They would bring" [*meitan*].

יִשְׁפּוּטוּ הֵם – *They decided*: The form *yishputu* is simply a variant of *yishpotu* [meaning "they would judge"]. We find a similar construction in the verse *Do not go away [taavuri] from here* (Ruth 2:8) where the verb is synonymous with the more common *taavori*. Note the Targum's translation, "they would judge [dayenin innun]. Above [in verse 22], these verbs all had the sense of a command: "They should judge," "they should bring," which is why the Targum translates them differently: *vidunun, yayton, yedunun*. But in the current verse, the text describes the fulfillment of those directions.

◀

כג אִם־אֶת־הַדָּבָר הַזֶּה תַּעֲשֶׂה וְצִוְּךָ אֱלֹהִים וְיָכָלְתָּ עֲמֹד
שלישי כד וְגַם כָּל־הָעָם הַזֶּה עַל־מְקֹמוֹ יָבֹא בְשָׁלוֹם: וַיִּשְׁמַע
מֹשֶׁה לְקוֹל חֹתְנוֹ וַיַּעַשׂ כֹּל אֲשֶׁר אָמָר: וַיִּבְחַר מֹשֶׁה
אַנְשֵׁי־חַיִל מִכָּל־יִשְׂרָאֵל וַיִּתֵּן אֹתָם רָאשִׁים עַל־הָעָם
שָׂרֵי אֲלָפִים שָׂרֵי מֵאוֹת שָׂרֵי חֲמִשִּׁים וְשָׂרֵי עֲשָׂרֹת:
כו וְשָׁפְטוּ אֶת־הָעָם בְּכָל־עֵת אֶת־הַדָּבָר הַקָּשֶׁה יְבִיאוּן
כז אֶל־מֹשֶׁה וְכָל־הַדָּבָר הַקָּטֹן יִשְׁפּוּטוּ הֵם: וַיְשַׁלַּח
מֹשֶׁה אֶת־חֹתְנוֹ וַיֵּלֶךְ לוֹ אֶל־אַרְצוֹ:
רביעי יט א בַּחֹדֶשׁ הַשְּׁלִישִׁי לְצֵאת בְּנֵי־יִשְׂרָאֵל מֵאֶרֶץ
ב מִצְרַיִם בַּיּוֹם הַזֶּה בָּאוּ מִדְבַּר סִינָי: וַיִּסְעוּ מֵרְפִידִים

כו וַיֵּלֶךְ לוֹ אֶל־אַרְצוֹ. לְגַיֵּר בְּנֵי מִשְׁפַּחְתּוֹ:

יט א בַּיּוֹם הַזֶּה. בְּרֹאשׁ חֹדֶשׁ. לֹא הָיָה צָרִיךְ לִכְתֹּב אֶלָּא 'בַּיּוֹם הַהוּא', מַהוּ 'בַּיּוֹם הַזֶּה'? שֶׁיִּהְיוּ דִּבְרֵי תוֹרָה חֲדָשִׁים עָלֶיךָ כְּאִלּוּ הַיּוֹם נִתְּנוּ:

ב וַיִּסְעוּ מֵרְפִידִים. מַה תַּלְמוּד לוֹמַר לַחֲזֹר וּלְפָרֵשׁ מֵהֵיכָן נָסְעוּ? וַהֲלֹא כְבָר כָּתַב שֶׁבִּרְפִידִים הָיוּ חוֹנִים (לעיל יז, א), בְּיָדוּעַ שֶׁמִּשָּׁם נָסְעוּ! אֶלָּא לְהַקִּישׁ נְסִיעָתָן מֵרְפִידִים לְבִיאָתָן לְמִדְבַּר סִינַי; מַה בִּיאָתָן לְמִדְבַּר סִינַי בִּתְשׁוּבָה אַף נְסִיעָתָן מֵרְפִידִים בִּתְשׁוּבָה:

וַיִּחַן־שָׁם יִשְׂרָאֵל. כְּאִישׁ אֶחָד בְּלֵב אֶחָד, אֲבָל שְׁאָר כָּל הַחֲנִיּוֹת בְּתַרְעֹמֶת וּבְמַחֲלֹקֶת:

27| וַיֵּלֶךְ לוֹ אֶל־אַרְצוֹ – *He went forth, back to his own land*: Yitro returned to Midyan to convert his family to the Israelite faith.

19 1| בַּיּוֹם הַזֶּה – *On that day*: The verse refers to the first day of the third month. Nevertheless, why does the Torah write *bayom hazeh* ["on this day"] as opposed to *bayom hahu* ["on that day"]? It teaches that the words of the Torah [which would soon be given] should always be as new and fresh to us as if they were delivered this very day.

2| וַיִּסְעוּ מֵרְפִידִים – *Setting out from Refidim*: Once the Torah states that Israel arrived at Mount Sinai, why bother telling us where they came from? After all, we already know that the nation had previously encamped at Refidim [as reported in 17:1]. The message of the verse compares Israel's setting out from Refidim to their encampment at Mount Sinai: Just as Israel reached Mount Sinai in a state of repentance, that was their attitude when they abandoned Refidim.

וַיִּחַן־שָׁם יִשְׂרָאֵל – *And there Israel camped*: [The verb "camped" – *vayiḥan* – is singular in the Hebrew.] When Israel encamped at Mount Sinai, they were united in purpose like a single individual. Israel's other departures and arrivals, on the other hand, were characterized by complaints and disputes.

◀

3 the wilderness, and there Israel camped, facing the mountain, while Moshe went up to God. And the LORD called to him from the mountain: "This is what you shall say to the house 4 of Yaakov, what you shall tell the people of Israel: You your-selves have seen what I did to the Egyptians: how I lifted 5 you up on eagles' wings and brought you to Me. Now, if you

נֶגֶד הָהָר. לְמִזְרָחוֹ, וְכָל מָקוֹם שֶׁאַתָּה מוֹצֵא 'נֶגֶד' – פָּנִים לַמִּזְרָח:

נֶגֶד הָהָר – *Facing the mountain*: Israel pitched camp to the east of the mountain. The term *neged* always connotes an eastward orientation.

ג| **וּמֹשֶׁה עָלָה. בַּיּוֹם הַשֵּׁנִי**, וְכָל עֲלִיּוֹתָיו בְּהַשְׁכָּמָה הָיוּ, שֶׁנֶּאֱמַר: "וַיַּשְׁכֵּם מֹשֶׁה בַּבֹּקֶר" (להלן לד, ד):

3| **וּמֹשֶׁה עָלָה** – *While Moshe went up*: Moshe ascended the mountain on the second day. [He cannot have gone up on the very day of Israel's arrival because we know from the Midrash that] each time Moshe climbed the hill he did so first thing in the morning, as the verse states: *And he rose early in the morning, and climbed Mount Sinai* (34:4).

כֹּה תֹאמַר. בַּלָּשׁוֹן הַזֶּה וְכַסֵּדֶר הַזֶּה:

כֹּה תֹאמַר – *This is what you shall say*: Repeat My message to Israel in precisely this language and relate My points in the same sequence.

לְבֵית יַעֲקֹב. אֵלּוּ הַנָּשִׁים, תֹּאמַר לָהֶן בְּלָשׁוֹן רַכָּה:

לְבֵית יַעֲקֹב – *To the house of Yaakov*: This refers to the nation's women, who should be addressed in soft language.

וְתַגֵּיד לִבְנֵי יִשְׂרָאֵל. עֳנָשִׁין וְדִקְדּוּקִין פָּרֵשׁ לַזְּכָרִים, דְּבָרִים הַקָּשִׁין כְּגִידִין:

וְתַגֵּיד לִבְנֵי יִשְׂרָאֵל – *Tell the people of Israel*: Inform the menfolk of the laws' particulars and the punishments for disobedience. These are matters which are difficult to hear and hard as sinews [*gidin*, echoing *vetaggeid*].

ד| **אַתֶּם רְאִיתֶם. וְלֹא מָסֹרֶת הִיא בְּיֶדְכֶם בִּדְבָרִים אֲשֶׁר עָשִׂיתִי בְמִצְרָיִם, עַל כַּמָּה עֲבֵרוֹת הָיוּ חַיָּבִין לִי קֹדֶם שֶׁנִּזְדַּוְּגוּ לָכֶם, וְלֹא נִפְרַעְתִּי מֵהֶם אֶלָּא עַל יֶדְכֶם:**

4| **אַתֶּם רְאִיתֶם** – *You yourselves have seen*: What I did in Egypt is not a story that you possess through received tradition [rather, you witnessed the events yourselves]. Know that the Egyptians long ago deserved to be penalized for their transgressions before Me. But I withheld My punishments from them until they encountered you, and exacted retribution against them only because of you [so that Israel would witness God's wonders and miracles].

וָאֶשָּׂא אֶתְכֶם. זֶה יוֹם שֶׁבָּאוּ יִשְׂרָאֵל לְרַעְמְסֵס, שֶׁהָיוּ יִשְׂרָאֵל מְפֻזָּרִין בְּכָל אֶרֶץ גֹּשֶׁן, וּלְשָׁעָה קַלָּה כְּשֶׁבָּאוּ לִסַּע וְלַעֲלוֹת נִקְבְּצוּ כֻלָּם לְרַעְמְסֵס:

וָאֶשָּׂא אֶתְכֶם – *I lifted you up*: This refers to the moment the entire nation was gathered together at Ramesses [in 12:37]. For the Israelite nation had been spread throughout the land of Goshen, yet all the people assembled at Ramesses ready to leave in virtually no time. Now Onkelos renders the verb

◀

וַיָּבֹ֙אוּ֙ מִדְבַּ֣ר סִינַ֔י וַיַּחֲנ֖וּ בַּמִּדְבָּ֑ר וַיִּֽחַן־שָׁ֥ם יִשְׂרָאֵ֖ל
נֶ֥גֶד הָהָֽר: וּמֹשֶׁ֥ה עָלָ֖ה אֶל־הָֽאֱלֹהִ֑ים וַיִּקְרָ֙א
אֵלָ֤יו יְהֹוָה֙ מִן־הָהָ֣ר לֵאמֹ֔ר כֹּ֤ה תֹאמַר֙ לְבֵ֣ית
יַעֲקֹ֔ב וְתַגֵּ֖יד לִבְנֵ֥י יִשְׂרָאֵֽל: אַתֶּ֣ם רְאִיתֶ֔ם אֲשֶׁ֥ר
עָשִׂ֖יתִי לְמִצְרָ֑יִם וָאֶשָּׂ֤א אֶתְכֶם֙ עַל־כַּנְפֵ֣י נְשָׁרִ֔ים
וָאָבִ֥א אֶתְכֶ֖ם אֵלָֽי: וְעַתָּ֗ה אִם־שָׁמ֤וֹעַ תִּשְׁמְעוּ֙

וְאוּנְקְלוֹס תִּרְגֵּם "וְאֶשָׂא" כְּמוֹ וְאַסִּיעַ אֶתְכֶם: "וְאַטֵּלִית יָתְכוֹן", תִּקֵּן אֶת הַדִּבּוּר דֶּרֶךְ כָּבוֹד לְמַעְלָה:

עַל־כַּנְפֵי נְשָׁרִים. כַּנֶּשֶׁר הַנּוֹשֵׂא גּוֹזָלָיו עַל כְּנָפָיו, שֶׁכָּל שְׁאָר הָעוֹפוֹת נוֹתְנִים אֶת בְּנֵיהֶם בֵּין רַגְלֵיהֶם, לְפִי שֶׁמִּתְיָרְאִין מֵעוֹף אַחֵר שֶׁפּוֹרֵחַ עַל גַּבֵּיהֶם, אֲבָל הַנֶּשֶׁר הַזֶּה אֵינוֹ מִתְיָרֵא אֶלָּא מִן הָאָדָם, שֶׁמָּא יִזְרֹק בּוֹ חֵץ, לְפִי שֶׁאֵין עוֹף פּוֹרֵחַ עַל גַּבֵּי, לְכָךְ נוֹתְנוֹ עַל כְּנָפָיו, אוֹמֵר: מוּטָב יִכָּנֵס הַחֵץ בִּי וְלֹא בִּבְנִי. אַף אֲנִי עָשִׂיתִי כֵן: "וַיִּסַּע מַלְאַךְ הָאֱלֹהִים וְגוֹ' וַיָּבֹא בֵּין מַחֲנֵה מִצְרַיִם" וְגוֹ' (לעיל יד, יט-כ), וְהָיוּ מִצְרַיִם זוֹרְקִים חִצִּים וְאַבְנֵי בַּלִיסְטְרָאוֹת וְהֶעָנָן מְקַבְּלָם:

וָאָבִא אֶתְכֶם אֵלָי. כְּתַרְגּוּמוֹ:

ה] וְעַתָּה. אִם עַתָּה תְּקַבְּלוּ עֲלֵיכֶם יֶעֱרַב לָכֶם מִכָּאן וְאֵילָךְ, שֶׁכָּל הַתְחָלוֹת קָשׁוֹת:

va'esa [meaning "lifted you up"] as *ve'attelit yatekhon*, meaning "I caused you to journey." This is poetic license on the part of the Targum, taken out of respect for God [since it would be awkward to state that God carried people Himself].

עַל־כַּנְפֵי נְשָׁרִים – *On eagles' wings*: I carried you in a manner similar to the eagle, which transports its eaglets on top of its wings. In contrast to all other bird species, which carry their chicks between their legs to protect them from birds of prey swooping down from above, the eagle fears no other bird. The only enemies which frighten her are human beings, who try to fell the bird by shooting arrows at it. Since no other bird can attack the eagle by flying higher, it reasons that it is better to position its young on top of its wings, believing: I would rather be shot by man's arrow than see my chicks so injured. So too did God behave [during the battle at the Sea of Reeds] as the verse states: *Then the angel of God who had been traveling ahead of the Israelite camp…came between the Egyptian and the Israelite camps* (14:19–20). In their efforts to attack Israel, the Egyptians shot arrows and catapulted stones in the direction of their former slaves. But God's protective cloud absorbed the missiles and spared the people from harm.

וָאָבִא אֶתְכֶם אֵלָי – *Brought you to Me*: This clause should be understood as the Targum translates it ["I have brought you near to My service"; the implication is that since God is transcendent, human beings cannot actually be close to Him].

5| **וְעַתָּה** – *Now*: If you now determine to accept My commandments, things will start to become sweeter for you. The start of any enterprise is difficult.

◀

faithfully heed My voice and keep My covenant, you will be
My treasure among all the peoples, although the whole earth
6 is Mine. A kingdom of priests and a holy nation you shall be
to Me. These are the words you must speak to the Israelites."
7 So Moshe came and summoned the elders of the people, and ḤAMISHI
8 set before them all that the Lord had commanded him. And
the people answered as one – "All that the Lord has spoken
we will do." Moshe brought their answer back to the Lord.
9 Then the Lord said to Moshe, "I will come to you in a dense
cloud, that the people may hear Me speaking to you. They will
then believe you forever." When Moshe reported the words of
10 the people to the Lord, the Lord said to Moshe, "Go to the
people and consecrate them today and tomorrow; let them

וּשְׁמַרְתֶּם אֶת־בְּרִיתִי. שֶׁאֶכְלֹת עִמָּכֶם עַל שְׁמִירַת הַתּוֹרָה:

וּשְׁמַרְתֶּם אֶת־בְּרִיתִי – *And keep my covenant*: The covenant that I will now establish with you concerning the observance of the Torah.

סְגֻלָּה. אוֹצָר חָבִיב, כְּמוֹ: "וּסְגֻלַּת מְלָכִים" (קהלת ב, ח), כְּלֵי יָקָר וַאֲבָנִים טוֹבוֹת שֶׁהַמְּלָכִים גּוֹנְזִים אוֹתָם, כָּךְ אַתֶּם לִי סְגֻלָּה מִשְּׁאָר אֻמּוֹת, וְלֹא תֹאמְרוּ, אַתֶּם לְבַדְּכֶם שֶׁלִּי וְאֵין לִי אֲחֵרִים עִמָּכֶם, וּמַה יֶּשׁ לִי עוֹד שֶׁאֶתְהַא חִבַּתְכֶם נִכֶּרֶת? – "כִּי לִי כָּל הָאָרֶץ", וְהֵם בְּעֵינַי וּלְפָנַי לִכְלוּם:

סְגֻלָּה – *Treasure*: You will be My precious treasure, as the verse states: *I gathered also silver and gold, and the treasure of kings* (Ecclesiastes 2:8) – referring to the expensive items and valuable gems that monarchs collect. That is what you will be like for Me – a people favored among all nations. Now lest you argue that Israel cannot be God's preferred nation since they are God's only possession – what else does God own that could give some basis for comparison? Recognize that in fact *the whole earth is Mine*, and still I hold a particular fondness for Israel beyond any other group.

ו| וְאַתֶּם תִּהְיוּ־לִי מַמְלֶכֶת כֹּהֲנִים. שָׂרִים, כְּמָה דְּאַתְּ חָמֵר: "וּבְנֵי דָוִד כֹּהֲנִים הָיוּ" (שמואל ב' ח, יח):

וְאַתֶּם תִּהְיוּ־לִי מַמְלֶכֶת כֹּהֲנִים |6 – *A kingdom of priests you shall be to Me*: The term *kohanim* [translated here as "priests"] in this instance means "rulers," as in the verse *The sons of David were ministers [kohanim] of state* (II Samuel 8:18).

אֵלֶּה הַדְּבָרִים. לֹא פָחוֹת וְלֹא יוֹתֵר:

אֵלֶּה הַדְּבָרִים – *These are the words*: No more and no less.

ח| וַיָּשֶׁב מֹשֶׁה אֶת־דִּבְרֵי הָעָם וְגו'. בְּיוֹם הַמָּחֳרָת שֶׁהוּא שְׁלִישִׁי, שֶׁהֲרֵי בְּהַשְׁכָּמָה עָלָה. וְכִי צָרִיךְ הָיָה מֹשֶׁה לְהָשִׁיב? אֶלָּא בָּא הַכָּתוּב לְלַמֶּדְךָ דֶּרֶךְ אֶרֶץ מִמֹּשֶׁה, שֶׁלֹּא אָמַר: הוֹאִיל וְיוֹדֵעַ מִי שֶׁשְּׁלָחַנִי, אֵינִי צָרִיךְ לְהָשִׁיב:

וַיָּשֶׁב מֹשֶׁה אֶת־דִּבְרֵי הָעָם |8 – *Moshe brought their answer back*: Moshe conveyed the people's response back to God on the third day. [After the nation said: *All that the Lord has spoken we will do* (19:8) on the second day, Moshe waited until the next day and] ascended to God early in the morning. Now why did Moshe have to inform God what the people said [if God is omniscient]? Moshe thereby teaches us appropriate manners,

◀

בְּקֹלִי וּשְׁמַרְתֶּם אֶת־בְּרִיתִי וִהְיִיתֶם לִי סְגֻלָּה מִכָּל־
הָעַמִּים כִּי־לִי כָּל־הָאָרֶץ: וְאַתֶּם תִּהְיוּ־לִי מַמְלֶכֶת טו
כֹּהֲנִים וְגוֹי קָדוֹשׁ אֵלֶּה הַדְּבָרִים אֲשֶׁר תְּדַבֵּר אֶל־
בְּנֵי יִשְׂרָאֵל: וַיָּבֹא מֹשֶׁה וַיִּקְרָא לְזִקְנֵי הָעָם וַיָּשֶׂם חמישי
לִפְנֵיהֶם אֵת כָּל־הַדְּבָרִים הָאֵלֶּה אֲשֶׁר צִוָּהוּ יְהוָה:
וַיַּעֲנוּ כָל־הָעָם יַחְדָּו וַיֹּאמְרוּ כֹּל אֲשֶׁר־דִּבֶּר יְהוָה
נַעֲשֶׂה וַיָּשֶׁב מֹשֶׁה אֶת־דִּבְרֵי הָעָם אֶל־יְהוָה: וַיֹּאמֶר
יְהוָה אֶל־מֹשֶׁה הִנֵּה אָנֹכִי בָּא אֵלֶיךָ בְּעַב הֶעָנָן
בַּעֲבוּר יִשְׁמַע הָעָם בְּדַבְּרִי עִמָּךְ וְגַם־בְּךָ יַאֲמִינוּ
לְעוֹלָם וַיַּגֵּד מֹשֶׁה אֶת־דִּבְרֵי הָעָם אֶל־יְהוָה: וַיֹּאמֶר
יְהוָה אֶל־מֹשֶׁה לֵךְ אֶל־הָעָם וְקִדַּשְׁתָּם הַיּוֹם וּמָחָר

ט | בְּעַב הֶעָנָן. בְּמַעֲבֶה הֶעָנָן, וְזֶהוּ עֲרָפֶל:

וְגַם־בְּךָ. גַּם בַּנְּבִיאִים הַבָּאִים אַחֲרֶיךָ:

וַיַּגֵּד מֹשֶׁה אֶת דִּבְרֵי וְגוֹ'. בַּיּוֹם הַמָּחֳרָת שֶׁהוּא רְבִיעִי לַחֹדֶשׁ:

אֶת־דִּבְרֵי הָעָם וְגוֹ'. תְּשׁוּבָה עַל דָּבָר זֶה שָׁמַעְתִּי מֵהֶם, שֶׁרְצוֹנָם לִשְׁמֹעַ מִמְּךָ, אֵינוֹ דוֹמֶה הַשּׁוֹמֵעַ מִפִּי שָׁלִיחַ לַשּׁוֹמֵעַ מִפִּי הַמֶּלֶךְ, רְצוֹנֵנוּ לִרְאוֹת אֶת מַלְכֵּנוּ:

י | וְקִדַּשְׁתָּם. וְזִמַּנְתָּם, שֶׁיָּכִינוּ עַצְמָם "הַיּוֹם וּמָחָר":

for he could have reasoned: Since the One who sent Me surely knows what the people said, I need not trouble to deliver the message myself.

9| בְּעַב הֶעָנָן – *In a dense cloud*: The phrase means "in a dense cloud," i.e., fog.

וְגַם־בְּךָ – *You*: [Literally, "also you." Rashi explains the word "also" – *gam*]. The nation will believe both in you and in the prophets who follow you.

וַיַּגֵּד מֹשֶׁה אֶת־דִּבְרֵי – *Moshe reported the words*: On the next day, the fourth of the month.

אֶת־דִּבְרֵי הָעָם – *The words of the people*: [God first offered to speak directly to the people. To this Moshe said:] I have heard from the people that they would prefer to hear the law from You. There is no comparison between receiving a communication firsthand from the king and hearing the declaration from His messenger. We desire to see our king.

10| וְקִדַּשְׁתָּם – *And consecrate them*: [Although the word literally means "to consecrate," here it more generally means to] prepare the people. Have them make themselves ready today and tomorrow.

◄

11 wash their clothes and be ready for the third day, for on that third day the Lᴏʀᴅ will descend on Mount Sinai before all
12 the peoples' eyes. Set a boundary for the people around the mountain; tell them to take care not to ascend to it, not even touch its edge. Anyone who touches the mountain must be
13 put to death. No hand shall touch him: he shall be stoned or shot with arrows; beast or man, he shall not live. When the ram's horn sounds a long blast – only then may they go up
14 on the mountain." So Moshe came down from the mountain to the people; he consecrated them and they cleansed their
15 clothes. "Be ready for the third day," he told them, "and do not

---

יא | וְהָיוּ נְכֹנִים. מְחֻשָּׁה:

לַיּוֹם הַשְּׁלִישִׁי. שֶׁהוּא שִׁשָּׁה בַּחֹדֶשׁ, וּבַחֲמִישִׁי בָּנָה מֹשֶׁה אֶת הַמִּזְבֵּחַ תַּחַת הָהָר וּשְׁתֵּים עֶשְׂרֵה מַצֵּבָה, כָּל הָעִנְיָן הָאָמוּר בְּפָרָשַׁת וְאֵלֶּה הַמִּשְׁפָּטִים (להלן פרק כד), וְאֵין מֻקְדָּם וּמְאֻחָר בַּתּוֹרָה:

לְעֵינֵי כָל־הָעָם. מְלַמֵּד שֶׁלֹּא הָיָה בָּהֶם סוּמָא, שֶׁנִּתְרַפְּאוּ כֻּלָּם:

יב | וְהִגְבַּלְתָּ. קְבַע לָהֶם תְּחוּמִין לְסִימָן, שֶׁלֹּא יִקְרְבוּ מִן הַגְּבוּל וָהָלְאָה:

לֵאמֹר. הַגְּבוּל אוֹמֵר לָהֶם: הִשָּׁמְרוּ מֵעֲלוֹת מִכָּאן וּלְהַלָּן, וְאַתָּה הַזְהִירֵם עַל כָּךְ:

וּנְגֹעַ בְּקָצֵהוּ. אֲפִלּוּ בְּקָצֵהוּ:

יג | יָרֹה יִיָּרֶה. מִכָּאן לַנִּסְקָלִין שֶׁהֵם נִדְחִין לְמַטָּה מִבֵּית הַסְּקִילָה, שֶׁהָיָה גָּבוֹהַּ שְׁתֵּי קוֹמוֹת:

יִיָּרֶה. יִשָּׁלַךְ לְמַטָּה לָאָרֶץ, כְּמוֹ "יָרָה בַיָּם" (לעיל טו, ד):

---

11 | וְהָיוּ נְכֹנִים – *And be ready*: [The men should separate themselves] from their wives [see 19:15].

לַיּוֹם הַשְּׁלִישִׁי – *For the third day*: The third day following the preparation would be the sixth of the month. On the fifth day, Moshe occupied himself with building an altar at the foot of the mountain and erecting the twelve monuments mentioned in Parashat Mishpatim (24:4). Those events occurred now, but the Torah does not insist on presenting events precisely in the sequence that they transpired.

לְעֵינֵי כָל־הָעָם – *Before all the peoples' eyes*: This verse proves that there were no blind individuals among the Israelites, for God had healed all those with impaired vision.

12 | וְהִגְבַּלְתָּ – *Set a boundary*: Mark off the area so that the people do not cross the line.

לֵאמֹר – *Tell them*: [Literally, "saying."] It is the boundary itself which will announce: Take care not to ascend the mountain at this point! You, Moshe, will warn them of the punishment.

וּנְגֹעַ בְּקָצֵהוּ – *Not even touch its edge*: [Literally, "nor touch its edge." Rashi explains that the prohibition is not of touching the edge specifically but any part of the mountain,] "even its edge."

13 | יָרֹה יִיָּרֶה – *Or shot with arrows*: [Rashi understands this term as meaning "or hurled down."] This verse teaches that when a court stones a criminal to death, he is first pushed off the roof of a two-story building.

יִיָּרֶה – *Shot*: [Differing from the translation here, Rashi holds that this term means] "hurled down to the ground." The

◀

יא וְכִבְּסוּ שִׂמְלֹתָם וְהָיוּ נְכֹנִים לַיּוֹם הַשְּׁלִישִׁי כִּי ׀
בַּיּוֹם הַשְּׁלִשִׁי יֵרֵד יְהוָה לְעֵינֵי כָל־הָעָם עַל־הַר
יב סִינָי: וְהִגְבַּלְתָּ אֶת־הָעָם סָבִיב לֵאמֹר הִשָּׁמְרוּ לָכֶם
עֲלוֹת בָּהָר וּנְגֹעַ בְּקָצֵהוּ כָּל־הַנֹּגֵעַ בָּהָר מוֹת יוּמָת:
יג לֹא־תִגַּע בּוֹ יָד כִּי־סָקוֹל יִסָּקֵל אוֹ־יָרֹה יִיָּרֶה אִם־
בְּהֵמָה אִם־אִישׁ לֹא יִחְיֶה בִּמְשֹׁךְ הַיֹּבֵל הֵמָּה
יד יַעֲלוּ בָהָר: וַיֵּרֶד מֹשֶׁה מִן־הָהָר אֶל־הָעָם וַיְקַדֵּשׁ
טו אֶת־הָעָם וַיְכַבְּסוּ שִׂמְלֹתָם: וַיֹּאמֶר אֶל־הָעָם הֱיוּ

verb is the same as that in the verse *He hurled [yara] into the sea* (15:4).

בִּמְשֹׁךְ הַיֹּבֵל – *When the ram's horn sounds a long blast*: When a long blast is heard from a ram's horn, that will signal that the Divine Presence has departed and that the voice of God has stopped speaking. Once I have departed from the mountain, the people will be allowed to ascend it.

הַיֹּבֵל – *The ram's horn*: A yovel is a ram's horn, for in Arabic a ram is referred to as a *yuvela* [see Rosh HaShana 26a]. The sound would be produced from the horn of the ram sacrificed in the episode of the binding of Yitzḥak [in Genesis 22].

14| מִן־הָהָר אֶל־הָעָם – *From the mountain to the people*: [Although the words "to the people" appear to be superfluous, in fact] they teach something: When Moshe descended from the mountain, he did not attend to his own business, but went immediately to the people in order to sanctify them.

15| הֱיוּ נְכֹנִים לִשְׁלֹשֶׁת יָמִים – *Be ready for the third day*: [Literally, "be ready for three days." Simply understood, this means:] "Be ready following three days of preparation," i.e., for the fourth day [in contrast to God's directive in verse 11 to prepare for the "third day"]. Moshe thus added an extra day of his own volition. Such is the opinion of Rabbi Yosei [who in the Talmud argues that revelation took place on the seventh day of the month]. But according to the opinion that the Ten Commandments were pronounced on the sixth day of the month, Moshe did not add an extra day to Israel's preparation. Rather, the phrase in our verse simply means "be ready for the third day."

בִּמְשֹׁךְ הַיֹּבֵל. כְּשֶׁיִּמְשֹׁךְ הַיּוֹבֵל קוֹל אָרֹךְ, הוּא סִימָן סִלּוּק שְׁכִינָה וְהַפְסָקַת הַקּוֹל, וְכֵיוָן שֶׁאֶסְתַּלֵּק הֵם רַשָּׁאִין לַעֲלוֹת:

הַיֹּבֵל. הוּא שׁוֹפָר שֶׁל אַיִל, שֶׁכֵּן בַּעֲרָבְיָא קוֹרִין לִדְכְרָא "יוּבְלָא". וְשׁוֹפָר שֶׁל אֵילוֹ שֶׁל יִצְחָק הָיָה:

יד| מִן־הָהָר אֶל־הָעָם. מְלַמֵּד שֶׁלֹּא הָיָה מֹשֶׁה פּוֹנֶה לַעֲסָקָיו, חֶלָּא מִן הָהָר אֶל הָעָם:

טו| הֱיוּ נְכֹנִים לִשְׁלֹשֶׁת יָמִים. לְסוֹף שְׁלֹשֶׁת יָמִים, הוּא יוֹם רְבִיעִי, שֶׁהוֹסִיף מֹשֶׁה יוֹם אֶחָד מִדַּעְתּוֹ, כְּדִבְרֵי רַבִּי יוֹסֵי. וּלְדִבְרֵי הָאוֹמֵר בְּשִׁשָּׁה בַּחֹדֶשׁ נִתְּנוּ עֲשֶׂרֶת הַדִּבְּרוֹת, לֹא הוֹסִיף מֹשֶׁה כְּלוּם, וְ"לִשְׁלֹשֶׁת יָמִים" כְּמוֹ 'לַיּוֹם הַשְּׁלִישִׁי':

16 draw close to your wives." The third day came; and that morning there was thunder and lightning and a dense cloud on the mountain and the sound of a ram's horn, intensely loud,
17 and all the people in the camp shook. Then Moshe led the people out of the camp to meet God, and they stood at the
18 foot of the mountain. Mount Sinai was enveloped in smoke because the LORD had descended on it in fire. Smoke billowed up from it as if from a furnace, and the mountain shook

אַל־תִּגְּשׁוּ אֶל־אִשָּׁה. כָּל שְׁלֹשֶׁת יָמִים הַלָּלוּ, כְּדֵי שֶׁיִּהְיוּ הַנָּשִׁים טוֹבְלוֹת לַיּוֹם הַשְּׁלִישִׁי וְיִהְיוּ טְהוֹרוֹת לְקַבֵּל תּוֹרָה, שֶׁאִם יִשְׁמְּשׁוּ תּוֹךְ שְׁלֹשָׁה שֶׁמָּא תִּפְלֹט הָאִשָּׁה שִׁכְבַת זֶרַע לְאַחַר טְבִילָתָהּ וְתַחֲזוֹר וְתִטָּמֵא, אֲבָל מִשֶּׁשָּׁהֲתָה שְׁלֹשָׁה יָמִים כְּבָר הַזֶּרַע מַסְרִיחַ וְאֵינוֹ רָאוּי לְהַזְרִיעַ, וְטָהוֹר מִלְּטַמֵּא אֶת הַפּוֹלֶטֶת:

טז| בִּהְיֹת הַבֹּקֶר. מְלַמֵּד שֶׁהִקְדִּים עַל יָדָם, מַה שֶּׁאֵין דֶּרֶךְ בָּשָׂר וָדָם לַעֲשׂוֹת כֵּן שֶׁיְּהֵא הָרַב מַמְתִּין לַתַּלְמִיד. וְכֵן מָצִינוּ בִּיחֶזְקֵאל: "קוּם צֵא אֶל הַבִּקְעָה... וָאָקוּם וָאֵצֵא אֶל הַבִּקְעָה וְהִנֵּה שָׁם כְּבוֹד ה' עֹמֵד" (יחזקאל ג, כב-כג):

יז| לִקְרַאת הָאֱלֹהִים. מַגִּיד שֶׁהַשְּׁכִינָה יוֹצְאָה לִקְרָאתָם כְּחָתָן הַיּוֹצֵא לִקְרַאת כַּלָּה, וְזֶהוּ שֶׁנֶּאֱמַר: "ה' מִסִּינַי בָּא" (דברים לג, ב) וְלֹא נֶאֱמַר: 'לְסִינַי בָּא':

בְּתַחְתִּית הָהָר. לְפִי פְּשׁוּטוֹ בְּרַגְלֵי הָהָר. וּמִדְרָשׁוֹ, שֶׁנִּתְלַשׁ הָהָר מִמְּקוֹמוֹ וְנִכְפָּה עֲלֵיהֶם כְּגִיגִית:

אַל־תִּגְּשׁוּ אֶל־אִשָּׁה – *Do not draw close to your wives*: Israel must separate from their wives during the three preparatory days, so that after three days the women may immerse and enter a state of purity before receiving the Torah. There was concern that if a couple were intimate during that period, the woman might expel residual semen after having immersed, which would make her impure again. However, if all women were to stay apart from their husbands for three days, any semen in their bodies from beforehand would surely have already putrefied and lost the ability to fertilize – and hence would no longer be impure – by the time of revelation.

16| בִּהְיֹת הַבֹּקֶר – *That morning*: We learn from this phrase that God arrived at the mountain before His audience did. This is never appropriate when a teacher addresses his students – it is most improper for a rabbi to have to sit and wait for his class. Yet we find a similar occurrence described elsewhere: *And the hand of the LORD was there upon me; and He said to me, Arise, go out into the plain, and I will talk with you there. Then I arose, and went out into the plain: and, behold, the glory of the LORD stood there, as the glory which I saw by the river Kevar: and I fell on my face* (Ezekiel 3:22–23).

17| לִקְרַאת הָאֱלֹהִים – *To meet God*: This phrase informs us that the Divine Presence went out to greet Israel like a groom hurries to receive his bride. This explains Moshe's later declaration: *The LORD came from Sinai* (Deuteronomy 33:2), for that verse does not say that God came to Sinai but from Sinai.

בְּתַחְתִּית הָהָר – *At the foot of the mountain*: [Alternatively, "under the mountain."] The straightforward meaning of this phrase is that Israel stood at the bottom of the hill. But the Midrash explains that God uprooted the mountain and held

◀

טו נְכֹנִים לִשְׁלֹשֶׁת יָמִים אַל־תִּגְּשׁוּ אֶל־אִשָּׁה: וַיְהִי
בַיּוֹם הַשְּׁלִישִׁי בִּהְיֹת הַבֹּקֶר וַיְהִי קֹלֹת וּבְרָקִים
וְעָנָן כָּבֵד עַל־הָהָר וְקֹל שֹׁפָר חָזָק מְאֹד וַיֶּחֱרַד כָּל־
יז הָעָם אֲשֶׁר בַּמַּחֲנֶה: וַיּוֹצֵא מֹשֶׁה אֶת־הָעָם לִקְרַאת
יח הָאֱלֹהִים מִן־הַמַּחֲנֶה וַיִּתְיַצְּבוּ בְּתַחְתִּית הָהָר: וְהַר
סִינַי עָשַׁן כֻּלּוֹ מִפְּנֵי אֲשֶׁר יָרַד עָלָיו יהוה בָּאֵשׁ וַיַּעַל

---

it above the Israelites' head like a barrel [threatening to destroy the people should they refuse to accept His Torah].

18 | עָשַׁן כֻּלּוֹ – *Was enveloped in smoke*: The word *ashan* ["smoke"] is not a noun in this verse, for the vowel beneath the letter *shin* is a *pataḥ*. Rather the term is a simple verb [literally, "smoked"], like the words *amar* ["said"], *shamar* ["guarded"], and *shama* ["heard"]. Hence the Targum renders this phrase *tanen kulleih* ["wholly smoked"] and not *tanna* [the noun "smoke"]. Elsewhere in Scripture, the term *ashan* is vocalized with a *kamatz*, since it is a noun.

הַכִּבְשָׁן – *A furnace*: A furnace made of lime. Now since the text uses this metaphor, we might have thought that the mountain burned just like a normal, everyday furnace. But a separate verse elaborates: *And you came near and stood under the mountain; and the mountain burned with fire to the heart of heaven* (Deuteronomy 4:11). Why then does our text employ the image of a furnace? To help the reader understand the event by appealing to our experience. We similarly read the verse: *They shall walk after the Lord, who shall roar like a lion* (Hosea 11:10). Is it not God himself who gives the lion the power to roar? And yet, the prophet is content to compare Him to a lion! Rather, Scripture uses imagery of God's own creatures to help us grasp what we essentially cannot know. Again, we find the verse: *And His voice was like the sound of many waters* (Ezekiel 43:2) – did God Himself not provide the waters with their sound? How does the text describe Him in terms of His creations, which are lesser than Him? This too is written to be accessible to our understanding.

יח| עָשַׁן כֻּלּוֹ. אֵין 'עָשַׁן' זֶה שֵׁם דָּבָר, שֶׁהֲרֵי נָקוּד הַשִּׁי"ן פַּתָּח, אֶלָּא לְשׁוֹן פָּעַל, כְּמוֹ אָמַר, שָׁמַר, שָׁמַע. לְכָךְ תַּרְגּוּמוֹ: "תְּנַן כֻּלֵּיהּ" וְלֹא תִרְגֵּם 'תְּנָנָא'. וְכָל 'עָשַׁן' שֶׁבַּמִּקְרָא נְקוּדִים קָמַץ, מִפְּנֵי שֶׁהֵם שֵׁם דָּבָר:

הַכִּבְשָׁן. שֶׁל סִיד. יָכוֹל כְּכִבְשָׁן זֶה וְלֹא יוֹתֵר? תַּלְמוּד לוֹמַר: "בֹּעֵר בָּאֵשׁ עַד לֵב הַשָּׁמַיִם" (דברים ד, יא). וּמַה תַּלְמוּד לוֹמַר: "כְּבִשְׁן"? לְשַׂבֵּר אֶת הָאֹזֶן מַה שֶּׁהִיא יְכוֹלָה לִשְׁמֹעַ, נוֹתֵן לַבְּרִיּוֹת סִימָן הַנִּכָּר לָהֶם. כַּיּוֹצֵא בּוֹ: "כְּאַרְיֵה יִשְׁאָג" (הושע יא, י) וְכִי מִי נָתַן כֹּחַ בָּאֲרִי אֶלָּא הוּא, וְהַכָּתוּב מוֹשְׁלוֹ כָּאַרְיֵה? אֶלָּא אָנוּ מְכַנִּין וּמְדַמִּין אוֹתוֹ לִבְרִיּוֹתָיו כְּדֵי לְשַׂבֵּר אֶת הָאֹזֶן מַה שֶּׁיְּכוֹלָה לִשְׁמֹעַ. כַּיּוֹצֵא בּוֹ: "יְקוֹלוֹ כְּקוֹל מַיִם רַבִּים" (יחזקאל מג, ב), וְכִי מִי נָתַן קוֹל לַמַּיִם אֶלָּא הוּא, וְאַתָּה מְכַנֶּה אוֹתוֹ לְדַמּוֹתוֹ לִבְרִיּוֹתָיו, כְּדֵי לְשַׂבֵּר אֶת הָאֹזֶן:

19 violently as one. As the sound of the ram's horn grew louder
and louder, Moshe spoke and God answered him aloud.
20 And the LORD descended on Mount Sinai, to the top of the   SHISHI
mountain, and called Moshe to the mountaintop, and Moshe
21 ascended. The LORD told Moshe, "Go back down – warn the
people not to force their way through to look at the LORD, or
22 many will die. Even priests who come near to the LORD must
first consecrate themselves, or the LORD will break out against

19| הוֹלֵךְ וְחָזֵק מְאֹד – *Grew louder and louder*: Normally, as a person continues to blow a horn, the sound becomes weaker and muted as the musician becomes winded. However, in this case, the sound grew increasingly stronger. And why did the tone start off softer and become louder? Because the people would not have been able to cope with such a powerful noise to begin with.

מֹשֶׁה יְדַבֵּר – *Moshe spoke*: The people heard only the first two commandments directly from God – *I am the LORD your God who brought you out of the land of Egypt, out of the house of slaves,* and *Have no other gods than Me* (20:2–3). The other statements were first conveyed to Moshe, who then repeated the information to the nation. Meanwhile, God amplified Moshe's voice when he addressed Israel so that everyone could hear him.

יַעֲנֶנּוּ בְקוֹל – *Answered him aloud*: The phrase means "answered him with a voice" [the letter *bet* prefixed to the word *vekol* means "with" or "by"]. We similarly find the verse *And the God that answers by fire [va'esh], let him be God* [I Kings 18:24; describing the demonstration on Mount Carmel], meaning that the God who answers by bringing down the fire.

20| וַיֵּרֶד יהוה עַל־הַר סִינַי – *And the LORD descended on Mount Sinai*: One might suppose that God actually came down onto the mountain, had not a different verse stated: *You yourselves have seen that I, from the heavens, have spoken to you* (20:19). How can we reconcile these two descriptions? By saying that God folded the upper and the lower heavens and spread them on the mountain like one would lay out a blanket on a bed. Thereupon the divine throne descended and rested upon these layers of sky.

יט עָשַׁן֙ כָּעֶ֣שֶׁן הַכִּבְשָׁ֔ן וַיֶּחֱרַ֥ד כָּל־הָהָ֖ר מְאֹֽד: וַיְהִי֙
קֹ֣ול הַשֹּׁפָ֔ר הוֹלֵ֖ךְ וְחָזֵ֣ק מְאֹ֑ד מֹשֶׁ֣ה יְדַבֵּ֔ר וְהָאֱלֹהִ֖ים
כ יַעֲנֶ֥נּוּ בְקֽוֹל: וַיֵּ֧רֶד יְהֹוָ֛ה עַל־הַ֥ר סִינַ֖י אֶל־רֹ֣אשׁ הָהָ֑ר
וַיִּקְרָ֨א יְהֹוָ֧ה לְמֹשֶׁ֛ה אֶל־רֹ֥אשׁ הָהָ֖ר וַיַּ֥עַל מֹשֶֽׁה:
כא וַיֹּ֤אמֶר יְהֹוָה֙ אֶל־מֹשֶׁ֔ה רֵ֖ד הָעֵ֣ד בָּעָ֑ם פֶּן־יֶהֶרְס֤וּ
כב אֶל־יְהֹוָה֙ לִרְא֔וֹת וְנָפַ֥ל מִמֶּ֖נּוּ רָֽב: וְגַ֧ם הַכֹּהֲנִ֛ים
הַנִּגָּשִׁ֥ים אֶל־יְהֹוָ֖ה יִתְקַדָּ֑שׁוּ פֶּן־יִפְרֹ֥ץ בָּהֶ֖ם יְהֹוָֽה:

שני

שלישי

כא| **הָעֵ֣ד בָּעָ֑ם.** הַתְרֵה בָּהֶם שֶׁלֹּא
לַעֲלוֹת בָּהָר:

פֶּן־יֶהֶרְסוּ וְגו'. שֶׁלֹּא יֶהֶרְסוּ אֶת
מַצָּבָם עַל יְדֵי שֶׁתַּאֲוָתָם "אֶל ה'
לִרְאוֹת" וְיִקְרְבוּ לְצַד הָהָר:

וְנָפַל מִמֶּנּוּ רָב. כָּל מַה שֶׁיִּפֹּל מֵהֶם,
וַאֲפִלּוּ הוּא יְחִידִי, חָשׁוּב לְפָנַי רָב:

פֶּן־יֶהֶרְסוּ. כָּל הֲרִיסָה מַפְרֶדֶת
אֲסִיפַת הַבִּנְיָן, אַף הַנִּפְרָדִין מִמַּעֲמַד
אֲנָשִׁים הוֹלְכִים אֵת הַמַּעֲמָד:

כב| **וְגַם הַכֹּהֲנִים.** אַף הַבְּכוֹרוֹת
שֶׁהָעֲבוֹדָה בָּהֶם:

הַנִּגָּשִׁים אֶל־יְהֹוָה. לְהַקְרִיב
קָרְבָּנוֹת, אַף הֵם אַל יִסְמְכוּ עַל
חֲשִׁיבוּתָם לַעֲלוֹת:

יִתְקַדָּשׁוּ. יִהְיוּ מְזֻמָּנִים לְהִתְיַצֵּב עַל
עָמְדָּן:

פֶּן־יִפְרֹץ. לְשׁוֹן פִּרְצָה, יַהֲרֹג בָּהֶם
וְיַעֲשֶׂה בָּהֶם פִּרְצָה:

21| הָעֵד בָּעָם – *Warn the people:* Caution Israel not to climb up the mountain.

פֶּן־יֶהֶרְסוּ – *Not to force their way:* [Literally, "lest they destroy."] Rashi explains the sense of the verb:] Lest they impair their position by approaching the mountain through their desire to "look at the Lord."

וְנָפַל מִמֶּנּוּ רָב – *Or many will die:* Even if only a single person should die due to such an infraction, I deem it to be too many.

פֶּן־יֶהֶרְסוּ – *Not to force their way:* Scripture uses the term *harisa* in the sense of disassembling component parts of a structure. Here too, the verb connotes that violators will upset the cohesion of the nation.

22| וְגַם הַכֹּהֲנִים – *Even priests:* This refers to the firstborn sons of Israel, who were initially charged with performing the sacrificial service [before being replaced by the sons of Aharon and the Levites; see Numbers 3:12].

הַנִּגָּשִׁים אֶל־יְהֹוָה – *Who come near to the Lord:* Even priests, who generally are permitted to approach God for the sake of offering sacrifices, must not trust in their status and ascend the mountain.

יִתְקַדָּשׁוּ – *Must first consecrate themselves:* The priests should prepare themselves to take up their positions.

פֶּן־יִפְרֹץ – *Will break out:* The verb means "to breach" – God might kill some of them and create a gap in the nation.

23 them." Moshe replied to the LORD, "The people cannot climb
Mount Sinai. You Yourself warned us to set a boundary
24 around the mountain and consecrate it." The LORD said to
him, "Go down, and come back together with Aharon. But do
not let the priests or people force their way through to come
25 up to the LORD, or He will break out against them." So Moshe
20 1 went down to the people and told them.   Then God
2 spoke all these words: "I am the LORD your God
who brought you out of the land of Egypt, out of the house of

כג| **לֹא־יוּכַל הָעָם.** אֵינִי צָרִיךְ
לְהָעִיד בָּהֶם, שֶׁהֲרֵי מֻתְרִין וְעוֹמְדִין
הֵם הַיּוֹם שְׁלֹשָׁה יָמִים, וְלֹא יוּכְלוּ
לַעֲלוֹת, שֶׁאֵין לָהֶם רְשׁוּת:

כד| **לֶךְ־רֵד.** וְהָעֵד בָּהֶם שְׁנִיָּה,
שֶׁמַּזְהִירִין אֶת הָאָדָם קֹדֶם מַעֲשֶׂה
וְחוֹזְרִין וּמַזְהִירִין אוֹתוֹ בִּשְׁעַת מַעֲשֶׂה:

וְעָלִיתָ אַתָּה וְאַהֲרֹן עִמָּךְ וְהַכֹּהֲנִים.
יָכוֹל אַף הֵם "עִמָּךְ"? תַּלְמוּד
לוֹמַר: "וְעָלִיתָ אַתָּה". אֱמֹר מֵעַתָּה,
אַתָּה מְחִצָּה לְעַצְמְךָ, וְאַהֲרֹן מְחִצָּה
לְעַצְמוֹ; מֹשֶׁה נִגַּשׁ יוֹתֵר מֵאַהֲרֹן
וְאַהֲרֹן יוֹתֵר מִן הַכֹּהֲנִים, "וְהָעָם"
כָּל עִקָּר "אַל יֶהֶרְסוּ" אֶת מַצָּבָם
"לַעֲלֹת אֶל ה'":

פֶּן־יִפְרָץ־בָּם. אַף עַל פִּי שֶׁהוּא
נָקוּד חֲטַף קָמָץ אֵינוֹ זָז מִגִּזְרָתוֹ. כָּךְ
דַּרְכָּהּ כָּל תֵּבָה שֶׁנְּקֻדָּתָהּ מְלֹאפֻם,
כְּשֶׁהִיא סְמוּכָה בְּמַקָּף מִשְׁתַּנֶּה
הַנִּקּוּד לַחֲטַף קָמָץ:

כה| **וַיֹּאמֶר אֲלֵהֶם.** הַתְרָאָה זוֹ:

23| **לֹא־יוּכַל הָעָם** – *The people cannot:* Moshe assured God that
he need not warn the nation again, for they had remained on
notice for three days and would not ascend the mountain
without permission.

24| **לֶךְ־רֵד** – *Go down:* God instructed Moshe to return to the
people and to warn them a second time, for it is advisable to
caution a person in advance and then once again when the
warning becomes applicable.

וְעָלִיתָ אַתָּה וְאַהֲרֹן עִמָּךְ וְהַכֹּהֲנִים – *And come back together with
Aharon, but the priests:* [Literally, "and you come back, etc."]
Lest Moshe err and think that Aharon and the priests were to
stand on the mountain together with him, God emphasized
the word "you." Moshe was to position himself at his own
designated spot on the mountain, Aharon at his specific place,
and the priests at theirs. And so, Moshe penetrated further into
the cloud than did Aharon, who in turn proceeded beyond the
limit set for the priests. The rest of the nation was not permitted to ruin the satiation by "forcing their way through" even a
bit "to come up to the LORD."

פֶּן־יִפְרָץ־בָּם – *Or He will break out against them:* Even though
this word features a *kamatz katan*, the word *yifrotz* has exactly
the same meaning as if it had been written with a *ḥolam* [Both
vowels are transliterated *o* here. The alternative spelling of this
word appears in verse 22.] For indeed, whenever a word that is
vocalized with a *ḥolam* is followed by a *makaf* [similar to a hy-
phen, as in our verse], the *ḥolam* changes into a *kamatz katan*.

25| **וַיֹּאמֶר אֲלֵהֶם** – *And told them:* He repeated the warning
as instructed.

כג וַיֹּאמֶר מֹשֶׁה אֶל־יהוה לֹא־יוּכַל הָעָם לַעֲלֹת אֶל־הַר
סִינָי כִּי־אַתָּה הַעֵדֹתָה בָּנוּ לֵאמֹר הַגְבֵּל אֶת־הָהָר
כד וְקִדַּשְׁתּוֹ: וַיֹּאמֶר אֵלָיו יהוה לֶךְ־רֵד וְעָלִיתָ אַתָּה
וְאַהֲרֹן עִמָּךְ וְהַכֹּהֲנִים וְהָעָם אַל־יֶהֶרְסוּ לַעֲלֹת אֶל־
כה יהוה פֶּן־יִפְרָץ־בָּם: וַיֵּרֶד מֹשֶׁה אֶל־הָעָם וַיֹּאמֶר
כ א אֲלֵהֶם: וַיְדַבֵּר אֱלֹהִים אֵת כָּל־הַדְּבָרִים
ב הָאֵלֶּה לֵאמֹר: אָנֹכִי יהוה אֱלֹהֶיךָ אֲשֶׁר

Hebrew Rashi column:

כ א| וַיְדַבֵּר אֱלֹהִים. אֵין "אֱלֹהִים" אֶלָּא דַיָּן, לְפִי שֶׁיֵּשׁ פָּרָשִׁיּוֹת בַּתּוֹרָה שֶׁאִם עֲשָׂאָן אָדָם מְקַבֵּל שָׂכָר וְאִם לָאו אֵינוֹ מְקַבֵּל עֲלֵיהֶם פֻּרְעָנִית, יָכוֹל אַף עֲשֶׂרֶת הַדִּבְּרוֹת כֵּן? תַּלְמוּד לוֹמַר: "וַיְדַבֵּר אֱלֹהִים", דַּיָּן לִפָּרַע:

אֵת כָּל־הַדְּבָרִים הָאֵלֶּה. מְלַמֵּד שֶׁאָמַר הַקָּדוֹשׁ בָּרוּךְ הוּא עֲשֶׂרֶת הַדִּבְּרוֹת בְּדִבּוּר אֶחָד, מַה שֶּׁאִי אֶפְשָׁר לְאָדָם לוֹמַר כֵּן. אִם כֵּן מַה תַּלְמוּד לוֹמַר עוֹד "אָנֹכִי" וְ"לֹא יִהְיֶה לְךָ"? שֶׁחָזַר וּפֵרֵשׁ עַל כָּל דִּבּוּר וְדִבּוּר בִּפְנֵי עַצְמוֹ:

לֵאמֹר. מְלַמֵּד שֶׁהָיוּ עוֹנִין עַל הֵן - הֵן, וְעַל לָאו - לָאו:

ב| אֲשֶׁר הוֹצֵאתִיךָ מֵאֶרֶץ מִצְרָיִם. כְּדַאי הִיא הַהוֹצָאָה שֶׁתִּהְיוּ מְשֻׁעְבָּדִים לִי. דָּבָר אַחֵר, לְפִי שֶׁנִּגְלָה בַּיָּם כְּגִבּוֹר מִלְחָמָה וְנִגְלָה כָּאן כְּזָקֵן מָלֵא רַחֲמִים, שֶׁנֶּאֱמַר: "וְתַחַת רַגְלָיו כְּמַעֲשֵׂה לִבְנַת הַסַּפִּיר" (להלן כד, י), זוֹ הָיְתָה לְפָנָיו

English commentary column:

20 1| וַיְדַבֵּר אֱלֹהִים – *Then God spoke*: Throughout Scripture, the term "God" [*Elohim*] means "judge." Sometimes, the Torah discusses actions that merit reward should a person perform them, but which incur no punishment if ignored. Lest one think that the Ten Commandments fall into such a category, straightaway the Torah states: *Then God spoke* – implying that retribution will attend violation of these laws, since God is a judge who punishes.

אֵת כָּל־הַדְּבָרִים הָאֵלֶּה – *All these words*: The addition of the word "all" [*kol*] teaches that God spoke all Ten Commandments in a single utterance, a feat of which the human mouth is incapable. But if that were so, why does the text proceed to record the separate statements, *I am the Lord your God, Have no other gods etc.* (20:2–14)? After enunciating the entire text simultaneously, God repeated the material sentence by sentence.

לֵאמֹר – *Saying*: [The term *lemor* – literally, "to say," and untranslated in this edition – can be understood as a directive to the listener to repeat what is being said. Rashi explains:] The word *lemor* teaches that after every positive commandment Israel responded "yes," and "no" after every negative commandment.

2| אֲשֶׁר הוֹצֵאתִיךָ מֵאֶרֶץ מִצְרָיִם – *Who brought you out of the land of Egypt*: My saving you from Egypt is reason enough for you to serve Me. Another interpretation [for God's mention of the exodus here]: At the Sea of Reeds, God revealed Himself to the people as a fierce warrior, whereas here He appeared to them as a compassionate elder [and so this was a reminder that it was the same God speaking]. Hence the later verse, *They saw a vision of the God of Israel, and beneath His feet what looked*

³
⁴ slaves. Have no other gods than Me. Do not make for yourself any carved image or likeness of any creature in the heavens
⁵ above or the earth beneath or the water beneath the earth. Do not bow down to them or worship them, for I the Lord your God demand absolute loyalty. For those who hate Me, I hold

like a lapis lazuli pavement (24:10), a description that on the one hand recalls the Israelites' slavery [when the unfortunates were forced to build and pave cities], but which also continues: *As clear as the sky itself*, reflecting the nation's redemption. Now God cautioned the people: Just because I manifest Myself before you with different attributes, dare not infer from that that there exist multiple gods in the world! Rather, I am the same *Lord your God who brought you out of the land of Egypt*, and the very God who acted on your behalf at the sea. Another interpretation for this verse: During the experience of revelation, Israel heard multiple sounds, as the verse states: *Every one of the people witnessed the thunder [or "sounds" – kolot]* (20:15), which arrived from the four corners of the world and the heavens. There was a danger that the people might conclude they were hearing the voices of many deities [hence, God affirms that He is the only speaker]. Now why does God use the term "your God" [*Elohekha*, as if spoken to an individual rather than to a group]? God expressed Himself this way so as to provide Moshe with an argument in Israel's defense later, when the nation creates the golden calf. When Moshe says to God: *Why, O Lord, unleash Your anger against Your people* (32:11), he meant: "You did not command all of them: 'You shall have no other gods than Me.' Rather, when You delivered the Ten Commandments, You were speaking to me alone."

מִבֵּית עֲבָדִים – *Out of the house of slaves*: I removed you from Pharaoh's house, where you toiled as his slaves. You might think that the phrase "house of slaves" indicates that the Israelites worked as slaves in the homes of other slaves. However, a later verse states: *He redeemed you from the house of slaves, from the grip of Pharaoh, king of Egypt* (Deuteronomy 7:8), which demonstrates that the Hebrews were the king's slaves and not servants' slaves.

3| **לֹא־יִהְיֶה לְךָ** – *Have no*: Why is this phrase used? Since the subsequent verse states: *Do not make for yourself any carved image etc.* (20:4), we might have thought that it is merely the

בִּשְׁעַת הַשִּׁעְבּוּד, "וּכְעֶצֶם הַשָּׁמַיִם" (שם) מְשֶׁנְּגְאֲלוּ. הוֹאִיל וַאֲנִי מִשְׁתַּנֶּה בְּמַרְאוֹת, אַל תֹּאמְרוּ שְׁתֵּי רָשֻׁיּוֹת הֵן! אָנֹכִי הוּא אֲשֶׁר הוֹצֵאתִיךָ מִמִּצְרַיִם וְעַל הַיָּם. דָּבָר אַחֵר, לְפִי שֶׁהָיוּ שׁוֹמְעִין קוֹלוֹת הַרְבֵּה, שֶׁנֶּאֱמַר "אֶת הַקּוֹלֹת" (להלן פסוק טו), קוֹלוֹת בָּאִין מֵאַרְבַּע רוּחוֹת וּמִן הַשָּׁמַיִם וּמִן הָאָרֶץ, אַל תֹּאמְרוּ רָשֻׁיּוֹת הַרְבֵּה הֵן! וְלָמָּה אָמַר לְשׁוֹן יָחִיד, "אֱלֹהֶיךָ"? לִתֵּן פִּתְחוֹן פֶּה לְמֹשֶׁה לְלַמֵּד סַנֵּגוֹרְיָא בְּמַעֲשֵׂה הָעֵגֶל, וְזֶה הוּא שֶׁאָמַר: "לָמָּה ה' יֶחֱרֶה אַפְּךָ בְּעַמֶּךָ" (להלן לב, יא), לֹא לָהֶם צִוִּיתָ "לֹא יִהְיֶה לָכֶם אֱלֹהִים אֲחֵרִים", אֶלָּא לִי לְבַדִּי:

מִבֵּית עֲבָדִים. מִבֵּית פַּרְעֹה שֶׁהֱיִיתֶם עֲבָדִים לוֹ. אוֹ אֵינוֹ אוֹמֵר אֶלָּא "מִבֵּית עֲבָדִים" שֶׁהָיוּ עֲבָדִים לַעֲבָדִים? תַּלְמוּד לוֹמַר: "וַיִּפְדְּךָ מִבֵּית עֲבָדִים מִיַּד פַּרְעֹה מֶלֶךְ מִצְרַיִם" (דברים ז, ח), אֱמֹר מֵעַתָּה, עֲבָדִים לַמֶּלֶךְ הָיוּ וְלֹא עֲבָדִים לַעֲבָדִים:

ג| **לֹא־יִהְיֶה לְךָ.** לָמָּה נֶאֱמַר? לְפִי שֶׁנֶּאֱמַר: "לֹא תַעֲשֶׂה לְךָ", אֵין לִי אֶלָּא שֶׁלֹּא יַעֲשֶׂה, הֶעָשׂוּי כְּבָר מִנַּיִן

ג הוֹצֵאתִ֛יךָ מֵאֶ֥רֶץ מִצְרַ֖יִם מִבֵּ֣ית עֲבָדִֽים: לֹֽא־יִהְיֶ֥ה
ד לְךָ֛ אֱלֹהִ֥ים אֲחֵרִ֖ים עַל־פָּנָֽי: לֹֽא־תַעֲשֶׂ֨ה לְךָ֥ פֶ֣סֶל֙
וְכָל־תְּמוּנָ֡ה אֲשֶׁ֣ר בַּשָּׁמַ֣יִם מִמַּ֗עַל וַֽאֲשֶׁ֤ר בָּאָ֨רֶץ֙
ה מִתַּ֔חַת וַֽאֲשֶׁ֥ר בַּמַּ֖יִם מִתַּ֥חַת לָאָֽרֶץ: לֹֽא־תִשְׁתַּחֲוֶ֤ה
לָהֶם֙ וְלֹ֣א תָֽעָבְדֵ֔ם כִּ֣י אָֽנֹכִ֞י יְהֹוָ֤ה אֱלֹהֶ֨יךָ֙ אֵ֣ל קַנָּ֔א

English column:

act of creating the idol which is prohibited. How would we know that we may not possess such items that have been fashioned by other people? Therefore the verse states: *Have no other gods than Me.*

אֱלֹהִ֥ים אֲחֵרִ֖ים – *Other gods:* They are not actually "gods"; rather, "others" have simply crafted them and turned them into objects of belief. [Hence the phrase should properly be translated "gods of others."] It is impossible to explain this phrase as actually meaning "other gods" for it would be disgraceful to equate false deities to God, and to categorize them all as divinities. Another interpretation for this phrase: "gods which are foreign" to their worshippers. For these mistaken people pray to their false gods and are ignored. Their deities thereby give the impression that their followers are strangers [aherim] to them, whom they have never met.

עַל־פָּנָֽי – *Other than Me:* [Literally, "before Me."] You may never worship other gods, as long as I exist [i.e., ever]. It was necessary to include this detail, lest future Jews argue that only the first generation of Israelites, whom God "brought out of the land of Egypt," (20:2) were required to abide by this rule.

4| **פֶ֣סֶל** – *Any carved image:* A statue [*pesel*] is so called because it has been carved [*nifsal*] from wood or stone to resemble something that is *in the heavens, etc.*

5| **אֵ֣ל קַנָּ֔א** – *Demand absolute loyalty:* [Literally, "am a jealous God."]: God will act zealously to punish idolaters, and He will act mercifully to forgive those who worship false gods. The term *kana* is equivalent to the Old French word *emportment*, that is, a determination to punish.

לְשׂנְאָי – *For those who hate Me:* This verse should be understood as the Targum renders it: [God will *hold the descendants to account for the sins of the fathers* only] "when the children

---

Hebrew Rashi column:

שֶׁלֹּא יְקַיֵּם? תַּלְמוּד לוֹמַר: "לֹא יִהְיֶה לְךָ":

אֱלֹהִים אֲחֵרִים. שֶׁאֵינָן אֱלֹהוּת, אֶלָּא אֲחֵרִים עֲשָׂאוּם אֱלֹהִים עֲלֵיהֶם. וְלֹא יִתָּכֵן לְפָרֵשׁ "אֱלֹהִים אֲחֵרִים" זוּלָתִי, שֶׁגְּנַאי הוּא כְּלַפֵּי מַעֲלָה לִקְרוֹתָם אֱלֹהוּת אֶצְלוֹ. דָּבָר אַחֵר, "אֱלֹהִים אֲחֵרִים", שֶׁהֵם אֲחֵרִים לְעוֹבְדֵיהֶם, צוֹעֲקִים אֲלֵיהֶם וְאֵינָן עוֹנִין אוֹתָם, וְדוֹמֶה כְּאִלּוּ הוּא אַחֵר שֶׁאֵינוֹ מַכִּירוֹ מֵעוֹלָם:

עַל־פָּנָי. כָּל זְמַן שֶׁאֲנִי קַיָּם, שֶׁלֹּא תֹאמַר, לֹא נִצְטַוּוּ עַל עֲבוֹדָה זָרָה אֶלָּא אוֹתוֹ הַדּוֹר:

ד| **פֶּסֶל.** עַל שֵׁם שֶׁנִּפְסָל כָּל תְּמוּנַת דָּבָר "אֲשֶׁר בַּשָּׁמַיִם" וְגוֹ':

ה| **אֵל קַנָּא.** מְקַנֵּא לִפָּרַע וְאֵינוֹ עוֹבֵר עַל מִדָּתוֹ לִמְחוֹל עַל עֲבוֹדָה זָרָה. כָּל לְשׁוֹן "קַנָּא" אנ״פרדמנ״ט בְּלַעַז, נוֹתֵן לֵב לִפָּרַע:

לְשׂנְאָי. כְּתַרְגּוּמוֹ, כְּשֶׁאוֹחֲזִין מַעֲשֵׂה אֲבוֹתֵיהֶם בִּידֵיהֶם. וְאוֹמֵר חֶסֶד שֶׁאָדָם עוֹשֶׂה, לְשַׁלֵּם שָׂכָר עַד לַאֲלָפִים דּוֹר.

the descendants to account for the sins of the fathers to the
6 third and fourth generation, but to those who love Me and
keep My commands – I shall act with faithful love for thou-
7 sands.   Do not speak the name of the LORD your
God in vain, for the LORD will not hold guiltless those who
speak His name in vain.
8
9 Remember the Sabbath to keep it holy. Six days you shall work,
10 and carry out all your labors, but the seventh is a Sabbath to the
LORD your God. On it, do no work – neither you, nor your son

נְמַצֵאת מִדָּה טוֹבָה יְתֵרָה עַל מִדַּת
פֻּרְעָנוּת אַחַת עַל חֲמֵשׁ מֵאוֹת, שֶׁזוֹ
לְאַרְבָּעָה דוֹרוֹת וְזוֹ לַאֲלָפִים:

persist in sinning as their parents did." God rewards for two
thousand generations the kindnesses that people perform.
What emerges is that God bestows goodness at a ratio that is
five hundred times greater than the amount of punishment He
dispenses. For up to two thousand generations of descendants
enjoy the benefits of good deeds, whereas only four generations suffer the effects of wickedness.

ז| לַשָּׁוְא. חִנָּם, לַהֶבֶל. וְאֵי זֶהוּ
שְׁבוּעַת שָׁוְא? נִשְׁבַּע לְשַׁנּוֹת אֶת
הַיָּדוּעַ, עַל עַמּוּד שֶׁל אֶבֶן שֶׁהוּא
שֶׁל זָהָב:

7| לַשָּׁוְא – In vain: The word means "for no purpose," or "in
vain." What constitutes an oath taken in vain? That is when
somebody swears contrary to what everybody knows – for
example, if using the name of God a person insists that a stone
pillar is really made of gold.

ח| זָכוֹר. "זָכוֹר" וְ"שָׁמוֹר" בְּדִבּוּר
אֶחָד נֶאֶמְרוּ. וְכֵן: "מְחַלְלֶיהָ מוֹת
יוּמָת" (להלן לא, יד), "וּבְיוֹם הַשַּׁבָּת שְׁנֵי
כְבָשִׂים" (במדבר כח, ט), וְכֵן: "לֹא תִלְבַּשׁ
שַׁעַטְנֵז", "גְּדִלִים תַּעֲשֶׂה לָּךְ" (דברים
כב, יא-יב), וְכֵן: "עֶרְוַת אֵשֶׁת אָחִיךָ"
(ויקרא יח, טז), "יְבָמָהּ יָבֹא עָלֶיהָ" (דברים
כה, ה); הוּא שֶׁנֶּאֱמַר: "אַחַת דִּבֶּר
אֱלֹהִים שְׁתַּיִם זוּ שָׁמָעְתִּי" (תהלים סב,
יב). "זָכוֹר" לְשׁוֹן פָּעוֹל הוּא, כְּמוֹ:
"אָכוֹל וְשָׁתוֹ" (ישעיה כב, יג), "הָלוֹךְ
וּבָכֹה" (שמואל ב' ג, טז), וְכֵן פִּתְרוֹנוֹ:
תְּנוּ לֵב לִזְכֹּר תָּמִיד אֶת יוֹם הַשַּׁבָּת,
שֶׁאִם נִזְדַּמֵּן לְךָ חֵפֶץ יָפֶה תְּהֵא
מַזְמִינוֹ לַשַּׁבָּת:

8| זָכוֹר – Remember: God uttered simultaneously the comple-
mentary statements Remember the Sabbath to keep it holy
and Guard the Sabbath day to keep it holy (Deuteronomy 5:12).
As well, the Torah contains several pairs of commandments
which seem to contradict each other [and yet, God communicated both instructions]. For example, one verse states:
Keep the Sabbath, for it is holy to you. Whoever profanes it shall
be put to death (Exodus 31:14), and yet the generally prohibited
labor of slaughtering is demanded by another verse: And on
the Sabbath day two lambs of the first year without blemish....
This is the burnt offering of every Sabbath (Numbers 28:9). In a
second case, the Torah first warns: You shall not wear a garment
of diverse kinds, of wool and linen together (Deuteronomy 22:11),
but that is quickly followed by the statement: You shall make
you fringes upon the four corners of your covering [Deuteronomy
22:12; according to tradition, it is permitted to tie a wool fringe
onto a linen garment]. Finally, the Torah warns: You shall not
uncover the nakedness of your brother's wife (Leviticus 18:16),
but later seems to contradict that by ordering: If brothers dwell
together, and one of them die, and have no child, the wife of the

◀

פֹּקֵד עֲוֹן אָבֹת עַל־בָּנִים עַל־שִׁלֵּשִׁים וְעַל־רִבֵּעִים
לְשֹׂנְאָי: וְעֹשֶׂה חֶסֶד לַאֲלָפִים לְאֹהֲבַי וּלְשֹׁמְרֵי
מִצְוֹתָי: ס   לֹא תִשָּׂא אֶת־שֵׁם־יהוה אֱלֹהֶיךָ
לַשָּׁוְא כִּי לֹא יְנַקֶּה יהוה אֵת אֲשֶׁר־יִשָּׂא אֶת־שְׁמוֹ
לַשָּׁוְא: ס
זָכוֹר אֶת־יוֹם הַשַּׁבָּת לְקַדְּשׁוֹ: שֵׁשֶׁת יָמִים תַּעֲבֹד
וְעָשִׂיתָ כָּל־מְלַאכְתֶּךָ: וְיוֹם הַשְּׁבִיעִי שַׁבָּת לַיהוה
אֱלֹהֶיךָ לֹא־תַעֲשֶׂה כָל־מְלָאכָה אַתָּה וּבִנְךָ וּבִתֶּךָ

dead shall not marry abroad to a stranger: her husband's brother shall go in to her, and take her to him to wife (Deuteronomy 25:5). All of these cases should be understood within the framework of the verse, *God has spoken once: twice I have heard this* (Psalms 62:12). Now the verb *zakhor* represents the infinitive absolute functioning as an imperative. Similar constructions appear in the verses, *Let us eat [akhol] and drink [veshato] for tomorrow we shall die* (Isaiah 22:13); *And her husband went along [halokh] with her weeping [uvakho] behind her* (II Samuel 3:16). In our verse the term *zakhor* means: Pay attention to always have the Sabbath on your mind, even during the week. If you perchance come across a choice food in the market – buy it in anticipation of your Sabbath meal.

9| וְעָשִׂיתָ כָּל־מְלַאכְתֶּךָ – *And carry out all your labors*: When the Sabbath begins, imagine that you really have finished all of your labors [thus driving them from your thoughts].

10| אַתָּה וּבִנְךָ וּבִתֶּךָ – *Neither you, nor your son or daughter*: Prevent your young ones from performing labors on the Sabbath. But is it not possible that the text refers to adult children? No, since the verse has already warned them how to behave on the holy day [that is, the opening word "you" is directed at all adults]. Rather, the text proceeds to caution parents – they must also guide their youngsters to avoid forbidden actions. Hence the Talmud teaches (Shabbat 121a): If a minor attempts to extinguish a candle on the Sabbath, he must be stopped, since adults must ensure that their children "rest" on the Sabbath too.

ט| וְעָשִׂיתָ כָּל־מְלַאכְתֶּךָ. כְּשֶׁתָּבוֹא שַׁבָּת יְהֵא בְּעֵינֶיךָ כְּאִלּוּ כָּל מְלַאכְתֶּךָ עֲשׂוּיָה, שֶׁלֹּא תְהַרְהֵר אַחַר מְלָאכָה:

י| אַתָּה וּבִנְךָ וּבִתֶּךָ. אֵלּוּ קְטַנִּים. אוֹ אֵינוֹ אֶלָּא גְדוֹלִים? אָמַרְתָּ, הֲרֵי כְבָר מֻזְהָרִין הֵם, אֶלָּא לֹא בָּא אֶלָּא לְהַזְהִיר הַגְּדוֹלִים עַל שְׁבִיתַת הַקְּטַנִּים, וְזֶהוּ שֶׁשָּׁנִינוּ: קָטָן שֶׁבָּא לְכַבּוֹת אֵין שׁוֹמְעִין לוֹ, מִפְּנֵי שֶׁשְּׁבִיתָתוֹ עָלֶיךָ:

or daughter, your male or female servant, your livestock, or the
11 migrant within your gates. For in six days the LORD made heaven and earth, the sea, and all that they contain, and He rested
on the seventh day. And so the LORD blessed the Sabbath day
12 and made it holy.　　　　　　　Honor your father and mother.
Then you will live long in the land that the LORD your God is
13 giving you.　　　Do not murder.　　　Do not
commit adultery.　　Do not steal.　　　Do not
14 bear false witness against your neighbor.　　Do not
crave your neighbor's house.　　　Do not
crave your neighbor's wife, his male or female servant, his ox,
his donkey, or anything else that is your neighbor's."
15 Every one of the people witnessed the thunder and lightning　SHEVI'I

יא | וַיָּנַח בַּיּוֹם הַשְּׁבִיעִי. כִּבְיָכוֹל הִכְתִּיב בְּעַצְמוֹ מְנוּחָה, לִלְמֹד הֵימֶנּוּ קַל וָחֹמֶר לָאָדָם שֶׁמְּלַאכְתּוֹ בְּעָמָל וּבִיגִיעָה שֶׁיָּנֹחַ נַח בַּשַׁבָּת:

בֵּרַךְ... וַיְקַדְּשֵׁהוּ. בֵּרְכוֹ בַּמָּן, לְכַפְּלוֹ בַּשִּׁשִּׁי לֶחֶם מִשְׁנֶה, וְקִדְּשׁוֹ בַּמָּן, שֶׁלֹּא הָיָה יוֹרֵד בּוֹ:

יב | לְמַעַן יַאֲרִכוּן יָמֶיךָ. אִם תְּכַבֵּד – יַאֲרִיכוּן, וְאִם לָאו – יִקְצְרוּן, שֶׁדִּבְרֵי תּוֹרָה נוֹטָרִיקוֹן הֵם נִדְרָשִׁים, מִכְּלַל הֵן לָאו וּמִכְּלַל לָאו הֵן:

יג | לֹא תִּנְאָף. אֵין נִאוּף אֶלָּא בְּאֵשֶׁת אִישׁ, שֶׁנֶּאֱמַר: "מוֹת יוּמַת הַנּוֹאֵף וְהַנּוֹאָפֶת" (ויקרא כ, י), וְאוֹמֵר: "הָאִשָּׁה הַמְּנָאֶפֶת תַּחַת אִישָׁהּ תִּקַּח אֶת זָרִים" (יחזקאל טז, לב):

11| וַיָּנַח בַּיּוֹם הַשְּׁבִיעִי – And He rested on the seventh day: God wrote this about Himself to give the impression that He rests. He did that to construct an a fortiori argument on our behalf. [If God, who neither requires nor takes any respite, nevertheless is said to rest, then certainly] people who strive and toil to exhaustion should rest on the Sabbath.

בֵּרַךְ... וַיְקַדְּשֵׁהוּ – Blessed...and made it holy: God blessed the Sabbath by providing Israel with manna beforehand to prepare for it. And He made it holy by withholding manna on the Sabbath itself.

12| לְמַעַן יַאֲרִכוּן יָמֶיךָ – Then you will live long: If you honor your parents, your days will be lengthened; but if you disrespect them, your days will be shortened. Many statements in the Torah are meant to imply their converse – sometimes a positive promise of reward implies a negative threat of punishment, or vice versa.

13| לֹא תִּנְאָף – Do not commit adultery: The term "adultery" specifically denotes sex with a woman who is married to another man. We know to this to be so because the verse that defines the couple's punishment states: And the man who commits adultery with another man's wife, who commits adultery with his neighbor's wife, the adulterer and the adulteress shall surely be put to death (Leviticus 20:10). And a later verse reads: Rather like a wife who commits adultery, who takes strangers instead of her husband (Ezekiel 16:32).

עַבְדְּךָ וַאֲמָתְךָ וּבְהֶמְתֶּךָ וְגֵרְךָ אֲשֶׁר בִּשְׁעָרֶיךָ:

יא כִּי שֵׁשֶׁת־יָמִים עָשָׂה יהוה אֶת־הַשָּׁמַיִם וְאֶת־
הָאָרֶץ אֶת־הַיָּם וְאֶת־כָּל־אֲשֶׁר־בָּם וַיָּנַח בַּיּוֹם
הַשְּׁבִיעִי עַל־כֵּן בֵּרַךְ יהוה אֶת־יוֹם הַשַּׁבָּת

יב וַיְקַדְּשֵׁהוּ: כַּבֵּד אֶת־אָבִיךָ וְאֶת־אִמֶּךָ
לְמַעַן יַאֲרִכוּן יָמֶיךָ עַל הָאֲדָמָה אֲשֶׁר־יהוה אֱלֹהֶיךָ

יג נֹתֵן לָךְ: לֹא תִרְצָח׃ לֹא
תִנְאָף׃ לֹא תִגְנֹב׃ לֹא

יד תַעֲנֶה בְרֵעֲךָ עֵד שָׁקֶר: לֹא
תַחְמֹד בֵּית רֵעֶךָ׃ לֹא

תַחְמֹד אֵשֶׁת רֵעֶךָ וְעַבְדּוֹ וַאֲמָתוֹ וְשׁוֹרוֹ וַחֲמֹרוֹ וְכֹל
אֲשֶׁר לְרֵעֶךָ:

טו וְכָל־הָעָם רֹאִים אֶת־הַקּוֹלֹת וְאֶת־הַלַּפִּידִם וְאֵת   שביעי

לֹא תִגְנֹב. בְּגוֹנֵב נְפָשׁוֹת הַכָּתוּב מְדַבֵּר. "לֹא תִּגְנֹבוּ" (ויקרא יט, יא) בְּגוֹנֵב מָמוֹן. אוֹ אֵינוֹ אֶלָּא זֶה בְּגוֹנֵב מָמוֹן וּלְהַלָּן בְּגוֹנֵב נְפָשׁוֹת? אָמַרְתָּ, דָּבָר לָמֵד מֵעִנְיָנוֹ, "לֹא תִרְצָח, לֹא תִנְאָף" מִיתַת בֵּית דִּין, אַף "לֹא תִגְנֹב" דָּבָר שֶׁחַיָּבִין עָלָיו מִיתַת בֵּית דִּין:

טו) וְכָל־הָעָם רֹאִים. מְלַמֵּד שֶׁלֹּא הָיָה בָּהֶם אֶחָד סוּמָא. וּמִנַּיִן שֶׁלֹּא הָיָה בָּהֶם אִלֵּם? תַּלְמוּד לוֹמַר: "וַיַּעֲנוּ כָל הָעָם" (לעיל יט, ח). וּמִנַּיִן שֶׁלֹּא הָיָה בָּהֶם חֵרֵשׁ? תַּלְמוּד לוֹמַר: "נַעֲשֶׂה וְנִשְׁמָע" (להלן כד, ז):

לֹא תִגְנֹב – *Do not steal*: This is a warning against kidnapping and selling human beings, whereas a separate statement, *You shall not steal* (Leviticus 19:11), prohibits stealing property. How do we know that it is not the reverse: the current verse forbidding theft, and the second proscribing kidnapping? We invoke the exegetical principle of learning a thing from its context. The text in question is juxtaposed with the prohibitions of murder and adultery, which are capital offenses. Hence, the commandment *Do not steal* must also refer to a crime that warrants capital punishment [the penalty for kidnapping and selling people – see Exodus 21:16].

15| **וְכָל־הָעָם רֹאִים** – *Every one of the people witnessed*: [Literally, "saw."] This description teaches that no one was blind among the Israelites. Furthermore, we know that no one was mute among the people, since the verse states: *And the people answered as one – "All that the Lord has spoken we will do"* (19:8). Finally, nobody suffered an inability to hear, as the verse states: *They replied, "All that the Lord has spoken we shall do and we shall heed"* (24:7).

and the sound of the ram's horn and the smoke-covered mountain; they saw and they shook – and they stood at a dis-
16 tance, and said to Moshe, "Speak to us yourself and we will listen, but let not God say any more to us, or we will die."
17 "Do not be afraid," said Moshe to the people, "God has come to lift you up, so that the awe of Him will be with you always,
18 keeping you from sin." But the people remained at a distance while Moshe approached the thick darkness where God
19 was.   Then the LORD said to Moshe, "This is what you   MAFTIR
shall tell the Israelites: You yourselves have seen that I, from

---

רֹאִים אֶת־הַקּוֹלֹת. רוֹאִים אֶת הַנִּשְׁמָע, שֶׁאִי אֶפְשָׁר לִרְאוֹת בְּמָקוֹם אַחֵר:

אֶת־הַקּוֹלֹת. הַיּוֹצְאִין מִפִּי הַגְּבוּרָה:

וַיָּנֻעוּ. אֵין 'נוֹעַ' חָלָף זִיעַ:

וַיַּעַמְדוּ מֵרָחֹק. הָיוּ נִרְתָּעִין לַאֲחוֹרֵיהֶם שְׁנֵים עָשָׂר מִיל כְּאֹרֶךְ מַחֲנֵיהֶם, וּמַלְאֲכֵי הַשָּׁרֵת בָּאִין וּמְסִיעִין אוֹתָן לְהַחֲזִירָם, שֶׁנֶּאֱמַר: "מַלְכֵי צְבָאוֹת יִדְּדוּן יִדֹּדוּן" (תהלים סח, יג):

יז| לְבַעֲבוּר נַסּוֹת אֶתְכֶם. לְגַדֵּל אֶתְכֶם בָּעוֹלָם, שֶׁיֵּצֵא לָכֶם שֵׁם בָּאֻמּוֹת שֶׁהוּא בִּכְבוֹדוֹ נִגְלָה עֲלֵיכֶם:

נַסּוֹת. לְשׁוֹן הֲרָמָה וּגְדֻלָּה, כְּמוֹ: "הָרִימוּ נֵס" (ישעיה סב, י), "אָרִים נִסִּי" (שם מט, כב), "וְכַנֵּס עַל הַגִּבְעָה" (שם ל, יז) שֶׁהוּא זָקוּף:

וּבַעֲבוּר תִּהְיֶה יִרְאָתוֹ. עַל יְדֵי שֶׁרְאִיתֶם אוֹתוֹ יָרְאוּי וּמְאֻיָּם, תֵּדְעוּ כִּי אֵין זוּלָתוֹ וְתִירְאוּ מִפָּנָיו:

רֹאִים אֶת־הַקּוֹלֹת – *Witnessed the thunder:* The Israelites actually saw sounds during their experience, something which is otherwise impossible.

אֶת־הַקּוֹלֹת – *The thunder:* [Literally, "sounds" or "voices."] They saw the sounds emanating from the mouth of God.

וַיָּנֻעוּ – *And they shook:* The verb *noa* denotes trembling.

וַיַּעַמְדוּ מֵרָחֹק – *And they stood at a distance:* The entire nation leapt backward a distance of twelve miles, the entire length of the Israelite camp. But the ministering angels descended and guided them back to their places, as the verse states: *Kings [malkhei] of armies flee [yiddodun], they flee* [Psalms 68:13; the midrash Rashi cites reads *malkhei* as *malakhei* – "angels," and *yiddodun* as *yidaddun* – "lead them back"].

17| **לְבַעֲבוּר נַסּוֹת אֶתְכֶם** – *To lift you up:* Your reputation will grow among the nations, for God will make you great as the world learns that He has revealed Himself to you in all His glory.

נַסּוֹת – *To lift up:* The verb *lenasot* means to raise or to exalt, as in the verses *Lift up a standard [nes] for the people* (Isaiah 62:10); *Behold, I will lift up My hand to the nations, and set up My standard [nisi] to the peoples* (Isaiah 49:22); and *As a banner [kanes] on a hill* (Isaiah 30:17). A banner or standard stands tall and erect.

וּבַעֲבוּר תִּהְיֶה יִרְאָתוֹ – *So that the awe of Him will be:* Once you have seen God as fearsome and threatening, you will understand that He is unique in all the world. You will therefore continue to fear His presence even afterward.

◀

קוֹל הַשֹּׁפָר וְאֶת־הָהָר עָשֵׁן וַיַּרְא הָעָם וַיָּנֻעוּ וַיַּעַמְדוּ

יט מֵרָחֹק: וַיֹּאמְרוּ אֶל־מֹשֶׁה דַּבֵּר־אַתָּה עִמָּנוּ וְנִשְׁמָעָה

יז וְאַל־יְדַבֵּר עִמָּנוּ אֱלֹהִים פֶּן־נָמוּת: וַיֹּאמֶר מֹשֶׁה

אֶל־הָעָם אַל־תִּירָאוּ כִּי לְבַעֲבוּר נַסּוֹת אֶתְכֶם בָּא

הָאֱלֹהִים וּבַעֲבוּר תִּהְיֶה יִרְאָתוֹ עַל־פְּנֵיכֶם לְבִלְתִּי

יח תֶחֱטָאוּ: וַיַּעֲמֹד הָעָם מֵרָחֹק וּמֹשֶׁה נִגַּשׁ אֶל־הָעֲרָפֶל

יט אֲשֶׁר־שָׁם הָאֱלֹהִים: וַיֹּאמֶר יהוה אֶל־ מפטיר

מֹשֶׁה כֹּה תֹאמַר אֶל־בְּנֵי יִשְׂרָאֵל אַתֶּם רְאִיתֶם כִּי

יח | נִגַּשׁ אֶל־הָעֲרָפֶל – Approached the thick darkness: Moshe passed through three barriers to reach the presence of God: darkness [ḥoshekh], cloud [anan], and thick darkness [arafel]. A later verse lists these: *The mountain burned with fire to the heart of heaven, with darkness, clouds, and thick darkness* (Deuteronomy 4:11). The term *arafel* connotes a thick cloud, as the verse states: *Then the Lord said to Moshe, "I will come to you in a dense cloud"* (19:9).

יט | כֹּה תֹאמַר – This is what you shall tell: Use these words exactly.

אַתֶּם רְאִיתֶם – You yourselves have seen: What a person hears described by others cannot compare to what he sees with his own eyes. For one receives only a secondhand report, one is unsure whether to believe it or not.

כִּי מִן־הַשָּׁמַיִם דִּבַּרְתִּי – I, from the heavens, have spoken: Our verse claims that God addressed Israel from the heavens, while a previous verse states: *And the Lord descended on Mount Sinai, to the top of the mountain* (19:20). How can these descriptions be reconciled? By a third verse, which states: *Out of heaven He made you hear His voice, that He might instruct you: and upon earth He showed you His great fire; and you did hear His words out of the midst of the fire* (Deuteronomy 4:36). This shows that while God's glory remained in the heavens, His fire and His might descended to earth. Another possible resolution: God folded the heavens and spread them on top of the mountain, as the verse states: *He bowed the heavens also, and came down* (II Samuel 22:10).

יח | נִגַּשׁ אֶל־הָעֲרָפֶל. לִפְנִים מִשָּׁלֹשׁ מְחִצּוֹת: חֹשֶׁךְ, עָנָן וַעֲרָפֶל, שֶׁנֶּאֱמַר: "וְהָהָר בֹּעֵר בָּאֵשׁ עַד לֵב הַשָּׁמַיִם חֹשֶׁךְ עָנָן וַעֲרָפֶל" (דברים ד, יא). עֲרָפֶל הוּא עַב הֶעָנָן, שֶׁאָמַר לוֹ: "הִנֵּה אָנֹכִי בָּא אֵלֶיךָ בְּעַב הֶעָנָן" (לעיל יט, ט):

יט | כֹּה תֹאמַר. בַּלָּשׁוֹן הַזֶּה:

אַתֶּם רְאִיתֶם. יֵשׁ הֶפְרֵשׁ בֵּין מַה שֶּׁאָדָם רוֹאֶה לְמַה שֶׁאֲחֵרִים מְשִׂיחִין לוֹ, שֶׁמַּה שֶּׁאֲחֵרִים מְשִׂיחִין לוֹ פְּעָמִים שֶׁלִּבּוֹ חָלוּק מִלְּהַאֲמִין:

כִּי מִן־הַשָּׁמַיִם דִּבַּרְתִּי. וְכָתוּב אֶחָד אוֹמֵר: "וַיֵּרֶד ה' עַל הַר סִינַי" (לעיל יט, כ)! בָּא הַכָּתוּב הַשְּׁלִישִׁי וְהִכְרִיעַ בֵּינֵיהֶם: "מִן הַשָּׁמַיִם הִשְׁמִיעֲךָ אֶת קֹלוֹ לְיַסְּרֶךָּ וְעַל הָאָרֶץ הֶרְאֲךָ אֶת אִשּׁוֹ הַגְּדוֹלָה" (דברים ד, לו), כְּבוֹדוֹ בַּשָּׁמַיִם וְאִשּׁוֹ וּגְבוּרָתוֹ עַל הָאָרֶץ. דָּבָר אַחֵר, הִרְכִּין שָׁמַיִם וּשְׁמֵי שָׁמַיִם וְהִצִּיעָן עַל הָהָר, וְכֵן הוּא אוֹמֵר: "וַיֵּט שָׁמַיִם וַיֵּרַד" (שמואל ב כב, י):

20 the heavens, have spoken to you. Have no others alongside
21 Me; make yourselves no silver gods, no golden gods. Make for
Me an altar of earth and on that sacrifice your burnt offerings
and peace offerings, your sheep and your cattle. Wherever I
cause My name to be invoked, I will come to you and I will
22 bless you. If you make Me an altar of stones, do not build it
of hewn stone, for in wielding a sword upon it, you profane

כ| **לֹא תַעֲשׂוּן אִתִּי.** לֹא תַעֲשׂוּן
דְּמוּת שַׁמָּשַׁי הַמְשַׁמְּשִׁים לְפָנַי
בַּמָּרוֹם:

אֱלֹהֵי כֶסֶף. בָּא לְהַזְהִיר עַל
הַכְּרוּבִים שֶׁאַתָּה עוֹשֶׂה לַעֲמֹד אִתִּי
שֶׁלֹּא יִהְיוּ שֶׁל כֶּסֶף, שֶׁאִם שִׁנִּיתָם
לַעֲשׂוֹתָם שֶׁל כֶּסֶף הֲרֵי הֵן לְפָנַי
כֵּאלֹהוּת:

וֵאלֹהֵי זָהָב. בָּא לְהַזְהִיר שֶׁלֹּא
יוֹסִיף עַל שְׁנַיִם, שֶׁאִם עֲשִׂיתָ אַרְבָּעָה
הֲרֵי הֵן לְפָנַי כֵּאלֹהֵי זָהָב:

לֹא תַעֲשׂוּ לָכֶם. שֶׁלֹּא תֹאמַר, הֲרֵינִי
עוֹשֶׂה כְּרוּבִים בְּבָתֵּי כְנֵסִיּוֹת וּבְבָתֵּי
מִדְרָשׁוֹת כְּדֶרֶךְ שֶׁאֲנִי עוֹשֶׂה בְּבֵית
עוֹלָמִים, לְכָךְ נֶאֱמַר: "לֹא תַעֲשׂוּ
לָכֶם":

כא| **מִזְבַּח אֲדָמָה.** מְחֻבָּר בָּאֲדָמָה,
שֶׁלֹּא יִבְנֶנּוּ עַל גַּבֵּי עַמּוּדִים אוֹ עַל
גַּבֵּי כִּפִּים. דָּבָר אַחֵר, שֶׁהָיָה מְמַלֵּא
אֶת חֲלַל מִזְבַּח הַנְּחֹשֶׁת אֲדָמָה
בִּשְׁעַת חֲנִיָּתָן:

תַּעֲשֶׂה-לִּי. שֶׁתְּהֵא תְּחִלַּת עֲשִׂיָּתוֹ
לִשְׁמִי:

וְזָבַחְתָּ עָלָיו. אֶצְלוֹ, כְּמוֹ: "וְעָלָיו מַטֵּה
מְנַשֶּׁה" (במדבר ב, כ). אוֹ אֵינוֹ אֶלָּא
עָלָיו מַמָּשׁ? תַּלְמוּד לוֹמַר: "הַבָּשָׂר
וְהַדָּם עַל מִזְבַּח ה' אֱלֹהֶיךָ" (דברים
יב, סז), וְאֵין שְׁחִיטָה בְּרֹאשׁ הַמִּזְבֵּחַ:

20| **לֹא תַעֲשׂוּן אִתִּי** – *Have no others alongside Me*: Do not create images of My celestial servants who labor for Me in the heavens.

אֱלֹהֵי כֶסֶף – *Silver gods*: This is a warning against fashioning the Tabernacle's cherubim, which will stand "alongside Me" [adorning the cover of the Ark of the Covenant], out of silver [rather than the prescribed gold]. If you do deviate from My instructions and make them out of silver, I will consider them to be idolatrous.

וֵאלֹהֵי זָהָב – *Golden gods*: This is a warning against adding more cherubim to the two that I mandate. If you make four, for example, I will consider them to be gods of gold.

לֹא תַעֲשׂוּ לָכֶם – *Make yourselves no*: Do not permit yourselves to place cherubim in your synagogues or in your study halls, seeing those of the Tabernacle as a model and a precedent. This is the sense of the prohibition *Make yourselves no silver gods, no golden gods* [that is, within your own precincts].

21| **מִזְבַּח אֲדָמָה** – *An altar of earth*: [Although the Tabernacle's altar was made out of acacia wood covered in bronze, and not out of earth, this verse commands only that] the altar that you construct shall be attached to the earth. That is, do not build it on pillars or positioned on a stone foundation. Another interpretation: The hollow space within the bronze altar was filled with earth whenever Israel reached a new camp site.

תַּעֲשֶׂה-לִּי – *Make for Me*: From the start of its construction, the altar should be dedicated to Me.

וְזָבַחְתָּ עָלָיו – *On that sacrifice*: [Literally, "slaughter on it." While sacrifices were never slaughtered directly atop the altar, but rather next to it, Rash argues that] the preposition *alav* can mean "next to it" as in the verse: *On the west side shall be the standard of the camp of Efrayim by their hosts…. And by him*

◀

כ מִן־הַשָּׁמַ֔יִם דִּבַּ֖רְתִּי עִמָּכֶ֑ם לֹ֣א תַעֲשׂ֣וּן אִתִּ֔י אֱלֹ֤הֵי
כא כֶ֨סֶף֙ וֵאלֹהֵ֣י זָהָ֔ב לֹ֥א תַעֲשׂ֖וּ לָכֶֽם׃ מִזְבַּ֣ח אֲדָמָה֘
תַּעֲשֶׂה־לִּי֒ וְזָבַחְתָּ֣ עָלָ֗יו אֶת־עֹלֹתֶ֙יךָ֙ וְאֶת־שְׁלָמֶ֔יךָ
אֶת־צֹֽאנְךָ֖ וְאֶת־בְּקָרֶ֑ךָ בְּכָל־הַמָּקוֹם֙ אֲשֶׁ֣ר אַזְכִּ֣יר
כב אֶת־שְׁמִ֔י אָב֥וֹא אֵלֶ֖יךָ וּבֵרַכְתִּֽיךָ׃ וְאִם־מִזְבַּ֤ח אֲבָנִים֙
תַּעֲשֶׂה־לִּ֔י לֹֽא־תִבְנֶ֥ה אֶתְהֶ֖ן גָּזִ֑ית כִּ֣י חַרְבְּךָ֤ הֵנַ֙פְתָּ֙

[ve'alav] shall be the tribe of Menashe (Numbers 2:18, 20). And how do we know that the animals are not in fact to be slaughtered on top of the altar, and that the term alav does not mean "on it"? For a later verse states: The meat and the blood, upon the altar of the Lord your God (Deuteronomy 12:27), showing that it is only the meat and the blood that are placed on the altar, and not the whole animal while it is still alive.

אֶת־עֹלֹתֶ֙יךָ֙ וְאֶת־שְׁלָמֶ֔יךָ. אֲשֶׁ֣ר מִצֹּאנְךָ֖ וּמִבְּקָרְךָ֑. "אֶת צֹאנְךָ֖ וְאֵת בְּקָרְךָ֑" פֵּרוּשׁ לְ"אֵת עֹלֹתֶ֙יךָ֙ וְאֵת שְׁלָמֶ֔יךָ":

אֶת־עֹלֹתֶ֙יךָ֙ וְאֶת־שְׁלָמֶ֔יךָ – Your burnt offerings and peace offerings: These offerings shall be brought from your sheep and cattle. The phrase "your sheep and your cattle" is not to be read as distinct from "your burnt offerings and peace offerings," but rather as an explanation thereof.

בְּכָל־הַמָּקוֹם֙ אֲשֶׁ֣ר אַזְכִּ֣יר אֶת־שְׁמִ֔י. אֲשֶׁ֣ר אֶתֵּ֖ן לְךָ֖ לָשׂ֥וּת לְהַזְכִּ֖יר שֵׁ֥ם הַמְפֹרָ֥שׁ שֶׁלִּ֔י, שָׁ֥ם "אָב֥וֹא אֵלֶ֖יךָ", אֲשָׁרָ֥ה אֶ֥ת שְׁכִינָתִ֖י, "וּבֵרַכְתִּֽיךָ". מִכָּ֣אן חַתָּ֔ה לָמַ֖ד שֶׁלֹּ֥א נִתַּ֖ן לָשׂ֥וּת לְהַזְכִּ֖יר שֵׁ֥ם הַמְפֹרָ֥שׁ אֶלָּ֖א בַּמָּק֖וֹם שֶׁהַשְּׁכִינָ֖ה בָּאָ֖ה שָׁ֥ם, וְזֶ֥הוּ בֵּ֥ית הַבְּחִירָ֖ה, שָׁ֥ם נִתַּ֖ן לָשׂ֥וּת לַכֹּהֲנִ֖ים לְהַזְכִּ֖יר שֵׁ֥ם הַמְפֹרָ֥שׁ בִּנְשִׂיא֖וּת כַּפַּ֖יִם וּלְבָרֵ֥ךְ אֶ֥ת הָעָ֖ם:

בְּכָל־הַמָּקוֹם֙ אֲשֶׁ֣ר אַזְכִּ֣יר אֶת־שְׁמִ֔י – Wherever I cause My name to be invoked: In every location where I grant you permission to utter My ineffable name, that is where I will come to you and I will bless you by manifesting My Divine Presence. Thus we learn that Israel was only permitted to pronounce the tetragrammaton at the site where the Divine Presence appears. And that location is the Temple. Only there were the priests allowed to utter this name when they raised their hands to bless the nation.

כב וְאִם־מִזְבַּ֤ח אֲבָנִים֙. רַבִּ֣י יִשְׁמָעֵ֥אל אוֹמֵ֔ר: כָּל־אִ֥ם וְאִ֥ם שֶׁבַּתּוֹרָ֖ה לָשׂ֥וּת חוּץ מִשְּׁלֹשָׁ֥ה: "וְאִ֥ם מִזְבַּ֤ח אֲבָנִים֙ תַּעֲשֶׂה־לִּ֔י", הֲרֵ֥י 'אִ֥ם' זֶ֥ה מְשַׁמֵּ֥שׁ בִּלְשׁ֥וֹן 'כַּאֲשֶׁ֔ר', וְכַאֲשֶׁ֥ר תַּעֲשֶׂ֥ה לִ֥י מִזְבַּ֤ח אֲבָנִים֙ "לֹֽא־תִבְנֶ֥ה אֶתְהֶ֖ן גָּזִ֑ית", שֶׁהֲרֵ֥י חוֹבָ֖ה עָלֶ֖יךָ

22 | וְאִם־מִזְבַּ֤ח אֲבָנִים֙ – If an altar of stones: Rabbi Yishmael taught: when the Torah uses the word "if," it always introduces an optional action, save in three cases: The first one is the statement, If you make Me an altar of stones, where the term "if" really means "when": "When you make Me an altar of stones, do not build it of hewn stone." For the mandate certainly is for Israel to construct the altar out of stone, as another verse states: You shall build the altar of the Lord your God of whole

◀

23 it. Do not ascend to My altar with steps, for your nakedness must not be exposed on it.

i

לִבְנוֹת מִזְבַּח אֲבָנִים, שֶׁנֶּאֱמַר: "אֲבָנִים שְׁלֵמוֹת תִּבְנֶה" (דברים כז, ו). וְכֵן: "חָס כֶּסֶף תַּלְוֶה" (להלן כב, כד) חוֹבָה הוּא, שֶׁנֶּאֱמַר: "וְהַעֲבֵט תַּעֲבִיטֶנּוּ" (דברים טו, ח), וְאַף זֶה מְשַׁמֵּשׁ בִּלְשׁוֹן 'כַּאֲשֶׁר'. וְכֵן: "וְאִם תַּקְרִיב מִנְחַת בִּכּוּרִים" (ויקרא ב, יד), זוֹ מִנְחַת הָעֹמֶר שֶׁהִיא חוֹבָה. וְעַל כָּרְחֲךָ אֵין 'אִם' הַלָּלוּ תְּלוּיִין חֶלָּא וַדָּאִין, וּבִלְשׁוֹן 'כַּאֲשֶׁר' הֵם מְשַׁמְּשִׁים:

stones (Deuteronomy 27:6). The second instance appears in the verse *If you lend money to one of My people who is poor, do not act with him as a harsh creditor, and do not charge him interest* (Exodus 22:24). We know that Jews are obliged to lend money to the poor, because a later verse states: *If there be among you a poor man…you shall surely lend him sufficient for his need, in that which he lacks* (Deuteronomy 15:8). Here too then, the term "if" means "when." And the third such case appears in the verse: *And if you offer a meal offering of your first fruits to the LORD, you shall offer for the meal offering of your first fruits ears of grain dried by the fire, grain beaten out of fresh ears* (Leviticus 2:14), a text that describes the mandatory practice of the Omer offering. In all three cases, we must conclude that the term "if" does not suggest an optional action but a required one, meaning "when."

גָּזִית. לְשׁוֹן גְּזִיזָה, שֶׁפּוֹסְקָן וּמְכַתְּתָן בְּבַרְזֶל:

גָּזִית – *Hewn stone*: The word *gazit* derives from the term *geziza* [meaning "cutting"], and denotes stones that are chiseled and cut with an iron tool.

כִּי חַרְבְּךָ הֵנַפְתָּ עָלֶיהָ. הֲרֵי "כִּי" זֶה מְשַׁמֵּשׁ בִּלְשׁוֹן 'פֶּן' שֶׁהוּא 'דִּלְמָא', פֶּן תָּנִיף חַרְבְּךָ עָלֶיהָ:

כִּי חַרְבְּךָ הֵנַפְתָּ עָלֶיהָ – *For in wielding a sword upon it*: Here the term *ki* means "lest" – lest you will place your sword upon the sacred altar. [According to this understanding, the verse would more properly be translated: "lest you wield a sword upon it and profane it."]

וַתְּחַלְלֶהָ. הָא לָמַדְתָּ שֶׁאִם הֵנַפְתָּ עָלֶיהָ בַּרְזֶל – חִלַּלְתָּ, שֶׁהַמִּזְבֵּחַ נִבְרָא לְהַאֲרִיךְ יָמָיו שֶׁל אָדָם וְהַבַּרְזֶל נִבְרָא לְקַצֵּר יָמָיו שֶׁל אָדָם, אֵין זֶה בְּדִין שֶׁיּוּנַף הַמְקַצֵּר עַל הַמַּאֲרִיךְ. וְעוֹד, שֶׁהַמִּזְבֵּחַ

וַתְּחַלְלֶהָ – *You profane it*: We learn from here that placing an iron tool upon the altar profanes it. Why is this so? Because the purpose of the altar is to extend people's lives [sins sacrifices can atone for sin], whereas the nature of iron [weapons] is to shorten a person's life. Hence these two things are incompatible, and it is inappropriate for the latter to be placed upon

◄

כג עָלֶיהָ וַתְּחַלְלֶהָ: וְלֹא־תַעֲלֶה בְמַעֲלֹת עַל־מִזְבְּחִי
אֲשֶׁר לֹא־תִגָּלֶה עֶרְוָתְךָ עָלָיו:

מַטִּיל שָׁלוֹם בֵּין יִשְׂרָאֵל לַאֲבִיהֶם
שֶׁבַּשָּׁמַיִם, לְפִיכָךְ לֹא יָבֹא עָלָיו
בֹּרֵת וּמְחַבֵּל. וַהֲרֵי דְּבָרִים קַל
וָחֹמֶר: וּמָה אֲבָנִים שֶׁאֵינָן רוֹאוֹת
וְלֹא שׁוֹמְעוֹת וְלֹא מְדַבְּרוֹת, עַל
יְדֵי שֶׁמַּטִּילוֹת שָׁלוֹם אָמְרָה תּוֹרָה:
"לֹא תָנִיף עֲלֵיהֶם בַּרְזֶל" (דברים כז),
ה, הַמַּטִּיל שָׁלוֹם בֵּין אִישׁ לְאִשְׁתּוֹ,
בֵּין מִשְׁפָּחָה לְמִשְׁפָּחָה, בֵּין אָדָם
לַחֲבֵרוֹ, עַל אַחַת כַּמָּה וְכַמָּה שֶׁלֹּא
תְבוֹאֵהוּ פֻּרְעָנוּת:

כג| וְלֹא־תַעֲלֶה בְמַעֲלֹת. כְּשֶׁאַתָּה
בּוֹנֶה כֶּבֶשׁ לַמִּזְבֵּחַ לֹא תַעֲשֵׂהוּ
מַעֲלוֹת מַעֲלוֹת, אשקלונ"ש בְּלַעַז,
אֶלָּא חָלָק יְהֵא וּמְשֻׁפָּע:

אֲשֶׁר לֹא־תִגָּלֶה עֶרְוָתְךָ. שֶׁעַל יְדֵי
הַמַּעֲלוֹת אַתָּה צָרִיךְ לְהַרְחִיב
פְּסִיעוֹתֶיךָ. וְאַף עַל פִּי שֶׁאֵינוֹ גִּלּוּי
עֶרְוָה מַמָּשׁ, שֶׁהֲרֵי כְּתִיב: "וַעֲשֵׂה
לָהֶם מִכְנְסֵי בָד" (להלן כח, מב), מִכָּל
מָקוֹם הַרְחָבַת הַפְּסִיעוֹת קְרוֹב
לְגִלּוּי עֶרְוָה הוּא, וְאַתָּה נוֹהֵג בָּם
מִנְהַג בִּזָּיוֹן. וַהֲרֵי דְּבָרִים קַל וָחֹמֶר:
וּמָה אֲבָנִים הַלָּלוּ שֶׁאֵין בָּהֶם דַּעַת
לְהַקְפִּיד עַל בִּזְיוֹנָן, אָמְרָה תּוֹרָה:
הוֹאִיל וְיֵשׁ בָּהֶם צֹרֶךְ לֹא תִנְהַג
בָּהֶם מִנְהַג בִּזָּיוֹן, חֲבֵרְךָ שֶׁהוּא
בִּדְמוּת יוֹצֶרְךָ וּמַקְפִּיד עַל בִּזְיוֹנוֹ,
עַל אַחַת כַּמָּה וְכַמָּה:

---

the former. Furthermore, since the altar stands as a mediator to create peace between Israel and their Father in Heaven, it cannot tolerate the presence of an item designed to cut down and destroy. We can learn a valuable lesson from this prohibition: Here we have an altar of stones, which lack the power of sight, hearing, and speech, and yet because this inanimate object is tasked with bringing God and Israel closer together, the Torah warns us not to wield a sword upon it. Consider then a counselor who mends a rift between a husband and wife, or resolves a feud between families, or bridges a gap between neighbors – such an intermediary must surely be protected from any kind of suffering.

23| וְלֹא־תַעֲלֶה בְמַעֲלֹת – *Do not ascend with steps*: When you construct the ramp that leads up to the altar, do not put steps – *eschelons* in Old French – on it. Rather, the surface should be a smooth incline.

אֲשֶׁר לֹא־תִגָּלֶה עֶרְוָתְךָ – *For your nakedness must not be exposed on it*: If ascending the altar meant climbing stairs, the priests who performed the service would have to take wide steps. And even though walking in this fashion would not really expose the individual, since the priests wore trousers, as the verse states, *Make them linen trousers to cover their nakedness, reaching from waist to thigh* (28:42), nevertheless, taking wide paces [to stretch to the stairs] is similar to exposing oneself, which would be disrespectful to the altar's stones. This teaches us a lesson about how to act toward human beings. If the Torah is concerned with behaving modestly toward stones, which sense no feeling of shame, and yet warns us not to treat them discourteously, then certainly one must always consider the sensitivities of a fellow person created in the image of God.

THE TEN COMMANDMENTS

"I am the Lord your God who brought you out of the land of Egypt, out of the house of slaves. Have no other gods than Me. Do not make for yourself any carved image or likeness of any creature in the heavens above or the earth beneath or the water beneath the earth. Do not bow down to them or worship them, for I the Lord your God demand absolute loyalty. For those who hate Me, I hold the descendants to account for the sins of the fathers to the third and fourth generation, but to those who love Me and keep My commands – I shall act with faithful love for thousands. Do not speak the name of the Lord your God in vain, for the Lord will not hold guiltless those who speak His name in vain.

Remember the Sabbath to keep it holy. Six days you shall work, and carry out all your labors, but the seventh is a Sabbath to the Lord your God. On it, do no work – neither you, nor your son or daughter, your male or female servant, your livestock, or the migrant within your gates. For in six days the Lord made heaven and earth, the sea, and all that they contain, and He rested on the seventh day. And so the Lord blessed the Sabbath day and made it holy. Honor your father and mother. Then you will live long in the land that the Lord your God is giving you. Do not murder. Do not commit adultery. Do not steal. Do not bear false witness against your neighbor. Do not crave your neighbor's house. Do not crave your neighbor's wife, his male or female servant, his ox, his donkey, or anything else that is your neighbor's."

עשרת הדיברות
בטעם העליון

אָנֹכִי֙ יְהוָ֣ה אֱלֹהֶ֔יךָ

אֲשֶׁ֣ר הוֹצֵאתִ֩יךָ֩ מֵאֶ֨רֶץ מִצְרַ֜יִם מִבֵּ֣ית עֲבָדִ֗ים לֹֽא־יִהְיֶ֥ה לְךָ֛ אֱלֹהִ֥ים
אֲחֵרִ֖ים עַל־פָּנָֽ֒י לֹֽא־תַעֲשֶׂ֨ה לְךָ֥ פֶ֣סֶל ׀ וְכָל־תְּמוּנָ֡ה אֲשֶׁ֣ר בַּשָּׁמַ֣יִם
׀ מִמַּ֡עַל וַֽאֲשֶׁ֣ר בָּאָ֣רֶץ מִתַָּ֑֗חַת וַאֲשֶׁ֥ר בַּמַּ֖יִם ׀ מִתַּ֣חַת לָאָ֑רֶץ
לֹֽא־תִשְׁתַּחֲוֶ֥ה לָהֶ֖ם וְלֹ֣א תָעָבְדֵ֑ם כִּ֣י אָֽנֹכִ֞י יְהוָ֤ה אֱלֹהֶ֨יךָ֙ אֵ֣ל
קַנָּ֔א פֹּ֠קֵ֠ד עֲוֺ֨ן אָבֹ֧ת עַל־בָּנִ֛ים עַל־שִׁלֵּשִׁ֥ים וְעַל־רִבֵּעִ֖ים לְשֹׂנְאָֽ֑י
וְעֹ֥שֶׂה חֶ֖סֶד לַאֲלָפִ֑ים לְאֹהֲבַ֖י וּלְשֹׁמְרֵ֥י מִצְוֺתָֽי׃   לֹ֥א
תִשָּׂ֛א אֶת־שֵֽׁם־יְהוָ֥ה אֱלֹהֶ֖יךָ לַשָּׁ֑וְא כִּ֣י לֹ֤א יְנַקֶּה֙ יְהוָ֔ה אֵ֥ת
אֲשֶׁר־יִשָּׂ֥א אֶת־שְׁמ֖וֹ לַשָּֽׁוְא׃

זָכ֛וֹר֩ אֶת־י֥֨וֹם הַשַּׁבָּ֖ת לְקַדְּשֽׁ֑וֹ שֵׁ֤֣שֶׁת יָמִ֣ים֙ תַּֽעֲבֹ֔ד֮ וְעָשִׂ֣֖יתָ כָּל־
מְלַאכְתֶּֽךָ֒ וְי֙וֹם֙ הַשְּׁבִיעִ֔֜י שַׁבָּ֖֣ת ׀ לַיהוָ֣֥ה אֱלֹהֶ֑֗יךָ לֹֽ֣א־תַעֲשֶׂ֣֨ה כָ֣ל־
מְלָאכָ֡ה אַתָּ֣ה ׀ וּבִנְךָֽ֣־וּ֠בִתֶּ֗ךָ עַבְדְּךָֽ֤ וַאֲמָֽתְךָ֙ וּבְהֶמְתֶּ֔ךָ וְגֵרְךָ֖ אֲשֶׁ֥ר
בִּשְׁעָרֶ֑יךָ כִּ֣י שֵֽׁשֶׁת־יָמִים֩ עָשָׂ֨ה יְהוָ֜ה אֶת־הַשָּׁמַ֣יִם וְאֶת־הָאָ֗רֶץ
אֶת־הַיָּם֙ וְאֶת־כָּל־אֲשֶׁר־בָּ֔ם וַיָּ֖נַח בַּיּ֣וֹם הַשְּׁבִיעִ֑י עַל־כֵּ֗ן בֵּרַ֧ךְ
יְהוָ֛ה אֶת־י֥וֹם הַשַּׁבָּ֖ת וַֽיְקַדְּשֵֽׁהוּ׃   כַּבֵּ֥ד אֶת־אָבִ֖יךָ
וְאֶת־אִמֶּ֑ךָ לְמַ֙עַן֙ יַאֲרִכ֣וּן יָמֶ֔יךָ עַ֚ל הָֽאֲדָמָ֔ה אֲשֶׁר־יְהוָ֥ה אֱלֹהֶ֖יךָ
נֹתֵ֥ן לָֽךְ׃ לֹ֥א תִּרְצָֽ֖ח׃   לֹ֣א
תִּנְאָֽ֑ף׃   לֹ֣א תִּגְנֹֽ֔ב׃   לֹֽא־
תַעֲנֶ֥ה בְרֵעֲךָ֖ עֵ֥ד שָֽׁקֶר׃   לֹ֥א
תַחְמֹ֖ד בֵּ֣ית רֵעֶ֑ךָ   לֹֽא־
תַחְמֹ֞ד אֵ֣שֶׁת רֵעֶ֗ךָ וְעַבְדּ֤וֹ וַאֲמָתוֹ֙ וְשׁוֹר֣וֹ וַחֲמֹר֔וֹ וְכֹ֖ל אֲשֶׁ֥ר לְרֵעֶֽךָ׃

HAFTARAT YITRO

6 1 In the year in which King Uziyahu died I saw the LORD sitting on a high,   ISAIAH
2 raised throne, the hem of His clothing filling the Sanctuary. There were
seraphim standing above Him, each with six wings – with two they covered their faces, with two they covered their feet, and with two they were
3 flying. And they called out one to another – "Holy, holy, holy – the LORD
4 of Hosts – all the world's fullness His glory." The door pillars shook with
5 the voice of him who called – and smoke filled the House. And I said –
"This ache – I am condemned, for my mouth has been defiled, one man
among a people with their mouths defiled – and my eyes see the King,
6 the LORD of Hosts." One of the seraphim flew to me, and in his hand was
7 a coal, taken with tongs from the altar top. With this he touched my lips
and said, "When this has touched your lips, your iniquity is gone, and all
8 your sin forgiven." I heard the voice of the LORD saying, "Whom shall I
9 send, and who will go for Us?" And I said, "I am here. Send me." He said,
"Go – tell this people: Hear, you shall hear but understand it not, see it
10 all but know it not. Fatten the heart of this people; make their ears heavy;
coat their eyes with plaster, lest they see with their eyes and hear with
11 their ears, and their hearts understand and they return – and are healed." I
said, "My LORD, how long?" And He said, "Until the towns are stripped of
all who live in them, houses left without people, the land stripped waste,
12 and the LORD dispatches man far hence, and swaths of land will be for-
13 saken; if a tenth there will survive, it will return and will be burnt like
the terebinth and oak tree that drop their leaves, and yet the trunk re-
7 1 mains – and the trunk is holy seed."   In the days of Aḥaz son of   *Sepharadim*
Yotam son of Uziyahu, king of Yehuda, Retzin, king of Aram, and Pekaḥ   *end here*
  Yemenites
son of Remalyahu, king of Israel, launched an attack on Jerusalem, but   *continue from*
2 they could not conquer it. The House of David was told, "Aram is allied   *chapter 9*
with Efrayim." And his heart swayed, and the hearts of his people, as trees
3 of the forest will sway with the wind.   And the LORD said to Yeshaya-
hu: Go out now to meet Aḥaz, you and She'ar Yashuv your son, to the end
4 of the Upper Pool's conduit, by the road to the Washer's Field. And say to
him: Be guarded, stay still, do not fear, and let your heart not soften before
these smoking tails of firebrands, before the rage of Retzin and Aram and

הפטרת יתרו

ישעיה

א בִּשְׁנַת־מוֹת הַמֶּלֶךְ עֻזִּיָּהוּ וָאֶרְאֶה אֶת־אֲדֹנָי יֹשֵׁב עַל־כִּסֵּא רָם

ב וְנִשָּׂא וְשׁוּלָיו מְלֵאִים אֶת־הַהֵיכָל: שְׂרָפִים עֹמְדִים ׀ מִמַּעַל לוֹ
שֵׁשׁ כְּנָפַיִם שֵׁשׁ כְּנָפַיִם לְאֶחָד בִּשְׁתַּיִם ׀ יְכַסֶּה פָנָיו וּבִשְׁתַּיִם יְכַסֶּה

ג רַגְלָיו וּבִשְׁתַּיִם יְעוֹפֵף: וְקָרָא זֶה אֶל־זֶה וְאָמַר קָדוֹשׁ ׀ קָדוֹשׁ

ד קָדוֹשׁ יהוה צְבָאוֹת מְלֹא כָל־הָאָרֶץ כְּבוֹדוֹ: וַיָּנֻעוּ אַמּוֹת הַסִּפִּים

ה מִקּוֹל הַקּוֹרֵא וְהַבַּיִת יִמָּלֵא עָשָׁן: וָאֹמַר אוֹי־לִי כִי־נִדְמֵיתִי כִּי
אִישׁ טְמֵא־שְׂפָתַיִם אָנֹכִי וּבְתוֹךְ עַם־טְמֵא שְׂפָתַיִם אָנֹכִי יֹשֵׁב כִּי

ו אֶת־הַמֶּלֶךְ יהוה צְבָאוֹת רָאוּ עֵינָי: וַיָּעָף אֵלַי אֶחָד מִן־הַשְּׂרָפִים

ז וּבְיָדוֹ רִצְפָּה בְּמֶלְקַחַיִם לָקַח מֵעַל הַמִּזְבֵּחַ: וַיַּגַּע עַל־פִּי וַיֹּאמֶר

ח הִנֵּה נָגַע זֶה עַל־שְׂפָתֶיךָ וְסָר עֲוֺנֶךָ וְחַטָּאתְךָ תְּכֻפָּר: וָאֶשְׁמַע
אֶת־קוֹל אֲדֹנָי אֹמֵר אֶת־מִי אֶשְׁלַח וּמִי יֵלֶךְ־לָנוּ וָאֹמַר הִנְנִי

ט שְׁלָחֵנִי: וַיֹּאמֶר לֵךְ וְאָמַרְתָּ לָעָם הַזֶּה שִׁמְעוּ שָׁמוֹעַ וְאַל־תָּבִינוּ

י וּרְאוּ רָאוֹ וְאַל־תֵּדָעוּ: הַשְׁמֵן לֵב־הָעָם הַזֶּה וְאָזְנָיו הַכְבֵּד וְעֵינָיו
הָשַׁע פֶּן־יִרְאֶה בְעֵינָיו וּבְאָזְנָיו יִשְׁמָע וּלְבָבוֹ יָבִין וָשָׁב וְרָפָא לוֹ:

יא וָאֹמַר עַד־מָתַי אֲדֹנָי וַיֹּאמֶר עַד אֲשֶׁר אִם־שָׁאוּ עָרִים מֵאֵין יוֹשֵׁב

יב וּבָתִּים מֵאֵין אָדָם וְהָאֲדָמָה תִּשָּׁאֶה שְׁמָמָה: וְרִחַק יהוה אֶת־

יג הָאָדָם וְרַבָּה הָעֲזוּבָה בְּקֶרֶב הָאָרֶץ: וְעוֹד בָּהּ עֲשִׂרִיָּה וְשָׁבָה
וְהָיְתָה לְבָעֵר כָּאֵלָה וְכָאַלּוֹן אֲשֶׁר בְּשַׁלֶּכֶת מַצֶּבֶת בָּם זֶרַע קֹדֶשׁ

הספרדים
מסיימים כאן
התימנים
ממשיכים בפרק ט

ז א מַצַּבְתָּהּ:* וַיְהִי בִּימֵי אָחָז בֶּן־יוֹתָם בֶּן־עֻזִּיָּהוּ מֶלֶךְ
יְהוּדָה עָלָה רְצִין מֶלֶךְ־אֲרָם וּפֶקַח בֶּן־רְמַלְיָהוּ מֶלֶךְ־יִשְׂרָאֵל

ב יְרוּשָׁלִַם לַמִּלְחָמָה עָלֶיהָ וְלֹא יָכֹל לְהִלָּחֵם עָלֶיהָ: וַיֻּגַּד לְבֵית
דָּוִד לֵאמֹר נָחָה אֲרָם עַל־אֶפְרָיִם וַיָּנַע לְבָבוֹ וּלְבַב עַמּוֹ כְּנוֹעַ

ג עֲצֵי־יַעַר מִפְּנֵי־רוּחַ: וַיֹּאמֶר יהוה אֶל־יְשַׁעְיָהוּ צֵא־נָא
לִקְרַאת אָחָז אַתָּה וּשְׁאָר יָשׁוּב בְּנֶךָ אֶל־קְצֵה תְּעָלַת הַבְּרֵכָה

ד הָעֶלְיוֹנָה אֶל־מְסִלַּת שְׂדֵה כוֹבֵס: וְאָמַרְתָּ אֵלָיו הִשָּׁמֵר וְהַשְׁקֵט
אַל־תִּירָא וּלְבָבְךָ אַל־יֵרַךְ מִשְּׁנֵי זַנְבוֹת הָאוּדִים הָעֲשֵׁנִים הָאֵלֶּה

5 the son of Remalyahu. For Aram has conspired to harm you, along with
6 Efrayim and Remalyahu's son: "We shall go up to Jerusalem, bring about
her end, we shall break her walls open for ourselves and set a new king
over her: the son of Taval."

9 5 For a child is born to us, a son is given us; leadership rests on his shoulders, and he shall be called Mighty God Is Planning Wonders; Eternal
6 Father; Prince of Peace. To instill great leadership, peace without end, on
the throne of David, and over his kingdom, founding and supporting it
with justice and with righteousness now and forever; the passion of the
LORD of Hosts will bring all this to be.

ה בַּחֲרִי־אַף רְצִין וַאֲרָם וּבֶן־רְמַלְיָהוּ: יַעַן כִּי־יָעַץ עָלֶיךָ אֲרָם רָעָה

ו אֶפְרַיִם וּבֶן־רְמַלְיָהוּ לֵאמֹר: נַעֲלֶה בִיהוּדָה וּנְקִיצֶנָּה וְנַבְקִעֶנָּה
אֵלֵינוּ וְנַמְלִיךְ מֶלֶךְ בְּתוֹכָהּ אֵת בֶּן־טָבְאַל:

ט כִּי־יֶלֶד יֻלַּד־לָנוּ בֵּן נִתַּן־לָנוּ וַתְּהִי הַמִּשְׂרָה עַל־שִׁכְמוֹ וַיִּקְרָא

י שְׁמוֹ פֶּלֶא יוֹעֵץ אֵל גִּבּוֹר אֲבִי־עַד שַׂר־שָׁלוֹם: לְמַרְבֵּה הַמִּשְׂרָה לְמַרְבֵּה
וּלְשָׁלוֹם אֵין־קֵץ עַל־כִּסֵּא דָוִד וְעַל־מַמְלַכְתּוֹ לְהָכִין אֹתָהּ
וּלְסַעֲדָהּ בְּמִשְׁפָּט וּבִצְדָקָה מֵעַתָּה וְעַד־עוֹלָם קִנְאַת יהוה
צְבָאוֹת תַּעֲשֶׂה־זֹּאת:

חומש קורן מקראות הדורות
THE KOREN MIKRAOT HADOROT

פרשת יתרו
PARASHAT YITRO

KOREN

THE ROHR FAMILY EDITION

חומש קורן מקראות הדורות
THE KOREN MIKRAOT HADOROT

THE ZAHAVA AND MOSHAEL STRAUS EDITION OF SEFER SHEMOT

פרשת יתרו עם מפרשים
PARASHAT YITRO WITH COMMENTARIES

TORAH TRANSLATION BY
Rabbi Lord Jonathan Sacks שליט״א
FROM THE MAGERMAN EDITION OF THE KOREN TANAKH

COMMENTARIES COLLECTED AND ABRIDGED BY
Rabbi Shai Finkelstein, EDITOR-IN-CHIEF

COMMENTARIES TRANSLATED BY
Rabbi Jonathan Mishkin

MANAGING EDITOR
Rabbi Yedidya Naveh

•

KOREN PUBLISHERS JERUSALEM

The Koren Mikraot HaDorot, The Rohr Edition
Volume 17: Parashat Yitro
First Edition, 2020

Koren Publishers Jerusalem Ltd.
POB 4044, Jerusalem 9104001, ISRAEL
POB 8531, New Milford, CT 06776, USA

www.korenpub.com

Torah Translation © 2019, Jonathan Sacks
Koren Tanakh Font © 1962, 2020 Koren Publishers Jerusalem Ltd.

Commentary © Koren Publishers Jerusalem Ltd., except as noted:
Commentaries of Philo, used with permission of Kodesh Press
Commentaries Rabbi Joseph B. Soloveitchik, used with permission of the OU Press
Commentaries of Nehama Leibowitz, used with permission of the World Zionist Organization

The Tanakh translation is excerpted from the Magerman Edition of The Koren Tanakh.

The creation of this work was made possible with the generous support
of the Jewish Book Trust Inc.

Printed in ISRAEL

ISBN 978 965 7760 72 7
KMDYT01

The Rohr Family Edition of
The Koren Mikraot HaDorot
pays tribute to the memory of

Mr. Sami Rohr ז״ל
ר׳ שמואל ב״ר יהושע אליהו ז״ל

who served his Maker with joy
and whose far-reaching vision, warm open hand, love of Torah,
and love for every Jew were catalysts for the revival and growth of
vibrant Jewish life in the former Soviet Union
and in countless communities the world over

and to the memory of his beloved wife

Mrs. Charlotte Rohr (née Kastner) ע״ה
שרה בת ר׳ יקותיאל יהודה ע״ה

who survived the fires of the Shoah to become
the elegant and gracious matriarch,
first in Colombia and later in the United States,
of three generations of a family
nurtured by her love and unstinting devotion.
She found grace in the eyes of all those whose lives she touched.

Together they merited to see all their children
build lives enriched by faithful commitment
to the spreading of Torah and *Ahavat Yisrael.*

Dedicated with love by
The Rohr Family
NEW YORK, USA

עֲטֶרֶת זְקֵנִים בְּנֵי בָנִים
(משלי יז, ו)

Grandchildren
are the crowning glory of the aged
(*Proverbs 17:6*)

May the learning and traditions of our people
be strengthened by our future generations.
In honor of our wonderful grandchildren

Zahava and Moshael Straus

CONTENTS

FOR THE COMPLETE RASHI AND HAFTARA
TURN TO THE OTHER END OF THIS VOLUME.

PUBLISHER'S PREFACE

The genius of Jewish commentary on the Torah is one of huge and critical import. Jewish life and law for millennia have been directed by our interpretations of the Torah, and each generation has looked to its rabbinic leadership for a deeper understanding of its teachings, its laws, its stories.

For centuries, *Mikraot Gedolot* have been a core part of understanding the Ḥumash; the words of Rashi, Ibn Ezra, Ramban, Rashbam, Ralbag, and other classic commentators illuminate and help us understand the Torah. But traditional editions of *Mikraot Gedolot* present only a slice in time and a small selection of the corpus of Jewish commentators. Almost every generation has produced rabbinic scholars who speak to their times, from Philo and Onkelos two thousand years ago, to Rabbi Joseph B. Soloveitchik, Rabbi Aharon Kotler, the Lubavitcher Rebbe, and Nehama Leibowitz in ours.

The Koren Mikraot HaDorot – Scriptures or Interpretations for the Generations – brings two millennia of Torah commentary into the hands and homes of Jews around the world. Readers will be able not only to encounter the classic commentators, but to gain a much broader sense of the issues that scholars grappled with in their time and the inspiration they drew from the ancient texts. We see, for example, how Philo speaks to an assimilating Greek Jewish audience in first-century Alexandria, and how similar yet different it is from Rabbi Samson Raphael Hirsch's approach to an equally assimilating nineteenth-century German readership; how the perspectives of Rabbi Soloveitchik and Rabbi Kotler differ in a post-Holocaust world; how Rav Se'adya Gaon interpreted the Torah for the Jews of Babylonia. It is an exciting journey through Jewish history via the unchanging words of the Torah.

The text of the Torah features the exceptional new translation of Rabbi Lord Jonathan Sacks, together with the celebrated and meticulously accurate Koren Hebrew text. Of course, with the exception of Rashi – for whom we present an entirely new translation in full – the commentaries are selected. We offer this anthology not to limit our reader's exploration but rather as a gateway for further learning of Torah and its commentaries on a broader and deeper level than space here permits. We discuss below how to use this book.

We must thank **Pamela and George Rohr** of New York, who recognized the unique value of *The Koren Mikraot HaDorot* and its ability to communicate historical breadth and context to the reader. For my colleagues here at Koren, we thank you; for the many generations of users who will find this a continuing source of new learning, we are forever in your debt.

We also are indebted to **Zahava and Moshael Straus**, true leaders of this Jewish generation in so many fields, who have invested not only in *Parashat Yitro* but the entire book of Shemot. Together, we were thus able to launch this innovative and unique project.

We are honored to acknowledge and thank **Debra and David Magerman**, whose support for the Koren Ḥumash with Rabbi Sacks's exemplary translation and commentary laid the foundation for the core English text of this work.

Finally, I must personally thank **Rabbi Marvin Hier**, with whom I had a special breakfast some years ago at the King David Hotel. During the meal, he raised the problem that so few people knew the writings of Rabbi Joseph B. Soloveitchik and Rabbi Aharon Kotler on the Torah; and I, who had just read some of Philo's work, had the same reaction. From that conversation came the seed for this project.

HOW TO USE *THE KOREN MIKRAOT HADOROT*

The Koren Mikraot HaDorot will be a fifty-five-volume edition of the Ḥumash (one for each *parasha* plus a companion volume). Each of the fifty-four volumes of the *parashot* can be read from right to left (Hebrew opening side), and left to right (English opening side).

Opening from the Hebrew side offers:

- ▸ the full Torah text, the translation of Rabbi Sacks, and the full commentary of Rashi in both Hebrew and the new English translation
- ▸ all *haftarot* associated with the *parasha* of the volume, including Rosh Ḥodesh and special readings, both in Hebrew and English

Opening from the English side presents four sections:

▸ THE TIME OF THE SAGES – includes commentaries from the Second Temple period and the talmudic period

▸ THE CLASSIC COMMENTATORS – quotes selected explanations by Rashi as well as most of the commentators found in traditional *Mikraot Gedolot*

▸ CONFRONTING MODERNITY – selects commentaries from the eighteenth century to the close of the twentieth century

▸ THE BIBLICAL IMAGINATION – features essays surveying some of the broader conceptual ideas as a supplement to the linear, text-based commentary

The first three of these sections each feature the relevant verses, in Hebrew and English, on the page alongside their respective commentaries, in chronological order, providing the reader with a single window onto the text without excessive page turning.

In addition to being a valuable resource in a Jewish home or synagogue library, we conceived of these volumes as a weekly accompaniment in the synagogue. There is scope for the reader to study each *parasha* on a weekly basis in preparation for the reading on Shabbat. One may select a particular group of commentators for study that week, or perhaps alternate between ancient and modern viewpoints. Some readers may choose to delve into the text through verse-by-verse interpretation, while others may prefer a conceptual perspective on the *parasha* as a whole. The broad array of options for learning means this is a series which can be returned to year after year, always presenting new insights and new approaches to understanding the text.

ACKNOWLEDGMENTS

The creation of this book was possible only thanks to the small but exceptional team here at Koren Jerusalem. We are grateful to:

▸ Rabbi Tzvi Hersh Weinreb, שליט״א, who conceptualized the structure of the project and provides both moral and halakhic leadership at Koren

▸ Rabbi Shai Finkelstein, whose encyclopedic knowledge of Torah and its interpreters is equaled only by his community leadership, formerly in Memphis and today in Jerusalem

▸ Rabbi Yedidya Naveh, whose knowledge, organizational skills, and superb leadership brought the disparate elements together

▸ Rabbi Jonathan Mishkin, translator of the commentaries, who crafted a fluent, accurate, and eloquent English translation

Our design, editing, typesetting, and proofreading staff, including Tani Bayer, Esther Be'er, Debbie Ismailoff, Estie Dishon, Tomi Mager, and Carolyn Budow Ben David, enabled an attractive, user-friendly, and accurate edition of these works.

> "One silver basin" (Numbers 7:13) was brought as a symbol of the Torah, which has been likened to wine, as the verse states: "And drink of the wine which I have mingled" (Proverbs 9:5). Because it is customary to drink wine in a basin – as we see in the verse "that drink wine in basins" (Amos 6:6) – he therefore brought a basin. "Of seventy shekels, after the shekel of the sanctuary" (Numbers 7:13). Why? Because just as the numerical value of "wine" [*yayin*] is seventy, so there are seventy modes of expounding the Torah. (Bemidbar Rabba 13:16)

Each generation produces exceptional rabbinic, intellectual leadership. It has been our purpose to enable all Jews to taste the wine of those generations, in the hope of expanding the breadth and depth of their knowledge. Torah is our greatest treasure, and we need the wisdom of those generations to better understand this bountiful gift from God. We hope that we at Koren can deepen that understanding for all who seek it.

Matthew Miller, Publisher
Jerusalem, 5780 (2019)

EDITOR'S INTRODUCTION

Over the course of millennia, the Jewish people have watched while the surrounding society and its values have changed unceasingly. For the Jews, the steadfast response to an evolving world has always been the study of Torah, specifically engagement with the weekly *parasha*. Devotees of Jewish learning have always looked to the weekly Torah portion for spiritual and intellectual guidance through life's challenges. And in every generation, commentaries on the Ḥumash have debated the precise interpretation of the verses therein. These scholars have continuously asked what message God is trying to convey to Israel and the world through the Torah's narratives and laws. Their explanations have struggled to identify the correct ways to apply its lessons to our daily lives.

Throughout, all these authors have approached the Torah text from their own unique perspectives, shaped in no small measure by the eras and environments they lived in. Naturally, the pantheon of commentaries present widely different styles in their writings. Occasionally the commentators will subject a particular verse to piercing scrutiny as a self-contained unit. At other times they present interpretations that seem to stray from the straightforward meaning of the text. Ultimately, all commentaries demand that a verse provide readers with theological meaning and direction for communal and social life.

Recognition of the wisdom embedded in the vast literature of commentary on the Torah spanning the various eras of Jewish history planted the seeds of the project whose fruit you now hold. We have called this publication *Mikraot HaDorot* – Readings of the Generations. This window into the world of Torah commentaries is not simply an upgrade of the classical *Mikraot Gedolot* collections, which give readers merely a handful of familiar

interpretations. *The Koren Mikraot HaDorot* instead presents a plethora of exegetical contributions, with more than forty scholars spanning Jewish teachings from the past two thousand years represented on its pages.

Each volume of the *Koren Mikraot HaDorot* series can be opened from both the right (Hebrew) side and left (English) side. The Hebrew opening side includes the Hebrew and a new English text of the *parasha*, translated by Rabbi Lord Jonathan Sacks, with a full, new translation of Rashi and the *haftarot*. The English opening side contains the bulk of the commentaries, and is divided into four parts: The first, THE TIME OF THE SAGES, comprises commentaries from antiquity – ranging from Philo to the Yalkut Shimoni. These figures lived mainly in the land of Israel, Egypt, and Babylonia. The second, THE CLASSIC COMMENTATORS, contains interpretations from the Middle Ages – starting from Rav Se'adya Gaon and Rashi and continuing through time to the work of Rabbi Shlomo Efrayim of Luntschitz, author of the *Keli Yakar*. The authors included here represent the rich traditions of both Sephardic (Spanish and North African) and Ashkenazic (central and eastern European) schools of exegesis. The third section, CONFRONTING MODERNITY, offers the work of both Old World and New World scholars who lived between the eighteenth and twentieth centuries. Before each of these three sections we include a time line that specifies the chronological relationships between the commentators and the places they lived.

In the final section, THE BIBLICAL IMAGINATION, we provide three in-depth investigations of particular ideas through the writings of the various commentaries. There are several goals to these essays. First, we aim to reveal common threads weaving across the generations of Torah scholarship. Second, we hope to illustrate how the various authors were influenced by their lives and times, and that the lessons they transmitted to their communities reflected their environments. Finally, each essay highlights for the reader some central issues that the commentaries have grappled with. We trust that this tool will facilitate the reader's understanding of the words of the commentaries themselves.

Three principles have governed the decision making in our work on *The Koren Mikraot HaDorot*:

▸ Chronological order: We have striven to sketch out the historical development of Torah exegesis, an enterprise that has occupied innumerable communities of Jews in far-flung lands for centuries.

▸ Economy of selection: In compiling the excerpts used in this work, we have gone through the authors' works and isolated those sections which most directly address the particular question, issue, or difficulty that confronted the scholar.

▸ Objectivity of presentation: This book presents ideas of the commentaries authentically, never censoring them or smoothing them over in light of our own positions or perspectives. We always strove to faithfully transmit the legal, conceptual, social, and ethical messages of the commentators.

The modern world constantly challenges us as individuals, as a society, and as communal leaders, teachers, and parents. The values and culture of the society that surrounds us force thinking Jews to seriously consider and reconsider their ideas and priorities on a regular basis as we struggle to find the correct path through life. Furthermore, we constantly must ask ourselves what teachings we wish to transmit to future generations. It is our hope that the *Koren Mikraot HaDorot* project will help guide its readers as they grapple with these very real problems. The world of Torah commentary is wide and deep beyond measure. It contains innumerable answers to the questions that face the individual, the family, the generation, and indeed all of humanity.

Rabbi Shai Finkelstein, Editor-in-Chief
Jerusalem, 5780 (2019)

A NOTE ON THE TRANSLATION

The terse writing style prevalent in Jewish scholarship over most of history can be difficult for the modern reader to decipher. Since our goal in the *Koren Mikraot HaDorot* series is to make thousands of years of Torah commentary accessible to a modern, English-speaking audience, we have opted for a relatively loose translation style that accurately presents the content of the Hebrew commentary while not necessarily mirroring its exact syntax. We have also resorted occasionally to paraphrase in instances where a literal translation would be opaque in English. As any student of Torah exegesis will recognize, draconian insistence on a word-for-word translation would result in an English text that was unreadable and that preserved neither the clarity nor the majesty of the original Hebrew.

Many of the commentaries' discussions focus on the meanings of words and phrases that are ambiguous in the Hebrew text of the *parasha*. The beautiful new translation of the Torah by Rabbi Lord Jonathan Sacks that we include here often dispels these ambiguities in the interest of clarity, necessarily coming down on one side or the other of a disagreement between commentators. The reader of the commentaries should therefore view the Torah translation presented here as one possible reading of the often-cryptic Hebrew original. In a similar vein, the significance of certain interpretations may seem unclear, or their points obvious, until one encounters another commentary with a starkly different read of the same verse. These contrasts, and the realization that themes and meanings we thought to be clear are actually ambiguous and multifaceted, are the essence of *The Koren Mikraot HaDorot*.

We have, as far as possible, allowed each text to speak for itself, and have left editorial comments to a minimum. Nevertheless, the commentaries

often assume the reader's knowledge of other biblical episodes, midrashim, or Hebrew grammar beyond what might be expected from the English-speaking public today. To ensure clarity, we have therefore interpolated brief editor's notes where we deemed it necessary, setting them off from the original text in square brackets.

Throughout Jewish history, the text of the Tanakh has been viewed as the apogee of the Hebrew language. For many commentators, especially those of the Middle Ages, it served as a fountain of language from which they drew numerous idioms and phrases. The result is that the Hebrew text of many commentaries is shot through with snippets of biblical prose or poetry to such an extent that almost every sentence can be viewed as a quote or allusion. Marking and citing all of these would make for a cluttered translation and would hinder rather than enhance the reader's understanding. We have therefore opted to cite only those quotes which are brought by the author as explicit evidence to further the point being made, and not those that supply only a turn of phrase.

The Hebrew side of this volume contains a complete and unabridged translation of Rashi's commentary. For those who wish to follow the *parasha* on the English side of the book, we have also reprinted many of Rashi's explanations alongside those of the other classic commentators. This will allow the reader to compare Rashi's interpretation to those of Rashbam, Ibn Ezra, and others, as well as appreciate how Rashi's commentary often serves to define the issues that will be addressed by later exegetes.

The text of the commentaries is of course abridged. We have not included ellipses to mark every point where text has been omitted, to maintain a clutter-free translation. However, we have included ellipses at points where the subject of discussion would otherwise appear to have changed abruptly and inexplicably, to save the reader confusion. We have also not adhered strictly to the original heading, or s.v. (*dibbur hamat-ḥil*) of every text, changing it in instances where it would help to focus the reader on those words that are the actual subject of discussion, and adding it to texts that did not originally have it.

Most of the commentaries that we quote in this series were originally organized by chapter and verse. Therefore, anyone who wishes to consult the original Hebrew text of a given commentary can simply open to the verse in question. However, not all sources are organized this way. The midrashim in particular are often ordered loosely; an important interpretation of a verse in Exodus might be found in a midrash on Deuteronomy. For the reader's convenience in locating the original Hebrew source, we have

provided citations for those works not organized sequentially, as well as for commentaries originally composed on verses other than the one under discussion. These citations can be found outside of the final punctuation at the end of the excerpt in question.

Our translation has generally relied upon the Hebrew text found in the Bar-Ilan Responsa Project and the online compendia Sefaria and AlHatorah. org, as well as the standard printed editions of commentaries not found in any of these. The Responsa Project contains more than one edition of several midrashim (Midrash Tanḥuma, Midrash Rabba, and Avot DeRabbi Natan). For these works, our citations should be understood as referring to the standard editions published in Vilna and Warsaw unless otherwise indicated. Aside from this, please note:

- Text from Mekhilta DeRabbi Shimon is understood to be from the Epstein-Melamed edition unless otherwise indicated.
- Excerpts from Ibn Ezra are almost always taken from his Long Commentary on Exodus, and we have marked those instances where we quote from his Short Commentary.
- Passages from Philo are quoted with permission from *Torah from Alexandria: Philo as a Biblical Commentator,* edited by Rabbi Michael Leo Samuel (New York: Kodesh Press, 2015).
- Selected commentaries of Rabbi Joseph B. Soloveitchik are printed with permission from *Chumash Mesoras HaRav,* edited by Dr. Arnold Lustiger (New York: OU Press and Ohr Publishing Inc., 2017).
- The commentaries of the Lubavitcher Rebbe are quoted from *The Torah, with an Interpolated Translation and Commentary Based on the Works of the Lubavitcher Rebbe,* edited by Rabbi Chaim Nochum Cunin and Rabbi Moshe Yaakov Wisnefsky (New York: Kehot Publication Society, 2017).
- The commentaries of Nehama Leibowitz are translated, with generous permission, from the Hebrew *Iyyunim Ḥadashim BeSefer Shemot* (14th edition), published by the World Zionist Organization Department for Torah Education and Culture in the Diaspora.

While we have thus done our best to aid the reader in finding and consulting the original Hebrew text of the commentaries we have translated, we emphasize that this is not a critical edition, and the scope and readership of the series do not permit us to fully cite every allusion and internal reference

that authors make to midrashim and other commentaries. Still, we have made a supreme effort to provide citations of talmudic passages, and of course biblical verses, quoted or referred to in the material included here.

Yedidya Naveh, Managing Editor
Jerusalem, 5780 (2019)

1ST CENTURY BCE

1ST CENTURY CE ——— PHILO, 25 BCE – 50 CE

2ND CENTURY

3RD CENTURY

HALAKHIC MIDRASHIM, 3RD CENTURY
(MEKHILTA, SIFRA, SIFREI)

4TH CENTURY
SEDER ELIYAHU, 3RD CENTURY

TALMUD YERUSHALMI, 3RD – 5TH CENTURY

TALMUD BAVLI, 3RD – 6TH CENTURY

5TH CENTURY ——— MIDRASH TANḤUMA, 5TH CENTURY

PESIKTA DERAV KAHANA,
6TH CENTURY   5TH – 6TH CENTURY

7TH CENTURY

8TH CENTURY ——— AVOT DERABBI NATAN, 7TH – 9TH CENTURY

9TH CENTURY ——— MIDRASH RABBA, 5TH – 12TH CENTURY

PESIKTA RABBATI, 9TH CENTURY
AGGADAT BERESHIT, 9TH CENTURY
10TH CENTURY   MIDRASH SHMUEL, 9TH – 11TH CENTURY

11TH CENTURY ——— BERESHIT RABBATI, 11TH CENTURY
MIDRASH LEKAḤ TOV, 11TH CENTURY

12TH CENTURY ——— MIDRASH SEKHEL TOV, 1139
MIDRASH AGGADA, 12TH – 13TH CENTURY

13TH CENTURY ——— YALKUT SHIMONI, 13TH CENTURY

פרשת יתרו
PARASHAT YITRO

THE **TIME**
OF THE **SAGES**

יח א וַיִּשְׁמַע יִתְרוֹ כֹהֵן מִדְיָן חֹתֵן מֹשֶׁה אֵת כָּל־אֲשֶׁר עָשָׂה יד
אֱלֹהִים לְמֹשֶׁה וּלְיִשְׂרָאֵל עַמּוֹ כִּי־הוֹצִיא יהוה אֶת־יִשְׂרָאֵל
ב מִמִּצְרָיִם: וַיִּקַּח יִתְרוֹ חֹתֵן מֹשֶׁה אֶת־צִפֹּרָה אֵשֶׁת מֹשֶׁה
ג אַחַר שִׁלּוּחֶיהָ: וְאֵת שְׁנֵי בָנֶיהָ אֲשֶׁר שֵׁם הָאֶחָד גֵּרְשֹׁם

CHAPTER 18, VERSE 1

─────────────────── MEKHILTA DERABBI SHIMON ───────────────────

וַיִּשְׁמַע יִתְרוֹ – *Yitro heard:* Yitro was originally called Yeter [see 4:18], but as recognition of his pleasant acts, the letter *vav* was added to his name, making it "Yitro". [As one of the letters of God's name, the *vav* signifies sanctity.]

─────────────────── SEDER ELIYAHU RABBA ───────────────────

יִתְרוֹ כֹהֵן מִדְיָן חֹתֵן מֹשֶׁה – *Moshe's father-in-law Yitro, priest of Midyan:* We learn from this story that a man should insist on marrying off his daughter to a Torah scholar, no matter how high the dowry. For we see that Yitro was only blessed [with fame and fortune] due to the merits of Moshe.

─────────────────── TALMUD YERUSHALMI, ───────────────────

וַיִּשְׁמַע יִתְרוֹ – *Yitro heard:* What did Yitro hear? Ḥizkiya taught: He heard about the splitting of the sea. (Megilla 1:11)

─────────────────── TALMUD BAVLI ───────────────────

וַיִּשְׁמַע יִתְרוֹ כֹהֵן מִדְיָן – *Yitro, priest of Midyan heard:* What did Yitro hear that led him to meet up with Israel and convert to their religion? Rabbi Yehoshua taught: He heard about Israel's military victory against Amalek, for the text immediately prior to this chapter states: *And Yehoshua overcame Amalek and his people by the sword* (17:13). Rabbi Elazar HaModa'i taught: Yitro heard the Torah being given. For when God spoke to Israel at Mount Sinai, the sound of His voice traveled the length and breadth of the world. (Zevaḥim 116a)

─────────────────── TANḤUMA ───────────────────

וַיִּשְׁמַע יִתְרוֹ – *Yitro heard:* After Yitro heard about Israel's success, he made a decision that benefited him. Originally Yitro had been a priest in the service of idolatry, but he gave it all up to come and join Moshe's mission. In reward he was taken under the wings of the Divine Presence and credited with introducing Israel's system of justice. (Yitro 2) **וַיִּשְׁמַע יִתְרוֹ** – *Yitro heard:* Said the Holy One, blessed be He, to Moshe: I am the One who created the world through speech alone. And I am the One who brings close the distant ones without distancing those who are already close, as the verse states: *Am I a God near at hand, says the Lord, and not a God far off?* (Jeremiah 23:23). Just as I embraced Yitro who came from afar rather than rebuff him, you too should adopt a similar attitude. Should a gentile approach you wishing to convert, you should welcome him and not discourage him. Immediately, *Moshe went out to greet his father-in-law* (18:7). Said our Sages, of blessed memory: Moshe did not set out alone, but was accompanied by Aharon, Nadav, Avihu, and all the elders of Israel. Thus does the verse state: *The wise inherit honor* (Proverbs 3:35). (Yitro 6)

18 1 Moshe's father-in-law Yitro, priest of Midyan, heard about all
that God had done for Moshe and for His people Israel when
2 the Lᴏʀᴅ brought Israel out of Egypt. Yitro had received
3 Moshe's wife Tzipora after he had sent her home, together
with her two sons. One was named Gershom, for Moshe had

VERSE 2
MEKHILTA DERABBI SHIMON

אַחַר שִׁלּוּחֶיהָ – *After he had sent her home:* When had Moshe sent his wife back to Midyan? After God commanded him to descend to Egypt and to lead the Israelites out of that country, Moshe saddled up his wife and sons, and traveled with them on a donkey to see his compatriots. At the same time, God directed Aharon to set out to meet his brother in the wilderness. Upon their reunion, Moshe and Aharon began to hug and kiss each other. Said Aharon: "Moshe, my brother – where have you been all these years?" Moshe answered: "I have been living in Midyan." "And

who are these people you have with you?" Aharon asked. Said Moshe: "They are my wife and children." "Where then are you taking them?" continued his brother. "To Egypt, of course," said Moshe. Said Aharon: "Here we are distressed over the fate of the Hebrews who are already ensnared in that horrid country, and you wish to introduce more people into bondage?" As soon as Moshe heard that, he addressed Tzipora and told her to turn around and head back home to her father. And so she did, which explains the verses *After he had sent her home, together with her two sons* (18:2–3).

VERSE 3
MEKHILTA DERABBI SHIMON

גֵּר הָיִיתִי בְּאֶרֶץ נָכְרִיָּה – *I have been a stranger in a foreign land:* Rabbi Yehoshua taught: Moshe felt like an outsider in Midyan, where he knew no one. Rabbi Elazar HaModa'i taught: What Moshe meant by this statement was

that all the citizens of Midyan worshipped idols – gods that were foreign to his belief, while He served the One who spoke and created the world.

SEKHEL TOV

וְאֵת שְׁנֵי בָנֶיהָ – *Together with her two sons:* Gershom and Eliezer are referred to as Tzipora's sons rather than Moshe's because their father

had sent them back to Midyan upon Aharon's advice. The language of the verse emphasizes that the two were raised by their mother.

MIDRASH AGGADA

שֵׁם הָאֶחָד גֵּרְשֹׁם – *One was named Gershom:* Yitro forced Moshe to agree to circumcise just one of his sons, and to leave the other one uncircumcised. Hence the occurrence at

the lodging place, where *the Lᴏʀᴅ confronted Moshe and was about to kill him* (4:24). Eliezer was the boy who had not been circumcised back in Midyan.

ד כִּי אָמַר גֵּר הָיִיתִי בְּאֶרֶץ נָכְרִיָּה: וְשֵׁם הָאֶחָד אֱלִיעֶזֶר כִּי־
ה אֱלֹהֵי אָבִי בְּעֶזְרִי וַיַּצִּלֵנִי מֵחֶרֶב פַּרְעֹה: וַיָּבֹא יִתְרוֹ חֹתֵן
מֹשֶׁה וּבָנָיו וְאִשְׁתּוֹ אֶל־מֹשֶׁה אֶל־הַמִּדְבָּר אֲשֶׁר־הוּא חֹנֶה
ו שָׁם הַר הָאֱלֹהִים: וַיֹּאמֶר אֶל־מֹשֶׁה אֲנִי חֹתֶנְךָ יִתְרוֹ בָּא

VERSE 4

MEKHILTA DERABBI SHIMON

וַיַּצִּלֵנִי מֵחֶרֶב פַּרְעֹה – *Saving me from Pharaoh's sword:* When exactly did God save Moshe from Pharaoh's sword? Rabbi Yehoshua taught: This happened during the episode of the quarreling Israelites, when Datan criticized Moshe, saying: *Who made you a ruler and judge over us?* (2:14). Rabbi Eleazar HaModa'i said: Once Moshe's killing of the Egyptian became known, he was arrested and taken up to the platform for execution. The soldiers bound him and bowed his neck under the sword. At that moment an angel descended from heaven disguised as Moshe. At once the guard turned from Moshe and seized his lookalike. Rabbi Eliezer taught: In punishing the soldiers

who had arrested Moshe, God divided them into three groups. He turned some of them mute, made others deaf, and afflicted the rest with blindness. The sightless soldiers shouted at their colleagues: Where has Moshe escaped to? But those who had become deaf could not hear them, and those who suddenly lacked the faculty of speech could not answer. Meanwhile, of course, the blind men could not locate Moshe, who easily escaped. It is to this salvation that God referred when He said to Moshe: *Who gives man speech? Who makes people dumb or deaf? Who gives them sight or blindness? Is it not I, the LORD?* (4:11).

TALMUD YERUSHALMI

וַיַּצִּלֵנִי מֵחֶרֶב פַּרְעֹה – *Saving me from Pharaoh's sword:* Early in Moshe's story, the Torah reports that *Moshe fled from Pharaoh's presence* (2:15), as if it were possible for a person to escape the reach of the empire! Rather, this is what happened: Moshe was arrested by the king's men, whereupon Pharaoh decreed that he be executed. But when the executioner brought his sword down upon Moshe's neck it first became dull and then broke into pieces. Indeed,

it is Moshe's neck that the verse refers to when it states: *Your neck is like a tower of ivory* (Song of Songs 7:5). Rabbi Yehuda HaNasi taught in the name of Rabbi Evyatar: Not only did the soldier's knife ricochet off Moshe's neck but it flew back at his own and killed him. This is what the verse means when it states: *Saving me from Pharaoh's sword* – He rescued me while dispatching the executioner. (Berakhot 9:1)

BEMIDBAR RABBA

וְשֵׁם הָאֶחָד אֱלִיעֶזֶר – *And the other, Eliezer:* Rabbi Aḥa said in the name of Rabbi Ḥanina: When Moshe went up to the heavens, he heard the Holy One, blessed be He, sitting and studying the passage of the red heifer (Numbers 19), and citing a teaching: Said God:

Rabbi Eliezer taught: The animal used in the ceremony of the heifer whose neck is broken [see Deuteronomy 21:1–9] must be a year old, while the cow used in the rite of the red heifer must be two years old. Said Moshe to God: Master of the Universe! May it be your will that

4 said, "I have been a stranger in a foreign land," and the other,
Eliezer, for he had said, "My father's God has helped me, sav-
5 ing me from Pharaoh's sword." And now Moshe's father-in-law
Yitro came to Moshe in the desert, bringing his sons and his
6 wife, to where he was encamped by the mountain of God. Yitro
sent word to Moshe, "I am coming to you – your father-in-law

———————————— BEMIDBAR RABBA *(cont.)* ————————————

this scholar should be a descendant of mine. *the other, Eliezer,* alluding to the other, future
Whereupon God vowed to him: I swear by Rabbi Eliezer. (Ḥukat 19:7)
your life that he will! Thus the verse states: *And*

VERSE 5

———————————— MEKHILTA DERABBI SHIMON ————————————

אֶל־הַמִּדְבָּר – *In the desert:* The text recounts him as a leader of his community. But he gave
a shocking transition made by Yitro. Here was all of that up to live in the wilderness, where he
a man who lived his life in luxury in Midyan, would have nothing. This is why the text em-
where he enjoyed the honor lavished upon phasizes that Yitro *came to Moshe in the desert.*

———————————— SEKHEL TOV ————————————

הַר הָאֱלֹהִים – *The mountain of God:* The verse he visits. Rather, it is due to an illustrious visitor
refers to Mount Ḥorev, where God would soon that a place becomes respected. Thus the site
reveal Himself. The phrase teaches us that a is called "the mountain of God" [because of
person is never honored through the places God's presence there at that time].

VERSE 6

———————————— LEKAḤ TOV ————————————

בָּא אֵלֶיךָ – *Coming to you:* It is polite to always בָּא אֵלֶיךָ – *Coming to you:* I am coming out
announce one's arrival when going to visit a of love for you. If you choose to venerate
friend. This is illustrated by Yitro, who sent a me, come out to receive me. And if not for
message saying: *I am coming to you – your* my sake, then walk out to accept your wife.
father-in-law Yitro. Our Sages learn from this And if you do not wish to honor her, then at
that just as a person should never burst into least come out to see her two sons. This is
his own home [for fear of startling his family], why Yitro emphasized that he had traveled
he should certainly not behave thus when *together with your wife and both of your sons.*
coming to a friend's house. (Genesis 46:28) (Exodus 18:6)

———————————— MIDRASH AGGADA ————————————

בָּא אֵלֶיךָ – *Coming to you:* Why did Yitro need a message tied to it, saying: *I am coming to*
to identify himself? This shows that Yitro tried *you – your father-in-law.* Moshe immediately
to penetrate the miraculous cloud surround- walked through the cloud and came out to
ing Israel's camp but found that he was unable greet his father-in-law.
to do so. Instead, he shot in an arrow with

אֵלֶיךָ וְאִשְׁתְּךָ וּשְׁנֵי בָנֶיהָ עִמָּהּ: וַיֵּצֵא מֹשֶׁה לִקְרַאת חֹתְנוֹ
וַיִּשְׁתַּחוּ וַיִּשַּׁק־לוֹ וַיִּשְׁאֲלוּ אִישׁ־לְרֵעֵהוּ לְשָׁלוֹם וַיָּבֹאוּ
הָאֹהֱלָה: וַיְסַפֵּר מֹשֶׁה לְחֹתְנוֹ אֵת כָּל־אֲשֶׁר עָשָׂה יהוה
לְפַרְעֹה וּלְמִצְרַיִם עַל אוֹדֹת יִשְׂרָאֵל אֵת כָּל־הַתְּלָאָה אֲשֶׁר
מְצָאָתַם בַּדֶּרֶךְ וַיַּצִּלֵם יהוה: וַיִּחַדְּ יִתְרוֹ עַל כָּל־הַטּוֹבָה
אֲשֶׁר־עָשָׂה יהוה לְיִשְׂרָאֵל אֲשֶׁר הִצִּילוֹ מִיַּד מִצְרָיִם:

VERSE 7

MEKHILTA DERABBI SHIMON

לִקְרַאת חֹתְנוֹ – *To greet his father-in-law:* Note how astounding this story is. Here was a man who had previously spent every day offering sacrifices and burning incense in honor of his false deities. Yet now he brought burnt offerings and other sacrifices to God. Now why does the subsequent verse exclude Moshe when it states: *And Aharon and all the elders of Israel came to break bread with Moshe's father-in-law* (18:12) – had Moshe himself not gone out to greet his father-in-law? The verse signifies that while the others ate, Moshe stood and served them.

TANHUMA

וַיֵּצֵא מֹשֶׁה – *Moshe went out:* When Yitro arrived to visit, the text reports that *Moshe went out to greet his father-in-law.* At that moment, who could have seen Moshe leaving to honor his wife's father and not have joined the procession? Who would have seen the chiefs over the thousands, and the chiefs over the hundreds leaving and not joined them? Is there anyone who could have witnessed the seventy elders walking out of the camp and not followed them? And anyone who was left and saw Aharon the High Priest walking out – would he have not joined everybody else? In the end, the entire nation of Israel left the camp to greet Yitro. (Vayigash 7)

MIDRASH AGGADA

וַיִּשְׁאֲלוּ אִישׁ־לְרֵעֵהוּ לְשָׁלוֹם – *Each asked after the other's welfare:* [Literally, "one man asked after the other's welfare."] Who exactly asked after whose welfare? We can infer that Moshe our teacher was the considerate one. For here the verse here refers to a "man" [ish], while elsewhere the text states: *Now the man Moshe was very humble* (Numbers 12:3), which shows that the term "man" always refers to Moshe.

YALKUT SHIMONI

וַיֵּצֵא מֹשֶׁה לִקְרַאת חֹתְנוֹ – *Moshe went out to greet his father-in-law:* What does the verse imply when it states, *And Aharon and all the elders of Israel came to break bread with Moshe's father-in-law before God* (18:12)? The text teaches that when an individual goes out to greet his fellow, it is as if he is appearing before the Divine Presence. Rabbi Avin taught: Whenever a person partakes of a meal attended by a Torah scholar, it is as if he is basking in the glow of the Divine Presence. (Yitro 270)

7 Yitro – together with your wife and both of your sons." Moshe went out to greet his father-in-law and bowed down and kissed him. Each asked after the other's welfare, and they went inside

8 the tent. And Moshe told his father-in-law all that the LORD had done to Pharaoh and the Egyptians for Israel's sake, all the hardship they had encountered along the way, and how the

9 LORD had rescued them. Yitro delighted in all the good that the LORD had done for Israel, in His liberating them from the

VERSE 8

SEKHEL TOV

וַיְסַפֵּר מֹשֶׁה לְחֹתְנוֹ – *And Moshe told his father-in-law:* Moshe related all of Israel's previous adventures in order to draw Yitro toward the Torah. אֵת כָּל־אֲשֶׁר עָשָׂה יהוה –*All that the LORD had done:* Moshe wanted Yitro to thank God for Israel's salvation. אֵת כָּל־הַתְּלָאָה – *All the hardship:* The term *telaa* connotes toil and exhaustion [*lei'ut*]. אֲשֶׁר מְצָאָתַם – *They had encountered:* Moshe described to Yitro how Pharaoh and his cavalry had pursued Israel; he told him how Israel had become trapped

between the desert on one side and the sea on the other; he related Israel's arrival at Mara and the bitter water the people found there, their experience of hunger in the Sin Desert and their thirst for water in Refidim, and how the nation engaged Amalek in battle and were rescued by God. Moshe told his father-in-law that through all these trials God had sustained Israel and redeemed them from their state of need to a place of satisfaction.

YALKUT SHIMONI

אֵת כָּל־הַתְּלָאָה – *All the hardship:* This refers to the crisis at the Sea of Reeds. אֲשֶׁר מְצָאָתַם בַּדֶּרֶךְ – *They had encountered*

along the way: Here Moshe related the story of the war against Amalek [which immediately precedes this story]. (Yitro 268)

VERSE 9

PHILO

וַיִּחַדְּ יִתְרוֹ – *Yitro delighted:* Yitro is a blend of vanity and loves to associate with a city or commonwealth that is peopled by a

promiscuous horde. He moves about and follows whatever happens to be the popular opinion.

MEKHILTA DERABBI SHIMON

וַיִּחַדְּ יִתְרוֹ עַל כָּל־הַטּוֹבָה – *Yitro delighted in all the good:* Rabbi Yehoshua taught: Yitro was delighted when he heard about the manna, for this is how Moshe described it to him: "This manna that God is serving us contains a range of flavors to suit any palate. It tastes like bread to some people, like meat to others, while there are some individuals to whom it tastes

like fish, like locusts or like any other available taste in the world." We know that Moshe elaborated on the wonder of the manna due to the phrase "in all the good" [*al kol hatova*], which is especially wordy [the verse could have merely stated *batova* and suffered the same meaning]. Rabbi Elazar HaModa'i taught: Yitro was astounded to hear about the miracle of the

 י וַיֹּאמֶר יִתְרוֹ בָּרוּךְ יְהוָה אֲשֶׁר הִצִּיל אֶתְכֶם מִיַּד מִצְרַיִם
וּמִיַּד פַּרְעֹה אֲשֶׁר הִצִּיל אֶת־הָעָם מִתַּחַת יַד־מִצְרָיִם:
יא עַתָּה יָדַעְתִּי כִּי־גָדוֹל יְהוָה מִכָּל־הָאֱלֹהִים כִּי בַדָּבָר אֲשֶׁר

——————— MEKHILTA DERABBI SHIMON *(cont.)* ———————

well, which Moshe described to him as follows: "God has provided us with a well whose
water tastes different to different people. It
tastes like honey to some, like milk to others,
while there are still others to whom it tastes
like fresh or aged wine or like any other available taste in the world." We know that Moshe
elaborated on the wonder of the water due to
the phrase *al kol hatova.* Rabbi Eliezer taught:

Yitro was impressed to hear about the lands
which God planned to bequeath the Israelites,
for this is how Moshe described Israel's future:
"We will one day inherit the land of Israel, the
World to Come, and a new world governed
by the Davidic monarchy and guided by the
priestly class and the tribe of Levi." We know
that Moshe elaborated on this point due to
the phrase *al kol hatova.*

——————— TALMUD BAVLI ———————

וַיִּחַדְּ יִתְרוֹ עַל כָּל־הַטּוֹבָה – *Yitro delighted in
all the good:* Rav and Shmuel interpreted the
word *vayihad* in opposite ways. Rav taught:
The verse teaches that Yitro passed a sharp
[*hada*] knife over his flesh [that is, he circumcised himself in an act of conversion].

Whereas Shmuel taught: Yitro's flesh prickled
with goosebumps [*hadudim*, upon hearing
the fate of the Egyptians]. Rav replied: This
reaction of his would explain the aphorism
"Do not disparage a gentile to a convert even
after ten generations." (Sanhedrin 94a)

——————— TANHUMA ———————

וַיִּחַדְּ יִתְרוֹ עַל כָּל־הַטּוֹבָה – *Yitro delighted in all
the good:* Do not read the word as *vayihad*
but as *vayihad,* meaning that upon hearing of
Israel's miraculous ordeal, Yitro became a Jew
[*Yehudi*]. Now what did Yitro convey when he
said: *Blessed be the* LORD (18:10)? He declared: In

all my life there has not been a single foreign
deity whom I have neglected to worship, and
still I have never heard of a God like the God of
Israel. *Now I know that the* LORD *is greater than
all gods* (18:11).

——————— MIDRASH AGGADA ———————

וַיִּחַדְּ יִתְרוֹ עַל כָּל־הַטּוֹבָה – *Yitro delighted in all
the good:* [The obscure word *vayihad* signi-
fies] that Yitro's flesh felt like a sharp [*hada*]
sword had pricked it [he was terrified to hear

of the suffering the Egyptians had endured].
Another interpretation: The verse should be
taken at face value, meaning that the man was
overjoyed to hear Moshe's tale.

VERSE 10

——————— TALMUD BAVLI ———————

וַיֹּאמֶר יִתְרוֹ בָּרוּךְ יְהוָה – *And said, "Blessed be
the* LORD*":* A *tanna* taught in the name of Rabbi
Pappias: How embarrassing for Moshe and
his six hundred thousand compatriots that

nobody thought to declare: "Blessed be the
LORD," until Yitro arrived and made such a proclamation. (Sanhedrin 94a)

10 Egyptians – and said, "Blessed be the LORD who has rescued
you from Egypt and Pharaoh and liberated the people from
11 the Egyptians' hands. Now I know that the LORD is greater
than all gods – for He brought upon them what they schemed

——————————————— LEKAH TOV ———————————————

וַיֹּאמֶר יִתְרוֹ בָּרוּךְ יהוה – *And said, "Blessed be the LORD":* Because Yitro was the first to praise God by saying: "Blessed be the LORD," a statement that not a single Hebrew from among a nation of six hundred thousand thought to

utter, his descendants were rewarded with seats on the Sanhedrin in the Hall of the Hewn Stone [the great court chamber in the Temple; see I Chronicles 2:55 concerning the Kenites, who are linked to Yitro in Judges 1:16].

VERSE 11

——————————————— MEKHILTA DERABBI YISHMAEL ———————————————

עַתָּה יָדַעְתִּי – *Now I know:* Said Yitro to Moshe: In truth, I have long been aware of the existence of God, but now His greatness has been confirmed in my eyes since His reputation has spread throughout the world. For the very method that the Egyptians thought to use

to destroy the Israelites [i.e., drowning their children in the Nile] has been turned against them [at the Sea of Reeds]. Thus the verse states: *For He brought upon them what they schemed against others.* (Massekhta DeVayhi 6)

——————————————— MEKHILTA DERABBI SHIMON ———————————————

מִכָּל־הָאֱלֹהִים – *Than all gods:* What astonished Yitro was that no slave had ever escaped from Egypt before, yet now God had freed

a nation of six hundred thousand men from it. This is why he declared: *The LORD is greater than all gods.*

——————————————— TALMUD BAVLI ———————————————

בַּדָּבָר אֲשֶׁר זָדוּ עֲלֵיהֶם – *What they schemed against others:* What does the verse imply? It means that the Egyptians themselves were cooked in the pot they had boiled for others. [That is, they were drowned as punishment for drowning the Hebrew babies.] And how do we know that the term *zadu* connotes cooking? From the verse *And Yaakov cooked pottage [nazid]* (Genesis 25:29). Rabbi Ḥiyya bar Abba taught in the name of Rabbi Simai:

Three individuals were present when the plot to drown the Israelites babies was hatched: Bilam, Iyov and Yitro. Bilam was the one who came up with the idea, and for that he was killed [in Numbers 31:8]; Iyov was silent when he heard about it, and for failing to object he was stricken with torments; Yitro, who fled the horror of the Egyptians' plan, was rewarded by having his descendants sit in the Hall of the Hewn Stone [as members of the Sanhedrin]. (Sota 11a)

——————————————— KOHELET RABBA ———————————————

מִכָּל־הָאֱלֹהִים – *Than all gods:* Rabbi Yishmael taught: There was not a single religion whose faith Reuel, i.e., Yitro, had not considered and whose gods he had not worshipped in his earlier years. But eventually he was forced

to declare: *The LORD is greater than all gods,* a realization that led the man to convert and to thank the Holy One, blessed be He, for His efforts on Israel's behalf. (3:11)

יב זָדוּ עֲלֵיהֶם: וַיִּקַּח יִתְרוֹ חֹתֵן מֹשֶׁה עֹלָה וּזְבָחִים לֵאלֹהִים
וַיָּבֹא אַהֲרֹן וְכֹל ׀ זִקְנֵי יִשְׂרָאֵל לֶאֱכָל־לֶחֶם עִם־חֹתֵן מֹשֶׁה
יג לִפְנֵי הָאֱלֹהִים: וַיְהִי מִמָּחֳרָת וַיֵּשֶׁב מֹשֶׁה לִשְׁפֹּט אֶת־הָעָם
וַיַּעֲמֹד הָעָם עַל־מֹשֶׁה מִן־הַבֹּקֶר עַד־הָעָרֶב: וַיַּרְא חֹתֵן
מֹשֶׁה אֵת כָּל־אֲשֶׁר־הוּא עֹשֶׂה לָעָם וַיֹּאמֶר מָה־הַדָּבָר
הַזֶּה אֲשֶׁר אַתָּה עֹשֶׂה לָעָם מַדּוּעַ אַתָּה יוֹשֵׁב לְבַדֶּךָ וְכָל־
טו הָעָם נִצָּב עָלֶיךָ מִן־בֹּקֶר עַד־עָרֶב: וַיֹּאמֶר מֹשֶׁה לְחֹתְנוֹ

שני

VERSE 12

───────────── SIFREI ZUTA ─────────────

וַיָּבֹא אַהֲרֹן וְכֹל זִקְנֵי יִשְׂרָאֵל – *Aaron and all the elders of Israel came:* Rabbi Yosei taught: Yitro's name was originally Reuel, indicating that he was a companion [*rea*] to God. Thus the verse states: *And Aharon and all the elders of Israel came to break bread with Moshe's father-in-law before God.* (10:29)

───────────── TALMUD BAVLI ─────────────

לִפְנֵי הָאֱלֹהִים – *Before God:* Did the company really eat their meal before God rather than before Moshe? What the verse teaches is that whenever a person participates in a meal with a Torah scholar, it is as if he absorbs the glory of the Divine Presence. (Berakhot 64a)

───────────── BEMIDBAR RABBA ─────────────

עֹלָה וּזְבָחִים לֵאלֹהִים – *A burnt offering and sacrifices to God:* Rabbi Elazar and Rabbi Yosei bar Ḥanina disputed the timing of this episode. One believed that Yitro arrived at the Israelite camp before the giving of the Torah, while the other claimed that he only came after the Torah was given. Rabbi Ḥama taught in the name of Rabbi Ḥanina: According to the approach that Yitro came before the Torah was given, we must accept the position that Noahides [committed gentiles] would offer peace offerings [whose meat is eaten, and not only burnt offerings, which are consumed whole on the altar; the assumption is that since our verse mentions "sacrifices" apart from burnt offerings, this must refer to peace offerings]. But if Yitro did in fact arrive after the Torah had been given [and offered these sacrifices as part of the sacrificial rites of Israel ordained at Sinai], we can entertain the position that Noahides would only ever offer burnt offerings. (Naso 13:2)

VERSE 13

───────────── MEKHILTA DERABBI SHIMON ─────────────

וַיְהִי מִמָּחֳרָת – *The next day:* This was the day after Yom Kippur [when Moshe gave Israel the second set of tablets; now Moshe could begin to judge the people according to the newly given laws of the Torah].

───────────── TALMUD BAVLI ─────────────

מִן־הַבֹּקֶר עַד־הָעָרֶב – *From morning to evening:* Could Moshe really have sat and judged the people for the entire day? When would he have had time to study the Torah? Rather, the

12 against others." Then Yitro brought a burnt offering and sacrifices to God. And Aharon and all the elders of Israel came
13 to break bread with Moshe's father-in-law before God. The SHENI
next day Moshe sat to serve the people as judge. From morn-
14 ing to evening the people stood before him. When Moshe's father-in-law saw everything Moshe did for the people, he asked,
"What is this that you do for the people? Why do you sit alone
while all the people stand over you from morning to evening?"
15 "The people come to me to inquire of God," Moshe replied.

——————————— TALMUD BAVLI *(cont.)* ———————————

verse teaches that when a judge judges truthfully and accurately even for a single hour, the text assigns him credit as if he has partnered with the Holy One, blessed be He, in the creation of the world. For our verse states:

From morning to evening the people stood before him, while an earlier verse [concerning the creation] states: *And there was evening and there was morning, one day* (Genesis 1:5). (Shabbat 10a)

——————————— LEKAḤ TOV ———————————

וַיְהִי מִמָּחֳרָת – *The next day:* This was the day after the meal described in the previous verse. **וַיֵּשֶׁב מֹשֶׁה לִשְׁפֹּט אֶת־הָעָם** – *Moshe sat to serve the people as judge:* What sort of lawsuits did the people have? The mixed multitudes of gentiles who had left Egypt with Israel, sued the Israelites for some of the plunder they took

from the Egyptians. **וַיַּעֲמֹד הָעָם עַל־מֹשֶׁה** – *The people stood before Moshe:* We learn from this verse that parties in a law case must stand before their judges. The court can give them permission to sit down, but it may not allow one party to sit while the other remains standing.

VERSE 14

——————————— MEKHILTA DERABBI SHIMON ———————————

כָּל־אֲשֶׁר־הוּא עֹשֶׂה – *Everything Moshe did:* Said Yitro to Moshe: The way you sit before the people makes you seem like a king receiving

his subjects. Why do you sit alone while the entire nation stands before you?

——————————— SEKHEL TOV ———————————

כָּל־אֲשֶׁר־הוּא עֹשֶׂה – *Everything Moshe did:* Yitro pointed out to his son-in-law that because he spent his entire day occupied with judging the nation, he had no time to study

Torah. Furthermore, the task he had undertaken, to listen to and handle all of Israel's problems, was exhausting and surely taxed his mind.

VERSE 15

——————————— MIDRASH SHMUEL ———————————

לִדְרֹשׁ אֱלֹהִים – *To inquire of God:* Rabbi Yehoshua of Sikhnin taught in the name of Rabbi Levi: The Holy One, blessed be He, said to Moshe: You boast of Torah knowledge, saying: *The people come to me to inquire of God.* You will

yet see how you will be required to come to Me to seek the law. Thus a later verse states: *And when Moshe went later into the Tent of Meeting to speak with Him, he heard the voice speaking to him from on the covering* (Numbers 7:89). (9:7)

טו כִּי־יָבֹא אֵלַי הָעָם לִדְרֹשׁ אֱלֹהִים: כִּי־יִהְיֶה לָהֶם דָּבָר
בָּא אֵלַי וְשָׁפַטְתִּי בֵּין אִישׁ וּבֵין רֵעֵהוּ וְהוֹדַעְתִּי אֶת־חֻקֵּי
יז הָאֱלֹהִים וְאֶת־תּוֹרֹתָיו: וַיֹּאמֶר חֹתֵן מֹשֶׁה אֵלָיו לֹא־טוֹב
יח הַדָּבָר אֲשֶׁר אַתָּה עֹשֶׂה: נָבֹל תִּבֹּל גַּם־אַתָּה גַּם־הָעָם הַזֶּה
אֲשֶׁר עִמָּךְ כִּי־כָבֵד מִמְּךָ הַדָּבָר לֹא־תוּכַל עֲשֹׂהוּ לְבַדֶּךָ:
יט עַתָּה שְׁמַע בְּקֹלִי אִיעָצְךָ וִיהִי אֱלֹהִים עִמָּךְ הֱיֵה אַתָּה לָעָם

——————————— SEKHEL TOV ———————————

לִדְרֹשׁ אֱלֹהִים — *To inquire of God:* The people come to me to hear words of reproach and warnings that the Holy One, blessed be He, has conveyed to me.

VERSE 16

——————————— MEKHILTA DERABBI SHIMON ———————————

כִּי־יִהְיֶה לָהֶם דָּבָר — *When they have a dispute:* [Literally, "when they have a matter."] They come to pose questions regarding matters of impurity and purity. **וְשָׁפַטְתִּי בֵּין אִישׁ וּבֵין רֵעֵהוּ** — *And I judge between one neighbor and another:* I adjudicate matters that can have no compromise position, as well as quarrels which can be settled through mutual accommodation. In the latter cases, the disputants can go home as friends [*re'im*].

אֶת־חֻקֵּי הָאֱלֹהִים וְאֶת־תּוֹרֹתָיו — *God's laws and teachings:* According to Rabbi Yehoshua, "laws" [*ḥukkim*] refers to God's decrees [i.e., statutes whose rationales are not immediately apparent], while "teachings" [*torot*] connotes laws [the purposes of which are intuitive]. According to Rabbi Elazar HaModa'i, "laws" refers to rules prohibiting illicit sexual unions, and "teachings" indicates decrees.

VERSE 17

——————————— MEKHILTA DERABBI SHIMON ———————————

וַיֹּאמֶר חֹתֵן מֹשֶׁה אֵלָיו — *Moshe's father-in-law said to him:* Yitro was so respected that he is given credit for an entire Torah passage, that which deals with the appointment of Israel's judges. Now considering that the Holy One, blessed be He, well knew that establishing a court system was a reasonable step in the nation's development, why did He not instruct Moshe to arrange the matter before Yitro offered his advice? God suppressed such a command in order to allow Yitro to present his idea and thereby garner Moshe's and the Israelites' respect. Everyone would then say that Yitro must be a great man, since the Holy One, blessed be He, agreed to his plan! For his part, Yitro offered his suggestion only tentatively, saying that his scheme should really only be adopted if the Holy One, blessed be He, agreed that it was worthwhile. This is why he said: *If you do this, and God so commands* (18:23).

——————————— LEKAḤ TOV ———————————

וַיֹּאמֶר חֹתֵן מֹשֶׁה אֵלָיו — *Moshe's father-in-law said to him:* Yitro's words in this verse teach that a polite person speaks in a well-mannered way, for he said: *What you are doing is not good* [while he could have said: "What you are doing is bad"].

16 "When they have a dispute, they come to me and I judge between one neighbor and another, and I make God's laws and
17 teachings known." Moshe's father-in-law said to him, "What
18 you are doing is not good. You will be worn away, and this
people along with you. It is too heavy a burden for you. You
19 cannot carry it alone. Now listen to me, let me advise you; and

VERSE 18

MEKHILTA DERABBI SHIMON

נָבֹל תִּבֹּל גַּם־אַתָּה – *You will be worn away:* Rabbi Yehoshua taught: Yitro warned Moshe that the people would start to disrespect him and take advantage of him. Whereas according to Rabbi Elazar the statement suggests Moshe would become worn out and dried up like the autumn leaves on a fig tree. We find similar phrasing in the verse *All its hosts will wither away [yibbol] as leaves wither and fall from the vine, like a fig that falls too soon* (Isaiah 34:4). גַּם־אַתָּה – *You:* [Literally, "and you."] The term "you" refers to Moshe, while the word "and" connotes Aharon. גַּם־הָעָם הַזֶּה אֲשֶׁר עִמָּךְ – *And this people*

along with you: Rabbi Yehoshua taught: This means that even if the seventy elders [see Numbers 11:16] assisted Moshe, they would be quickly overwhelmed. According to Rabbi Elazar HaModa'i, Yitro also included Nadav and Avihu among those who would not be up to the task of constantly settling the Israelites' problems. כִּי־כָבֵד מִמְּךָ הַדָּבָר – *It is too heavy a burden for you:* Said Yitro to Moshe: Have a look at this beam. When it is saturated with water, it is much too heavy for a single person to carry. But when three or four men band together, they can shoulder it. Similarly, this *is too heavy a burden for you. You cannot carry it alone.*

SEKHEL TOV

גַּם־הָעָם הַזֶּה אֲשֶׁר עִמָּךְ – *And this people along with you:* Yitro here referred to the seventy elders, as well as to Nadav and Avihu. These men were not yet qualified judges, and they still served as Moshe's students and followed his instructions.

For a disciple still learning jurisprudence from his mentor is himself not authorized to rule, and so too did these individuals lack permission to judge on their own, for they had not been appointed to a position of responsibility.

VERSE 19

MEKHILTA DERABBI SHIMON

וִיהִי אֱלֹהִים עִמָּךְ – *And may God be with you:* If God agrees with this plan then you will find yourself able to endure; if God disapproves of this idea you will not be able to manage. הֱיֵה אַתָּה לָעָם מוּל הָאֱלֹהִים – *You*

speak for the people before God: You shall be to the people a vessel holding God's words. וְהֵבֵאתָ אַתָּה אֶת־הַדְּבָרִים אֶל־הָאֱלֹהִים – *And bring their concerns to Him:* And whatever you hear, you shall teach the people.

SHEMOT RABBA

עַתָּה שְׁמַע בְּקֹלִי אִיעָצְךָ – *Now listen to me, let me advise you:* The verse which states: *Rebuke one who has understanding, and he will gain knowledge* (Proverbs 19:25), refers to Moshe.

For when Yitro saw him sitting all day and judging the people of Israel, he said to him: *Why do sit alone…. You will be worn away* (18:14, 18). His father-in-law continued: "Do not

מוּל הָאֱלֹהִים וְהֵבֵאתָ אַתָּה אֶת־הַדְּבָרִים אֶל־הָאֱלֹהִים:
וְהִזְהַרְתָּה אֶתְהֶם אֶת־הַחֻקִּים וְאֶת־הַתּוֹרֹת וְהוֹדַעְתָּ לָהֶם
אֶת־הַדֶּרֶךְ יֵלְכוּ בָהּ וְאֶת־הַמַּעֲשֶׂה אֲשֶׁר יַעֲשׂוּן: וְאַתָּה
תֶחֱזֶה מִכָּל־הָעָם אַנְשֵׁי־חַיִל יִרְאֵי אֱלֹהִים אַנְשֵׁי אֱמֶת

SHEMOT RABBA (cont.)

act on my advice alone, but be sure to ask the Holy One, blessed be He, what He thinks." Thus

the verse states: *Now listen to me, let me advise you; and may God be with you.* (Yitro 27:6)

VERSE 20

MEKHILTA DERABBI SHIMON

אֶת־הַחֻקִּים וְאֶת־הַתּוֹרֹת – *With His precepts and laws:* According to Rabbi Yehoshua, "precepts" [*hukkim*] are statutes whose reasons are obscure, while "laws" [*torot*] refers to rational directives. Whereas Rabbi Elazar HaModa'i taught: *Ḥukkim* refers to forbidden sexual unions, as a later verse states: *Therefore shall you keep my ordinance, that you commit not any one of these abominable customs [ḥukkot] which were practiced before you* (Leviticus 18:30), and *torot* refers to statutes whose

reasons are unclear. אֶת־הַדֶּרֶךְ יֵלְכוּ בָהּ – *The path they are to walk:* This too refers to laws whose rationales are unknowable, which is why another verse must emphasize: *You shall walk in all the ways which the LORD your God has commanded you* [Deuteronomy 5:30; that is, even if you do not know their reasoning]. וְאֶת־הַמַּעֲשֶׂה אֲשֶׁר יַעֲשׂוּן – *And the way they must act:* This refers to good deeds; so teaches Rabbi Yehoshua.

TALMUD BAVLI

אֶת־הַדֶּרֶךְ יֵלְכוּ בָהּ – *The path they are to walk:* [Literally, "the path they are to walk on."] Rav Yosef learned: The phrase "make known to them" refers to teaching the Israelites how to earn a livelihood; "the path" means that Moshe should guide the people in practicing acts of righteousness; "they are to walk" alludes

to the necessity of visiting the sick; the word "on" [*vah*] teaches that people must bury their dead; "and the way" means that the nation should exercise strict justice when called for; "they must act" means that on occasion courts should allow judgments that bend the letter of the law. (Bava Metzia 30b)

LEKAH TOV

וְהִזְהַרְתָּה אֶתְהֶם – *And you must acquaint them:* Yitro here advises Moshe to teach Israel the Ten Commandments. This is the allusion hiding in the superfluous letter *heh* at the end of the word *vehizharta*, and that in the middle

of the word *ethem* [usually *otam*. The numerical value of the letter *heh* is five, and hence the two superfluous letters together hint at the number ten.]

MIDRASH AGGADA

אֶת־הַחֻקִּים – *His precepts:* By using the world "precepts" [*ḥukkim*], Yitro advised Moshe to

teach Israel the commandments governing the Sabbath; the word "laws" [*torot*] refers to

may God be with you. You speak for the people before God,
20 and bring their concerns to Him. And you must acquaint them
with His precepts and laws, and make known to them the
21 path they are to walk and the way they must act. You, as well,
must seek out among the people, capable men – God-fearing,

——————— MIDRASH AGGADA *(cont.)* ———————

the laws of permitted and prohibited actions and items, as the verse states: *This is the law [torah]: when a man dies in a tent, all that come into the tent, and all that is in the tent, shall be unclean seven days* (Numbers 19:14). And what is the connection between the term *torah* and the case of a person dying? We learn from here that only somebody who kills himself [metaphorically] in the pursuit of Torah study will find success in that area.

VERSE 21

——————— MEKHILTA DERABBI SHIMON ———————

תֶחֱזֶה מִכָּל־הָעָם – *Seek out among the people:* Rabbi Yehoshua taught: Moshe was to use the power of prophecy to divine who fit the specified criteria. Rabbi Elazar HaModa'i said: Moshe used the strength of his intellect in interviewing these men to look into their hearts, as kings are capable of doing.

——————— MIDRASH TANNA'IM DEVARIM ———————

אַנְשֵׁי־חַיִל יִרְאֵי אֱלֹהִים – *Capable men – God-fearing:* When Yitro suggested to Moshe that he sought outstanding judges, he listed seven attributes that Moshe was to look for. Alas, the leader was only able to find men with three of the necessary traits: capable, God-fearing, and trustworthy. Still, these are the seven characteristics that every judge should possess, even if he sits merely on a panel of three justices [a minor court that hears only monetary cases]: wisdom, fear of God, humility, indifference to personal gain, love of truth, fondness for people, and a fine reputation. How do we know that judges must be wise? From the verse: *So I took the chief of your tribes, wise men, and known* (Deuteronomy 1:15). We know that justices must fear God from the verse *You must seek out among the people, capable men – God-fearing* (Exodus 18:21). That they must be modest we learn from Moshe, about whom the verse states: *And the man Moshe was the most modest person ever to walk the face of the earth* (Numbers 12:3). Judges must despise money.

We know this is true from Yitro's advice to select people who "despise corruption" (Exodus 18:21). But not only must judges be impervious to bribery, they should care little for the money they already own and not be obsessed about protecting it or amassing great amounts of wealth. This same verse shows us that judges must be "trustworthy men" [literally, "men of truth"], meaning men who are committed to unearthing the truth for its own sake and who revile injustice. The phrase "chief of your tribes and known" (Deuteronomy 1:15) shows that judges must be personable. They demonstrate their love of people by acting generously and humbly toward them, they are friendly, and all of their business transactions are conducted pleasantly. Finally, the phrase "capable men" [anshei ḥayil] suggests that judges must possess solid reputations. They should be well-known for being industrious in observing the commandments, as masters of their own desires, and as being of impeccable character. Finally, judges must be brave enough to rescue

שֹׂנְאֵי בֶצַע וְשַׂמְתָּ עֲלֵהֶם שָׂרֵי אֲלָפִים שָׂרֵי מֵאוֹת שָׂרֵי
כב חֲמִשִּׁים וְשָׂרֵי עֲשָׂרֹת: וְשָׁפְטוּ אֶת־הָעָם בְּכָל־עֵת וְהָיָה
כָּל־הַדָּבָר הַגָּדֹל יָבִיאוּ אֵלֶיךָ וְכָל־הַדָּבָר הַקָּטֹן יִשְׁפְּטוּ־
כג הֵם וְהָקֵל מֵעָלֶיךָ וְנָשְׂאוּ אִתָּךְ: אִם אֶת־הַדָּבָר הַזֶּה תַּעֲשֶׂה
וְצִוְּךָ אֱלֹהִים וְיָכָלְתָּ עֲמֹד וְגַם כָּל־הָעָם הַזֶּה עַל־מְקֹמוֹ יָבֹא

────────────── MIDRASH TANNA'IM DEVARIM *(cont.)* ──────────────

victims of abuse and exploitation. This attribute of compassion for the weak is also learned from Moshe, as the verse states: *Shepherds arrived and started to drive the young women away. But Moshe stood up to defend them, and then water their flock* (2:17). (1:15)

VERSE 22

────────────── MEKHILTA DERABBI SHIMON ──────────────

וְשָׁפְטוּ אֶת־הָעָם בְּכָל־עֵת – *Serve as daily judges for the people:* Rabbi Yehoshua taught: the judges should be otherwise unemployed, so that they will always be available to hear the people's complaints. Rabbi Elazar HaModa'i taught: Yes, being unoccupied is important for judges, but it is also critical that they be learned in the Torah so that they may issue proper rulings for Israel. **כָּל־הַדָּבָר הַגָּדֹל יָבִיאוּ אֵלֶיךָ** – *Let them bring the major cases to you:* [The phrase hadavar hagadol – "major cases" – can also be interpreted as meaning "cases of important people."] Does the verse mean that weighty issues should be brought to Moshe for judgment, while the appointed judges should handle the less significant problems? Perhaps it suggests that cases involving important personages should be tried by Moshe, while disputes that trouble the common folk would be heard by the lower courts. A subsequent verse resolves this question, for when the plan is executed, the text states that *any major case [hadavar hakasheh] they brought to Moshe* [18:26; this phrasing is unambiguous].

────────────── TALMUD BAVLI ──────────────

וְנָשְׂאוּ אִתָּךְ – *And bear it together with you:* The goal was for Moshe to judge the people along with the justices, for the verse states: *They will bear it together with you.* According to Rabbi Yehuda, the phrase "with you" implies that the judges had to be like Moshe [and be of noble lineage]. (Sanhedrin 17a)

VERSE 23

────────────── MEKHILTA DERABBI SHIMON ──────────────

וְצִוְּךָ אֱלֹהִים וְיָכָלְתָּ עֲמֹד – *And God so commands, then you will endure:* Said Yitro to Moshe: Go and consult with God – if He approves of my plan, you should implement it, for then you will be able to manage the burden of judging Israel. However, if God disapproves of my idea, you will surely be unable to handle the task, since even God believes that even such assistance will not help you. **וְגַם כָּל־הָעָם הַזֶּה** – *And all these people:* Aharon, Nadav and Avihu, and all the elders of Israel, who until this point had also struggled to deal with the caseload, would be able to go home if they were replaced by an extensive court

trustworthy men, who despise corruption; and appoint them over the people as leaders of thousands, hundreds, fifties, and
22 tens. Have them serve as daily judges for the people; let them bring the major cases to you, but judge the minor ones themselves. In this way they will lighten your load, and bear it to-
23 gether with you. If you do this, and God so commands, then you will endure, and all these people will be able to go home in

──────── MEKHILTA DERABBI SHIMON *(cont.)* ────────

system. Rabbi Simai taught: One might think that when a judge adjudicates correctly and truthfully, he provokes jealousy among people [since the disputant who had exploited his fellow is now forced to reimburse him]. In reality, however, a carefully considered judgment is critical to resolving disputes and making peace between the quarreling parties, as the verse states: *These are the things that you shall do: Speak every man the truth to his neighbor; execute the judgment of truth and peace in your gates* (Zechariah 8:16). Now it is clear that the one who is awarded damages in a case is content, for his grievance has been vindicated, but why should the party who has to pay be at peace as well? Because he too will eventually realize that justice has been achieved, as the verse states: *And all these people will be able to go home in peace.* And how do we know that the satisfaction that the plaintiff and the defendant feel will also extend to rest of the nation? From the verse *That he may judge Your people with righteousness, and Your poor with justice. Let the mountains bring peace to the people, and the hills, by righteousness* [Psalms 72:2–3; i.e., by executing justice, the court assures that peace spreads throughout the

land]. And such contentment will be granted even to the animals and beasts of the field, as the verse states: *But with righteousness shall he judge the poor, and decide with equity for the meek of the earth.... And righteousness shall be the girdle of his loins, and faithfulness the girdle of his reins. The wolf also shall dwell with the lamb, and the leopard shall lie down with the kid.... They shall not hurt nor destroy in all My holy mountain: for the earth shall be full of the knowledge of the LORD, as the waters cover the sea* (Isaiah 11:4–9). And "knowledge" [*de'a*] in this verse refers to justice, as Yirmeyahu said to Shalum son of Yoshiyahu [king of Yehuda]: *Shall you reign, because you do compete in cedar? Did not your father eat and drink, and do judgment and justice, and then it was well with him? He judged the cause of the poor and needy; then it was well with him: was not this to know [hadaat] Me?* (Jeremiah 22:15–16). How powerful is true justice! For he who despises fairness will never be healed from his wounds, as the verse states: *Shall even one that hates right govern [yaḥavosh]?* (Job 34:17) – The term *yaḥavosh* connotes healing, as in the verse *He heals the brokenhearted, and binds up [umḥabbesh] their wounds* (Psalms 147:3).

──────── SEKHEL TOV ────────

וְכָלְתָּ עֲמֹד – *Then you will endure:* [Literally, "you will be able to stand."] If you free yourself from continuous judging, then you will be available to hear the commandments that the Divine Presence issues you. You will be

able to stand before the Holy One, blessed be He, as in the verse *As the LORD lives, before whom I stand [amadti]* (II Kings 5:16). We learn from here that when a person is engaged in judgment he may not sit while deliberating.

כד בְּשָׁלוֹם: וַיִּשְׁמַע מֹשֶׁה לְקוֹל חֹתְנוֹ וַיַּעַשׂ כֹּל אֲשֶׁר אָמָר: שלישי

כה וַיִּבְחַר מֹשֶׁה אַנְשֵׁי־חַיִל מִכָּל־יִשְׂרָאֵל וַיִּתֵּן אֹתָם רָאשִׁים עַל־הָעָם שָׂרֵי אֲלָפִים שָׂרֵי מֵאוֹת שָׂרֵי חֲמִשִּׁים וְשָׂרֵי

כו עֲשָׂרֹת: וְשָׁפְטוּ אֶת־הָעָם בְּכָל־עֵת אֶת־הַדָּבָר הַקָּשֶׁה

כז יְבִיאוּן אֶל־מֹשֶׁה וְכָל־הַדָּבָר הַקָּטֹן יִשְׁפּוּטוּ הֵם: וַיְשַׁלַּח מֹשֶׁה אֶת־חֹתְנוֹ וַיֵּלֶךְ לוֹ אֶל־אַרְצוֹ:

VERSE 24

——— MEKHILTA DERABBI SHIMON ———

וַיַּעַשׂ כֹּל אֲשֶׁר אָמָר – *And did all that he said:* According to Rabbi Yehoshua, this means that he followed Yitro's advice to the letter. According to Rabbi Elazar HaModa'i, this phrase signifies that Moshe waited for God's approval of the plan, and then obeyed His instructions.

VERSE 25

——— MEKHILTA DERABBI SHIMON ———

וַיִּבְחַר מֹשֶׁה אַנְשֵׁי־חַיִל – *Moshe chose capable men:* Moshe appointed judges over Israel and ordered them to suffer the travails of public service, as a later verse states: *And I charged your judges at that time, saying, Hear the causes between your brethren, and judge righteously between every man and his brother, and the stranger that is with him* (Deuteronomy 1:16). Simultaneously, Moshe commanded the people to treat their judges respectfully, as the verse states: *And I commanded you at that time all the things which you should do* (Deuteronomy 1:18).

——— LEKAH TOV ———

וַיִּבְחַר מֹשֶׁה אַנְשֵׁי־חַיִל – *Moshe chose capable men:* This verse abridges the list of qualifications that Moshe's appointees possessed. For when the text states that these men were "capable," it means that they were honest in financial matters, that they were possessed with a deep reverence of God, and that they were strict adherents of the Torah's commandments.

VERSE 26

——— MEKHILTA DERABBI SHIMON ———

אֶת־הַדָּבָר הַקָּשֶׁה – *Any major case:* Said the Holy One, blessed be He, to Moshe: Do you really think you are capable of adjudicating difficult matters? Look, the daughters of Tzelofhad put a request to you [see Numbers 27:1–4] that any schoolchild could have answered, and yet you were stymied by their demand! Instead of handily resolving the case, we read that *Moshe brought their cause before the Lord* (Numbers 27:5).

——— LEKAH TOV ———

וְשָׁפְטוּ אֶת־הָעָם בְּכָל־עֵת – *They judged the people every day:* [Literally, "at all times."] Because the judges were not otherwise employed, they were always available to sit in judgment of their compatriots. Now does the verse mean that the judges heard cases even at night? No, for a later

24 peace." Moshe listened to his father-in-law and did all that he   SHELISHI
25 said. Moshe chose capable men from all Israel and made them
chiefs over the people, leaders of thousands, hundreds, fifties,
26 and tens. They judged the people every day. Any major case
they brought to Moshe, but they decided every minor matter
27 themselves. Then Moshe parted from his father-in-law, and the
latter went forth, back to his own land.

LEKAḤ TOV *(cont.)*

verse describing a particular court proceeding states: *Then it shall be, on the day that he makes his sons to inherit that which he has…* (Deuteronomy 21:16), proving that monetary cases are only judged during the day, although a sentence may be issued at night.

SEKHEL TOV

אֶת־הַדָּבָר הַקָּשֶׁה – *Any major case:* Major cases are those that involve the judgment of entire tribes, alleged false prophets, and impious high priests. As we learn [Mishna Sanhedrin 1:4–5]: "Capital cases are heard by courts comprising twenty-three judges, whereas matters governing whole tribes or false prophets are brought before the supreme court of seventy-one."

VERSE 27

MEKHILTA DERABBI SHIMON

וַיְשַׁלַּח מֹשֶׁה אֶת־חֹתְנוֹ – *Then Moshe parted from his father-in-law:* Rabbi Yehoshua taught: Moshe saw Yitro off with great honor and fanfare. Rabbi Elazar HaModa'i added: Moshe presented his father-in-law with many gifts. Said Yitro to Moshe: "I am returning to my homeland, where I will labor to convert my fellow Midianites to the faith of Israel." Why did Yitro need to tell Moshe that? For Moshe had requested of his father-in-law: *Leave us not, I pray you; since you know how we are to encamp in the wilderness, and you may be to us instead of eyes* (Numbers 10:31). The Israelites pleaded with Yitro: "You have given us sound and wise advice, counsel that was approved by God Himself! Please do not abandon us now." Said he to them: "Consider the effect of a candle – does its power not lie in its ability to brighten the darkness? Of what use is a torch in the light provided by the sun and the moon – by which I mean Moshe and Aharon? But if I go home I will be able to influence my countrymen and draw them into the folds of the Divine Presence." And lest you think that Yitro left Israel permanently, a subsequent verse states: *And the children of the Kenite, Moshe's father-in-law, went up out of the city of palm trees with the children of Yehuda into the wilderness of Yehuda, which lies in the south of Arad; and they went and dwelt among the people* (Judges 1:16). In fact, Yitro rejoined the nation of Israel, bringing with him great numbers of his people whom he had succeeded in converting. Now Yitro told Moshe: *I will not go; but I will depart to my own land, and to my kindred* (Numbers 10:30). Why did Yitro insist on returning to his homeland? He reasoned: The land is suffering through a drought this year, and all along I have been supporting my destitute neighbors by sustaining them in these difficult times. If I do not return to pay their debts, I will cause a desecration of God's name. So I must head back in order to settle those accounts.

יט א בַּחֹדֶשׁ הַשְּׁלִישִׁי לְצֵאת בְּנֵי־יִשְׂרָאֵל מֵאֶרֶץ מִצְרָיִם בַּיּוֹם רביעי
ב הַזֶּה בָּאוּ מִדְבַּר סִינָי: וַיִּסְעוּ מֵרְפִידִים וַיָּבֹאוּ מִדְבַּר סִינַי
ג וַיַּחֲנוּ בַּמִּדְבָּר וַיִּחַן־שָׁם יִשְׂרָאֵל נֶגֶד הָהָר: וּמֹשֶׁה עָלָה
אֶל־הָאֱלֹהִים וַיִּקְרָא אֵלָיו יהוה מִן־הָהָר לֵאמֹר כֹּה

————————————— MIDRASH AGGADA —————————————

וַיְשַׁלַּח מֹשֶׁה אֶת־חֹתְנוֹ – *Then Moshe parted from his father-in-law:* Whoever shares in the anguish of the community is privileged to witness its moments of comfort. But because Yitro was not present during Israel's time of suffering [in the privations of the desert], he was not invited to witness their hour of greatest consolation – the giving of the Torah.

CHAPTER 19, VERSE 1

————————————— TALMUD BAVLI —————————————

בַּחֹדֶשׁ הַשְּׁלִישִׁי – *On the first day of the third month:* [The phrase could be understood to mean simply "in the third month."] Our Sages taught: The Ten Commandments were given to Israel on the sixth day of the month [i.e., of Sivan, the third month]. However, according to Rabbi Yosei, the revelation took place on the seventh of that month. Rava taught: Nevertheless, both sides agree that the nation arrived in the wilderness on the first day of the month. For here it is written: *bayom hazeh* [literally, "on that day"]. (Shabbat 86b)

————————————— PESIKTA DERAV KAHANA —————————————

בַּחֹדֶשׁ הַשְּׁלִישִׁי – *On the first day of the third month:* Israel was ready to receive the Torah as soon as they left their bondage in Egypt. On the other hand, the forced labor the people had been forced to perform with brick and mortar had resulted in various injuries and blemishes among the people. Said the Holy One, blessed be He: Israel has not yet been cleansed or healed from the indignities of slavery. I will allow them two or three months to recover and refresh themselves with water from the [miraculous] well, sustenance from the manna, and meat from the quail. After that recovery, the Israelites will be revived enough to receive the Torah. Thus the verse states: *On the first day of the third month etc.* (12) **בַּחֹדֶשׁ הַשְּׁלִישִׁי** – *On the third month:* Why did God wait until the third month to give Israel the Torah? This was done in order to preclude the nations of the world from boasting that had God given them His Torah they too would have willingly accepted it. Said the Holy One, blessed be He: Witness in what month I revealed My law to the Israelites – it was in the third month, during the influence of the constellation Gemini. This would have been a propitious hour for the descendants of the wicked Esav to repent and convert to their cousins' faith. Had they decided to join the Israelites and devote themselves to study of the Torah, they surely would have been welcomed. This is why the Torah was presented in the third month. [Needless to say, the gentile progeny of Esav did not accept the invitation.] And why was the Torah given in the heart of the wilderness? This was done to teach that only one who clears his mind and empties it like the desert can truly absorb the Torah. For like the wilderness, the Torah is without limit and requires a great expanse to host it. (12)

19 1 On the first day of the third month after the Israelites had left   REVI'I
   2 Egypt they came to the Sinai Desert. Setting out from Refidim
     they had arrived at the Sinai Desert, encamping in the wil-
   3 derness, and there Israel camped, facing the mountain, while
     Moshe went up to God. And the LORD called to him from the
     mountain: "This is what you shall say to the house of Yaakov,

---

MIDRASH AGGADA

בַּחֹדֶשׁ הַשְּׁלִישִׁי – *On the first day of the third month:* The number three is heavily represented in Jewish literature and practice. Firstly, the Scriptures are divided into three sections: The Torah, the Prophets, and the Writings. The Mishna comprises three main types of material: laws, exegesis [*midrash*], and rabbinic tales [*aggadot*]. God appointed three intermediaries to represent Him before Israel: Moshe, Aharon and Miriam. The Jews worship God three times a day: at night, in the morning, and in the afternoon. Three times is God declared to be sanctified in the verse *Holy, holy, holy is the LORD of Hosts* (Isaiah 6:3). The nation of Israel, which received the Torah, is divided into three classes: Priests, Levites and Israelites. There are three patriarchs: Avraham, Yitzḥak and Yaakov. And the preparatory period prior to the giving of the Torah comprised three days, as the verse states: *Be ready for the third day* (19:11). And the event took place in the third month.

VERSE 2

MEKHILTA DERABBI SHIMON

וַיָּבֹאוּ מִדְבַּר סִינַי – *They had arrived at the Sinai Desert:* Had God given the Torah to the nation after they arrived in the land of Israel, the people would have argued that its message belonged to them exclusively [and outsiders have no right to study it]. And had the Torah been revealed in some other land [such as in Egypt or Moav] that place's inhabitants would have claimed ownership over the Torah. Therefore the Torah was given in the heart of a barren and unclaimed wilderness, so that anyone can feel welcome to come and acquire the book and its teachings. Indeed, the Torah is accessible to all who desire it.

VAYIKRA RABBA

וַיִּסְעוּ מֵרְפִידִים – *Setting out from Refidim:* All throughout their travels, the Israelites set up and broke camp in strife and division. This explains why the verbs which normally describe those actions [as in our verse] are expressed in the plural form – *vayisu* (they journeyed) and *vayaḥanu* (they encamped). However when the people arrived at Mount Sinai to receive the Torah, they were united in purpose and orientation, as the verse states: *And there Israel camped [vayiḥan, in the singular].* (Tzav 9:9)

VERSE 3

MEKHILTA DERABBI SHIMON

כֹּה תֹאמַר לְבֵית יַעֲקֹב – *This is what you shall say to the house of Yaakov:* On the one hand, the verse states: *Say to the house of Yaakov,* indicating that it was due to the merits accrued by Yaakov that his descendants were given the Torah. On the other hand, the verse

ד תֹאמַר לְבֵית יַעֲקֹב וְתַגֵּיד לִבְנֵי יִשְׂרָאֵל: אַתֶּם רְאִיתֶם
אֲשֶׁר עָשִׂיתִי לְמִצְרָיִם וָאֶשָּׂא אֶתְכֶם עַל־כַּנְפֵי נְשָׁרִים

———————— MEKHILTA DERABBI SHIMON *(cont.)* ————————

continues: *Tell the people of Israel,* which shows that it was thanks to their own merits that the Israelites received the word of God. Another explanation for the shift in the verse's terminology: The phrase *Say to the house of Yaakov* refers to the patriarch's original name. However, the subsequent clause *Tell the people of Israel* reminds us that because the man strove with God, he was rewarded with great name Yisrael.

———————— TALMUD BAVLI ————————

וּמֹשֶׁה עָלָה אֶל־הָאֱלֹהִים – *While Moshe went up to God:* Rabbi Yosei taught: The Divine Presence never descended to earth, nor did Moshe or the prophet Eliyahu ever ascend to the heavens. For the psalmist writes: *The heavens are the heavens of the Lord: but He has given the earth to the children of men* (Psalms 115:16). But how can Rabbi Yosei declare that God never came down to earth, when a verse clearly states: *And the Lord descended on Mount Sinai* (Exodus 19:20)? God did come down, but He stopped short ten handbreadths from the top of the hill. But how can Rabbi Yosei declare that Moshe and Eliyahu never went up to the heavens, when a verse clearly states: *Moshe went up to God,* while later we read: *There* appeared a chariot of fire, and horses of fire… and Eliyahu went up by a storm of wind into heaven (II Kings 2:11)? Both men did go up, but they each stopped ten handbreadths short of heaven. But does another verse not claim: *He seizes hold of the face of His throne, and He spreads His cloud upon him* (Job 26:9), which Rabbi Tanḥum said describes God spreading some of His divine radiance and His cloud over Moshe? Nevertheless, that took place at least ten handbreadths from heaven. How can this be when the verse claims that Moshe grabbed hold of the celestial throne [which must be in heaven itself]? The throne was lowered from its normal height for Moshe, who then seized hold of it. (Sukka 5a)

———————— TANḤUMA ————————

לְבֵית יַעֲקֹב – *To the house of Yaakov:* [The term "house" is traditionally understood to connote Israel's women.] The women of Israel received the Torah before the men did, for first the verse states: *Say to the house of Yaakov,* which refers to the women, and only then does God instruct Moshe: *Tell the people of Israel,* meaning the men. (Buber, Metzora 18)

———————— SHEMOT RABBA ————————

וּמֹשֶׁה עָלָה אֶל־הָאֱלֹהִים – *While Moshe went up to God:* What does the verse mean when it states: *You have ascended on high, you have led captivity captive* (Psalms 68:19)? It means that Moshe was exalted since he contended with the celestial angels [a midrashic idea that Moshe was forced to convince the angels that the Torah was better suited for Israel than for them; see Shabbat 88b]. Another interpretation: No human being ever achieved such heights as Moshe did. Rabbi Berekhya taught: The tablets containing the Ten Commandments were six handbreadths long. The Creator gripped two handbreadths of the stones,

4 what you shall tell the people of Israel: You yourselves have
seen what I did to the Egyptians: how I lifted you up on eagles'

——————————— SHEMOT RABBA *(cont.)* ———————————

so to speak, while Moshe held two hand-breadths of the tablets from their other side, with two handbreadths separating the two pairs of hands. [That is, what Moshe took captive were the tablets which he managed to wrest away from God.] Another interpretation for the verse: Usually, when a thief steals into a

city, he tries to make off with something that nobody is guarding. But Moshe went straight up to heaven and lifted the Torah while the eyes of all the angels were looking right at it. Thus the verse states: *You have ascended on high, you have led captivity captive.* (Yitro 28:1)

——————————— DEVARIM RABBA ———————————

וּמֹשֶׁה עָלָה אֶל־הָאֱלֹהִים – *While Moshe went up to God:* The Holy One, blessed be He, created the upper worlds and populated them with celestial beings, and He fashioned the lower worlds and filled with them earthly life forms, as the verse states: *The heavens are the heavens*

of the LORD, *but He has given the earth to the children of men* (Psalms 115:16). But Moshe came along and reversed that arrangement, as the Torah reports: *Moshe went up to God,* and: *The LORD descended on Mount Sinai* (19:20). (Haazinu 10:2)

VERSE 4

——————————— SIFREI DEVARIM ———————————

וָאֶשָּׂא אֶתְכֶם עַל־כַּנְפֵי נְשָׁרִים – *I lifted you up on eagles' wings:* Before an eagle returns to its nest, it alerts the eaglets by the furious flapping of its wings as it flies between one tree or building and another. It does this to prepare its young for its arrival. Similarly, when the Holy One, blessed be He, made ready to present Israel with the Torah, He did not reveal

His presence immediately from a single direction, but presented Himself from four different angles, as the verses states: *The LORD came from Sinai, and rose up from Se'ir to them; He shone forth from Mount Paran* (Deuteronomy 33:2), and: *God comes from Teiman, and the Holy One from Mount Paran* (Habakkuk 3:3). (Haazinu 314)

——————————— LEKAḤ TOV ———————————

וָאֶשָּׂא אֶתְכֶם עַל־כַּנְפֵי נְשָׁרִים – *I lifted you up on eagles' wings:* The eagle fears no other bird in the sky as it flies. Nevertheless, because it is wary of the arrows of men, it carries its young on top of its pinions, as the verse states: *As an eagle stirs up her nest, broods over her young,*

spreads abroad her wings, takes them, bears them on her pinions (Deuteronomy 32:11). The mother bird says to herself: I would rather that people shoot me than my chicks, as the verse states: *For he that touches you touches the apple of His eye* (Zechariah 2:12).

——————————— MIDRASH AGGADA ———————————

וָאֶשָּׂא אֶתְכֶם עַל־כַּנְפֵי נְשָׁרִים – *I lifted you up on eagles' wings:* This is how God carried Israel

from Goshen to Ramesses [the start of their journey in 12:37].

ה וְאָבִא אֶתְכֶם אֵלָי: וְעַתָּה אִם־שָׁמוֹעַ תִּשְׁמְעוּ בְּקֹלִי
וּשְׁמַרְתֶּם אֶת־בְּרִיתִי וִהְיִיתֶם לִי סְגֻלָּה מִכָּל־הָעַמִּים כִּי־לִי
כָּל־הָאָרֶץ: וְאַתֶּם תִּהְיוּ־לִי מַמְלֶכֶת כֹּהֲנִים וְגוֹי קָדוֹשׁ אֵלֶּה טו
הַדְּבָרִים אֲשֶׁר תְּדַבֵּר אֶל־בְּנֵי יִשְׂרָאֵל: וַיָּבֹא מֹשֶׁה וַיִּקְרָא חמישי
לְזִקְנֵי הָעָם וַיָּשֶׂם לִפְנֵיהֶם אֵת כָּל־הַדְּבָרִים הָאֵלֶּה אֲשֶׁר

VERSE 5

──── MEKHILTA DERABBI YISHMAEL ────

וִהְיִיתֶם לִי סְגֻלָּה – *You will be My treasure:* You will be devoted to me and will spend your time studying Torah, not having to trouble yourself with other matters. And just as a person cherishes a treasure, so will you be beloved to Me.

──── MEKHILTA DERABBI SHIMON ────

אִם־שָׁמוֹעַ תִּשְׁמְעוּ בְּקֹלִי – *If you faithfully heed My voice:* [The repetitive phrase *shamoa tishme'u*] teaches that all processes are difficult at first. But once a person begins to heed God's commands, he will find that it becomes easier. If the person begins to practice one commandment, he will find himself ready to move on to other areas of Jewish practice. Once the individual has shown a willingness to listen to the words of the Written Torah, he will become open to hearing the teachings of the Sages. **וּשְׁמַרְתֶּם אֶת־בְּרִיתִי** – *And keep My covenant:* Rabbi Eliezer taught that this clause refers to the ritual of circumcision [called a "covenant" in Genesis 17:13], while Rabbi Akiva argued that it is actually the covenant of the Sabbath [called a "covenant" in Exodus 31:16]. The Rabbis however, argue that God is alluding to the prohibition of idolatry. **וִהְיִיתֶם לִי סְגֻלָּה** – *You will be My treasure:* A person's estate can pacify him when he is angry [viewing one's wealth has a calming effect on the troubled mind]. Similarly, the presence of Israel will serve to placate God. And just as human beings love their wealth, so does God have great affection for His people. There is an analogy that people use to describe this relationship: Consider a man who inherits great tracts of land, but nevertheless goes out and buys a separate field with his own money. Surely he cherishes the plot of earth that he has acquired through his own efforts more than the property that he has inherited. Similarly, although the Creator naturally owns the world and all its inhabitants, it is Israel, whom He molded to be His own, that He loves more than any other people. For they are the community He rescued from Egypt and redeemed from the house of bondage. Hence the verse states: *You will be My treasure among all the peoples, although the whole earth is Mine.*

──── BERESHIT RABBATI ────

וִהְיִיתֶם לִי סְגֻלָּה – *You will be My treasure:* The Holy One, blessed be He, distinguished Israel by giving them the Torah, while the rest of the nations stumble along in darkness. (Bereshit)

5 wings and brought you to Me. Now, if you faithfully heed My
voice and keep My covenant, you will be My treasure among
6 all the peoples, although the whole earth is Mine. A kingdom
of priests and a holy nation you shall be to Me. These are the
7 words you must speak to the Israelites." So Moshe came and   ḤAMISHI
summoned the elders of the people, and set before them all that

VERSE 6

MEKHILTA DERABBI SHIMON

וְגוֹי קָדוֹשׁ – *And a holy nation:* Before the debacle of the golden calf, all Israelites were eligible to eat sacrificial meat. But once the people perpetrated that sin, the right to partake of the holy food was taken from the populace and reserved for the priestly class. The singular form of the phrase "a holy nation" suggests that Israel stands as a united body with one interconnected soul. Thus the verse states: *And what one nation on earth is like Your people, like Israel?* (II Samuel 7:23). The implication of such a bond is that should one person sin, the entire nation will be punished. And so we read: *Did not Akhan the son of Zeraḥ commit a trespass in regard to the devoted property, and wrath fell on all the congregation of Israel? That man perished not alone in his iniquity* [Joshua 22:20; the

transgression of Akhan had led indirectly to the deaths of thirty-six Israelite soldiers]. Similarly, when the verse states: *Israel is a scattered sheep* (Jeremiah 50:17), it draws that analogy because Israel is like a single sheep: Should one of its limbs be cut off, the whole body suffers. But gentiles rejoice at each other's downfall. **וְגוֹי קָדוֹשׁ** – *And a holy nation:* What does it mean that Israel is a holy nation? We learn from a subsequent verse, *For you are a holy people to the Lord your God* [Deuteronomy 14:2; the phrase is in the context of a list of laws], that Israel becomes sanctified through its observance of the laws of the Torah. For whenever the Holy One, blessed be He, demands that Israel perform one more commandment, He increases their level of holiness.

AGGADAT BERESHIT

מַמְלֶכֶת כֹּהֲנִים – *A kingdom of priests:* Rabbi Aḥa taught: Why were the names of Israel's tribes engraved on the stones of the High Priest's breastpiece? It is because at Mount Sinai all Israelites were declared to be priests, as the verse states: *A kingdom of priests and a holy nation you shall be to Me.* The Holy One, blessed be He, reasoned: It would be

impractical for the entire nation to participate in the sacrificial service. Rather, let the names of the tribes, representing all the people, be written above the High Priest's heart. Then, when that holy man enters the sanctuary to offer sacrifices before Me, it will be as if every individual Israelite is worshipping Me, clothed in the High Priest's vestments. (80)

VERSE 7

MEKHILTA DERABBI SHIMON

וַיִּקְרָא לְזִקְנֵי הָעָם – *And summoned the elders of the people:* This verse illustrates the respect

that Moshe accorded the elders. The text also indicates that the elders received preliminary

ה צִוָּהוּ יְהוָה: וַיַּעֲנוּ כָל־הָעָם יַחְדָּו וַיֹּאמְרוּ כָּל אֲשֶׁר־דִּבֶּר
ט יְהוָה נַעֲשֶׂה וַיָּשֶׁב מֹשֶׁה אֶת־דִּבְרֵי הָעָם אֶל־יְהוָה: וַיֹּאמֶר
יְהוָה אֶל־מֹשֶׁה הִנֵּה אָנֹכִי בָּא אֵלֶיךָ בְּעַב הֶעָנָן בַּעֲבוּר
יִשְׁמַע הָעָם בְּדַבְּרִי עִמָּךְ וְגַם־בְּךָ יַאֲמִינוּ לְעוֹלָם וַיַּגֵּד מֹשֶׁה

———————————— MEKHILTA DERABBI SHIMON *(cont.)* ————————————

instruction in the Torah before Moshe edu-
cated the rest of the nation, and that he tasked

the leaders of his generation with publicizing
the word of God to the people.

VERSE 8

———————————— MEKHILTA DERABBI SHIMON ————————————

וַיַּעֲנוּ כָל־הָעָם יַחְדָּו – *And the people answered
as one:* The people were not speaking obse-
quiously when they answered Moshe, nor
did they consult with each other before giving him their response. Rather, all the people
were of a single mind and eager to serve God.
כָּל אֲשֶׁר־דִּבֶּר יהוה נַעֲשֶׂה – *All that the LORD has
spoken we will do:* We assume responsibility
for all the demands God has made upon us.
וַיָּשֶׁב מֹשֶׁה אֶת־דִּבְרֵי הָעָם – *Moshe brought
the people's answer:* This took place on the
third day of Israel's encampment. Another

interpretation: Every time Moshe climbed
the mountain to report back to God, and
each time he returned to the people, he was
rewarded for his effort as the nation's intermediary. [This explains why Moshe repeatedly climbed up and down the hill.] Another
interpretation: We learn from this that even
the recipient knows what the content of his
messenger's report will be, it still behooves
the agent to return to inform his superior and
thereby complete his mission.

———————————— TALMUD BAVLI ————————————

וַיָּשֶׁב מֹשֶׁה אֶת־דִּבְרֵי הָעָם – *Moshe brought
the people's answer:* This verse states: *Moshe
brought [vayashev] their answer back to the LORD,*
while the next verse reports: *Moshe reported
[vayagged] the words of the people to the LORD*
[19:9, without specifying the content of that
message]. What did the Holy One, blessed be
He, say to Moshe, and what did Moshe tell the
people? How did the nation respond to Moshe,
and what did Moshe relate back to God? The
establishment of the boundaries [recorded in
verse 12] interposed between the two verses
in question [and it was the people's affirma-
tive response to this command that Moshe
conveyed in verse 9]. Such is the opinion of
Rabbi Yosei bar Yehuda. Rabbi Yehuda HaNasi
explains the verses as follows: At first Moshe

outlined to the people the punishments they
would incur for ignoring the commandments.
Hence the first verse uses the verb *vayashev*
["brought" understood homiletically as] meaning matters that shock [*meshabbevin*]. Subsequently however, Moshe described to Israel
the rewards they would receive for compliance with God's will. This explains the shift in
verb to *vayagged* ["reported"] – matters that
are pleasing to the ears like stories [*aggadot*].
Other scholars reverse the interpretations of
these two verses, claiming that Moshe began
by telling the people the good things that God
was prepared to bestow upon them should
they obey Him. Hence the verse states *vayashev* – matters that calm [*meshivin*] the mind.
But then he proceeded to warn the nation

8 the LORD had commanded him. And the people answered as one – "All that the LORD has spoken we will do." Moshe brought
9 their answer back to the LORD. Then the LORD said to Moshe, "I will come to you in a dense cloud, that the people may hear Me speaking to you. They will then believe you forever." When

——————————————— TALMUD BAVLI *(cont.)* ———————————————

about the price they would pay for disobedience. Hence *vayagged* – alluding to matters that are difficult to digest like wormwood [*gidin*]. (Shabbat 87a)

VERSE 9

——————————————— MEKHILTA DERABBI SHIMON ———————————————

הִנֵּה אָנֹכִי בָּא אֵלֶיךָ בְּעַב הֶעָנָן – *I will come to you in a dense cloud:* The term "cloud" in this context refers to a dense shroud of mist, as the verse states: *The third day came; and that morning there was thunder and lightning and a dense cloud on the mountain* (19:16). Rabbi Yosei the Galilean taught: Moshe went through a week-long process of sanctification on the mountain, as the verse states: *The glory of the LORD rested on Mount Sinai, and the cloud covered it for six days. On the seventh, He called to Moshe from within the cloud* (24:16). These days took place after the Ten Commandments had been delivered, and they represented the beginning of the forty days [Moshe spent on the mountain afterward]. Rabbi Akiva taught: When the text states that *the cloud covered it for six days,* it means that at the start of the month God called Moshe to be purified [before the Ten Commandments were given]. **בַּעֲבוּר יִשְׁמַע הָעָם בְּדַבְּרִי עִמָּךְ** – *That the people may hear Me speaking to you:* Rabbi Yehuda taught: The Holy One, blessed be He, said to Moshe: As Israel listens, I will address you and you will respond to Me, whereupon I will agree with your statements. Rabbi Yehuda HaNasi said: The purpose of this exercise was not to boost Moshe's standing. Rather, God's was now repeating to Moshe the commandments He had issued at Mara [so that the people could be sure that they were of divine origin].

Note that when the text reports that *Moshe came and summoned the elders of the people, and set before them all that the LORD had commanded him* (19:7) – rather than simply "all the LORD had commanded" – the word "him" emphasizes that when the leaders learned the Torah from Moshe, it was as if they were hearing it directly from God Himself. Furthermore, the involvement of the elders was meant to institute the practice of Jewish education. The nation would henceforth accept the word of their elders and prophets as being ultimately derived from God through Moshe. Hence the verse states: *They will then believe you forever.* **וַיַּגֵּד מֹשֶׁה אֶת־דִּבְרֵי הָעָם** – *Moshe reported the words of the people:* What message did the nation intend for Moshe to convey to God and what communication did God tell Moshe to transmit to the people? The people requested that God speak directly to them, arguing that there can be no comparison between hearing an edict directly from the king and receiving it second hand from his agent. Said the Holy One, blessed be He, to Moshe: "I will grant the people's request, and the nation will hear My voice when I address you." Thereupon Israel made a second demand: "We wish to see our King, since there can be comparison between hearing a speaker while seeing him and merely hearing a disembodied voice." Said the Holy One, blessed be He, to Moshe: "I will grant

י אֶת־דִּבְרֵי הָעָם אֶל־יהוה: וַיֹּאמֶר יהוה אֶל־מֹשֶׁה לֵךְ אֶל־
יא הָעָם וְקִדַּשְׁתָּם הַיּוֹם וּמָחָר וְכִבְּסוּ שִׂמְלֹתָם: וְהָיוּ נְכֹנִים
לַיּוֹם הַשְּׁלִישִׁי כִּי | בַּיּוֹם הַשְּׁלִשִׁי יֵרֵד יהוה לְעֵינֵי כָל־הָעָם
יב עַל־הַר סִינָי: וְהִגְבַּלְתָּ אֶת־הָעָם סָבִיב לֵאמֹר הִשָּׁמְרוּ
לָכֶם עֲלוֹת בָּהָר וּנְגֹעַ בְּקָצֵהוּ כָּל־הַנֹּגֵעַ בָּהָר מוֹת יוּמָת:

———————— MEKHILTA DERABBI SHIMON *(cont.)* ————————

this request as well." Thus the verse states: *For on that that third day, the L*ord *will descend on Mount Sinai before all the peoples' eyes* (19:11). Such an encounter will occur once more in

the future, and Israel will again see the face of the Divine Presence, as the verse states: *For they shall see eye to eye, the L*ord *returning to Zion* (Isaiah 52:8).

VERSE 10

———————— MEKHILTA DERABBI SHIMON ————————

וְקִדַּשְׁתָּם הַיּוֹם וּמָחָר – *Consecrate them today and tomorrow:* Moshe delivered this message on the fourth day of Israel's encampment at Sinai. Now it would have sufficed for the people to immerse themselves on the fifth day which would have brought the people to a state of purity and readiness for the sixth day [when the Torah was given]. And yet the verse states that the people were to immerse already on the fourth day. How then did they occupy themselves on the fifth day? Moshe spent that day recording the Torah as one would write memoirs in a notebook. The sixth day

itself is described in the text: *Early the next morning he rose and built an altar at the base of the mountain, and also twelve pillars for the twelve tribes of Israel* (24:4). Rabbi Yehuda says that each pillar served one of Israel's twelve tribes. However, the Rabbis argue that the pillars were all set up on behalf of the entire nation. Thus the following verse states: *Then he sent young men of Israel, and they sacrificed bulls as burnt offerings and peace offerings to the L*ord [24:5; the "young men of Israel" are mentioned as a single group, rather than being divided by tribe].

———————— AVOT DERABBI NATAN ————————

וְקִדַּשְׁתָּם הַיּוֹם וּמָחָר – *Consecrate them today and tomorrow:* Upon receiving the command from God, Moshe altered the instructions slightly. For although God had said to him: *Go to the people and consecrate them today and tomorrow,* Moshe was reluctant to pass along the message of the Holy One, blessed be He, verbatim. Rather, here is what he told them: *Make yourselves ready for three days, and do not draw close to your wives* [19:15; this is the literal meaning of that verse, notwithstanding the translation "be ready for the third day" in this volume], thereby adding a third day for Israel

to prepare themselves. Now Moshe was righteous and reasoned as follows: If the Israelite men are intimate with their wives before they begin to prepare, it could conceivably happen that on the third day a woman might expel semen from several days earlier. That would mean that such women would be impure at the very moment they are hearing the Torah at Mount Sinai for the first time. However, if Israel must observe an additional day of separation, the women will avoid such a circumstance. And hence all of Israel will be in a state of purity when they stand before God. (2)

10 Moshe reported the words of the people to the Lᴏʀᴅ, the Lᴏʀᴅ said to Moshe, "Go to the people and consecrate them
11 today and tomorrow; let them wash their clothes and be ready for the third day, for on that third day the Lᴏʀᴅ will descend
12 on Mount Sinai before all the peoples' eyes. Set a boundary for the people around the mountain; tell them to take care not to ascend to it, not even touch its edge. Anyone who touches

VERSE 11

MEKHILTA DERABBI SHIMON

וְהָיוּ נְכֹנִים לַיּוֹם הַשְּׁלִישִׁי – *And be ready for the third day:* The people arranged a meeting place to coordinate the preparations. **לְעֵינֵי כָל־הָעָם** – *Before all the peoples' eyes:* This verse signifies no Israelites were blind at the giving of the Torah. Rabbi Shimon ben Yehuda of Kefar Ikos taught: How do we know that had even one of the redeemed slaves not been present at the mountain, God would not have delivered His Torah to the nation? For the verse states: *The Lᴏʀᴅ will descend before all*

the peoples' eyes, meaning that every Israelite had to be there. Furthermore, the statement emphasizes that never before had there been such a generation, nor will there ever again be such a community, that was so qualified to receive the Torah [since the participation of every individual was critical]. It was regarding the people of that era that the verse states: *He is a shield to those who walk uprightly, to keep the paths of justice* (Proverbs 2:7).

LEKAḤ TOV

וְהָיוּ נְכֹנִים לַיּוֹם הַשְּׁלִישִׁי – *And be ready for the third day:* This refers to the sixth day of the

month [of Sivan], when the Torah was given. The revelation took place on the Sabbath.

VERSE 12

MEKHILTA DERABBI SHIMON

וְהִגְבַּלְתָּ אֶת־הָעָם – *Set a boundary for the people:* Boundary markers were established to show the Israelites how far they were permitted to go. Now from a later description, *No one else should be seen anywhere on the mountain, nor may flocks or herds graze near the mountain* (34:3) we might have inferred that Israel was forbidden from approaching the mountain only on its eastern side. [The assumption is that this is where the Israelites were encamped]. How do we know that the people were forbidden from climbing Sinai on its north, south, and west sides as well? From our verse, which states: *Set a boundary for the people around the mountain,* which

indicates that all sides of the hill were off limits. **הִשָּׁמְרוּ לָכֶם עֲלוֹת בָּהָר** – *Take care not to ascend to it:* This statement has the force of a formal prohibition. Lest you think that the Israelites were only forbidden from ascending the mountain, and that they were still permitted to touch it, the verse continues: *Tell them to take care…not even touch its edge.* What's more, any Israelite going up the mountain in a carriage would have violated the decree as well. [Such an person would not be able to argue that the vehicle interposed between him and the mountain.] Thus, when the verse states: *Take care not to ascend to it,* it means the people were not allowed to ascend in any manner.

יג לֹא־תִגַּע בּוֹ יָד כִּי־סָקוֹל יִסָּקֵל אוֹ־יָרֹה יִיָּרֶה אִם־בְּהֵמָה
יד אִם־אִישׁ לֹא יִחְיֶה בִּמְשֹׁךְ הַיֹּבֵל הֵמָּה יַעֲלוּ בָהָר: וַיֵּרֶד
מֹשֶׁה מִן־הָהָר אֶל־הָעָם וַיְקַדֵּשׁ אֶת־הָעָם וַיְכַבְּסוּ שִׂמְלֹתָם:
טו וַיֹּאמֶר אֶל־הָעָם הֱיוּ נְכֹנִים לִשְׁלֹשֶׁת יָמִים אַל־תִּגְּשׁוּ אֶל־

VERSE 13

── TALMUD BAVLI ──

בִּמְשֹׁךְ הַיֹּבֵל – *When the ram's horn sounds a long blast:* When a decree has been instituted by a majority vote, it can only be rescinded through a subsequent majority vote. [The Talmud refers to mandates issued by a human court. The text continues to apply the axiom to divine laws as well.] Rav Yosef taught: What is the source for this principle? It is the verse *Go say to them, "Return again to your tents"* [Deuteronomy 5:27. The Israelite men had previously been told to separate from their wives for three days; this second command was required to allow them to return home.] Similarly, in our verse, Israel is told: *When the ram's horn sounds a long blast* – only then may they go up on the mountain. [That is, permission

had to be expressly given to rescind the prohibition on approaching the mountain.] (Beitza 5a) **הֵמָּה יַעֲלוּ בָהָר** – *Only then may they go up on the mountain:* Rabbi Yosei taught: It is never a location that lends honor to an individual, rather it is the place itself that is honored by the presence of a distinguished person. For so we find regarding Mount Sinai, that as long as the Divine Presence rested on the hill, the space was completely restricted, as the verse states: *No one else should be seen anywhere on the mountain, nor may flocks or herds graze near the mountain* (34:3). But as soon as the Divine Presence departed, the people were permitted to *go up on the mountain.* (Taanit 21b)

── YALKUT SHIMONI ──

לֹא־תִגַּע בּוֹ יָד – *No hand shall touch him:* This prohibition did not apply to the Tabernacle at Shilo. Nor were the Israelites subject to the death penalty for touching the Tent of Meeting in the desert, or the Temple in Jerusalem. How do we know that an individual who touched Mount Sinai would be put to death by being hurled from a high place? The verse states: *He shall be hurled down* [*yaro yiyyareh,* in this edition translated "shot with arrows"; the midrash understands this phrase as instead signifying that the person would himself be thrown; see commentary on 15:4]. And how do we know that such a

transgressor would be stoned with rocks? The verse states: *He shall be stoned.* How do we know that both punishments would befall the trespasser together? We know this because the verse states: *He shall be stoned or hurled down.* And how do we know that if he expired after falling from the height, that that would be sufficient [and his body would not be stoned]? The verse uses the word "or." Finally, how do we know that courts should follow the same procedure [in executing criminals] throughout the generations? The verse adds the future forms *yissakel* and *yiyyareh.* (Yitro 280)

13 the mountain must be put to death. No hand shall touch him:
he shall be stoned or shot with arrows; beast or man, he shall
not live. When the ram's horn sounds a long blast – only then
14 may they go up on the mountain." So Moshe came down from
the mountain to the people; he consecrated them and they
15 cleansed their clothes. "Be ready for the third day," he told them,

---

VERSE 14

──────────── MEKHILTA DERABBI SHIMON ────────────

מִן־הָהָר אֶל־הָעָם – *From the mountain to the people:* Based on this phrasing, we understand that upon his descent from the hill, Moshe did not first head home to attend to personal matters, but went directly to the people to convey to them God's instructions. Subsequently, when Moshe returned to God to report that he had fulfilled his mission, he did so first thing in the morning. A later verse attests to Moshe's conscientiousness when it states: *So Moshe carved two stone tablets like the first. He rose early in the morning and climbed Mount Sinai, as the Lord had commanded him* (34:4). Moshe was careful to always follow this practice of fulfilling God's word first thing in the morning. וַיְקַדֵּשׁ אֶת־הָעָם וַיְכַבְּסוּ שִׂמְלֹתָם – *He consecrated them and they cleansed their clothes:* The verse means that the Israelites cleaned their soiled clothing. But how do we know that they then immersed them in a ritual bath as well? We can infer this by building an *a fortiori* argument: In normal circumstances, when clothes need to be purified, they must be immersed in a ritual bath, but they need not be cleaned first. Now Moshe demanded that the clothes needed to be cleaned; all the more so they should be immersed as well.

VERSE 15

──────────── MIDRASH AGGADA ────────────

אַל־תִּגְּשׁוּ אֶל־אִשָּׁה – *Do not draw close to your wives:* When Moshe separated from his wife, he did not do so of his own free will, but was following a divine instruction. [Moshe is understood to have lived apart from his wife in order to always be ready to receive prophecy; see Rashi on Numbers 12:1.] This is what God implied in that incident when He said: *I speak with him mouth to mouth* (Numbers 12:8). What textual evidence supports the claim that the Holy One, blessed be He, so ordered Moshe? For the verse states [following the revelation at Sinai]: *Go say to* them, "Return again to your tents" (Deuteronomy 5:27), meaning that then the Israelites were allowed to reunite with their wives, but Moshe was not [since the order is addressed only to the people]. Previously, God had commanded: *Do not draw close to your wives* [an order to which Moshe was subject], but that decree restricting the Israelites was now rescinded. Moshe, on the other hand, was told: *As for you, stand here by Me, and I will speak to you all the commandments, and the statutes, and the judgments* (Deuteronomy 5:28). (Numbers 12:7)

טז אִשָּׁה: וַיְהִי בַיּוֹם הַשְּׁלִישִׁי בִּהְיֹת הַבֹּקֶר וַיְהִי קֹלֹת וּבְרָקִים
וְעָנָן כָּבֵד עַל־הָהָר וְקֹל שֹׁפָר חָזָק מְאֹד וַיֶּחֱרַד כָּל־הָעָם
יז אֲשֶׁר בַּמַּחֲנֶה: וַיּוֹצֵא מֹשֶׁה אֶת־הָעָם לִקְרַאת הָאֱלֹהִים

VERSE 16

SHIR HASHIRIM RABBA

וַיְהִי בַיּוֹם הַשְּׁלִישִׁי – *The third day came:* The Holy One, blessed be He, arrived at the mountain before the Israelites. Israel slept through the entire previous night, for nighttime in the season of Shavuot is pleasant, and the nights are short. Rabbi Yudan taught: The sleep of the people was not even disturbed by the presence of a flea biting them. But when the Holy One, blessed be He, came and found all the Israelites fast asleep, He began to wake them up with the sound of trumpets. Thus the verse states: *The third day came; and that morning there was thunder and lightning.* At the same time Moshe went through the camp rousing his charges to greet the King of Kings, the Holy One, blessed be He, as the verse states: *Then Moshe led the people out of the camp to meet God* (19:17). And then the Holy One, blessed be He, walked before Israel until He reached Mount Sinai, as the verse states: *Mount Sinai was enveloped in smoke because the Lord had descended on it in fire* (19:18). (1:2)

YALKUT SHIMONI

וַיְהִי קֹלֹת וּבְרָקִים – *There was thunder and lightning:* Lest you think that revelation took place at night and in silence, the verse states: *The third day came; and that morning there was thunder and lightning* (19:16). And do not think that Israel was unable to hear the voice of God, for a later verse states: *The voice of the Lord is powerful; the voice of the Lord is full of majesty* (Psalms 29:4). (Yitro 275)

וַיְהִי קֹלֹת וּבְרָקִים – *There was thunder and lightning:* Announcing God's revelation at Mount Sinai were different varieties of thunder and a range of lightning displays [the Hebrew phrase is plural, literally, "thunders and lightnings"]. **וְעָנָן כָּבֵד עַל־הָהָר** – *And a dense cloud on the mountain:* The verse here refers to the thick darkness mentioned later in the text: *But the people remained at a distance while Moshe approached the thick darkness where God was* (20:18). **וְקֹל שֹׁפָר חָזָק מְאֹד** – *And the sound of a ram's horn, intensely loud:* It is customary when people sound a horn for the quality to deteriorate as the musician tires. But here the sound grew in strength and vehemence. The call of the ram's horn was presented this way so as not to overwhelm Israel with a sudden surge of sound. **וַיֶּחֱרַד כָּל־הָעָם** – *And all the people shook:* The Israelites trembled at the experience. Rabbi Ḥelbo taught: If a person partakes of a wedding feast and yet is remiss in his obligation to delight the bride and groom, he violates five separate "voices": *The voice of joy, and the voice of gladness, the voice of the bridegroom, and the voice of the bride, the voice of them that shall say, Praise the Lord of Hosts: for the Lord is good* (Jeremiah 33:11). But if a guest does contribute to the couple's happiness, he will merit understanding of the Torah, for the Torah too was given with five "voices" [*kolot*. The term *kol* appears twice in verse 16, and twice in verse 19, but the first reference is plural, suggesting two – for a total of five.] (Yitro 282)

16 "and do not draw close to your wives." The third day came; and
that morning there was thunder and lightning and a dense
cloud on the mountain and the sound of a ram's horn, intensely
17 loud, and all the people in the camp shook. Then Moshe led
the people out of the camp to meet God, and they stood at the

VERSE 17

MEKHILTA DERABBI SHIMON

בְּתַחְתִּית הָהָר – *At the foot of the mountain:*
The entire nation of Israel crowded and
huddled around the bottom of the mountain. This scene is alluded to in the verse: *My
dove, who is in the clefts of the rock, in the secret
places of the cliff* (Song of Songs 2:14). Another
interpretation: We learn from here that the
Holy One, blessed be He, held the mountain
above Israel's heads like an inverted barrel [the
verse's language can be understood to mean
"underneath the mountain"] and declared: "If
you accept my Torah, all will be well; but if
you refuse, this will be your burial place." At
once the entire nation began to pour out their
hearts in expressions of repentance. It was
then that they declared: *All that the Lord has
spoken we shall do and we shall heed* (24:7).
Said the Holy One, blessed be He: "I require
guarantors who will agree to be punished in
the event that you transgress the Torah." Israel

responded: "The heavens and the earth will
guarantee our compliance [and will be destroyed should Israel not uphold the Torah]."
Said God to them: "The heavens and earth are
destined to vanish, and so they cannot serve
as your guarantors." [The midrash refers to the
prophecy *For the heavens shall vanish away like
smoke, and the earth shall grow old like a garment* – Isaiah 51:6] Israel then suggested: "Our
ancestors will guarantee our compliance." But
God answered: "That company is too occupied to ensure that you behave." "Then our
young children will be our guarantors," said
Israel [pledging to bind their children's lives
to their own observance of the command-
ments]. Thus the verses state: *From the coos
of little ones and babies You founded power*
(Psalms 8:3), and *Seeing you have forgotten the
Torah of your God, I will also forget your children*
(Hosea 4:6).

TALMUD BAVLI

בְּתַחְתִּית הָהָר – *At the foot of the mountain:*
[The phrase can be understood to mean
"underneath the mountain."] Rav Avdimi bar
Ḥama bar Ḥassa taught: We learn from this
phrase that the Holy One, blessed be He, held
the mountain above Israel's heads like an
inverted barrel and declared: "If you accept
my Torah, all will be well; but if you refuse,
this will be your burial place!" Rav Aḥa bar
Yaakov responded: That is a severe complaint

against the Torah! [If it were only accepted
under duress, one could argue that it is not
really binding.] Rava answered: Nevertheless,
the nation of Israel later accepted the Torah
willingly in the time of Aḥashverosh, as the
verse states: *The Jews confirmed, and took
upon themselves* (Esther 9:27), meaning that
the Jews reaffirmed what they had already
taken upon themselves. (Shabbat 88a).

TANḤUMA

וַיִּתְיַצְּבוּ – *And they stood:* When the people
of Israel left Egypt, the nation included some

individuals who were blind, deaf, and lame. Said
the Holy One, blessed be He: The Torah itself is

יח מִן־הַמַּחֲנֶה וַיִּתְיַצְּבוּ בְּתַחְתִּית הָהָר: וְהַר סִינַי עָשַׁן כֻּלּוֹ
מִפְּנֵי אֲשֶׁר יָרַד עָלָיו יהוה בָּאֵשׁ וַיַּעַל עֲשָׁנוֹ כְּעֶשֶׁן הַכִּבְשָׁן
יט וַיֶּחֱרַד כָּל־הָהָר מְאֹד: וַיְהִי קוֹל הַשֹּׁפָר הוֹלֵךְ וְחָזֵק מְאֹד

———————————— TANHUMA *(cont.)* ————————————

whole, as the verse states: *The Torah of the Lord is perfect, restoring the soul* (Psalms 19:8). So, the Holy One, blessed be He, determined to heal all the handicapped Israelites prior to giving them the Torah. Proof of this miracle comes from the text itself, for the verse states: *Every one of the people witnessed the thunder and lighting* (20:15) which shows that no one was blind. And a later verse states: *They replied, "All that the Lord has spoken we shall do and we shall heed"* (24:7) – this illustrates that no one was deaf. Finally, our verse proves that all the lame people had been healed, for the text states: *And they stood at the foot of the mountain.*

VERSE 18

———————————— MEKHILTA DERABBI SHIMON ————————————

בָּאֵשׁ – *In fire:* This verse teaches that the fire lapped at the skies and then descended onto Mount Sinai, setting it ablaze. The presence of fire at the moment of revelation was a metaphor for the Torah's teachings. Just as fire supports life in this world, so is Torah critical to sustaining human existence. Similarly, a person who gets too close to Torah is burned, just as if he had abused actual fire. And a person who distances himself too much from Torah will freeze. And just as with fire, a tiny match can set a hefty log alight, while a conflagration will consume little twigs, so too in the study of Torah can a child spark the interest of an adult, and an experienced scholar teach a novice. Whoever immerses himself in the Torah's fire in this world will merit an invitation to the next world, And how can we achieve that? Follow the verse which states: *He that walks righteously, and speaks uprightly; he that despises the gain of oppressions, that shakes his hands from holding of bribes . . . he shall dwell on high* (Isaiah 33:15). Fire is like Torah in another way too: Just as it is easy to discern those who work with fire [their faces and clothes are blackened], so too we can always tell who is a Torah scholar by the way he talks, by his humble gait, and by how he is wrapped in a tallit even when appearing in the market. וַיַּעַל עֲשָׁנוֹ כְּעֶשֶׁן הַכִּבְשָׁן – *Smoke billowed up from it as if from a furnace:* The comparison of Mount Sinai to a furnace presents the oven as a metaphor for teachings of the Torah. For a furnace is often used to test the strength of various utensils – the applied heat indicates when a given item is suitable for wine or for oil, while the severe heat will expose a flawed and cracked container as such. Engagement with Torah provides a parallel test to its students' mettle [individuals who are unworthy of its challenges are soon discovered]. Hence the verse states: *As for God, His ways are perfect* (Psalms 18:31), meaning that the Torah's commandments are intended to refine and perfect their adherents. Now one might think that when the verse states: *Smoke billowed up from it as if from a furnace,* it is to be taken literally. However, note the phrasing "as if from a furnace," which means that while the substance had the appearance of smoke, it was in reality a spiritual phenomenon. This exemplifies how the Torah takes pains to employ language that its readers can understand.

18 foot of the mountain. Mount Sinai was enveloped in smoke because the LORD had descended on it in fire. Smoke billowed up from it as if from a furnace, and the mountain shook violently
19 as one. As the sound of the ram's horn grew louder and louder,

---

LEKAH TOV

וְהַר סִינַי – *Mount Sinai:* Why was the site called "Sinai"? Because the event that occurred there caused the nations of the world to feel hatred [*sina*]. For the idolaters would forever be envious of Israel, who received the Torah while they did not.

YALKUT SHIMONI

וְהַר סִינַי – *Mount Sinai:* The area had five distinct names. It was called the Tzin Desert, because that was where the Israelites were commanded [*nitztavvu*] regarding God's laws. The place was also known as the Kadesh Desert, because the people were sanctified [*nitkaddeshu*] there. Another name was the Kedemot Desert, because it was there that the Torah, which is more ancient [*keduma*] than creation, was given. It was called the Paran Desert, recalling that Israel was fruitful [*paru*] and multiplied there. And finally, the place's most common name – the Sinai Desert – alludes to how it aroused hatred [*sina*] in the world [see Lekah Tov]. Meanwhile, its true name was Horev. Rabbi Abbahu, on the other hand, believed that the mountain's accepted name was Sinai, and that it was occasionally referred to as Horev in remembrance of the desolation [*hurva*] that descended there for the nations of the world. (Yitro 284)

VERSE 19

MEKHILTA DERABBI SHIMON

הוֹלֵךְ וְחָזֵק – *Grew louder and louder:* It is normal that when a ram's horn is blown, the tone progressively diminishes as the musician becomes winded. But when the Creator sounds an instrument, the music grows louder and louder. This is a metaphor for Torah scholars – the more wizened they become, the more clear-minded and intelligent they are. Thus does the verse state: *With aged men is wisdom; and length* of days brings understanding (Job 12:12). מֹשֶׁה יְדַבֵּר וְהָאֱלֹהִים יַעֲנֶנּוּ בְקוֹל – *Moshe spoke and God answered him aloud:* Rabbi Elazar HaModa'i taught: This was a great honor that the Holy One, blessed be He, extended to Moshe. For God waited to address the nation until He received the signal from Moshe, who told Him: You can speak now, for Your children have acknowledged that they willingly accept Your message to them.

TALMUD BAVLI

יַעֲנֶנּוּ בְקוֹל – *Answered him aloud:* Rabbi Shimon ben Pazi taught: How do we know that a translator [translating the public Torah reading from Hebrew into Aramaic] may not speak louder than the one reading from the scroll? For the verse states: *Moshe spoke and God answered him aloud.* The term "aloud" appears superfluous in this verse, but its presence teaches that God spoke in a voice no stronger than Moshe's. (Berakhot 45a)

שׁשׁי

כ מֹשֶׁה יְדַבֵּר וְהָאֱלֹהִים יַעֲנֶנּוּ בְקוֹל: וַיֵּרֶד יהוה עַל־הַר סִינַי
אֶל־רֹאשׁ הָהָר וַיִּקְרָא יהוה לְמֹשֶׁה אֶל־רֹאשׁ הָהָר וַיַּעַל
כא מֹשֶׁה: וַיֹּאמֶר יהוה אֶל־מֹשֶׁה רֵד הָעֵד בָּעָם פֶּן־יֶהֶרְסוּ
כב אֶל־יהוה לִרְאוֹת וְנָפַל מִמֶּנּוּ רָב: וְגַם הַכֹּהֲנִים הַנִּגָּשִׁים

──────────── TANHUMA ────────────

יַעֲנֶנּוּ בְקוֹל – *Answered him aloud:* What does the term "aloud" indicate? It teaches that God addressed Moshe in a voice that the prophet could tolerate. Thus the verse states: *The voice of the Lord is powerful* [Psalms 29:4; literally,

"the voice of the Lord is in strength"] – meaning that the voice matched the strength of every individual. Pregnant women heard God speak in a voice that they could endure, as did every other person.

VERSE 20

──────────── MEKHILTA DERABBI YISHMAEL ────────────

וַיֵּרֶד יהוה עַל־הַר סִינַי – *The Lord descended on Mount Sinai:* Rabbi Akiva taught: On the one hand, we have a verse that states: *I, from the heavens, have spoken to you* (20:19). On the other hand, this earlier statement claims: *And*

the Lord descended on Mount Sinai. To resolve the contradiction, we must say that the Holy One, blessed be He, bowed the heavens down to the mountain and spoke to Israel from the sky as it met the earth.

──────────── AVOT DERABBI NATAN ────────────

וַיֵּרֶד יהוה עַל־הַר סִינַי – *The Lord descended on Mount Sinai:* The Divine Presence made ten descents to earth [of which nine are listed here]: The first was in the Garden of Eden, as the verse states: *And they heard the voice of the Lord God walking in the garden in the breeze of the day* (Genesis 3:8). The second took place at the Tower of Babel, as the verse states: *And the Lord came down to see the city and the tower that the children of men were building* (Genesis 11:5). The next appearance of God on earth was prior to the destruction of Sodom, as the verse reports: *I will go down now and see whether they have done altogether according to the cry of it which has come to Me* (Genesis 18:21). An additional descent took place in Egypt, as the text relates: *So I have come to rescue them from the hand of the Egyptians* (Exodus 3:8). This was followed by God's appearance at the Sea of Reeds, as we read:

He bowed the heavens also, and came down (II Samuel 22:10). Israel experienced the arrival of the Divine Presence at Sinai as the verse states: *And the Lord descended on Mount Sinai.* God is said to have come down in a pillar of cloud, as the verse states: *And the Lord came down in a cloud, and spoke to him, and took of the spirit that was upon him, and gave it to the seventy elders* (Numbers 11:25). The Divine Presence descended in the Temple, as the verse states: *Then the Lord said to me: This gate shall be shut, it shall not be opened, and no man shall enter in by it; because the Lord, the God of Israel, has entered in by it, therefore it shall be shut* (Ezekiel 44:2). And in the future, during the battle of Gog and Magog, we can expect one final appearance, as the verse states: *And His feet shall stand on that day upon the Mount of Olives, which is before Jerusalem on the east* (Zechariah 14:4). (34)

20 Moshe spoke and God answered him aloud. And the Lord   SHISHI
descended on Mount Sinai, to the top of the mountain, and
21 called Moshe to the mountaintop, and Moshe ascended. The
Lord told Moshe, "Go back down – warn the people not to
force their way through to look at the Lord, or many will die.
22 Even priests who come near to the Lord must first consecrate

——————————— PESIKTA RABBATI ———————————

וַיֵּרֶד יהוה עַל־הַר סִינַי – *The Lord descended on
Mount Sinai:* When the verse states: *A man's
pride shall bring him low* (Proverbs 29:23), it alludes to Mount Tavor and Mount Carmel [two
prominent mountains in the land of Israel],
who both traveled to the site of Israel's national revelation, each believing itself worthy
of hosting the event. "Because of our great
heights," they boasted, "we are certain that the
Holy One, blessed be He, will choose one of
us as the site for the giving of the Torah." But

when that verse continues: *But the humble
in spirit shall attain honor,* it refers to Mount
Sinai, who humbly disparaged itself saying:
"I am far too low and insignificant a hill to at-
tract God's attention." It was that modest spirit
that caused the Holy One, blessed be He, to
select Mount Sinai as the place to deliver His
Torah. Thus was the lowly hilltop granted the
privilege of hosting the Divine Presence, as
the verse states: *And the Lord descended on
Mount Sinai.* (7)

VERSE 21

——————————— MEKHILTA DERABBI SHIMON ———————————

רֵד הָעֵד בָּעָם – *Go back down – warn the people:* Those who were later permitted to ascend
partway up the mountain [such as Nadav and
Avihu; see 24:9] were warned not to look at the
manifestation of the Divine Presence; everyone

else was told to avoid even approaching the
mountain. **וְנָפַל מִמֶּנּוּ רָב** – *Or many will die:* The
term "many" here suggests an entire popula-
tion. If any single person perishes, it is as if the
entire people has been destroyed.

——————————— LEKAH TOV ———————————

רֵד הָעֵד בָּעָם – *Go back down – warn the
people:* The nation was warned not to push
forward to the mountain in order to glimpse

the glory of God. **וְנָפַל מִמֶּנּוּ רָב** – *Or many will
die:* We learn from this that God had granted
free rein to the angels of destruction.

VERSE 22

——————————— MEKHILTA DERABBI SHIMON ———————————

וְגַם הַכֹּהֲנִים – *Even priests:* Rabbi Yehoshua ben
Korha taught: This verse refers to the firstborn
sons of Israel [and not the sons of Aharon who

later replaced them]. Rabbi Yehuda HaNasi
said: The verse is talking about Nadav and
Avihu [the sons of Aharon].

——————————— LEKAH TOV ———————————

וְגַם הַכֹּהֲנִים – *Even priests:* The term "even" intimates that Israel's elders were included in this
precaution.

כג אֶל־יהוה יֶהֶרְסוּ פֶּן־יִפְרֹץ בָּהֶם יהוה: וַיֹּאמֶר מֹשֶׁה אֶל־
יהוה לֹא־יוּכַל הָעָם לַעֲלֹת אֶל־הַר סִינָי כִּי־אַתָּה הַעֵדֹתָה
כד בָּנוּ לֵאמֹר הַגְבֵּל אֶת־הָהָר וְקִדַּשְׁתּוֹ: וַיֹּאמֶר אֵלָיו יהוה
לֶךְ־רֵד וְעָלִיתָ אַתָּה וְאַהֲרֹן עִמָּךְ וְהַכֹּהֲנִים וְהָעָם אַל־
כה יֶהֶרְסוּ לַעֲלֹת אֶל־יהוה פֶּן־יִפְרָץ־בָּם: וַיֵּרֶד מֹשֶׁה אֶל־
כ א הָעָם וַיֹּאמֶר אֲלֵהֶם: וַיְדַבֵּר אֱלֹהִים אֵת כָּל־

VERSE 23

──────────── MEKHILTA DERABBI SHIMON ────────────

וַיֹּאמֶר מֹשֶׁה – *Moshe replied:* Rabbi Yehuda taught: The Holy One, blessed be He, said to Moshe: I have told you something; now you argue with me, and I concede and change my mind. For Moshe said: *You Yourself warned us to set a boundary around the mountain* – the people have already marked off the territory and are carefully maintaining their distance. [Therefore God did not continue to insist that Moshe warn the people again.]

VERSE 24

──────────── MEKHILTA DERABBI SHIMON ────────────

וְעָלִיתָ אַתָּה וְאַהֲרֹן עִמָּךְ – *Come back together with Aharon:* While God invited select individuals to ascend the hill, such permission was not granted to the entire nation, as the verse states: *Do not let the priests or people force their way through.* Even Aharon was allowed only a modest ascent and was not permitted to climb as far as Moshe into the dark cloud, as the verse states: *Moshe alone shall approach the LORD* (24:2) – Aharon had his own boundary, and Moshe had license to advance further.

──────────── LEKAH TOV ────────────

לֶךְ־רֵד – *Go down:* The Holy One, blessed be He, responded to Moshe: You did well by establishing a perimeter for the people. [Hence God dropped the insistence on an additional warning to the whole nation that He had expressed in verses 21–22.]

VERSE 25

──────────── LEKAH TOV ────────────

וַיֹּאמֶר אֲלֵהֶם – *And told them:* Moshe said to the nation: Prepare to willingly accept the rulership of God. Another interpretation: Moshe prepared Israel to respond affirmatively to the positive commandments, and negatively to the prohibitions.

CHAPTER 20, VERSE 1

──────────── MEKHILTA DERABBI YISHMAEL ────────────

אֶת־כָּל־הַדְּבָרִים הָאֵלֶּה – *All these words:* This introductory clause teaches that the entire text of the Ten Commandments was pronounced simultaneously, in a manner that a human voice could never imitate. However, the subsequent verses give the impression that

23 themselves, or the LORD will break out against them." Moshe replied to the LORD, "The people cannot climb Mount Sinai. You Yourself warned us to set a boundary around the moun-
24 tain and consecrate it." The LORD said to him, "Go down, and come back together with Aharon. But do not let the priests or people force their way through to come up to the LORD,
25 or He will break out against them." So Moshe went down to
20 1 the people and told them.   Then God spoke all these

──────────────── MEKHILTA DERABBI YISHMAEL *(cont.)* ────────────────

indeed each of the commandments was re-cited singly. In fact, the experience unfolded as follows: Initially, God pronounced the en-tirety of the oration in one utterance. He then proceeded to state each precept distinctly. Does this mean that the rest of the Torah's laws were similarly conveyed in this way? No, for our verse emphasizes that *God spoke all these words* – only these words were com-municated first as one articulation and then as separate messages; the remainder of the commandments were given one at a time.

──────────────── SIFREI BEMIDBAR ────────────────

וַיְדַבֵּר אֱלֹהִים – *Then God spoke:* How do we know that if a person embraces foreign gods, it is as if he has rejected all the Ten Commandments? For the Torah states: *And if you have erred, and not observed all these commandments, which the LORD spoke to Moshe* [Numbers 15:22; this verse is understood by the Midrash to refer to idolatry], when an ear-lier verse had used similar language: *Then God spoke all these words.* (Shelaḥ 111)

──────────────── TANḤUMA ────────────────

וַיְדַבֵּר אֱלֹהִים – *Then God spoke:* On one occa-sion, Rabbi Akiva was petitioned by the com-munity to ascend the podium and to read the Torah in public, but he refused. Said his students to him: "Master, have you not taught us that the Torah is our lives and the length of our days? Why have you turned down the request to read the Torah for us?" Rabbi Akiva answered: "I swear by the Temple service that I am only unwilling because I have not re-viewed the text two and three times. And I maintain that a person may not pronounce words of Torah before the community unless he has practiced his speech two and three times in private." For even though the Holy One, blessed be He, grants man the power of elocution, and He has total mastery of the To-rah, He did not immediately communicate the Ten Commandments to the Israelites. When it came time for Him to give the Torah to Israel, first *he saw it, and declared it; he established it, and searched it out* (Job 28:27). Only then did "He say unto man" (Job 28:28). This is why the verse states: *Then God spoke all these words,* adding the final word *lemor* [literally, "saying"], meaning that He insisted on "speaking" mate-rial to Himself before "saying" it to the people. (Yitro 15) אֵת כָּל־הַדְּבָרִים הָאֵלֶּה – *All these words:* When the Holy One, blessed be He, dic-tated the Torah to Moshe, He recited to him, in sequence, the following works: The Torah, the Mishna, the Aggadah, and the Talmud, as the verse states: *Then God spoke all these words.* At that time, the Holy One, blessed be He, even related to Moshe what future students would ask their rabbis. (Buber, Ki Tisa 17)

ב הַדְּבָרִים הָאֵלֶּה לֵאמֹר: אָנֹכִי יהוה אֱלֹהֶיךָ
ג אֲשֶׁר הוֹצֵאתִיךָ מֵאֶרֶץ מִצְרַיִם מִבֵּית עֲבָדִים: לֹא־יִהְיֶה
ד לְךָ אֱלֹהִים אֲחֵרִים עַל־פָּנָי: לֹא־תַעֲשֶׂה לְךָ פֶסֶל וְכָל־
תְּמוּנָה אֲשֶׁר בַּשָּׁמַיִם מִמַּעַל וַאֲשֶׁר בָּאָרֶץ מִתַּחַת וַאֲשֶׁר

───────────────── BEMIDBAR RABBA ─────────────────

אֶת כָּל־הַדְּבָרִים הָאֵלֶּה – *All these words:* The term *baalei asufot* [a term appearing in Ecclesiastes 12:11 and meaning "masters of collections"] refers to scholars, who sit in groups and engage in Torah study. Some of these authorities tend to rule that objects are impure, while others are inclined to declare things pure. Some usually forbid while others permit; some disqualify while others label items as fit. Now this situation might bewilder a Jew trying to obey God's law – how can one follow the Torah when there are so many contrasting opinions? Hence you must remember that even these disparate approaches were all taught by a single shepherd [Moshe]. God pronounced all these possible interpretations; they were all transmitted by a single Creator, blessed be He, as the verse states: *Then God spoke all these words.* (Naso 14:4)

VERSE 2

───────────── MEKHILTA DERABBI SHIMON ─────────────

אָנֹכִי יהוה אֱלֹהֶיךָ – *I am the Lord your God:* During Israel's forty-year journey through the wilderness, the Ark of the Covenant and Yosef's sarcophagus traveled side by side. Meanwhile, wayfarers coming from the other direction would stop and ask what was inside the two boxes. "One represents the Divine Presence," they were told, "and the other contains a corpse." But the strangers would protest: "How is it fitting to carry a dead body alongside the Divine Presence?" "You must understand," they were told, "that the person who occupied this body embodied the message contained in this ark [i.e., inscribed on the Tablets of the Covenant]." We know that this is so because the Ten Commandments begins with the statement *I am the Lord your God,* whereas toward the end of his life, Yosef insisted: *Am I in the place of God?* (Genesis 50:19). The tablets contain the law *Have no other gods than Me,* and Yosef declared, *I fear God* (Genesis 42:18). (13:19) אָנֹכִי יהוה אֱלֹהֶיךָ – *I am the Lord your God:* I am the God of all the earth's creatures.

Nevertheless, do not imagine that Israel and the nations of the world are on equal footing, for God is referred to as the "God of Israel" [for example, in 5:1]. Still, do not believe that He is the Jews' private deity, for He states, "I am the Lord," meaning: I am God of all of humanity. How can we reconcile these two understandings? Although He is the God of every person and nation, His name is associated with Israel specifically. Another interpretation: What does the verse mean when it states: *I am the Lord your God?* Said the Holy One, blessed be He: When Israel honors My will, I will be their "Lord," as the verse states, *The Lord, the Lord, God compassionate and gracious* (34:6; i.e., that divine name connotes the divine attribute of Compassion). However, should the Israelites choose a path of disobedience, I will treat them as their "God" and exact punishment from them, for that divine name is associated with the attribute of Justice. Another interpretation: The statement *I am the Lord your God* alludes to the tradition that prior to the revelation, the Holy

2 words: "I am the Lᴏʀᴅ your God who brought you
3 out of the land of Egypt, out of the house of slaves. Have no
4 other gods than Me. Do not make for yourself any carved image or likeness of any creature in the heavens above or the earth

──────────── MEKHILTA DERABBI SHIMON *(cont.)* ────────────

One, blessed be He, offered the Torah to each of the world's nations and they all declined His overture. But then He approached Israel and declared: *I am the Lᴏʀᴅ your God.* (20:2)

──────────── BERESHIT RABBA ────────────

אָנֹכִי יהוה אֱלֹהֶיךָ – *I am the Lᴏʀᴅ your God:* Rabbi Elazar bar Ḥanina taught in the name of Rabbi Aḥa: For twenty-six generations [from the creation of the world to the revelation at Sinai], the letter *alef* harangued the Holy One, blessed be He, complaining that since he is the first letter of the alphabet, God ought to have employed him when He began to create the world [since the story of creation begins with a *bet*]. Said the Holy One, blessed be He, to him: Surely you know that I have created the entire world only for the sake of the Torah, as the verse states: *The Lᴏʀᴅ by wisdom founded the earth; by understanding He established the heavens* (Proverbs 3:19). Tomorrow I will arrive at Sinai to bestow the Torah upon Israel, and it will open with an *alef.* Hence the verse states: *I am [anokhi] the Lᴏʀᴅ your God.* (Bereshit 1:10)

──────────── LEKAḤ TOV ────────────

אָנֹכִי יהוה אֱלֹהֶיךָ – *I am the Lᴏʀᴅ your God:* The word "I" connotes consolation from suffering, as in the verse *I, even I, am He that comforts you* (Isaiah 51:12). But it also implies a warning, as in the verse *I am He who knows, and I am a witness, says the Lᴏʀᴅ* (Jeremiah 29:23). In addition, it represents assistance as we read: *I will go down with you into Egypt* (Genesis 46:4).... Why were the Ten Commandments expressed in singular form? [Starting with the word *Elohekha* – your God – the text appears to be addressed to the individual rather than to the community.] This was done so that every Israelite should believe that the Ten Commandments were given to him or to her personally, so that he or she should feel a private obligation to fulfill their demands. No Jew should be able to say that is suffices for someone else to observe the commandments.

──────────── MIDRASH AGGADA ────────────

אָנֹכִי יהוה אֱלֹהֶיךָ – *I am the Lᴏʀᴅ your God:* The word *anokhi* is spelled *alef-nun-kaf-yod.* The *alef,* with a numerical value of one, represents God, who is singular in this world. The letters *nun-kaf,* with a combined numerical value of seventy, indicate that the Holy One, blessed be He, chose Israel over all the other seventy nations of the world. Finally, the letter *yod* [with a value of ten] is an allusion to the Ten Commandments.

VERSE 4

──────────── MEKHILTA DERABBI SHIMON ────────────

לֹא־תַעֲשֶׂה לְךָ פֶסֶל – *Do not make for yourself any carved image:* Lest you think that you can make your own image to worship, the Torah warns: *Do not make for yourself any carved* image. How do we know that creating images of people is forbidden? For the verse states: *Lest you become corrupt, and make a carved idol, the similitude of any figure, the likeness*

ה בַּמַּיִם מִתַּחַת לָאָרֶץ: לֹא־תִשְׁתַּחֲוֶה לָהֶם וְלֹא תָעָבְדֵם
כִּי אָנֹכִי יהוה אֱלֹהֶיךָ אֵל קַנָּא פֹּקֵד עֲוֹן אָבֹת עַל־בָּנִים
ו עַל־שִׁלֵּשִׁים וְעַל־רִבֵּעִים לְשֹׂנְאָי: וְעֹשֶׂה חֶסֶד לַאֲלָפִים

——————— MEKHILTA DERABBI SHIMON *(cont.)* ———————

of male or female (Deuteronomy 4:16). How do we know that the prohibition extends to stone with no likeness? For the verse states: *You shall make no idols, nor shall you erect a carved idol, or a pillar, nor shall you install a figured stone in your land, to bow down upon it* (Leviticus 26:1). How do we know that the prohibition includes trees? The verse states: *Do not plant a sacred tree of any kind beside the altar that you make for the Lord your God,* (Deuteronomy 16:21). How do we know that creating images of fish is forbidden? For the verse states: *The likeness of any fish that is in the waters beneath the earth* (Deuteronomy

4:18). How do we know that creating images of birds is forbidden? For the verse proscribes *the likeness of any winged bird that flies in the air* (Deuteronomy 4:17). How do we know that creating images of animals is forbidden? From the same verse, which begins: *The likeness of any beast that is on the earth.* How do we know that creating images of angels is forbidden? From our verse, which mentions the *likeness of any creature in the heavens.* And how do we know that creating images of entities of the deep is forbidden? From the same verse, which states: *Or the water beneath the earth.*

VERSE 5

——————— MEKHILTA DERABBI SHIMON ———————

לֹא־תִשְׁתַּחֲוֶה לָהֶם – *Do not bow down to them:* Considering that bowing down before idols is only one of many acts prohibited in this regard, why was it singled out for specific mention? Because bowing was chosen to serve as an archetype for all idolatrous service. A person is liable simply for bowing, even when it is not performed in conjunction with another act [like sacrificing], and whether or not bowing is the accepted form of worship of the god in question. Similarly, one transgresses the decree against idolatry if he behaves toward another deity in any manner reserved for the service of God, whether this is the normal way to worship that false god or not. For God "demands absolute loyalty." ... Agrippas the Elder put the following problem to Rabban Gamliel: Is it not true that a person is only

jealous of others whom he views as rivals? And yet the verse states: *Know therefore this day, and consider it in your heart, that the Lord He is God in heaven above, and upon the earth beneath: there is no other* (Deuteronomy 4:39). Rabban Gamliel answered: In truth, those of whom God is jealous are not greater than He, nor are they His equals. They are lesser than Him, as the verse states: *For My people have committed two evils; they have forsaken Me the fountain of living waters...* (Jeremiah 2:13). Had Israel merely abandoned Me, their source of life, they would have been in a miserable state. Yet they have made things even worse, since they *have hewn them out cisterns, broken cisterns, that can hold no water* [i.e., false and worthless gods].

5 beneath or the water beneath the earth. Do not bow down to them or worship them, for I the LORD your God demand absolute loyalty. For those who hate Me, I hold the descendants to account for the sins of the fathers to the third and fourth gen-
6 eration, but to those who love Me and keep My commands –

──────────── MIDRASH AGGADA ────────────

עֲוֹן אָבֹת – *The sins of the fathers:* One verse states: *Fathers shall not be put to death for children, neither shall children be put to death for fathers: every man shall be put to death for his own sin* (Deuteronomy 24:16). On the other hand, our verse reads: *I hold the descendants to account for the sins of the fathers.* How are these to be reconciled? Whenever children perpetuate the sins of their fathers, they are held accountable for the behavior of their parents. But if children do not imitate their fathers' sins, *neither shall children be put to death for fathers.*

VERSE 6

──────────── TALMUD BAVLI ────────────

חֶסֶד לַאֲלָפִים – *Faithful love for thousands:* Rabbi Shimon ben Elazar taught: One who serves God out of love is greater than one who serves Him out of fear. For the reward of the latter endures for a thousand generations, whereas the merit accrued by the former extends for two thousand generations. With regard to acting out of love, the verse states: *But to those who love Me I shall act with faithful love for thousands* [the word "thousands" is plural, the minimum of which is two]. On the other hand, a later verse argues: *Know therefore that the LORD your God, He is God, the faithful God, Who keeps covenant and mercy with those who love Him and keep His commandments to a thousand generations* (Deuteronomy 7:9). – But does not that verse also refer to those "who love him"? In the former verse [Exodus 20:6] the stated reward appears immediately juxtaposed to the words "to those who love Me" [it is thus in the Hebrew, although not in the English translation here]. In the verse in Deuteronomy, it is the clause "those who keep His commandments" that is linked to the assurance of a thousand blessed generations [suggesting even those who behave out of fear of punishment]. (Sota 31a)

──────────── LEKAH TOV ────────────

לְאֹהֲבַי וּלְשֹׁמְרֵי מִצְוֹתָי – *To those who love Me and keep My commands:* We see from this verse that those who observe God's commands are considered His beloved. Another interpretation: The verse refers to those who are martyred in the sanctification of God's name. Why would gentiles cut off the head of a Jew? Because a father circumcised his son. Why would they burn a Jew to death? Because he studied from the Torah. Why would a Jew be crucified? Because he ate matza on Passover. Why would a gentile court sentence a Jew to one hundred lashes of the whip? Because he raised his lulav on Sukkot. And why do Jews ever face such hatred and violence? Because they refuse to renounce their Creator. That is what the text means when it refers to *those who love Me and keep My commands.*

לְאֹהֲבַי וּלְשֹׁמְרֵי מִצְוֹתָי: לֹא תִשָּׂא אֶת־שֵׁם־
יְהוָה אֱלֹהֶיךָ לַשָּׁוְא כִּי לֹא יְנַקֶּה יְהוָה אֵת אֲשֶׁר־יִשָּׂא אֶת־
שְׁמוֹ לַשָּׁוְא:

ח זָכוֹר אֶת־יוֹם הַשַּׁבָּת לְקַדְּשׁוֹ: שֵׁשֶׁת יָמִים תַּעֲבֹד וְעָשִׂיתָ

VERSE 7

TALMUD BAVLI

לַשָּׁוְא – *In vain:* One violates the prohibition of saying God's name in vain if he recites an unnecessary blessing. (Berakhot 33a)

לֹא תִשָּׂא – *Do not speak:* One who violates any of the Torah's commandments incurs thirty-nine lashes, on condition that the transgression was an active one. If the sin involves no physical act it is not punishable by lashes. Exceptions to this rule are swearing falsely, exchanging [i.e., verbally redesignating a sacrificial animal by substituting another for it],

and cursing one's fellow in the name of God. How do we know that swearing falsely does incur lashes? Rabbi Yoḥanan said in the name of Rabbi Shimon bar Yoḥai: The Torah states: *Do not speak the name of the LORD your God in vain, for the LORD will not hold guiltless etc.* That is, although the heavenly court will not render such a person guiltless [that is, will not clear him], a human court must impose lashes on the violator and thereby clear him of his guilt. (Shevuot 21a)

LEKAḤ TOV

אֶת־שֵׁם־יהוה אֱלֹהֶיךָ – *The name of the LORD your God:* This refers to the Tetragrammaton.

לַשָּׁוְא – *In vain:* The term "in vain" appears twice in this verse, once referring to futile oaths

and once warning against false oaths. A futile or unnecessary oath is, for example, when one swears to something that is commonly known, such as that a certain pillar is made of stone.

MIDRASH AGGADA

לֹא תִשָּׂא – *Do not speak:* [Literally, "do not bear."] Do not pretend that you are a righteous

person [one who bears God's name] when you are really not.

VERSE 8

MEKHILTA DERABBI SHIMON

זָכוֹר אֶת־יוֹם הַשַּׁבָּת לְקַדְּשׁוֹ – *Remember the Sabbath to keep it holy:* [Literally, "the Sabbath day"] Rabbi Yehuda ben Beteira taught: How do we know that the days of the week should be called by their position relative to the Sabbath – that is, Day One of the Sabbath [*Rishon BaShabbat* – Hebrew for Sunday], Day Two of the Sabbath, Day Three of the Sabbath, Day Four of the Sabbath, Day Five of the Sabbath, and Sabbath Eve? We learn this practice from

the Torah's command to "remember the Sabbath" [that is, one remembers the Sabbath day whenever he or she mentions one of the week's other days]. Now, when the verse states: *Remember the Sabbath day,* it would seem that one is required to sanctify the holy time during the day [that is, to recite *Kiddush* in the daytime]. How do we know that *Kiddush* should be proclaimed at night [on Friday evening at the Sabbath's start]? We learn this rule from

7 I shall act with faithful love for thousands.   Do not speak the name of the LORD your God in vain, for the LORD will not hold guiltless those who speak His name in vain.

$\genfrac{}{}{0pt}{}{8}{9}$ Remember the Sabbath to keep it holy. Six days you shall work,

———————————— MEKHILTA DERABBI SHIMON *(cont.)* ————————————

the words "to keep it holy" [i.e., at the hour of its sanctification, at the time when it becomes distinguished from the rest of the week]. Why then does the verse employ the word "day"? To emphasize that greater care should be taken in honoring the day than the night [e.g., by reserving the best food and wine for the day's meal]. How do we know that if one has neglected to recite *Kiddush* at night, he should proceed to do so during the day? For the verse states: *Remember the Sabbath day to keep it holy.* Another interpretation for the

phrase "to keep it holy": How does one sanctify the day? By enjoying good meals and wines and by dressing in fancy clothes. This means that one should not eat the same foods on the Sabbath as one would during the week, and one should not wear weekday clothes on the holy day. How do we know that even impoverished Jews should make sure to indulge in a special food on the Sabbath, and conversely that wealthy Jews should not serve Sabbath-style fare during the week? This is the power of the verse *Remember the Sabbath to keep it holy.*

———————————— TALMUD BAVLI ————————————

זָכוֹר אֶת־יוֹם הַשַּׁבָּת – *Remember the Sabbath:* Rava taught: Regarding the Sabbath, the Torah states both: *Remember [zakhor] the Sabbath,* and: *Keep [shamor] the Sabbath* (Deuteronomy 5:12). Those who must keep the Sabbath are correspondingly required to remember the Sabbath. Since women are obligated to keep the Sabbath [by abstaining from performing work], they are similarly required to express the day's remembrance [by reciting *Kiddush* and *Havdala*]. (Berakhot 20b) זָכוֹר אֶת־יוֹם הַשַּׁבָּת לְקַדְּשׁוֹ – *Remember*

the Sabbath to keep it holy: Remember the day by reciting *Kiddush* over wine at the day's start. (Pesaḥim 106a) זָכוֹר אֶת־יוֹם הַשַּׁבָּת לְקַדְּשׁוֹ – *Remember the Sabbath to keep it holy:* When God addressed Israel He recited the two commands *Remember [zakhor] the Sabbath* and *Keep [shamor] the Sabbath* (Deuteronomy 5:12) in a single utterance, a feat that a human mouth could never achieve. And yet, at that moment, Israel was able to distinguish the two words [*zakhor* and *shamor*], something which is usually impossible. (Shevuot 20b)

VERSE 9

———————————— MEKHILTA DERABBI YISHMAEL ————————————

שֵׁשֶׁת יָמִים תַּעֲבֹד – *Six days you shall work:* On the one hand, the Torah states: *Six days through shall work be done* [31:15, using the passive voice], while another verse proclaims: *Six days you shall work.* How can these two statements be reconciled? As long as Israel fulfills the will of God, their work will be performed by others, as the verse states: *And*

strangers shall stand and feed your flocks, and the sons of the alien shall be your ploughmen and your vinedressers (Isaiah 61:5). However, when the Jewish people ignore God's commandments, they will have to labor for themselves during the six weekdays. What's more, Israel will then be compelled to do the work of others as well.

י כָּל־מְלַאכְתֶּךָ: וְיוֹם֙ הַשְּׁבִיעִ֔י שַׁבָּ֖ת לַיהוָ֣ה אֱלֹהֶ֑יךָ לֹֽא־
תַעֲשֶׂ֣ה כָל־מְלָאכָ֡ה אַתָּ֣ה ׀ וּבִנְךָֽ־וּ֠בִתֶּ֗ךָ עַבְדְּךָ֤ וַאֲמָֽתְךָ֙
יא וּבְהֶמְתֶּ֔ךָ וְגֵרְךָ֖ אֲשֶׁ֥ר בִּשְׁעָרֶֽיךָ: כִּ֣י שֵֽׁשֶׁת־יָמִים֩ עָשָׂ֨ה
יְהוָ֜ה אֶת־הַשָּׁמַ֣יִם וְאֶת־הָאָ֗רֶץ אֶת־הַיָּם֙ וְאֶת־כָּל־
אֲשֶׁר־בָּ֔ם וַיָּ֖נַח בַּיּ֣וֹם הַשְּׁבִיעִ֑י עַל־כֵּ֗ן בֵּרַ֧ךְ יְהוָ֛ה אֶת־י֥וֹם
הַשַּׁבָּ֖ת וַֽיְקַדְּשֵֽׁהוּ: יב כַּבֵּ֥ד אֶת־אָבִ֖יךָ וְאֶת־אִמֶּ֑ךָ

AVOT DERABBI NATAN

שֵׁשֶׁת יָמִים תַּעֲבֹד – *Six days you shall work:* A person should love to work; it is unseemly to hate toil. For just as the Torah was given to Israel as a covenant, so too was work given as a covenant, as the verse states: *Six days you shall work, and carry out all your labors, but the seventh is a Sabbath to the Lord your God* (20:9–10). Rabbi Akiva taught: There are times when a person works and those efforts save his life; on other occasions, a person is idle, and heaven sentences him to death for his sloth. How so? Consider a man who sits and wastes time the entire week. Come Sabbath eve, he finds that he has nothing to eat for the holy day. What might such a person do? He will take some money that he has previously dedicated to the Temple and use it to buy food, thereby incurring a punishment of death. If that same individual had been a laborer working to construct the Temple and had been paid his wages with sanctified money, he could use that cash to feed himself and stave off starvation. (11)

VERSE 10

PHILO

עַבְדְּךָ וַאֲמָתְךָ – *Your male of female servant:* The Sabbath also teaches the servants not to despair of better times that lay ahead. Indeed, having a day of relaxation can serve as a spark and kindling of freedom.

MEKHILTA DERABBI YISHMAEL

לֹא־תַעֲשֶׂה כָל־מְלָאכָה – *Do no work:* When the Torah forbids that work be done, it refers to the thirty-nine principal labors. But how do we know that rabbinic prohibitions [such as engaging in commerce on the Sabbath] must also be respected? The verse which states: *You shall keep My Sabbaths* (Leviticus 19:30), alludes to behavior proscribed by the Sages as well.

MEKHILTA DERABBI SHIMON

לֹא־תַעֲשֶׂה כָל־מְלָאכָה – *Do no work:* Our verse warns Israel against performing work on the Sabbath, while a later text similarly uses the term "work" [*melakha*] when discussing the construction of the Tabernacle [see 35:21]. The latter usage clarifies the meaning of the word to teach that only planned and creative work is prohibited on the Sabbath, for only such activity was employed to build the Tabernacle.

10 and carry out all your labors, but the seventh is a Sabbath to the
LORD your God. On it, do no work – neither you, nor your son
or daughter, your male or female servant, your livestock, or the
11 migrant within your gates. For in six days the LORD made heav-
en and earth, the sea, and all that they contain, and He rested
on the seventh day. And so the LORD blessed the Sabbath day
12 and made it holy. Honor your father and mother.

LEKAḤ TOV

וְיוֹם הַשְּׁבִיעִי שַׁבָּת לַיהוה – *But the seventh is a Sabbath to the LORD:* When a person desists from labor on the Sabbath, his behavior is a testament to his belief that the Holy One, blessed be He, created the world in six days. **לֹא־תַעֲשֶׂה כָל־מְלָאכָה** – *Do no work:* This represents the Torah's warning against labor on the Sabbath. For it is an established principle that no punishment can be imposed unless a warning has first been issued. Another interpretation: Although the verse states that the "day"

is holy [the word *yom* appears in the Hebrew, though not in the translation], no labor may be performed during the Sabbath at night either. **אַתָּה וּבִנְךָ וּבִתֶּךָ** – *Neither you, nor your son or daughter:* This refers to children, meaning that adults are instructed to guide the young ones in proper Sabbath behavior. **עַבְדְּךָ וַאֲמָתְךָ** – *Your male or female servant:* Israelite slaves may not perform labor on the Sabbath [though gentile slaves may]. **וְגֵרְךָ** – *The migrant:* This refers to sincere converts to Judaism.

VERSE 11

MEKHILTA DERABBI SHIMON

בֵּרַךְ... וַיְקַדְּשֵׁהוּ – *Blessed...and made it holy:* In what way did God bless and sanctify the day? He blessed and sanctified the day by providing the Israelites with a double portion of manna on Friday. For on every day of the week, the people collected *an omer for every person* (16:16), but in honor of the Sabbath,

they gathered a double portion, two omers each (16:22). Furthermore, during the week, manna that was kept overnight *became worm-infested and stank* (16:20), but when the Israelites held on to the extra food on Sabbath eve, *it did not stink, nor did worms infest it* (16:24).

BERESHIT RABBA

כִּי שֵׁשֶׁת־יָמִים – *For in six days:* The verse states: *And by the seventh day God ended His work which He had done* (Genesis 2:2). But did God have to work? Did not Rabbi Berekhya teach in the name of Rabbi Yehuda bar Simon: The Holy One, blessed be He, required

no labor or toil to create His world? That verse appears to condemn the wicked who destroy the world that God labored to create, and to reward the righteous who sustain the earth that God labored to create. (Albeck, Bereshit 10)

VERSE 12

TALMUD YERUSHALMI

כַּבֵּד אֶת־אָבִיךָ וְאֶת־אִמֶּךָ – *Honor your father and mother:* Rabbi Shimon ben Yoḥai taught:

The commandment to honor one's father and mother is so important that the Holy

לְמַ֗עַן יַאֲרִכ֣וּן יָמֶ֔יךָ עַ֚ל הָ֣אֲדָמָ֔ה אֲשֶׁר־יהוה אֱלֹהֶ֖יךָ
נֹתֵ֥ן לָֽךְ׃ לֹ֥א תִרְצָ֖ח לֹ֥א
תִנְאָ֑ף לֹ֥א תִגְנֹ֖ב לֹֽא־

—————— TALMUD YERUSHALMI *(cont.)* ——————

One, blessed be He, indicates it is preferable to honoring Him. For our verse states: *Honor your father and mother* [without qualification], whereas regarding God, the verse states: *Honor the LORD with your substance, and with the first fruits of all your increase* (Proverbs 3:9). Now how does one show honor to God? By spending money to feed the poor and in the performance of commandments. Firstly, a farmer must abandon a corner of his field's crops to the hungry, and may not retrieve forgotten sheaves or individual stalks, but must leave them for the poor to collect. Secondly, produce must be separated as *teruma* [a donation] to the priests, as a tithe [to the Levites], as a second tithe [to be eaten in celebration in Jerusalem], and as an additional tithe to the poor, while some of a baker's dough is taken out as a gift for the priests. Next, the Jew must spend money to build a sukka, to acquire a lulav, a shofar, tefillin, and tzitzit. And all Jews must bear the costs of feeding the hungry and providing water for the thirsty. Note that all of these obligations are only incurred when one can afford them; they are not required of a Jew who is himself destitute. However, when it comes to honoring one's parents, every child is responsible for fulfilling the obligation regardless of financial status. A person must provide for his father and mother even when it means begging for charity to attain the necessary sustenance. (Kiddushin 1:7)

—————— TALMUD BAVLI ——————

כַּבֵּד אֶת־אָבִיךָ וְאֶת־אִמֶּךָ – *Honor your father and mother:* Ulla the Great lectured at the entrance to the Nasi's house and said: What is meant by the verse *All the kings of the earth shall give You thanks, O LORD, when they hear the words of Your mouth* (Psalms 138:4)? Note that the verse does not say "the word of Your mouth," but "the words of Your mouth." This should be understood as follows: When the Holy One, blessed be He, addressed Israel and declared: *I am the LORD your God* and *Do not make for yourself any carved image* (20:2–3), the nations of world scoffed and said: See how all of His rules are about demanding honor for himself! But as soon as they heard God's command *Honor your father and mother*, the gentiles retracted their mockery and admitted that the first precepts were also valid. Rava taught: This process is also attested to by the verse *The beginning of Your word is true* (Psalms 119:160). Is it only the beginning of God's communication that is true, and not the end? Rather, by reading the end of God's message, we see that the opening words are true as well. (Kiddushin 31a)

—————— LEKAH TOV ——————

כַּבֵּד אֶת־אָבִיךָ וְאֶת־אִמֶּךָ – *Honor your father and mother:* Rabbi Yehuda HaNasi taught: The Creator is well aware of human nature. As such, He knows that a child has a tendency to honor his mother more than his father, because the former spoils him and woos him with words. To counter this inclination, the verse mentions the father before the mother,

Then you will live long in the land that the Lᴏʀᴅ your God is
13 giving you.   Do not murder.   Do not
commit adultery.   Do not steal.   Do not

———————————— LEKAḤ TOV *(cont.)* ————————————

instructing that the parent who is listed first should be honored first. אֶת־אָבִיךָ – *Your father:* The additional word *et* teaches that one must honor even one's stepfather. וְאֵת־אִמֶּךָ – *And your mother:* Here, the word *et* teaches that one must honor one's stepmother. וְאֵת־אִמֶּךָ – *And your mother:* The additional letter *vav* [which starts the word *ve'et*] teaches that one must honor even one's firstborn brother.

VERSE 13

———————————— SIFREI DEVARIM ————————————

לֹא תִרְצָח לֹא תִנְאָף לֹא תִגְנֹב – *Do not murder. Do not commit adultery. Do not steal:* When the Holy One, blessed be He, determined to reveal His Torah, He did not offer His work to Israel alone, but proffered the law to all the nations of the world. He first approached the descendants of Esav and said: "Would you like to accept My Torah?" Said they: "It depends – what is written in it?" Answered God: "In the Torah it states, *Do not murder.*" They responded: "But our entire culture is based on our ancestor's murderous character, as the verse states: *By your sword shall you live* (Genesis 27:40)." God moved on to the peoples of Amon and Moav and asked them: "Would you like to accept My Torah?" Said they: "It depends – what is written in it?" Answered God: "In the Torah it states: *Do not commit adultery.*" They responded, "But our entire culture is based on licentiousness, for so the verse states of our ancestors: *Thus were both the daughters of Lot with child by their father* (Genesis 19:36)." Next, God appealed to the descendants of Yishmael, asking them: "Would you like to accept My Torah?" Said they: "It depends – what is written in it?" Answered God: "In the Torah it states: *Do not steal.*" They said, "But stealing is our way of life, which we have learned from our progenitor, as the verse states: *And he will be a wild man; his hand will be against every man, and every man's hand against him* (Genesis 16:12)." And so God appealed to nation after nation, group after group, trying to convince them to accept His Torah. Indeed, even the seven Noahide laws that humanity had already accepted were no longer observed and were shunted to Israel. It was only when the Holy One, blessed be He, approach Israel that He met with success. It was only they who were prepared to accept the Torah with all its interpretations and details. (Vezot HaBerakha 343)

———————————— TALMUD YERUSHALMI ————————————

לֹא־תַעֲנֶה בְרֵעֲךָ עֵד שָׁקֶר – *Do not bear false witness against your neighbor:* Rabbi Levi taught: The Holy One, blessed be He, said: When an individual gives false testimony against his fellow, I consider that as severe as if he had testified that I did not create the heavens and the earth. (Berakhot 1:5)

———————————— TALMUD BAVLI ————————————

לֹא תִגְנֹב – *Do not steal:* When the Torah states: *Do not steal,* that represents the prohibition of kidnapping human beings. One might have thought that it was a warning against

יד תַּעֲנֶה בְרֵעֲךָ עֵד שָׁקֶר:
לֹא
תַחְמֹד בֵּית רֵעֶךָ
לֹא־
לֹא תַחְמֹד אֵשֶׁת רֵעֶךָ וְעַבְדּוֹ וַאֲמָתוֹ וְשׁוֹרוֹ וַחֲמֹרוֹ וְכֹל אֲשֶׁר
לְרֵעֶךָ:
טו וְכָל־הָעָם רֹאִים אֶת־הַקּוֹלֹת וְאֶת־הַלַּפִּידִם וְאֵת קוֹל הַשֹּׁפָר שביעי

—————————— TALMUD BAVLI *(cont.)* ——————————

stealing money. But apply one of the thirteen exegetical principles used to interpret the Torah, specifically the one that explains a verse's meaning by its context, and the correct understanding will present itself. Since the other prohibitions in this verse – murder and adultery – are capital crimes, we can infer that the decree against stealing is also of that variety. [Abduction is the only kind of theft that warrants the death penalty.] (Sanhedrin 86a)

—————————— MIDRASH AGGADA ——————————

לא תרצח – *Do not murder:* Transpose the letters of the word *tirtzaḥ* to read the prohibition as *lo tirḥatz* – do not wash. For we read after Kayin's murder of Hevel: *The voice of your brother's blood cries to me from the ground* (Genesis 4:10) – the Torah warns not to wash in the blood of another. Compare to the imagery in the verse: *The righteous shall rejoice when he sees vengeance: He shall wash his feet in the blood of the wicked* (Psalms 58:11).

VERSE 14

—————————— MEKHILTA DERABBI SHIMON ——————————

לא תחמד – *Do not crave:* This account of the Ten Commandments uses only the verb "crave," whereas a later telling uses the additional verb "desire" (Deuteronomy 5:18). This teaches that there are two distinct prohibitions: craving and desiring. One violates the command *Do not desire* by merely thinking: Oh, if I only I possessed…, whereas one violates *Do not crave* when he hatches a concrete plan to wrest the object from its owner. Now, how is it possible for one individual to unfairly obtain all these things at once? If a man desires a married woman and lies with her, he could father a son with the neighbor's wife. Thinking thē son is his, the husband bequeaths all of his possessions to the boy, giving him his house, his field, his male and female servants, his ox, his donkey, and everything else he owns. Lest one think that he is only liable for violating the commandments in these verses once he transgresses all of them, the text states repetitively: *Do not murder. Do not commit adultery. Do not steal. Do not bear false witness. Do not crave* [indicating that each prohibition stands on its own.] Why then does the later version of the Ten Commandments state: *Do not murder. And do not commit adultery. And do not steal. And do not bear false witness. And do not crave. And do not desire* [Deuteronomy 5:17–18, repeating the word "and" several times]? The language of those verses teaches that performance of one sin invariably leads to the violation of the other crimes.

14 bear false witness against your neighbor. **Do not**
crave your neighbor's house. **Do not**
crave your neighbor's wife, his male or female servant, his ox,
his donkey, or anything else that is your neighbor's."

15 Every one of the people witnessed the thunder and light- sʜᴇvɪ'ɪ
ning and the sound of the ram's horn and the smoke-covered

———————————— TALMUD BAVLI ————————————

לֹא תַחְמֹד – *Do not crave:* The prohibition *Do not crave* is popularly understood to refer only to obtaining something without paying for it.

[In fact, it prohibits even conniving to take something and then pay restitution.] (Bava Metzia 5b)

VERSE 15

———————————— MEKHILTA DERABBI SHIMON ————————————

וְכָל־הָעָם רֹאִים אֶת־הַקּוֹלֹת – *Every one of the people witnessed the thunder:* People are usually unable to see sound, but during the experience of revelation, things were different. Just as the Israelites were able to see the lighting, they could visually perceive the thunder as well. **וַיַּרְא הָעָם** – *They saw:* What exactly did Israel see? They witnessed the tremendous

glory of God. Rabbi Eliezer taught: We see here that at that time an Israelite maidservant saw wonders that the greatest prophets of Israel were never privileged to see. **וַיָּנֻעוּ** – *And they shook:* The verb *vayanu'u* suggests that the people lost their minds somewhat, as the verse states: *The earth shall reel to and fro [noa tanua] like a drunkard* (Isaiah 24:20).

———————————— TANHUMA ————————————

וְכָל־הָעָם רֹאִים אֶת־הַקּוֹלֹת – *Every one of the people witnessed the thunder:* [Alternatively, "witnessed the voices."] Rabbi Yosei bar Hanina taught: All of the manna that descended to earth arrived in a uniform state, and yet, when it was eaten, it provided a different taste to each person based on his preferences. Similarly, when the voice of God emerged from the heavens, it too sounded

differently to each pair of ears. This was so because people possess different capabilities, and while the amplitude of a sound might be tolerable to one individual, it becomes harmful to another. Thus the verse states: *Every one of the people witnessed the voices* – note that it does not use the singular "voice," but "voices." (Shemot 25)

———————————— SHEMOT RABBA ————————————

וְכָל־הָעָם רֹאִים אֶת־הַקּוֹלֹת – *Every one of the people witnessed the thunder:* [Alternatively, "witnessed the voices."] Rabbi Yohanan taught: When God's voice emanated from Him, it divided into seventy distinct sounds, each in one of the world's seventy languages. [Hence the plural "voices."] This meant that

all the nations of the world were able to hear and understand the divine revelation. Now, when every nation heard the voice of God, their souls departed. Israel, however, was able to hear God's communication and remain unscathed. (Shemot 5:9)

טז וְאֶת־הָהָר עָשֵׁן וַיַּרְא הָעָם וַיָּנֻעוּ וַיַּעַמְדוּ מֵרָחֹק: וַיֹּאמְרוּ
אֶל־מֹשֶׁה דַּבֵּר־אַתָּה עִמָּנוּ וְנִשְׁמָעָה וְאַל־יְדַבֵּר עִמָּנוּ
יז אֱלֹהִים פֶּן־נָמוּת: וַיֹּאמֶר מֹשֶׁה אֶל־הָעָם אַל־תִּירָאוּ כִּי
לְבַעֲבוּר נַסּוֹת אֶתְכֶם בָּא הָאֱלֹהִים וּבַעֲבוּר תִּהְיֶה יִרְאָתוֹ
יח עַל־פְּנֵיכֶם לְבִלְתִּי תֶחֱטָאוּ: וַיַּעֲמֹד הָעָם מֵרָחֹק וּמֹשֶׁה נִגַּשׁ
יט אֶל־הָעֲרָפֶל אֲשֶׁר־שָׁם הָאֱלֹהִים: וַיֹּאמֶר יהוה   מפטיר
אֶל־מֹשֶׁה כֹּה תֹאמַר אֶל־בְּנֵי יִשְׂרָאֵל אַתֶּם רְאִיתֶם כִּי מִן־

VERSE 16

MEKHILTA DERABBI SHIMON

דַּבֵּר־אַתָּה עִמָּנוּ וְנִשְׁמָעָה – *Speak to us yourself and we will listen:* It was because of this request that God granted Israel the institution of the prophets, as the verse states: *The LORD your God* will raise up to you a prophet from the midst of you, of your brethren, like me; to him you shall hearken (Deuteronomy 18:15).

MIDRASH AGGADA

וְאַל־יְדַבֵּר עִמָּנוּ אֱלֹהִים – *But let not God say any more to us:* This verse proves that God spoke the entire text of the Ten Commandments in a single utterance. Such a feat is impossible for human beings, nor are people normally able to understand such a communication.

VERSE 17

MEKHILTA DERABBI SHIMON

לְבַעֲבוּר נַסּוֹת אֶתְכֶם – *To lift you up:* [Alternatively, "to test you" or "to make you experienced."] Said Moshe to the Israelites: Whenever you have sinned in the past, your behavior was considered inadvertent [since you did not yet know the commandments]. From now on, however, your sins will be deemed willful. In the past, you were unaware of the reward that awaits the righteous and the punishments facing the wicked. But now you know what the future holds for those who obey God's will and for those who flaunt it.

TALMUD BAVLI

וּבַעֲבוּר תִּהְיֶה יִרְאָתוֹ עַל־פְּנֵיכֶם – *So that awe of Him will be with you always:* Here Moshe expressed his hope that the people would forever be ashamed to sin in God's presence. We learn from here that shame leads to fear of sin, and hence it is a good thing for a person to be shamefaced. Indeed, some claim that no person who is easily humbled will be quick to sin, whereas one who is impudent certainly cannot have descended from those who stood at Sinai. (Nedarim 20a)

VERSE 18

MEKHILTA DERABBI SHIMON

וּמֹשֶׁה נִגַּשׁ אֶל־הָעֲרָפֶל – *While Moshe approached the thick darkness:* At first it is unclear which level of darkness Moshe entered – the inner or outer ring of the cloud. However, once

mountain; they saw and they shook – and they stood at a dis-
16 tance, and said to Moshe, "Speak to us yourself and we will lis-
17 ten, but let not God say any more to us, or we will die." "Do not
be afraid," said Moshe to the people, "God has come to lift you
up, so that the awe of Him will be with you always, keeping you
18 from sin." But the people remained at a distance while Moshe
19 approached the thick darkness where God was.   Then   MAFTIR
the LORD said to Moshe, "This is what you shall tell the Israelites: You yourselves have seen that I, from the heavens, have

──────────── MEKHILTA DERABBI SHIMON *(cont.)* ────────────

we read that he approached *where God was,* it
becomes clear that Moshe reached its inner-
most point. We can visualize this by picturing
two walls of darkness, with Moshe walking
between them until he reached the inner intensity. We find a similar description following

construction of Shlomo's Temple, when the
verse states: *Then spoke Shlomo, "The LORD
said that He would dwell in the thick darkness"*
(I Kings 8:12). How fortunate was Moshe [that
he was allowed that proximity to the Divine
Presence]!

──────────── LEKAḤ TOV ────────────

וַיַּעֲמֹד הָעָם מֵרָחֹק – *But the people remained
at a distance:* The people stood at a distance
of twelve miles, which was the length of
the entire Israelite camp. (Exodus 20:18)
וּמֹשֶׁה נִגַּשׁ אֶל־הָעֲרָפֶל – *While Moshe approached the thick darkness:* Why did Moshe
deserve such an honor as to be invited into
presence of God? It was a reward for his great
humility, as the verse states: *Now the man
Moshe was very modest* (Numbers 12:3). We

learn from here that any humble person can
expect to encounter the Divine Presence. For
so the prophet states: *The spirit of the LORD God
is upon me; because the LORD has anointed me to
announce good tidings to the meek; He has sent
me to bind up the broken hearted* (Isaiah 61:1).
(Exodus 20:18) **וּמֹשֶׁה נִגַּשׁ אֶל־הָעֲרָפֶל** – *While
Moshe approached the thick darkness:* At this
point, Moshe approached God by himself.
(Exodus 24:2)

VERSE 19

──────────── LEKAḤ TOV ────────────

אַתֶּם רְאִיתֶם – *You yourselves have seen:* A report
that one hears secondhand cannot compare
to what a person witnesses with his own eyes.
Whenever a person hears an event described
by others, he might believe the story and he
might not. But here, Moshe tells the people,
*You yourselves have seen that [God has] spoken
to you.* Furthermore, the language of the verse
emphasizes that while *you yourselves have seen*
revelation, the nations of the world were not
so privileged. **מִן־הַשָּׁמַיִם דִּבַּרְתִּי עִמָּכֶם** – *I, from
the heavens, have spoken to you:* A previous verse

reads: *And the LORD descended on Mount Sinai*
(19:20), while our verse states that God spoke
from the heavens. Rabbi Yishmael taught: Let a
third text come and reconcile the conflicting descriptions, for a later verse states: *Out of heaven
He made you hear His voice, that He might instruct
you: and upon earth He showed you His great fire*
(Deuteronomy 4:36). Rabbi Akiva described the
situation differently: The Holy One, blessed be
He, bent the upper heavens down to the summit of Mount Sinai and addressed Israel from
the skies.

ב הַשָּׁמַיִם דִּבַּרְתִּי עִמָּכֶם: לֹא תַעֲשׂוּן אִתִּי אֱלֹהֵי כֶסֶף וֵאלֹהֵי
כא זָהָב לֹא תַעֲשׂוּ לָכֶם: מִזְבַּח אֲדָמָה תַּעֲשֶׂה־לִּי וְזָבַחְתָּ עָלָיו
אֶת־עֹלֹתֶיךָ וְאֶת־שְׁלָמֶיךָ אֶת־צֹאנְךָ וְאֶת־בְּקָרֶךָ בְּכָל־

VERSE 20

———————————————— **TALMUD BAVLI** ————————————————

לֹא תַעֲשׂוּן אִתִּי – *Have no others alongside Me:* When the Torah pronounces the prohibition *Have no others alongside Me*, it forbids fashioning images of God's attendants who serve Him on high. Abbaye taught: This only refers to the beings with four faces [described in Ezekiel 1]. – But this would mean that it is permissible to fashion a human likeness with just one face. Why then has it been taught: One may reproduce an image of any kind of face save that of a person? Rav Huna son of Rav Idi taught: I heard the following teaching from Abbaye himself: Although the verse states: *Have no others alongside Me [itti]*, it should be understood as if it were "Do not make Me" [*oti*, i.e., the image of a human being, since humanity was created in the image of God]. – Still, is it permitted to create other images of God's [non-humanoid] attendants? Was it not taught: The prohibition *Have no others alongside Me* forbids fashioning images of God's ministering angels who serve Him on high such as *ofanim, serafim,* and the holy *ḥayyot*? Abbaye taught: This only refers to those beings who serve Him in the upper sphere. – But this would mean that it

is permissible to fashion a likeness of those beings who serve Him in the lower sphere [such as the sun and the moon]. Why then has it been taught: The verse that states: *Do not make for yourself any carved image or likeness of any creature in the heavens* (20:4) includes the sun, the moon, the stars and the constellations? – What the verse forbids is the creation of such images for the purpose of worshipping them. – But in that case, it should be prohibited to make an image even of smallest worm! – Indeed, that is so. As it has been taught: The verse that states: *Or the earth* (20:4) forbids fashioning a likeness of mountains, hills, seas, rivers, streams, and valleys, whereas the following word "beneath" extends the prohibition to the smallest worm. (Rosh HaShana 24b) **אֱלֹהֵי כֶסֶף** – *Silver gods:* The verse states: *Make yourselves no silver gods, no golden gods.* Does that mean that one may carve idols out of wood? Rav Ashi taught: No it does not. What the verse prohibits is appointing judges who have paid for their position with silver or gold. [The term *elohim* is also used to signify judges; see for example 21:6.] (Sanhedrin 7b)

———————————————— **LEKAH TOV** ————————————————

לֹא תַעֲשׂוּ לָכֶם – *Make yourselves no:* Israel might have reasoned that since they have been granted permission to fashion images in the Temple [the cherubim, which adorned the cover of the Ark of the Covenant, were images of gold], they may place such objects inside their synagogues and study halls.

Therefore, the text states: *Make yourselves no silver gods, no golden gods.* Furthermore, such representations may not even be constructed for decorative purposes, as communities do in other lands. Our Sages have employed this verse for homiletical purposes: When the text refers to "gods of silver" and "gods of gold," it

20 spoken to you. Have no others alongside Me; make yourselves
21 no silver gods, no golden gods. Make for Me an altar of earth
and on that sacrifice your burnt offerings and peace offerings,
your sheep and your cattle. Wherever I cause My name to be

———————————— LEKAH TOV *(cont.)* ————————————

alludes to judges [sometimes called *elohim*; see e.g., 21:6]. When a judge accepts silver in order to rule, he is called a god of silver, and when a judge accepts gold in order to rule, he

is called a god of gold. Thus our Sages rule: If a judge accepts money for adjudicating, all his rulings are null and void.

VERSE 21

———————————— MEKHILTA DERABBI SHIMON ————————————

מִזְבַּח אֲדָמָה תַּעֲשֶׂה־לִּי – *Make for Me an altar of earth:* Does this verse really mean that the altar must be made out of earth? No, for a subsequent verse states: *You shall build the altar of the* Lord *your God of whole stones* (Deuteronomy 27:6). Rather, Rabbi Yehuda taught: What our verse means is that when Israel

enters the land and constructs a permanent altar, it must be attached to the earth. Rabbi Meir taught: The floors beneath the Temple courtyards were hollow [that is, there were empty vaults beneath them], but earth was piled beneath the altar attaching it to the bedrock.

———————————— SIFREI BEMIDBAR ————————————

בְּכָל־הַמָּקוֹם אֲשֶׁר אַזְכִּיר אֶת־שְׁמִי – *Wherever I cause My name to be invoked:* Rabbi Yonatan taught: The verse containing God's promise to Israel, *Wherever I cause My name to be invoked, I will come to you and I will bless you,* should really have its clauses reversed. For really the sense of the text is that wherever God reveals

Himself to the nation becomes a site where the people should invoke His name. The Temple is just such a location. Indeed, the Israelites may only utter the divine name within the Temple precincts, pronouncing it is forbidden outside of its borders. (Naso 39)

———————————— TALMUD BAVLI ————————————

בְּכָל־הַמָּקוֹם אֲשֶׁר אַזְכִּיר אֶת־שְׁמִי – *Wherever I cause My name to be invoked:* Rav Ashi taught: If a person plans to perform a mitzva but is forcibly prevented from doing so, the Torah nevertheless gives him credit for having done

it. And how do we know that the Divine Presence descends even upon one who sits and studies Torah? For the verse states: *Wherever I cause My name to be invoked, I will come to you and I will bless you.* (Berakhot 6a)

———————————— AVOT DERABBI NATAN ————————————

בְּכָל־הַמָּקוֹם אֲשֶׁר אַזְכִּיר אֶת־שְׁמִי – *Wherever I cause My name to be invoked:* Hillel used to say: God promises Israel: If you come to My house, I shall come to your house. This refers to people who rise early in the morning and tarry late at night in the synagogues and the

study halls. For the Holy One, blessed be He, blesses them with a share in the World to Come, as the verse states: *Wherever I cause My name to be invoked, I will come to you and I will bless you.* (12)

כב הַמָּקוֹם אֲשֶׁר אַזְכִּיר אֶת־שְׁמִי אָבוֹא אֵלֶיךָ וּבֵרַכְתִּיךָ: וְאִם־
מִזְבַּח אֲבָנִים תַּעֲשֶׂה־לִּי לֹא־תִבְנֶה אֶתְהֶן גָּזִית כִּי חַרְבְּךָ
כג הֵנַפְתָּ עָלֶיהָ וַתְּחַלְלֶהָ: וְלֹא־תַעֲלֶה בְמַעֲלֹת עַל־מִזְבְּחִי
אֲשֶׁר לֹא־תִגָּלֶה עֶרְוָתְךָ עָלָיו:

YALKUT SHIMONI

מִזְבַּח אֲדָמָה תַּעֲשֶׂה־לִּי – *Make for Me an altar of earth:* Rav Ḥisda taught in the name of Rav: The altar that stood in Shilo [the location of the Tabernacle following Israel's entry into the land] was constructed out of stones. It was also taught in the name of Rabbi Yehuda HaNasi: Why does the term "stones" appear three times [in Exodus 20:22, Deuteronomy 27:5, and 27:6]? One alludes to the Tabernacle in Shilo [which stood for 369 years], one to the Tabernacle in Nov [which stood for thirteen years after the destruction of Shilo], while a third reference alludes to the altar in the eternal Temple.

VERSE 22

MEKHILTA DERABBI SHIMON

לֹא־תִבְנֶה אֶתְהֶן גָּזִית – *Do not build it of hewn stone:* Rabbi Yoḥanan ben Zakkai taught: Why does the Torah specifically rule out the use of iron among all metals for construction of the altar [see Deuteronomy 27:5]? Because iron is the metal of swords, and weapons are tools of punishment. The altar is a vehicle for atonement, and substance whose purpose is to inflict suffering should not be used to fashion the source of forgiveness. This requirement provides comfort for those who serve God. Consider how inanimate stones, which cannot see, or hear, or speak, but are nevertheless used to reconcile Israel with their Father in heaven. The Holy One, blessed be He, commanded that a sword not be wielded against them. How much more so should we expect that Torah scholars, who themselves provide atonement for the entire world through their study, will be protected from any sort of harm.

VERSE 23

MEKHILTA DERABBI SHIMON

לֹא־תִגָּלֶה עֶרְוָתְךָ עָלָיו – *Your nakedness must not be exposed on it:* Considering that a later verse commands [regarding the priests]: *Make them linen trousers to cover their nakedness,*

22 invoked, I will come to you and I will bless you. If you make Me
an altar of stones, do not build it of hewn stone, for in wielding
23 a sword upon it, you profane it. Do not ascend to My altar with
steps, for your nakedness must not be exposed on it.

———————————— MEKHILTA DERABBI SHIMON *(cont.)* ————————————

reaching from waist to thigh (28:42), why is this
warning necessary? What our verse teaches
is that when the priest ascends the altar, he
should not walk up the ramp with long strides;
rather, he should advance heel to toe [to avoid
exposing himself]. Now, the verse emphasizes
the appropriate gait only for the altar; how
do we also know that movement around the
courtyards should be similarly measured? For
the verse states: *Do not ascend to My altar with
steps, for your nakedness must not be exposed
on it [alav]*, and the [seemingly extraneous]

word *alav* connotes nearby areas. Support for
this interpretation comes from the verse *And
by him [ve'alav] shall be the tribe of Menashe*
[Numbers 2:20; in this context, the word *alav*
clearly cannot mean "on"]. Does the verse pro-
hibit the construction of steps throughout the
sanctuary and the courtyards? No, for the text
emphasizes: *Do not ascend to My altar with
steps,* meaning that it is forbidden only to ascend to the altar via steps; use of steps to access any other part of the Temple is permitted.

———————————— MIDRASH AGGADAH ————————————

וְלֹא־תַעֲלֶה בְמַעֲלֹת עַל־מִזְבְּחִי – *Do not ascend
to My altar with steps:* Do not read the word as
maalot ["steps"] but as *me'ilot* ["trespasses"],
meaning that a priest may not raise to the
altar any sacrifice upon which a trespass has
been committed [for example, an animal
that has been used for secular purposes].
לֹא־תִגָּלֶה עֶרְוָתְךָ עָלָיו – *Your nakedness must*

not be exposed on it: Do not bring such a dis-
qualified animal to my altar for sacrifice, since
I will not accept it. And when I reject the offering, your nakedness [i.e., shame] will be
exposed. For everybody standing there will
see that the smoke on the altar does not rise
straight up [as it did whenever a sacrifice was
accepted].

10TH CENTURY

11TH CENTURY

12TH CENTURY

RASHI, 1040 – 1105, FRANCE

RASHBAM, 1080 – 1160, FRANCE

RABBI AVRAHAM IBN EZRA,
1089, SPAIN – 1164, ENGLAND

RABBI YOSEF BEKHOR SHOR,
12TH CENTURY, FRANCE

13TH CENTURY

RABBI AVRAHAM BEN HARAMBAM,
1186 – 1237, EGYPT

RAMBAN, 1194, SPAIN – 1270, ISRAEL

RABBI ḤIZKIYA BEN MANOAḤ – *ḤIZKUNI*,
13TH CENTURY, FRANCE

14TH CENTURY

RABBEINU BAḤYA BEN ASHER,
1255 – 1340, SPAIN

RALBAG, 1288 – 1344, PROVENCE

15TH CENTURY

RABBI YITZḤAK ARAMA – *AKEDAT YITZḤAK*,
1420 – 1494, SPAIN

RABBI YITZḤAK ABARBANEL,
1437, PORTUGAL – 1508, ITALY

16TH CENTURY

RABBI OVADYA SFORNO, 1475 – 1550, ITALY

MAHARAL – *GUR ARYEH*,
1512 POLAND – 1609, BOHEMIA

17TH CENTURY

RABBI SHLOMO EFRAYIM LUNTSCHITZ –
KELI YAKAR, 1550, POLAND – 1619, BOHEMIA

פרשת יתרו
PARASHAT YITRO

THE **CLASSIC**
COMMENTATORS

יח א וַיִּשְׁמַ֞ע יִתְר֨וֹ כֹהֵ֤ן מִדְיָן֙ חֹתֵ֣ן מֹשֶׁ֔ה אֵת֩ כָּל־אֲשֶׁ֨ר עָשָׂ֤ה יד
אֱלֹהִים֙ לְמֹשֶׁ֔ה וּלְיִשְׂרָאֵ֖ל עַמּ֑וֹ כִּֽי־הוֹצִ֧יא יְהֹוָ֛ה אֶת־יִשְׂרָאֵ֖ל
ב מִמִּצְרָֽיִם: וַיִּקַּ֗ח יִתְרוֹ֙ חֹתֵ֣ן מֹשֶׁ֔ה אֶת־צִפֹּרָ֖ה אֵ֣שֶׁת מֹשֶׁ֑ה

CHAPTER 18, VERSE 1

RASHI

וַיִּשְׁמַע יִתְרוֹ – *Yitro heard:* What exactly did Yitro hear? He heard how God had split the Sea of Reeds and how Israel had defeated Amalek. **יִתְרוֹ** – *Yitro:* The man Yitro had seven names: Reuel, Yeter, Yitro, Hovav, Hever, Keini, and Putiel. He was called Yeter because he was responsible for adding [*yitter*] a passage to the Torah, namely, *You, as well, must seek out among the people, capable men etc.* (18:21). A letter [*vav*] was added to the name Yeter to produce the name Yitro after he converted to Judaism and started to observe the commandments. He was called Hovav because he loved [*hibbev*] the Torah. We know that Hovav and Yitro were one and the same, as attested by the verse *The children of Hovav the father-in-law of Moshe* (Judges 4:11). Some authorities, however, claim that Reuel was Yitro's father [see Numbers 10:29]. According to that approach, we must explain the verse *When they*

returned to Reuel their father [2:18, apparently indicating that Reuel was Moshe's wife's father] by positing that occasionally children refer to their grandfather as "father." Such is the understanding of the Sifrei (Behaalotekha 78). **חֹתֵן מֹשֶׁה** – *Moshe's father-in-law:* At this point, Yitro could boast of his connection to Moshe, saying: "I am the king's father-in-law." This contrasted with the past, when Moshe's honor came through his association with his wife's father, as the verse states: *Moshe left and returned to Yeter his father-in-law.* (4:18). **לְמֹשֶׁה וּלְיִשְׂרָאֵל** – *For Moshe and for Israel:* Moshe was equal in weight to all the rest of the nation. **אֵת כָּל־אֲשֶׁר עָשָׂה** – *All that God had done:* Yitro was impressed that God had provided manna for the people, brought water out of the rock, and defeated Amalek. **כִּֽי־הוֹצִיא יְהֹוָה** – *When the Lord brought:* This was the greatest achievement of all.

RASHBAM

וַיִּשְׁמַע יִתְרוֹ – *Yitro heard:* Yitro was astonished that Pharaoh had not managed to kill Moshe, and that God had raised the latter to such an exalted status in the eyes of the king of

Egypt and his officials. Furthermore, Yitro was pleased to learn of all the miracles that God had performed on Israel's behalf.

IBN EZRA

וַיִּשְׁמַע יִתְרוֹ – *Yitro heard:* Rav Se'adya Gaon believes that Yitro came to meet Israel before the giving of the Torah. But I maintain that Yitro only joined the nation in its second year, following the construction of the Tabernacle. For the text states: *Then Yitro brought a burnt offering and sacrifices to God* (18:12), without reporting that the man first built an altar

[suggesting that the Tabernacle's altar was at that point already in use]. Furthermore, Moshe tells Yitro: *When they have a dispute, they come to me and I judge between one neighbor and another, and I make God's laws and teachings known* (18:16), a statement which makes sense only after the giving of the Torah. Finally, the language of the text supports my contention,

18 1 Moshe's father-in-law Yitro, priest of Midyan, heard about all that God had done for Moshe and for His people Israel
2 when the LORD brought Israel out of Egypt. Yitro had received

——————————— IBN EZRA *(cont.)* ———————————

for it states: *And now Moshe's father-in-law Yitro came to Moshe in the desert, bringing his sons and his wife, to where he was encamped by the mountain of God* [18:5; since the Torah reports the people's arrival at Sinai only later, in 19:1, this proves that this passage has been placed out of chronological order].

——————————— RAMBAN ———————————

וַיִּשְׁמַע יִתְרוֹ – *Yitro heard:* I find the approach that Yitro traveled to meet Israel only after the revelation at Sinai [and this passage is out of chronological order] somewhat difficult. For the text states: *Yitro…heard about all that God had done for Moshe and for His people Israel when the LORD brought Israel out of Egypt.* If the man only arrived later, why would he not have heard also about the great wonders God performed at Sinai, when He presented Israel with the Torah? **כָּל־אֲשֶׁר עָשָׂה אֱלֹהִים** – *All that God had done:* Note that the verse mentions two names of God, starting with *Elohim* [the non-specific "God"], an appellation Yitro was familiar with from before. It then states: *The LORD [Adonai] brought Israel out of Egypt,* using God's great name, since this name had now been publicized by Moshe in connection with the signs he had performed.

VERSE 2

——————————— RASHI ———————————

אַחַר שִׁלּוּחֶיהָ – *After he had sent her home:* When the Holy One, blessed be He, said to Moshe in Midyan: *Go, return to Egypt* (4:19), the prophet obeyed, as the verse states: *Moshe took his wife and sons and put them on a donkey* (4:20). When Aharon came to meet his brother, as the verse states: *He went and met him at God's mountain, and kissed him* (4:27), he asked of him: "Who are these people with you?" Said Moshe: "This is my wife whom I married in Midyan, and these are our sons." But this distressed Aharon: "Where exactly are you taking them?" Answered Moshe: "I'm bringing them to Egypt with me." Aharon protested: "Here we are anxious about the Hebrews already trapped in Egypt; why would you bring more souls into bondage?" So Moshe turned his wife around and said: "Go back home to your father." So Tzipora took her two sons and left.

——————————— RAMBAN ———————————

אַחַר שִׁלּוּחֶיהָ – *After he had sent her home:* Even though Moshe had earlier sent her away, Yitro now returned his daughter to Moshe after learning all that God had done for him. For it was now appropriate for Tzipora to follow the leader of Israel wherever he may go.

——————————— RALBAG ———————————

אַחַר שִׁלּוּחֶיהָ – *After he had sent her home:* This clause refers to how at the lodging place [where the couple were last seen together, in 4:24], Moshe decided to send Tzipora home.

גּ אַחַר שִׁלּוּחֶיהָ: וְאֵת שְׁנֵי בָנֶיהָ אֲשֶׁר שֵׁם הָאֶחָד גֵּרְשֹׁם
ד כִּי אָמַר גֵּר הָיִיתִי בְּאֶרֶץ נָכְרִיָּה: וְשֵׁם הָאֶחָד אֱלִיעֶזֶר כִּי־
ה אֱלֹהֵי אָבִי בְּעֶזְרִי וַיַּצִּלֵנִי מֵחֶרֶב פַּרְעֹה: וַיָּבֹא יִתְרוֹ חֹתֵן

———————————— RALBAG *(cont.)* ————————————

For soon after the family reached the inn, Tzipora was required to circumcise her son, an
act which delayed the company's descent to
Egypt. Moshe determined that he could not

tarry longer while the baby recovered from
the operation, and he instructed his wife to
turn back and take her sons with her.

———————————— SFORNO ————————————

אַחַר שִׁלּוּחֶיהָ – *After he had sent her home:*
[Alternatively, "after he had sent her."] Yitro
had sent Tzipora to determine the location of
Israel's encampment. Moshe notified her that
the nation would not set up their camp until
they reached the mountain of God, where

they would serve Him. This had always been
the plan, as attested by God's prediction at
the burning bush, *You shall come to serve God
upon this mountain* (3:12). Hence Yitro waited
to join Moshe until he and the nation had
reached Mount Sinai.

———————————— KELI YAKAR ————————————

אֶת־צִפֹּרָה אֵשֶׁת מֹשֶׁה – *Moshe's wife Tzipora:*
There is a reason why the text bothers to relate the names of Moshe's wife and sons. For
Yitro sent a message to the leader, saying:
Come out to greet your wife Tzipora, for *as a
bird [tzippor] that wanders from her nest, so is
a man who wanders from his place* (Proverbs
27:8). Yitro thereby hinted to his son-in-law
the hardship his daughter had endured as
long as she had been away from her house.
And if Moshe was not prepared to venture
away from the camp for his wife's sake – for a
man is occasionally insensitive to the feelings
of his wife – perhaps he could be persuaded
to come out to greet the family for the sake
of Gershom. The latter was so named because
Moshe had *been a stranger [ger] in a foreign*

land (18:3). The name thus alluded to the pain
children feel when they do not sit at their
father's table and are essentially strangers to
him. After all, Moshe should know what it
feels like to be an outsider, for he too was
a "stranger in a foreign land." Finally, if even
this tactic did not convince Moshe to set
out to collect his family, Yitro appealed to
Moshe's sense of duty by mentioning Eliezer.
The latter was so called because Moshe had
remembered that *my father's God [Elohei] has
helped me [be'ezri], saving me from Pharaoh's
sword* (18:4). Yitro thereby reminded Moshe
that his son's name contained the name of
his Master [God], and that going out to greet
his son would be akin to receiving the Divine
Presence.

VERSE 3

———————————— RAMBAN ————————————

אֲשֶׁר שֵׁם הָאֶחָד גֵּרְשֹׁם – *One was named Gershom:* The naming of Moshe's sons is mentioned here, even though the Torah is not now

describing their births. This is because there
had been no opportunity until this point to
describe Eliezer's birth, as I have explained in

3 Moshe's wife Tzipora after he had sent her home, together
with her two sons. One was named Gershom, for Moshe had
4 said, "I have been a stranger in a foreign land," and the other,
Eliezer, for he had said, "My father's God has helped me, sav-
5 ing me from Pharaoh's sword." And now Moshe's father-in-law

CLASSIC COMMENTATORS

RAMBAN *(cont.)*

my commentary to Parashat Shemot (4:20). Here, however, the text takes the opportunity to recall the graciousness that God extended to Moshe, who had been a "stranger in a foreign land." [Regarding Eliezer,] Moshe wished to commemorate how God had saved him from Pharaoh's sword by aiding his escape [in chapter 2]. Furthermore [the name also conveys] Moshe's gratitude that God had made him ruler over Israel and drowned Pharaoh and his people in the sea.

VERSE 4

RASHI

וַיַּצִּלֵנִי מֵחֶרֶב פַּרְעֹה – *Saving me from Pharaoh's sword:* When Datan and Aviram revealed Moshe's murder of the Egyptian taskmaster to Pharaoh, the king sought to kill Moshe [as reported in 2:15. According to the Midrash, the two quarreling Hebrews in 2:13–14 were Datan and Aviram, who are only introduced by name in Numbers 16]. However, when the executioner attempted to decapitate Moshe, the prophet's neck turned into marble and the sword was rendered useless.

RABBEINU BAḤYA

וְשֵׁם הָאֶחָד – *And the other:* [Literally, "and the name of one."] After stating that the name of one of Moshe's sons was Gershom, the text should have said: "The name of the second one was Eliezer." The straightforward explanation for the verse's terminology is that one son was a favorite of his mother, and the other was preferred by his father. Gershom was his mother's firstborn son and hence she loved him most. And it was his life that she had saved in the verse *But Tzipora took a flint knife and cut off her son's foreskin* (4:25). Meanwhile, Moshe appreciated Eliezer, for his name recalled how God had saved him from Pharaoh's executioner.

SFORNO

וַיַּצִּלֵנִי מֵחֶרֶב פַּרְעֹה – *Saving me from Pharaoh's sword:* By the time Eliezer was born, the Egyptian king who had sought Moshe's life was dead, as the verse states: *Years passed, and the king of Egypt died* (2:23). It was only at that point that Moshe felt he had truly escaped Pharaoh's sword. For as long as the king was alive, Moshe believed that Pharaoh might still track him down wherever he might be.

VERSE 5

RASHI

אֶל־הַמִּדְבָּר – *In the desert:* Surely we already know that Moshe and the nation were encamped in the desert. Nevertheless, the text mentions this detail to praise Yitro for

מֹשֶׁה וּבָנָיו וְאִשְׁתּוֹ אֶל־מֹשֶׁה אֶל־הַמִּדְבָּר אֲשֶׁר־הוּא חֹנֶה
שָׁם הַר הָאֱלֹהִים: וַיֹּאמֶר אֶל־מֹשֶׁה אֲנִי חֹתֶנְךָ יִתְרוֹ בָּא
אֵלֶיךָ וְאִשְׁתְּךָ וּשְׁנֵי בָנֶיהָ עִמָּהּ: וַיֵּצֵא מֹשֶׁה לִקְרַאת חֹתְנוֹ
וַיִּשְׁתַּחוּ וַיִּשַּׁק־לוֹ וַיִּשְׁאֲלוּ אִישׁ־לְרֵעֵהוּ לְשָׁלוֹם וַיָּבֹאוּ
הָאֹהֱלָה: וַיְסַפֵּר מֹשֶׁה לְחֹתְנוֹ אֵת כָּל־אֲשֶׁר עָשָׂה יהוה

RASHI *(cont.)*

meeting them there. For Yitro was stirred to leave his comfortable home in Midyan for the desolate wilderness, just to hear the message of the Torah.

VERSE 6

RASHI

וַיֹּאמֶר אֶל־מֹשֶׁה – *Sent word to Moshe:* [Literally, "said to Moshe," although Yitro had not yet arrived. Rashi explains that this was] through an emissary. אֲנִי חֹתֶנְךָ יִתְרוֹ – *I – Your father-in-law Yitro:* If you will not come out to honor me, at least set out to greet "your wife." And if she is not worthy of your time, at least come out for the sake of "both of your sons."

BEKHOR SHOR

וַיֹּאמֶר אֶל־מֹשֶׁה – *Sent word to Moshe:* [Alternatively, "had sent."] Yitro had sent this message to Moshe in the past, when the latter had traveled to Egypt and dispatched his wife back to Midyan. For Moshe had communicated to his father-in-law: "I cannot myself return to Midyan, for the Holy One, blessed be He, has employed me to lead Israel out of Egypt." Yitro responded: "Do not concern yourself over Tzipora, for now that you have sent her back, I will eventually see to her and her children's return to you. When you free Israel, I, your father-in-law, will come to you when I learn of your location. And I will arrive *together with your wife and both of your sons.* And now that Moshe heard that Yitro was fulfilling his vow, he set out to greet his father-in-law.

RABBEINU BAHYA

וְאִשְׁתְּךָ וּשְׁנֵי בָנֶיהָ עִמָּהּ – *Together with your wife and both of your sons:* [Literally, "both of her sons."] Would it not have been proper for Yitro to say: "both of your sons?" After all the man did refer to himself as "your father-in-law" and to Tzipora as "your wife." Rather, it is customary for Scripture to associate sons with their mother, as the verse states: *These are the sons of Leah, whom she bore to Yaakov* (Genesis 46:15), and daughters with their father, as that verse continues: *With his daughter Dina.*

GUR ARYEH

בָּא אֵלֶיךָ – *Coming to you:* Rashi argues that Yitro appealed to Moshe to greet his family; if Moshe was reluctant to honor him, he ought to respect his wife and sons. And yet, some writers argue that it would have been unseemly for Yitro, who was an important personage in his own right, to seek honor through Moshe's greeting. Therefore, Yitro's request should not be understood as a pursuit of glory, but as an effort to avoid disrespect.

Yitro came to Moshe in the desert, bringing his sons and his
6 wife, to where he was encamped by the mountain of God. Yitro
sent word to Moshe, "I am coming to you – your father-in-law
7 Yitro – together with your wife and both of your sons." Moshe
went out to greet his father-in-law and bowed down and kissed
him. Each asked after the other's welfare, and they went inside
8 the tent. And Moshe told his father-in-law all that the LORD

———————————— GUR ARYEH *(cont.)* ————————————

For every person, no matter how righteous
and modest, resents being disparaged. And
since it is customary to honor one's guests,
especially one's father-in-law, Yitro felt that
were Moshe not to set out to greet him, it

would be an unpleasant slight. Hence, Yitro's
message was only out of a desire to avoid being mistreated, rather than an attempt to seek
honor or privilege.

VERSE 7

———————————————— RASHI ————————————————

וַיֵּצֵא מֹשֶׁה – *Moshe went out:* Yitro was greatly
honored at that time, for Moshe, Aharon, Nadav, and Avihu all went out to receive him.
And everybody who saw the entourage
leaving the camp to greet the approaching
dignitary, naturally joined the procession as
well. **וַיִּשְׁתַּחוּ וַיִּשַּׁק־לוֹ** – *Bowed down and*

kissed him: At first glance, the verse does not
reveal who bowed to whom. But it provides
a clue when it states that *each [ish] asked after
the other's welfare,* for we know that Moshe
is later referred to as an *ish* [in Numbers 12:3;
ish means "man" and carries connotations of
importance].

———————————————— IBN EZRA ————————————————

וַיֵּצֵא מֹשֶׁה – *Moshe went out:* Moshe set out
to welcome his father-in-law, honoring Yitro's
high standing and wisdom. It was not his wife

and sons whom he left the camp to meet,
for it is not customary for a national leader to
leave home to greet his wife or children.

——————————— RABBI AVRAHAM BEN HARAMBAM ———————————

וַיִּשַּׁק־לוֹ – *And kissed him:* Moshe kissed Yitro
out of love, but bowed to him as a sign of
etiquette. We see here that it is permitted to
bow to other people in a demonstration of

respect, as long as no worship is intended.
For the purpose of this passage is to teach us
correct behavior.

———————————————— SFORNO ————————————————

וַיֵּצֵא מֹשֶׁה – *Moshe went out:* Despite Moshe's
own prominence, he personally went out to

greet this man, who had treated him so well
during his time of turmoil.

VERSE 8

———————————————— RASHI ————————————————

וַיְסַפֵּר מֹשֶׁה לְחֹתְנוֹ – *Moshe told his father-in-
law:* Moshe related the entire narrative of the
exodus to Yitro, in order to draw him toward

the Torah. **אֵת כָּל־הַתְּלָאָה** – *All the hardship:*
This refers specifically to the crisis at the Sea
of Reeds and the battle with Amalek.

CLASSIC COMMENTATORS

לְפַרְעֹה וּלְמִצְרַיִם עַל אוֹדֹת יִשְׂרָאֵל אֵת כָּל־הַתְּלָאָה אֲשֶׁר
מְצָאָתַם בַּדֶּרֶךְ וַיַּצִּלֵם יהוה: וַיִּחַדְּ יִתְרוֹ עַל כָּל־הַטּוֹבָה
אֲשֶׁר־עָשָׂה יהוה לְיִשְׂרָאֵל אֲשֶׁר הִצִּילוֹ מִיַּד מִצְרָיִם:
וַיֹּאמֶר יִתְרוֹ בָּרוּךְ יהוה אֲשֶׁר הִצִּיל אֶתְכֶם מִיַּד מִצְרַיִם
וּמִיַּד פַּרְעֹה אֲשֶׁר הִצִּיל אֶת־הָעָם מִתַּחַת יַד־מִצְרָיִם:

───────── RASHBAM ─────────

אֵת כָּל־הַתְּלָאָה – *All the hardship:* Moshe related to Yitro the story of Pharaoh's pursuit of Israel, and how God had provided the nation with drinking water, manna, and meat.

───────── SFORNO ─────────

וַיַּצִּלֵם יהוה – *And how the LORD had rescued them:* These events demonstrated the providence that God extended to Israel. He granted them this beneficence because the nation was unanimously determined and prepared to serve Him.

VERSE 9

───────── RASHI ─────────

וַיִּחַדְּ יִתְרוֹ – *Yitro delighted:* The straightforward meaning of the verb *vayiḥad* means that Yitro rejoiced. But the homiletic interpretation is that the man's flesh bristled [*naasa ḥiddudin*] as he mourned the Egyptian destruction. This illustrates the popular adage: Do not insult gentiles in the presence of a convert or even of his descendant to the tenth generation [see Sanhedrin 94a]. **עַל כָּל־הַטּוֹבָה** – *In all the good:* Yitro was pleased with the manna, the [miraculous] well, and the Torah the people had been taught. Above all, he was impressed with how God had liberated Israel from Egypt. For until now not a single slave had succeeded in escaping from the Egyptian prison, yet God had now opened the country's doors to 600,000 men.

───────── BEKHOR SHOR ─────────

וַיִּחַדְּ יִתְרוֹ – *Yitro delighted:* Yitro rejoiced over Israel's providential rescue [but not over the punishment exacted from the Egyptians], because he was unaware that their enslavement by Pharaoh had been wrong and immoral.

───────── RABBI AVRAHAM BEN HARAMBAM ─────────

וַיִּחַדְּ יִתְרוֹ – *Yitro delighted:* One might surmise that Yitro's happiness was largely on behalf of his son-in-law Moshe. Nevertheless, God, who knows the thoughts of human beings, is well aware that in truth Yitro rejoiced over the success of Israel. For they were an exalted nation, and Yitro was right to celebrate all the good fortune and achievements such a people would enjoy.

───────── AKEDAT YITZHAK ─────────

וַיִּחַדְּ יִתְרוֹ – *Yitro delighted:* It is a sign of stellar character when one exults in positive developments rather than in the downfall of the wicked. Thus the verse states: *Have I*

had done to Pharaoh and the Egyptians for Israel's sake, all the
hardship they had encountered along the way, and how the
9 LORD had rescued them. Yitro delighted in all the good that
the LORD had done for Israel, in His liberating them from the
10 Egyptians – and said, "Blessed be the LORD who has rescued
you from Egypt and Pharaoh and liberated the people from

─────────────── AKEDAT YITZHAK *(cont.)* ───────────────

*any pleasure at all that the wicked should die?
says the Lord God: and not that he should return
from his ways, and live?* (Ezekiel 18:23). What
this means is that God would much prefer
that the wicked repent and abandon their
evil ways, than that they should be expunged

from the world. Hence Yitro proclaimed only:
*Blessed be the Lord who has rescued you from
Egypt* [18:10; ignoring the Egyptians' regret-
table destruction]. This statement illustrates
the man's righteousness.

─────────────── SFORNO ───────────────

וַיִּחַדְּ יִתְרוֹ – *Yitro delighted:* Yitro was in error
not to celebrate the destruction of the Egyp-
tians, for that would have been the true way
to stand up for the Creator's honor. As the
verse states: *The righteous shall rejoice when
he sees the vengeance: he shall wash his feet in*

*the blood of the wicked. So that a man shall say,
"Truly there is a reward for the righteous; truly
there is a God who judges in the earth"* (Psalms
58:11). Still, Yitro rejoiced over Israel's salvation, showing compassion for the tears of the
oppressed.

VERSE 10

─────────────── RASHI ───────────────

אֲשֶׁר הִצִּיל אֶתְכֶם מִיַּד מִצְרַיִם – *Who has
rescued you from Egypt:* A harsh nation.
וּמִיַּד פַּרְעֹה – *And Pharaoh:* A harsh king.
מִתַּחַת יַד־מִצְרָיִם – *From the Egyptians' hands:*
The term "hand" should be understood as the

Targum translates it [*marvat,* meaning "dominion"], referring to the tyranny and domination of the Egyptians. The oppressors held
Israel in a tight fist by imposing slavery upon
them.

─────────────── RASHBAM ───────────────

אֲשֶׁר הִצִּיל אֶתְכֶם – *Who rescued you:* Yitro here
refers specifically to Moshe and Aharon, who
escaped the wrath of Pharaoh, and then to the

liberation of "the people" from the Egyptian
slavery.

─────────────── RALBAG ───────────────

אֲשֶׁר הִצִּיל אֶתְכֶם – *Who rescued you:* It is possible that initially [with the word "you" in the
first clause of the verse], Yitro was addressing the elders and the tribal chiefs, who were
then in Moshe's company. These leaders had
not themselves suffered the hardship of the
slavery, nor had they been compelled to toil

with brick and mortar. As I have explained
in my commentary to Parashat Shemot, the
Egyptians did not force the entire Israelite
people to slave away in the fields. When Yitro
celebrates how *the Lord has rescued you from
Egypt and Pharaoh,* he therefore refers instead
to the lashes and torture that the oppressors

יא עַתָּה יָדַ֫עְתִּי כִּי־גָד֥וֹל יהוה מִכָּל־הָאֱלֹהִ֑ים כִּ֣י בַדָּבָ֔ר אֲשֶׁ֥ר
יב זָד֖וּ עֲלֵיהֶֽם: וַיִּקַּ֞ח יִתְר֨וֹ חֹתֵ֤ן מֹשֶׁה֙ עֹלָ֣ה וּזְבָחִ֖ים לֵֽאלֹהִ֑ים
וַיָּבֹ֨א אַהֲרֹ֜ן וְכֹ֣ל ׀ זִקְנֵ֣י יִשְׂרָאֵ֗ל לֶֽאֱכָל־לֶ֛חֶם עִם־חֹתֵ֥ן מֹשֶׁ֖ה

———————————— RALBAG *(cont.)* ————————————

had inflicted upon them [rather than hard labor, which the rest of the people had been obligated to perform]. On the other hand, it is possible that some of the Israelite leaders and elders had been conscripted into Pharaoh's labor force, and that Yitro addresses

their specific salvation separately since, as the most respected element of the society, they deserved special mention. Subsequently, Yitro turned his attention to recognizing God's emancipation of "the people" at large.

VERSE 11

———————————— RASHI ————————————

עַתָּה יָדַ֫עְתִּי – *Now I know:* Although I recognized God in the past, now I am even more convinced of His greatness. **מִכָּל־הָאֱלֹהִ֑ים** – *Than all gods:* Yitro was familiar with all the world's religions, for he had dabbled in all varieties of idolatry. **כִּ֣י בַדָּבָ֔ר אֲשֶׁ֥ר זָד֖וּ עֲלֵיהֶֽם** – *For He brought upon them what they schemed against others:* [Literally, "for what they schemed against them."] This clause should be understood in light of the Targum [which translates freely: "for the Egyptians were punished with

the punishment they plotted for Israel"]. The Egyptians had planned to destroy Israel by drowning them in water, but they themselves were punished that way. **אֲשֶׁ֥ר זָד֖וּ** – *What they schemed:* The word *zadu* means "acted wickedly." Our Sages associate the verb with the verse *And Yaakov cooked pottage [nazid]* (Genesis 25:29), meaning that the Egyptians cooked up a scheme to murder the Israelites, but in the end they were boiled in their own pot.

———————————— RASHBAM ————————————

מִכָּל־הָאֱלֹהִ֑ים – *Than all gods:* All other deities lack the power to avenge wrongs perpetrated against their adherents.

———————————— RAMBAN ————————————

בַדָּבָ֔ר אֲשֶׁ֥ר זָד֖וּ עֲלֵיהֶֽם – *What they had schemed against others:* Since it was God who had decreed that Israel should be oppressed, as He predicted to Avraham: *Your seed shall be a stranger in a land that is not theirs, and shall serve them; and they shall afflict them four hundred years* (Genesis 15:13), it surely would have been reasonable for the Egyptians be absolved of punishment. But the Egyptians exceeded God's mission and acted maliciously,

plotting to utterly destroy Israel, as the verse states: *Come, let us deal wisely with them in case they increase* (Exodus 1:10). This attitude found expression in Pharaoh's command to the midwives to strangle the Hebrew boys at birth [in 1:16], and the order to the entire Egyptian nation: *Throw every boy that is born into the Nile* (1:22). Because of these actions against Israel, Egypt deserved to be utterly annihilated, a consequence that God also foretells when He

11 the Egyptians' hands. Now I know that the LORD is greater
than all gods – for He brought upon them what they schemed
12 against others." Then Yitro brought a burnt offering and sacrifices to God. And Aharon and all the elders of Israel came

———————————— **RAMBAN** *(cont.)* ————————————

states: *And also that nation, whom they shall
serve, will I judge* (Genesis 15:14). Now God examined the Egyptians' thoughts and exercised
vengeance for the evil plans they contrived to

exacerbate the Israelites' suffering. For God is
privy to the thoughts of human beings and
executes judgment on behalf of the down-
trodden with a wrathful vengeance.

———————————— **SFORNO** ————————————

מִכָּל־הָאֱלֹהִים – *Than all gods:* God's emancipation of Israel demonstrated His superiority
over all other gods, for Yitro could not imagine
that any nation's deity could possibly avenge

them measure for measure as God had done
for His people. Still, Yitro believed that perhaps
individual deities might be able to act in their
specific areas of influence.

VERSE 12

———————————— **RASHI** ————————————

וַיָּבֹא אַהֲרֹן – *And Aharon came:* Where did
Moshe disappear to? Had he not gone out to
greet Yitro and to lead the procession honoring him? Actually, instead of eating with the
rest of the group, Moshe stood and served

Yitro, Aharon, and the elders [in a gesture of
respect]. לִפְנֵי הָאֱלֹהִים – *Before God:* We learn
from this verse that when one participates in
a meal attended by Torah scholars, it is as if
he basks in the glory of the Divine Presence.

———————————— **IBN EZRA** ————————————

עִם־חֹתֵן מֹשֶׁה לִפְנֵי הָאֱלֹהִים – *With Moshe's
father-in-law before God:* The sense of the verse

is that from this point onward Yitro accepted
and revered the LORD as his God.

———————————— **RAMBAN** ————————————

עֹלָה וּזְבָחִים – *A burnt offering and sacrifices:*
This entire episode took place before Israel's
arrival at Mount Sinai. [Yitro, a gentile, was
permitted to offer sacrifices, since the Torah,
which regulates such matters, had not yet
been given.] Alternatively, Yitro's complete
sojourn with Israel may have been condensed
into the single narrative that we have before
us, even though the distinct events recorded

in this chapter took place over a lengthy period. If so, Yitro brought sacrifices to God only
after his conversion, involving circumcision,
immersion, and the sprinkling of sacrificial
blood according to the Torah's law. And the
phrase *And Aharon and all the elders of Israel
came to break bread* describes the celebration
of Yitro's entry into the covenant of blood with
God [i.e., his conversion].

———————————— **RALBAG** ————————————

לִפְנֵי הָאֱלֹהִים – *Before God:* This expression
is similar to when the text refers to Sinai
as the "mountain of God," (3:1) because the

Divine Presence descended upon it. Since
some divine manifestation was always present in Moshe's tent, our verse states that the

יֹּ לִפְנֵי הָאֱלֹהִים: וַיְהִי מִמָּחֳרָת וַיֵּשֶׁב מֹשֶׁה לִשְׁפֹּט אֶת־הָעָם שני

———————— RALBAG *(cont.)* ————————

company ate bread with Yitro "before God." Alternatively, the verse means to say that the meal was comparable to one "before God,"

in that their behavior resembled a religious service and the offering of sacrifices under Moshe's guidance.

———————— ABARBANEL ————————

עֹלָה וּזְבָחִים לֵאלֹהִים – *A burnt offering and sacrifices to God:* At this point, Yitro was still untutored in the correct usage of God's various names. Hence the verse states that the man

brought a burnt offering and sacrifices to God *[Elohim]*, an appellation that never appears in conjunction with any sacrifice.

———————— SFORNO ————————

עֹלָה וּזְבָחִים לֵאלֹהִים – *A burnt offering and sacrifices to God:* The purpose of these sacrifices was to signal Yitro's acceptance of God's authority. We find a similar expression of devotion in the case of [the Aramean general] Naaman, who proclaimed: *Your servant will henceforth offer neither burnt offering nor sacrifice to other gods, but to the LORD* (II Kings 5:17). **לֶאֱכָל־לֶחֶם עִם־חֹתֵן מֹשֶׁה** – *To break bread with Moshe's father-in-law:* Yitro wished to celebrate with his son-in-law on the occasion

of his entering into a relationship with God, a sentiment expressed in the verse *Let Israel rejoice in Him who made him* (Psalms 149:2). **לִפְנֵי הָאֱלֹהִים** – *Before God:* This clause means that the company ate their meal before the altar upon which the sacrifices had been offered. This might have been the altar that Moshe fashioned following the defeat of Amalek, or a different structure whose construction is not mentioned in the text.

VERSE 13

———————— RASHI ————————

וַיְהִי מִמָּחֳרָת – *The next day:* According to the Mekhilta, this was the day following Yom Kippur [and not the day after the celebration reported in the previous verse]. Thus "the next day" means: "the day after Moshe descended from Mount Sinai [with the second tablets, as reported in 34:28–29]." We are forced to posit that Moshe waited until the day after Yom Kippur to judge the nation, because he would not have done so before the Torah had been given to them. And immediately after revelation, Moshe ascended the mountain and remained in God's presence for forty days until the seventeenth of Tamuz. On that day, Moshe smashed the tablets, and early the next day

he went back up the mountain to pray on Israel's behalf. There he stayed for an additional eighty days, finally descending on Yom Kippur. **וַיֵּשֶׁב מֹשֶׁה... וַיַּעֲמֹד הָעָם** – *Moshe sat... the people stood:* What disturbed Yitro was that Moshe sat like a king on a throne while the people remained standing. This arrangement was disrespectful to the people of Israel, which is why Yitro rebuked his son-in-law, saying: *Why do you sit alone* (18:14), i.e., while everybody else stands? **מִן־הַבֹּקֶר עַד־הָעָרֶב** – *From morning to evening:* Is it really possible that Moshe judged people all day? Rather, what the verse implies is that when a judge rules truthfully and correctly for even a single hour, the Torah

13 to break bread with Moshe's father-in-law before God. The   SHENI
next day Moshe sat to serve the people as judge. From morning

———————————————————— RASHI *(cont.)* ————————————————————

credits him with having sat and studied Torah the entire day. It is as if such an individual has become a partner in creation with the Holy

One, blessed be He, as the verse states: *And there was evening and there was morning, one day* (Genesis 1:5).

———————————————————— RASHBAM ————————————————————

לִשְׁפֹּט אֶת־הָעָם – *To serve the people as judge:* There should be no difficulty in arguing this episode occurred before the giving of the Torah, for matters of civil law were known to the people somewhat earlier. As our Sages have taught, the people were taught the details of monetary issues at Mara, as the verse states: *It was there that the LORD gave His people decree and law* (15:25). Still, it seems that the current passage actually took place after the Torah was given. For here the verse states that Yitro came *to where [Moshe] was encamped by the mountain of God* (18:5), but only subsequently does the Torah report: *On the first day of the*

third month after the Israelites had left Egypt they came to the Sinai Desert. Setting out from Refidim they had arrived at the Sinai Desert, encamping in the wilderness, and there Israel camped, facing the mountain (19:1–2). This suggests that the episode at Refidim [recorded in chapter 17], and Israel's encampment at the mountain, took place before the events described here occurred. Nevertheless, the description of Yitro's reunion with Moshe is recorded here in order not to interrupt the narrative of the commandments [that begins in the next chapter].

———————————————————— IBN EZRA ————————————————————

וַיְהִי מִמָּחֳרָת – *The next day:* This refers to the day after Yitro's arrival.

———————————————————— RAMBAN ————————————————————

וַיְהִי מִמָּחֳרָת – *The next day:* According to the Mekhilta, Yitro proffered his advice on a day following Yom Kippur. Now the Sages could not have meant that the phrase "the next day" actually alludes to the day immediately after Yom Kippur, since that holy day is nowhere explicitly mentioned in the text. Rather, what

the midrash means is simply that this event occurred some time after Yom Kippur, since between the day that Israel arrived at Mount Sinai until after Yom Kippur of that first year, Moshe had not a single available day to sit in judgment of Israel.

———————————————————— ABARBANEL ————————————————————

וַיְהִי מִמָּחֳרָת – *The next day:* The Torah emphasizes that the dialogue between Moshe and Yitro took place on the day following the latter's arrival, to teach that Moshe hardly took off any time at all from ruling the nation to attend to his family. Certainly on the day when his father-in-law, wife, and sons joined

the Israelites in the wilderness, Moshe busied himself with greeting them and settling them in. However, by the next morning he had returned to sitting in judgment of the nation, as the verse states: *From morning to evening the people stood before him.* Hearing the Israelites' issues and conflicts kept Moshe

CLASSIC COMMENTATORS

יד וַיַּעֲמֹד הָעָם עַל־מֹשֶׁה מִן־הַבֹּקֶר עַד־הָעָרֶב: וַיַּרְא חֹתֵן
מֹשֶׁה אֵת כָּל־אֲשֶׁר־הוּא עֹשֶׂה לָעָם וַיֹּאמֶר מָה־הַדָּבָר
הַזֶּה אֲשֶׁר אַתָּה עֹשֶׂה לָעָם מַדּוּעַ אַתָּה יוֹשֵׁב לְבַדֶּךָ וְכָל־
טו הָעָם נִצָּב עָלֶיךָ מִן־בֹּקֶר עַד־עָרֶב: וַיֹּאמֶר מֹשֶׁה לְחֹתְנוֹ

ABARBANEL *(cont.)*

---

occupied the entire day, while he paid no attention to the needs of his relatives. Now initially Yitro refrained from interrupting Moshe during his work, because he knew that before critiquing the behavior of a wise man, it is best to understand the reasons behind his actions. Hence Yitro suspected that perhaps Moshe harbored some unknown motive for his method of judging Israel, or even that God had commanded him to act the way he did. This is why he asked Moshe, *What is this that you do for the people* (18:14), meaning: What principles are guiding this system you have introduced?

VERSE 14

IBN EZRA

וַיַּרְא חֹתֵן מֹשֶׁה – *When Moshe's father-in-law saw:* Yitro was perturbed watching Moshe sit and receive the people from morning until evening. Rashi explains that Yitro found it inappropriate that Moshe alone should sit while all of the common folk stood before him. Thus, according to Rashi, Moshe's father-in-law was commenting on a matter of etiquette. However, I am certain that Yitro recognized Moshe's greatness and would not have taken exception to his allowing himself that minor honor. For even Moshe's brother Aharon, who was held in high esteem throughout Israel and was older than Moshe, nevertheless addressed the latter reverently: *Alas, my lord, I pray you* (Numbers 12:11). Indeed, Moshe behaved correctly, for it is proper for judges to sit while litigants stand before them and make their cases. This is what the Torah itself recommends: *Then both the men, between whom is the controversy, shall stand before the Lord, before the priests and the judges* (Deuteronomy 19:17). No, Yitro's objection to Moshe's behavior lay solely in how he was the lone magistrate hearing the myriad of cases the people brought before him, and that he had no other judges to assist him.

BEKHOR SHOR

כָּל־אֲשֶׁר־הוּא עֹשֶׂה לָעָם – *Everything Moshe did for the people:* Moshe's system created a difficulty for the nation, since the people had to wait in line all day in order to have their cases heard. This meant that some litigants ended up going home in frustration when their turn still had not been reached by evening.

ABARBANEL

מָה־הַדָּבָר הַזֶּה אֲשֶׁר אַתָּה עֹשֶׂה לָעָם – *What is this that you do for the people:* Moshe explained to his father-in-law the reason behind the practice he had observed: *The people come to me to inquire of God* (18:15). In other words, the Israelites asked Moshe to appeal to God

14 to evening the people stood before him. When Moshe's father-in-law saw everything Moshe did for the people, he asked, "What is this that you do for the people? Why do you sit alone while all the people stand over you from morning to evening?"
15 "The people come to me to inquire of God," Moshe replied.

———————————— ABARBANEL *(cont.)* ————————————

on their behalves to discover what their futures held. They posed such questions as: Will I recover from my illness? Will my lost donkeys be found? These were the sorts of issues that were best put to a prophet, and therefore the people lined up to present Moshe with their concerns. Additionally, the Israelites approached Moshe with logistical questions regarding the nation's travels and encampments and the particulars of communal organization. This is implied in the opening clause of the verse: *When they have a dispute*

[literally, "a matter"] *they come to me* (18:16). Thirdly, Moshe was Israel's address for settling disputes between quarreling parties, as he says: *I judge between one neighbor and another.* Finally, some Hebrews came to Moshe simply to learn the scope of God's laws and commandments which had been taught at Mara [see 15:25]. This is what Moshe meant when he said: *And I make God's laws and teachings known.* Thus Moshe was required to deal with four types of proceedings.

VERSE 15

———————————— RASHI ————————————

לִדְרֹשׁ אֱלֹהִים – *To inquire of God:* As the Targum translates, the people would come to "seek teaching" [*lemitba ulfan*] from God.

———————————— RASHBAM ————————————

כִּי־יָבֹא אֵלַי הָעָם לִדְרֹשׁ אֱלֹהִים – *The people come to me to inquire of God:* The people come

to me alone because I am the only one with direct access to God.

———————————— BEKHOR SHOR ————————————

לִדְרֹשׁ אֱלֹהִים – *To inquire of God:* This is similar to the verse *And she went to inquire of the Lord* (Genesis 25:22). On the one hand, the people sought clarifications regarding civic disputes of the nature described in the verse *Both*

parties' claims shall be brought to the court [el ha'elohim; alternatively, "to God."] (22:8). On the other hand, many came to Moshe simply to learn God's commandments.

———————————— SFORNO ————————————

לִדְרֹשׁ אֱלֹהִים – *To inquire of God:* The princes of Israel and the leaders of the generation consulted with Moshe to determine the best way to conduct public affairs. Moshe explained to Yitro that the leaders asked him to speak to God about these matters, since *according to*

the commandment of the Lord they remained encamped, and according to the commandment of the Lord they journeyed [Numbers 9:20. That is, all public issues were subject to divine decision].

טז כִּי־יָבֹא אֵלַי הָעָם לִדְרֹשׁ אֱלֹהִים: כִּי־יִהְיֶה לָהֶם דָּבָר
בָּא אֵלַי וְשָׁפַטְתִּי בֵּין אִישׁ וּבֵין רֵעֵהוּ וְהוֹדַעְתִּי אֶת־חֻקֵּי
יז הָאֱלֹהִים וְאֶת־תּוֹרֹתָיו: וַיֹּאמֶר חֹתֵן מֹשֶׁה אֵלָיו לֹא־טוֹב
יח הַדָּבָר אֲשֶׁר אַתָּה עֹשֶׂה: נָבֹל תִּבֹּל גַּם־אַתָּה גַּם־הָעָם הַזֶּה
אֲשֶׁר עִמָּךְ כִּי־כָבֵד מִמְּךָ הַדָּבָר לֹא־תוּכַל עֲשֹׂהוּ לְבַדֶּךָ:
יט עַתָּה שְׁמַע בְּקֹלִי אִיעָצְךָ וִיהִי אֱלֹהִים עִמָּךְ הֱיֵה אַתָּה לָעָם
מוּל הָאֱלֹהִים וְהֵבֵאתָ אַתָּה אֶת־הַדְּבָרִים אֶל־הָאֱלֹהִים:

VERSE 16

ḤIZKUNI

אֶת־חֻקֵּי הָאֱלֹהִים וְאֶת־תּוֹרֹתָיו – *God's laws and teachings:* Moshe refers to those commandments which God had already transmitted to Israel in the verse *It was there that the Lord gave His people decree and law* (15:25).

VERSE 17

RASHI

וַיֹּאמֶר חֹתֵן מֹשֶׁה – *Moshe's father-in-law said:* Although the text could have said merely: "his father-in-law said to him," the verse includes Moshe's name as a way of honoring Yitro, identifying him as the father-in-law of the king.

RALBAG

לֹא־טוֹב הַדָּבָר אֲשֶׁר אַתָּה עֹשֶׂה – *What you are doing is not good:* The way you are conducting matters is a sure recipe for exhaustion, both for you and *this people along with you* (18:18). There is no way that you will be able to adjudicate all the disputes that arise among your compatriots. Eventually the people will despair of bringing their complaints to you. Due to your fatigue, your rapport with God may weaken and your prophetic ability erode, making it difficult for you to resolve the people's questions.

VERSE 18

RASHI

נָבֹל תִּבֹּל – *You will be worn away:* The phrase *navol tibbol* should be understood as the Targum translates [*mila tilei* – "you will become worn out"]. We find a similar term in the verse *The leaf is withered [navel]* (Jeremiah 8:13).

גַּם־אַתָּה – *You:* [Literally, "also you."] The extra word "also" [*gam*] serves to include Aharon, Ḥur, and the seventy elders. [That is, even if they assist you, they will be worn out as well.]

RASHBAM

נָבֹל תִּבֹּל – *You will be worn away:* The verb in this clause is related to that used in the verse *Come, let us go down, and there confound [venavela] their language, that they may not understand one another's speech* (Genesis 11:7). Yitro was cautioning Moshe: If you try to communicate with several petitioners at once, your speech will become confused.

16 "When they have a dispute, they come to me and I judge between one neighbor and another, and I make God's laws and
17 teachings known." Moshe's father-in-law said to him, "What
18 you are doing is not good. You will be worn away, and this
people along with you. It is too heavy a burden for you. You
19 cannot carry it alone. Now listen to me, let me advise you; and
may God be with you. You speak for the people before God,

RASHBAM *(cont.)*

The people too will start to shout above each other to be heard, and you will be unable to discern what their complaints are. And on the other hand, you certainly have not the stamina to hear all the nation's cases one after the other.

VERSE 19

RASHI

אִיעָצְךָ וִיהִי אֱלֹהִים עִמָּךְ – *Let me advise you; and may God be with you:* Do not just take my advice; you ought to consult with God as well. הֱיֵה אַתָּה לָעָם מוּל הָאֱלֹהִים – *You speak for the people before God:* Moshe should act as a messenger and as an intermediary between the people and God, seeking His rulings on their behalf. אֶת־הַדְּבָרִים – *Their concerns:* [Literally, "the matters." Rashi specifies that this refers to] the people's quarrels.

RASHBAM

הֱיֵה אַתָּה לָעָם מוּל הָאֱלֹהִים – *You speak for the people before God:* There certainly are cases which require consultation with God. In those situations, you should listen to what He advises, and then direct the people how to act. This is what Yitro meant when he suggested: *Let them bring the major cases to you* (18:22). However, the minor issues can be handled by the sages of Israel, whom Moshe would appoint to lighten Moshe's case load.

IBN EZRA

וִיהִי אֱלֹהִים עִמָּךְ – *And may God be with you:* At the end of his counsel, Yitro told Moshe to seek God's approval for his plan. This is what the father-in-law meant when he said, *If you do this, and God so commands* (18:23). There is no doubt that Moshe followed this advice as well.

BEKHOR SHOR

וִיהִי אֱלֹהִים עִמָּךְ – *And may God be with you:* When you implement my scheme, your affairs will be conducted properly and will therefore be successful. Consequently, God will favor your endeavors and be with you.

RABBI AVRAHAM BEN HARAMBAM

עַתָּה שְׁמַע בְּקֹלִי – *Now listen to me:* The straightforward meaning of this verse is: You should listen to the following advice that I give you. However, Rav Se'adya Gaon interprets the phrase as conditional: If you listen to me, I will issue you advice. This is not the true sense of the verse. וִיהִי אֱלֹהִים עִמָּךְ – *And may God be with you:* If you accept my counsel, God will be with you. For if you implement my plan, your time will be freed up to work on perfecting your soul and its adherence to God.

כ וְהִזְהַרְתָּ֣ה אֶתְהֶ֔ם אֶת־הַֽחֻקִּ֖ים וְאֶת־הַתּוֹרֹ֑ת וְהוֹדַעְתָּ֣ לָהֶ֗ם
כא אֶת־הַדֶּ֙רֶךְ֙ יֵ֣לְכוּ בָ֔הּ וְאֶת־הַֽמַּעֲשֶׂ֖ה אֲשֶׁ֣ר יַעֲשֽׂוּן: וְאַתָּ֣ה
תֶחֱזֶ֣ה מִכָּל־הָעָ֡ם אַנְשֵׁי־חַ֩יִל֩ יִרְאֵ֨י אֱלֹהִ֜ים אַנְשֵׁ֥י אֱמֶ֛ת
שֹׂ֣נְאֵי בָ֑צַע וְשַׂמְתָּ֣ עֲלֵהֶ֗ם שָׂרֵ֤י אֲלָפִים֙ שָׂרֵ֣י מֵא֔וֹת שָׂרֵ֥י

————————————— ABARBANEL —————————————

וִיהִי אֱלֹהִים עִמָּךְ – *And may God be with you:* Yitro's intention was not that Moshe should develop Yitro's idea only if God agreed with it, since clearly Moshe would never execute a project that God disapproved of. Rather, what Yitro meant was that if Moshe accepted his father-in-law's plan, he would save valuable time which he could employ in communing with God. Then God would issue commandments to Moshe and direct him in how to behave. This is the meaning of the phrase *And may God be with you.* Additionally, the new arrangement would allow Moshe to tolerate the burden of judging the nation, which would then *be able to go home in peace* (18:23), not having had to stand before you all day to have their cases heard.

VERSE 20

————————————— IBN EZRA —————————————

וְהִזְהַרְתָּה אֶתְהֶם – *And you must acquaint them:* Yitro recognized that Moshe would have to teach the people about God's positive and negative commandments of the heart, and which are the most fundamental matters of religion. Examples of these are the obligation to love God and to cleave to Him, to revere Him, to walk in His ways, to *circumcise the foreskin of your heart* (Deuteronomy 10:16), not to loathe one's fellow Jew, or to seek revenge against him or to bear a grudge. These sorts of demands are meant by the verse *But the word is very near to you, in your mouth, and in your heart, that you may do it* (Deuteronomy 30:14), and many commandments fit into this category. **וְאֶת־הַמַּעֲשֶׂה אֲשֶׁר יַעֲשׂוּן** – *And the way they must act:* Here Yitro refers to the positive commandments that involve action. The significance of many of these does not lie in the acts themselves, but in their symbolism, as with the Sabbath, the festivals, the obligation to redeem the firstborn, to love the foreigner, to wear tzitzit, don tefillin, and affix the mezuza.

————————————— RAMBAN —————————————

וְהִזְהַרְתָּה אֶתְהֶם – *And you must acquaint them:* [Literally, "warn them."] You must show Israel the proper way to conduct themselves according to God's laws and commandments. Thus Yitro agreed with Moshe's statement that he was required to *make God's laws and teachings known* (18:16) and added that Moshe would have to caution his people strongly regarding the punishments that await disobedience. Such intense warnings were necessary because it was not Moshe who would be punishing the people for transgression [but God]. However, in matters of disagreement, regarding which Moshe explained: *When they have a dispute, they come to me and I judge between one neighbor and another* (18:16), Yitro

20 and bring their concerns to Him. And you must acquaint them
with His precepts and laws, and make known to them the
21 path they are to walk and the way they must act. You, as well,
must seek out among the people, capable men – God-fearing,
trustworthy men, who despise corruption; and appoint them
over the people as leaders of thousands, hundreds, fifties, and

——————————— RAMBAN *(cont.)* ———————————

advised that his son-in-law appoint additional
judges to serve alongside him. For the burden
of hearing the entire nation's complaints was
too heavy for a single man to bear. Such an arrangement would improve the situation both
for Moshe and for the people, as these other
men would *bear [the load] together with you*
(18:22). Now it is known that Moshe employed
bailiffs to conduct defendants to answer
claims brought against them, and officers

who compelled guilty parties to comply
with Moshe's verdicts. Many of these officials
were subsequently promoted to judgeships.
This is what Moshe means when he later
recalls: *So I took the chief of your tribes, wise
men, and known, and made them heads over
you* (Deuteronomy 1:15). These civil servants
are not mentioned in the current text since
their selection was not a function of Yitro's
advice.

——————————— RALBAG ———————————

וְהִזְהַרְתָּה אֶתְהֶם – *And you must acquaint
them:* [Literally, "warn them."] Yitro here refers
to the negative commandments, which could
only be known through the medium of prophecy. אֶת־הַדֶּרֶךְ יֵלְכוּ בָהּ – *The path they are to
walk :* This refers to appropriate ways for the
people to conduct themselves interpersonally.
It includes the demand that Israelites should

love each other, that they should refrain from
seeking revenge against their neighbors and
bearing grudges, and other similar ethical
norms. וְאֶת־הַמַּעֲשֶׂה אֲשֶׁר יַעֲשׂוּן – *And the way
they must act:* Here Yitro refers to positive commandments that require a physical act, such
as eating unleavened bread, sitting in a sukka,
donning tefillin, and wrapping oneself in tzitzit.

VERSE 21

——————————— RASHI ———————————

וְאַתָּה תֶחֱזֶה – *You must seek out:* Use your
divine inspiration to find these judges.
אַנְשֵׁי־חַיִל – *Capable men:* Rich men. Judges
who are wealthy will have no need to flatter
others or curry favor. אַנְשֵׁי אֱמֶת – *Trustworthy
men:* Individuals who have faith in God are
those whose words can be trusted. As such,
disputing parties will have confidence in their
judgments. שֹׂנְאֵי בָצַע – *Despise corruption:*
This refers to a reluctance to let any of their
own conflicts reach the stage of litigation

[always preferring to reach a negotiated set-
tlement]. As the Sages teach: Any judge who
has been compelled to pay money in court
is not a real judge. שָׂרֵי אֲלָפִים – *Leaders of
thousands:* Moshe was to appoint six hundred
men to have jurisdiction over the 600,000 Israelites who left Egypt. שָׂרֵי מֵאוֹת – *Leaders
of hundreds:* There were six thousand men
at this level. שָׂרֵי חֲמִשִּׁים – *Leaders of fifties:*
And twelve thousand men in this group.
וְשָׂרֵי עֲשָׂרֹת – *Leaders of tens:* Sixty thousand.

כב חֲמִשִּׁים וְשָׂרֵי עֲשָׂרֹת: וְשָׁפְטוּ אֶת־הָעָם בְּכָל־עֵת וְהָיָה
כָּל־הַדָּבָר הַגָּדֹל יָבִיאוּ אֵלֶיךָ וְכָל־הַדָּבָר הַקָּטֹן יִשְׁפְּטוּ־
כג הֵם וְהָקֵל מֵעָלֶיךָ וְנָשְׂאוּ אִתָּךְ: אִם אֶת־הַדָּבָר הַזֶּה תַּעֲשֶׂה
וְצִוְּךָ אֱלֹהִים וְיָכָלְתָּ עֲמֹד וְגַם כָּל־הָעָם הַזֶּה עַל־מְקֹמוֹ יָבֹא

IBN EZRA

שָׂרֵי אֲלָפִים – *Leaders of thousands:* It seems to me that the term "leaders of thousands" refers to men who each ruled over a thousand subjects such as slaves, young men, and hired workers. These people might have been the tribal heads, in which case there were only twelve of them. On the other hand, there were many more leaders of hundreds. The meaning of the term *leaders of fifties* is made clear by the verse: *And it came to pass after this, that Avshalom prepared him chariots and horses, and fifty men to run before him* [II Samuel 15:1; i.e., since fifty is a standard military unit, this term refers to minor officers in general, rather than implying that there was literally one for every fifty Israelites].

RABBI AVRAHAM BEN HARAMBAM

תֶּחֱזֶה מִכָּל־הָעָם – *Seek out among the people:* Do not direct your search efforts within the population of a single favored tribe. Rather, appoint as a judge any citizen who possesses the desirable attributes.

RAMBAN

אַנְשֵׁי־חַיִל – *Capable men:* [Literally, "men of *ḥayil*."] Yitro suggested that Moshe seek men who were capable of leading large numbers of people, for any assembly or gathering can be called a *ḥayil*, not only large military forces. In the realm of justice, a man of *ḥayil* is a wise, diligent, and honest individual. In the context of soldiering, the term would refer to someone who is strong, enterprising, and skilled at leading troops through military strategy. We also find the term "woman of *ḥayil*" [as in Proverbs 31:10], which refers to an industrious woman who knows how to run her household. אַנְשֵׁי אֱמֶת שֹׂנְאֵי בָצַע – *Trustworthy men who despise corruption:* The straightforward understanding of this is that Moshe is to unearth men who pursue truth and who loathe exploitation. These are the sort of people who recoil whenever they witness cruelty or violence, and whose first object is to rescue the despondent from the hands of the oppressor.

RABBEINU BAHYA

וְאַתָּה תֶחֱזֶה – *You must seek out:* [Literally, "you must see."] We might have expected Yitro to advise Moshe to "choose" men who fit the necessary requirements for judges. Indeed, this is the verb that describes how Moshe implemented his father-in-law's advice, as the verse states: *Moshe chose capable men from all of Israel* (18:25). Nevertheless, as expressed by God's claim that *a man looks on the outward appearance, but the LORD looks on the heart* (I Samuel 16:7), Moshe was required to employ his prophetic powers to select the right candidates. For the term *teḥezeh* is related to the terms *maḥazeh* and *ḥazon* [types of vision; the words are often used in association with prophecy].

22 tens. Have them serve as daily judges for the people; let them bring the major cases to you, but judge the minor ones themselves. In this way they will lighten your load, and bear it to-
23 gether with you. If you do this, and God so commands, then you will endure, and all these people will be able to go home in

VERSE 22

———— RASHBAM ————

כָּל־הַדָּבָר הַגָּדֹל – *The major cases:* Matters that require divine consultation.

———— RAMBAN ————

וְשָׁפְטוּ אֶת־הָעָם בְּכָל־עֵת – *Have them serve as daily judges:* Since there will be many different judges available to serve the nation, people with grievances will be able to appeal to an authority figure at any time without having to wait. Were Moshe to remain the sole justice for Israel, the average person would find it nearly impossible to reach him and to receive a hearing. Consequently, many individuals will simply give up hope for recompense, resigning themselves to enduring any injustice and violence perpetrated against them. People will not wish to abandon their work and other concerns to stand in line all day just for the moment Moshe becomes free to attend to their case. This is what Yitro meant when he said: *And all these people will be able to go home in peace* (18:23). Currently, the people whose complaints are not being addressed are dissatisfied. They are frustrated at the paucity of judges and their inability to talk to anyone about their problem whenever they wish. This lack of oversight leads to thieves running amok throughout the helpless population, and to dissent and unrest. But according to Yitro's plan, the nation would be able to feel secure wherever they lived.

VERSE 23

———— RASHI ————

וְצִוְּךָ אֱלֹהִים וְיָכָלְתָּ עֲמֹד – *If God so commands, then you will endure:* Ask God whether He commands you to establish the system I have described. If He does, then you will be able to handle the burden of the nation. If He rejects my approach, you will be unable to withstand the difficulty of judging the people. וְגַם כָּל־הָעָם הַזֶּה – *And all these people:* The inclusive word *vegam* [literally, "and also"] connotes Aharon, Nadav, Avihu, and the seventy elders – the men who have been sitting by you until now.

———— RASHBAM ————

וְצִוְּךָ אֱלֹהִים וְיָכָלְתָּ עֲמֹד – *If God so commands, then you will endure:* [Literally, "If God commands you, and you are able to endure." Rashbam parses the sentence differently from the translation here:] When God commands you to judge the people, and the aid that your colleagues provide allows you to shoulder the burden, then – *All these people,* i.e., those who *stand over you from morning to evening* (18:14), *will be able to go home in peace* – quickly and efficiently.

כד בְּשָׁלוֹם: וַיִּשְׁמַע מֹשֶׁה לְקוֹל חֹתְנוֹ וַיַּעַשׂ כֹּל אֲשֶׁר אָמָר: שלישי

כה וַיִּבְחַר מֹשֶׁה אַנְשֵׁי־חַיִל מִכָּל־יִשְׂרָאֵל וַיִּתֵּן אֹתָם רָאשִׁים
עַל־הָעָם שָׂרֵי אֲלָפִים שָׂרֵי מֵאוֹת שָׂרֵי חֲמִשִּׁים וְשָׂרֵי

כו עֲשָׂרֹת: וְשָׁפְטוּ אֶת־הָעָם בְּכָל־עֵת אֶת־הַדָּבָר הַקָּשֶׁה

כז יְבִיאוּן אֶל־מֹשֶׁה וְכָל־הַדָּבָר הַקָּטֹן יִשְׁפּוּטוּ הֵם: וַיְשַׁלַּח
מֹשֶׁה אֶת־חֹתְנוֹ וַיֵּלֶךְ לוֹ אֶל־אַרְצוֹ:

——————— IBN EZRA ———————

וְגַם כָּל־הָעָם הַזֶּה – *And all these people:* Under the current conditions, litigants who stood waiting for Moshe to resolve their conflicts were sometimes not able to reach him by the end of the day. This meant that they would return home angrier and more divided than before, with their dispute likely to flare up again when they reached their tents. However, under the new plan, disputants would be able to return relaxed, content, and at peace.

——————— SFORNO ———————

עַל־מְקֹמוֹ יָבֹא בְשָׁלוֹם – *Will be able to go home in peace:* After the law has been clarified in so many courts, the disputants will recognize that true justice has been served, and they will contend with each other no more.

VERSE 24

——————— IBN EZRA ———————

וַיִּשְׁמַע מֹשֶׁה – *Moshe listened:* Our passage mentions that Moshe followed Yitro's advice, but it does not state that Moshe acted on his own counsel as well. For Moshe improved upon his father-in-law's plan by appointing officers from the tribes who would be tasked with enforcing the courts' rulings.

——————— RABBI AVRAHAM BEN HARAMBAM ———————

וַיִּשְׁמַע מֹשֶׁה – *Moshe listened:* After receiving God's approval to implement Yitro's scheme, Moshe set about following the man's advice. Thus the verse states, *Moshe listened... and did all that he said.* Included within Yitro's directive was to make sure of God's agreement as a condition for making any changes. We learn from this story that a modest Torah scholar is always prepared to accept suggestions and ideas when they are true, though they may be issued by laymen. For we see that God permitted Moshe to make the alterations devised by Yitro, believing them to represent a wise strategy.

VERSE 25

——————— IBN EZRA ———————

וַיִּבְחַר מֹשֶׁה אַנְשֵׁי־חַיִל – *Moshe chose capable men:* The text informs us that Moshe selected men he deemed to be capable – an attribute that was easily discernible – but it does not report that he ascertained that the men were God-fearing [as Yitro had suggested in 18:21], since only God knows the hearts of men. When later reviewing this development in

24 peace." Moshe listened to his father-in-law and did all that he SHELISHI
25 said. Moshe chose capable men from all Israel and made them
   chiefs over the people, leaders of thousands, hundreds, fifties,
26 and tens. They judged the people every day. Any major case
   they brought to Moshe, but they decided every minor matter
27 themselves. Then Moshe parted from his father-in-law, and the
   latter went forth, back to his own land.

IBN EZRA *(cont.)*

Israelite society, Moshe recalls that he chose "wise" men on Israel's behalf (Deuteronomy 1:13), for the intelligence of a person is something that others can detect. However, there will always be clever people who do not in fact fear God. In the same verse, Moshe also mentions that he picked men who were *known among your tribes*, a detail the text omits here for considerations of space.

SFORNO

וַיִּבְחַר מֹשֶׁה אַנְשֵׁי־חַיִל – *Moshe chose capable men:* Actually, Moshe tried in vain to locate men who possessed all of the characteristics Yitro had listed [in 18:21]. And so he was forced to settle for men who were merely capable, expert, diligent, and committed to getting at the heart of a matter and reaching an equitable solution. Such minds were preferable over those that were God fearing but less capable. Thus do our Sages proclaim: Even if a scholar is vindictive and grudging as a snake, stand by him to learn from his teachings; but when a man, albeit righteous, is an ignoramus, do not even live in his neighborhood (Shabbat 63a).

VERSE 27

RASHI

וַיֵּלֶךְ לוֹ אֶל־אַרְצוֹ – *He went forth, back to his own land:* Yitro returned to Midyan to convert his family to the Israelite faith.

IBN EZRA

וַיְשַׁלַּח מֹשֶׁה אֶת־חֹתְנוֹ – *Then Moshe parted from his father-in-law:* Moshe saw Yitro off with honor, similar to how his ancestor had behaved, as the verse states: *And Avraham went with them [the three angels] to bring them on the way* (Genesis 18:16).

SFORNO

וַיְשַׁלַּח מֹשֶׁה אֶת־חֹתְנוֹ – *Then Moshe parted from his father-in-law:* Moshe and Yitro parted ways because the latter was reluctant to join the nation on its march to the land of Israel, as the verse later recounts: *I will not go, but I will depart to my own land, and to my kindred* (Numbers 10:30). Yitro's unwillingness to participate in Israel's continued adventure may have been a function of his old age. We find a similar protestation with Barzilai [an ally of David during Avshalom's rebellion], who protested: *Let your servant, I pray you, turn back again, that I may die in my own city, and be buried by the grave of my father and of my mother* (II Samuel 19:38). Nevertheless, it is clear that Yitro's sons did accompany the nation as they progressed to the promised land, as the verse states: *And the children of the Kenite, Moshe's*

CLASSIC COMMENTATORS

יט א בַּחֹדֶשׁ הַשְּׁלִישִׁי לְצֵאת בְּנֵי־יִשְׂרָאֵל מֵאֶרֶץ מִצְרָיִם בַּיּוֹם רביעי
הַזֶּה בָּאוּ מִדְבַּר סִינָי: וַיִּסְעוּ מֵרְפִידִים וַיָּבֹאוּ מִדְבַּר סִינַי ב

———————————— SFORNO *(cont.)* ————————————

father-in-law, went up out of the city of palm trees with the children of Yehuda into the wilderness of Yehuda, which lies in the south of Arad; | *and they went and dwelt among the people* (Judges 1:16).

CHAPTER 19, VERSE 1

———————————— RASHI ————————————

בַּיּוֹם הַזֶּה – *On that day:* The verse refers to the first day of the third month. Nevertheless, why is the phrase written *bayom hazeh* ["on this day"] as opposed to *bayom hahu* ["on that day"]? It teaches that the words of the Torah [which would soon be given] should always be as new and fresh to us as if they were delivered this very day.

———————————— RAMBAN ————————————

בַּחֹדֶשׁ הַשְּׁלִישִׁי – *On the first day of the third month:* Our chapter should have opened in a way similar to the statement that begins chapter 17, *Israel moved on after that from the desert of Sin…and they camped at Refidim* (17:1). Here too, the Torah could have written: "The Israelites departed from Refidim and camped in the Sinai Desert on the first day of the third month." However, the style of this opening verse expresses the foundational importance of Israel's arrival in the Sinai Desert and the great happiness that it brought the nation. After all, the people had anticipated this moment ever since their departure from Egypt; they knew that this was the site where they would receive the Torah from God. For Moshe had revealed to them the promise issued at the burning bush, *Proof that I have sent you will come when, having brought the people out of Egypt, you come to serve God upon this mountain* (3:12). Indeed, Israel's expectation of revelation was the first message that Moshe conveyed to Pharaoh, when he said: *Let us take a three-day journey into the wilderness and sacrifice to the Lord our God* (5:3). What Moshe described was the journey from

Egypt to Sinai. Hence, the chapter begins by reporting triumphantly: *On the first day of the third month after the Israelites had left Egypt they came to the Sinai Desert,* thereby fulfilling their national destiny. After this opening, the text reverts to its usual style that it employs in describing all of Israel's journeys: *Setting out from Refidim they had arrived at the Sinai Desert* (19:2). This second verse too requires some analysis, for we would have expected it to read: Setting out from Refidim they *encamped* in the Sinai Desert. The language of the verse implies that as soon as the nation "arrived" at the desert and saw the mountain looming over them, they pitched their tents right there. The people did not bother to look for a more desirable camp site, but were content to settle down in the wilderness of Ḥorev – a desolate landscape situated in front of the mountain. It is also possible that the Israelites separated themselves from the mixed multitudes who had taken advantage of the exodus to emigrate from Egypt with them. While the Hebrews advanced toward the foot of mountain and encamped there, the other groups who were with them stopped short.

19 **1** On the first day of the third month after the Israelites had REVI'I
2 left Egypt they came to the Sinai Desert. Setting out from
Refidim they had arrived at the Sinai Desert, encamping in

———— RAMBAN *(cont.)* ————

[This explains the apparent repetition in these two verses – they are describing the actions of two different groups of people.] For it was Israel alone who was slated to receive the Torah, as the next verse declares: *This is what you shall say to the house of Yaakov, what you shall tell the people of Israel* (19:3).

———— ḤIZKUNI ————

בְּחֹדֶשׁ הַשְּׁלִישִׁי – *On the first day of the third month:* Israel needed a grace period of three months before arriving at Mount Sinai because the nation had been previously enslaved and was now emancipated with the object of converting. This parallels the teaching of our Sages: A woman who converts to Judaism, a Jewish woman who had been taken captive by gentiles, and an emancipated female slave must all wait three months before marrying [to ensure that they were not pregnant prior to their marrying a Jewish man].

VERSE 2

———— RASHI ————

וַיִּסְעוּ מֵרְפִידִים – *Setting out from Refidim:* Once the Torah states that Israel arrived at Mount Sinai, why bother telling us where they came from? After all, we already know that the nation had previously encamped at Refidim [as reported in 17:1]. The message of the verse compares Israel's setting out from Refidim to their encampment at Mount Sinai: Just as Israel reached Mount Sinai in a state of repentance, that was their attitude when they abandoned Refidim. **וַיִּחַן־שָׁם יִשְׂרָאֵל** – *And there Israel camped:* [The verb "camped" – vayiḥan – is singular in the Hebrew.] When Israel encamped at Mount Sinai, they were united in purpose like a single individual. Israel's other departures and arrivals, on the other hand, were characterized by complaints and disputes. **נֶגֶד הָהָר** – *Facing the mountain:* Israel pitched camp to the east of the mountain. The term *neged* always connotes an eastward orientation.

———— ABARBANEL ————

וַיִּסְעוּ מֵרְפִידִים – *Setting out from Refidim:* The text mentions Israel's departure from Refidim to emphasize that the nation's encounter there did not traumatize them for the future. For one might have imagined that following the attack of Amalek that took place in Refidim, the people would have been reluctant to again set up camp in the wilderness, preferring to be more selective in their choice of camp sites. Israel could have been forgiven had they tried to ascend the mountain to protect themselves from enemies lurking in the wasteland. But in fact they did not seek shelter when they arrived in the Sinai Desert, but trusted in God to care for them, *encamping in the wilderness.*

———— KELI YAKAR ————

וַיָּבֹאוּ מִדְבַּר סִינַי – *They had arrived at the Sinai Desert:* This verse is replete with repetitions, for the text could have stated merely: "And Israel departed from Refidim and encamped

ג וַיִּחַן־שָׁם יִשְׂרָאֵל נֶגֶד הָהָר: וּמֹשֶׁה עָלָה
אֶל־הָאֱלֹהִים וַיִּקְרָא אֵלָיו יהוה מִן־הָהָר לֵאמֹר כֹּה
תֹאמַר לְבֵית יַעֲקֹב וְתַגֵּיד לִבְנֵי יִשְׂרָאֵל: אַתֶּם רְאִיתֶם ד
אֲשֶׁר עָשִׂיתִי לְמִצְרָיִם וָאֶשָּׂא אֶתְכֶם עַל־כַּנְפֵי נְשָׁרִים

———————————— KELI YAKAR *(cont.)* ————————————

in the Sinai Desert facing the mountain." Why does the verse use three different verbs: "arrived," "encamping," and "camped"? And is it not odd that the location is identified as "the Sinai Desert" but the hill itself as merely "the mountain"? It seems to me that the verse is teaching us that Israel only deserved to receive the Torah after they had united and were living together peacefully. For one verse alludes to Israel as *masters of collections; they [all of their teachings] are given by one shepherd* (Ecclesiastes 12:11), and regarding the Torah, the text states: *Her ways are ways of*

pleasantness, and all her paths are peace (Proverbs 3:17). Now, when one sees a given rabbi permitting an action or an object, and another scholar forbidding it, one might get the impression that there are multiple Torahs. Hence our chapter emphasizes that the people came to Sinai *on the first day of the third month* (19:1), for the constellation governing that period is Gemini, the sign of twins, which indicates the closeness and love that Israel required as a prerequisite to receiving the Torah. As the verse states, *Great peace have they who love Your Torah* (Psalms 119:165).

VERSE 3

———————————— RASHI ————————————

וּמֹשֶׁה עָלָה – *While Moshe went up:* Moshe ascended the mountain on the second day. [He cannot have gone up on the very day of Israel's arrival because we know from the Midrash that] each time Moshe climbed the hill he did so first thing in the morning, as the verse states: *And he rose early in the morning and climbed Mount Sinai* (34:4). **כֹּה תֹאמַר** – *This is what you shall say:* Repeat My message to

Israel in precisely this language and relate My points in the same sequence. **לְבֵית יַעֲקֹב** – *To the house of Yaakov:* This refers to the nation's women, who should be addressed in soft language. **וְתַגֵּיד לִבְנֵי יִשְׂרָאֵל** – *Tell the people of Israel:* Inform the menfolk of the laws' particulars and the punishments for disobedience. These are matters which are difficult to hear and hard as sinews [*gidin*, echoing *vetaggeid*].

———————————— IBN EZRA ————————————

לְבֵית יַעֲקֹב – *To the house of Yaakov:* God here refers to the masses of Israel present at Sinai, who would personally receive God's communication during revelation, and to their descendants who would follow them. **וְתַגֵּיד לִבְנֵי יִשְׂרָאֵל** – *Tell the people of Israel:*

Tell the elders the content of the following verses and they will convey that message to the rest of the nation. Thus we subsequently read: *So Moshe came and summoned the elders of the people.... And the people answered as one* (19:7–8).

the wilderness, and there Israel camped, facing the mountain,
3 while Moshe went up to God. And the LORD called to him
from the mountain: "This is what you shall say to the house
4 of Yaakov, what you shall tell the people of Israel: You yourselves have seen what I did to the Egyptians: how I lifted you

──────────────── BEKHOR SHOR ────────────────

וּמֹשֶׁה עָלָה אֶל־הָאֱלֹהִים – *While Moshe went up to God:* Moshe did not ascend the hill at his own initiative, but responded to the call of the Holy One, blessed be He, from atop the mountain.

──────────────── RAMBAN ────────────────

וּמֹשֶׁה עָלָה אֶל־הָאֱלֹהִים – *While Moshe went up to God:* A cloud covered Mount Sinai, where the presence of God's glory rested from the moment that the nation arrived at the site. This is described in the verse *The glory of the LORD rested on Mount Sinai, and the cloud covered it for six days* (24:16), meaning six days prior to revelation. When our verse states: *Moshe went up to God,* it means that he reached the edge of the mountain in preparation of communing with God, but he did not yet penetrate *the thick darkness where God was* (20:18). It was then that God called to Moshe from the top of the mountain saying, *This is what you shall say to house of Yaakov.*

VERSE 4

──────────────── RASHI ────────────────

אַתֶּם רְאִיתֶם – *You yourselves have seen:* What I did in Egypt is not a story that you possess through received tradition [rather, you witnessed the events yourselves]. Know that the Egyptians long ago deserved to be penalized for their transgressions before Me. But I withheld My punishments from them until they encountered you, and exacted retribution against them only because of you [so that Israel would witness God's wonders and miracles]. **וָאֶשָּׂא אֶתְכֶם** – *I lifted you up:* This refers to the moment the entire nation was gathered together at Ramesses [in 12:37]. For the Israelite nation had been spread throughout the land of Goshen, yet all the people assembled at Ramesses ready to leave in virtually no time. **עַל־כַּנְפֵי נְשָׁרִים** – *On eagles' wings:* I carried you in a manner similar to the eagle, which transports its eaglets on top of its wings. In contrast to all other bird species, which carry their chicks between their legs to protect them from birds of prey swooping down from above, the eagle fears no other bird. The only enemies which frighten her are human beings, who try to fell the bird by shooting arrows at it. Since no other bird can attack the eagle by flying higher, it reasons that it is better to position its young on top of its wings, believing: I would rather be shot by man's arrow than see my chicks so injured. So too did God behave [during the battle at the Sea of Reeds] as the verses state: *Then the angel of God who had been traveling ahead of the Israelite camp…came between the Egyptian and the Israelite camps* (14:19–20).

ה וָאָבִא אֶתְכֶם אֵלָי: וְעַתָּה אִם־שָׁמוֹעַ תִּשְׁמְעוּ בְּקֹלִי
וּשְׁמַרְתֶּם אֶת־בְּרִיתִי וִהְיִיתֶם לִי סְגֻלָּה מִכָּל־הָעַמִּים כִּי־

──────────── RASHBAM ────────────

עַל־כַּנְפֵי נְשָׁרִים – *On eagles' wings:* I transport-ed you across the sea on dry land, just like eagles traverse bodies of water through flight. Furthermore, I ensured no harm would come to you, as the verse states: *As an eagle stirs up her nest, broods over her young* (Deuteronomy 32:11). וָאָבִא אֶתְכֶם אֵלָי – *And brought you to Me:* So that I might be your God.

──────────── IBN EZRA ────────────

עַל־כַּנְפֵי נְשָׁרִים – *On eagles' wings:* The eagle flies higher than any other species of bird. And all other birds fear it, and it is intimidated by none of them. וָאָבִא אֶתְכֶם אֵלָי – *And brought you to Me:* My glory will descend from this summit, which is a sacred mountain.

──────────── BEKHOR SHOR ────────────

וָאֶשָּׂא אֶתְכֶם עַל־כַּנְפֵי נְשָׁרִים – *I lifted you up on eagles' wings:* I raised you to heights of great-ness and superiority when I rescued you from slavery. I subsequently brought you to Me so that you may serve Me, the King of Kings. You have attained such elevation and prominence that it is as if you are riding on the wings of eagles – creatures who surpass all other birds in the heights they reach.

──────────── ABARBANEL ────────────

אַתֶּם רְאִיתֶם – *You yourselves have seen:* God does not here elaborate on all the details of His successful rescue of Israel, because people are generally made uncomfortable by re-peated descriptions of the favors others have done for them. Constant reminders make the recipients of such beneficence feel belittled and dependent. And so God recalled Israel's salvation in the tersest terms.

──────────── SFORNO ────────────

אֲשֶׁר עָשִׂיתִי לְמִצְרָיִם – *What I did to the Egyp-tians:* I made every effort to persuade the Egyptians to repent of their evil ways, for I have no desire that the wicked should per-ish. But because of their stubbornness, I was forced to unleash many signs and wonders against the country to destroy the oppressors. וָאֶשָּׂא אֶתְכֶם עַל־כַּנְפֵי נְשָׁרִים – *I lifted you up on eagles' wings:* I carried you on paths that no man has ever crossed, just like eagles who transport their young to heights that no other bird can reach. I did this to distinguish you from the other nations, to separate you from the ways of other peoples, and thereby to make you Mine.

──────────── KELI YAKAR ────────────

וָאֶשָּׂא אֶתְכֶם עַל־כַּנְפֵי נְשָׁרִים – *I lifted you up on eagles' wings:* God describes three levels of His interaction with Israel. He first declares that He *lifted you up on eagles' wings,* carrying the nation the way a nurse carries a suckling child. At this stage, God is like a parent while Israel is comparable to the child. God then states that He *brought you to Me,* which presents Him

5 up on eagles' wings and brought you to Me. Now, if you faithfully heed My voice and keep My covenant, you will be My
treasure among all the peoples, although the whole earth is

———— KELI YAKAR *(cont.)* ————

and Israel as equals with the closeness of two brothers. Finally, God expresses His hope for the future: *A kingdom of priests and a holy nation shall you be to Me* (19:6), suggesting that

Israel will be a community of kings vis-à-vis God Himself, so to speak, as the verse states: *He that rules over men must be just, ruling in the fear of God* (II Samuel 23:3).

VERSE 5

———— RASHI ————

וְעַתָּה – *Now:* If you now determine to accept My commandments, things will start to become sweeter for you. The start of any enterprise is difficult. סְגֻלָּה – *Treasure:* You will be My precious treasure, as the verse states: *I gathered also silver and gold, and the treasure of kings* (Ecclesiastes 2:8) – referring to the expensive items and valuable gems that monarchs collect. That is what you will be like

for Me – a people favored among all nations. Now lest you argue that Israel cannot be God's preferred nation since they are God's only possession – what else does God own that could give some basis for comparison? Recognize that in fact *the whole earth is Mine*, and still I hold a particular fondness for Israel beyond any other group.

———— RASHBAM ————

כִּי־לִי כָּל־הָאָרֶץ – *Although the whole earth is mine:* Although I have created and possess all

of the world's nations, yours is the only one I have chosen to be My treasure.

———— RAMBAN ————

סְגֻלָּה – *Treasure:* You will be a treasure in My possession, like a valuable prize that a king would never entrust to anybody else. The term *segula* is used in a similar sense in the

verse *I gathered also silver and gold, and the treasure of [segulat] kings and of the provinces* (Ecclesiastes 2:8).

———— RALBAG ————

סְגֻלָּה – *Treasure:* Like a prized possession, I will protect and watch over you.

———— SFORNO ————

סְגֻלָּה מִכָּל־הָעַמִּים – *Treasure among all the peoples:* Now, the entire human race is beloved to Me, more important than the animal kingdom, since only people can possibly fulfill My purposes, as our Sages teach: Precious is man, for he was created in the image of God. Nevertheless, you, Israel, will be even more

special to Me. כִּי־לִי כָּל־הָאָרֶץ – *Although the whole earth is mine:* The distinction between you and other nations is but a small one. Because the whole world is mine, and the nations of the earth undoubtedly contain righteous individuals, they are dear to Me as well.

י לִי כָּל־הָאָרֶץ: וְאַתֶּם תִּהְיוּ־לִי מַמְלֶכֶת כֹּהֲנִים וְגוֹי קָדוֹשׁ טו
ז אֵלֶּה הַדְּבָרִים אֲשֶׁר תְּדַבֵּר אֶל־בְּנֵי יִשְׂרָאֵל: וַיָּבֹא מֹשֶׁה חמישי
וַיִּקְרָא לְזִקְנֵי הָעָם וַיָּשֶׂם לִפְנֵיהֶם אֵת כָּל־הַדְּבָרִים הָאֵלֶּה

VERSE 6

RASHI

מַמְלֶכֶת כֹּהֲנִים – *A kingdom of priests:* The term kohanim [translated here as "priests"] in this instance means "rulers," as in the verse *The*

sons of David were ministers [kohanim] of state (II Samuel 8:18). אֵלֶּה הַדְּבָרִים – *These are the words:* No more and no less.

IBN EZRA

מַמְלֶכֶת כֹּהֲנִים – *A kingdom of priests:* The nation of Israel will be the means through which My rulership is publicized throughout

the world. For you will act as My stewards in serving Me.

RABBI AVRAHAM BEN HARAMBAM

מַמְלֶכֶת כֹּהֲנִים – *A kingdom of priests:* What does God imply by referring to Israel as a kingdom of priests? In every community, the priest's role is to serve as the honorable leader and as the role model whom everyone strives to emulate. It is the priest who directs the people along life's correct path. Hence God's message to Israel is as follows: When you observe My Torah, you will elevate yourselves to the guardianship of the world, much in the way a priest teaches and shapes his flock. The other nations will study your behavior, mimic your actions, and walk in your ways. Now our Sages explain why God refers to Israel as "a kingdom of priests" and does not simply say: "You shall be priests to Me." According to them, Israel will possess both the respect and the authority that are the province of monarchs. Thus, God wants Israel to function as rulers and leaders

in the world. They will be priests for whomever chooses to learn from their example. But should some ignore the teachings that Israel promotes to humanity, our nation will be empowered by the sword of Moshe to impose God's true faith over all peoples. What I mean by this is that Israel has the right and obligation to ensure that people across the globe accept the unity of God and agree to abide by the seven Noahide laws, which are incumbent upon all human beings. God demands that the entirety of the Israelite nation become holy. It is insufficient for some people to live as righteous and elevated representatives of God's word while others remain licentious sinners. Rather, the entire nation is expected to observe God's commandments, since every distinct law promotes sanctity.

RAMBAN

וְגוֹי קָדוֹשׁ – *And a holy nation:* You have a responsibility to cleave to your holy God, as a later verse states: *You shall be holy: for I the Lord*

your God am holy (Leviticus 19:2). This would guarantee Israel's flourishing in this world as well as in the next.

6 Mine. A kingdom of priests and a holy nation you shall be
to Me. These are the words you must speak to the Israelites."

7 So Moshe came and summoned the elders of the people, ḤAMISHI
and set before them all that the LORD had commanded him.

ABARBANEL

מַמְלֶכֶת כֹּהֲנִים – *A kingdom of priests:* In one notable midrash, a Midianite is quoted as asking whether submission to a life of Torah observance provides the adherent with freedom and tranquility, or whether such obedience to God constitutes a life of slavery and surrender. The response to this was that because the halakhic lifestyle guides the individual toward the perfection of character and beliefs, acceptance of the system elevates rather than lowers the person. Hence God refers to Israel as a kingdom of priests: While the nation serves God and ministers to him like priests, they are exalted to a position of kingship. They thereby become the most honored people in the land, a free nation, and a class of princes.

SFORNO

מַמְלֶכֶת כֹּהֲנִים – *A kingdom of priests:* Once you become a kingdom of priests, you will be treasured by the rest of world, as you educate all of humanity to invoke the name of God and to serve Him exclusively. Such will be Israel's role in the future. **וְגוֹי קָדוֹשׁ** – *And a holy nation:* You will be a nation that endures forever among the other groups of the world, as the verse states: *And it shall come to pass, that he that is left in Zion, and he that remains in Jerusalem, shall be called holy* (Isaiah 4:3). Now when God gave Israel the Torah, that was His intention – that Israel be provided with only a good future. However, the construction of the golden calf corrupted their ways, as the verse states: *So the Israelites stripped themselves of their finery from Mount Ḥorev onward* (33:6).

VERSE 7

IBN EZRA

וַיָּבֹא מֹשֶׁה – *So Moshe came:* Moshe returned to the Israelite camp. There was no need for the Torah to state that he first came down from the mountain. **וַיָּשֶׂם לִפְנֵיהֶם** – *And set before them:* The terminology echoes the verse, *And this is the Torah which Moshe set before the children of Israel* (Deuteronomy 4:44). Rav Se'adya Gaon relates the verb to the verse *Now therefore write this poem for yourselves, and teach it the children of Israel: put [simah] it in their mouths* (Deuteronomy 31:19), implying that our verse too refers to the Oral Law which acts as an interpretation to the Written Law.

RAMBAN

וַיָּשֶׂם לִפְנֵיהֶם – *And set before them:* Moshe exclaimed to Israel: Behold! I have repeated to you all the words of God. Now you must decide today whether you will fulfill them or not. In response, the people proclaimed: *All that the LORD has spoken we will do* (19:8).

ח אֲשֶׁר־צִוָּהוּ יהוה: וַיַּעֲנוּ כָל־הָעָם יַחְדָּו וַיֹּאמְרוּ כָּל אֲשֶׁר־
דִּבֶּר יהוה נַעֲשֶׂה וַיָּשֶׁב מֹשֶׁה אֶת־דִּבְרֵי הָעָם אֶל־יהוה:
ט וַיֹּאמֶר יהוה אֶל־מֹשֶׁה הִנֵּה אָנֹכִי בָּא אֵלֶיךָ בְּעַב הֶעָנָן
בַּעֲבוּר יִשְׁמַע הָעָם בְּדַבְּרִי עִמָּךְ וְגַם־בְּךָ יַאֲמִינוּ לְעוֹלָם

VERSE 8

RASHI

וַיָּשֶׁב מֹשֶׁה אֶת־דִּבְרֵי הָעָם – *Moshe brought their answer back:* Moshe conveyed the people's response back to God on the third day. [After the nation said: *All that the Lord has spoken we will do* (19:8) on the second day, Moshe waited until the next day and] ascended to God early in the morning. Now why did Moshe have to inform God what the people said [if God is omniscient]? Moshe thereby teaches us appropriate manners, for he could have reasoned: Since the One who sent Me surely knows what the people said, I need not trouble to deliver the message myself.

BEKHOR SHOR

כֹּל אֲשֶׁר־דִּבֶּר יהוה נַעֲשֶׂה – *All that the Lord has spoken we will do:* We are ready to accept anything that God commands us to obey or decrees that we must do.

RAMBAN

וַיָּשֶׁב מֹשֶׁה אֶת־דִּבְרֵי הָעָם – *Moshe brought their answer back:* Moshe returned to God on the mountain, bringing with him Israel's response to God's proposition. Now everything is revealed before God, and He had not asked Moshe to bring him news of how the people reacted to His words. We can see God's omniscience in the verse *And the Lord heard the voice of your words, when you spoke to me* (Deuteronomy 5:25). [Therefore, what was the purpose of Moshe's report to God?] In fact, Moshe brought up the people's answer only in response to God's speech in the coming verse: *I will come to you in a dense cloud, that the people may hear Me speaking to you. They will then believe you forever* (Exodus 19:9). Hereupon Moshe said to God: Master of the Universe! Your children are already a nation of the faithful and they fully accept anything that you say to them.

RABBEINU BAHYA

נַעֲשֶׂה – *We will do:* Israel accepted and acknowledged the responsibility posed by the Torah and its commandments, and it did so willingly. Now, the rabbinic interpretation of this episode [see Shabbat 88a] claims that God suspended the mountain above the nation's heads like a barrel and threatened them, saying: If you agree to undertake all that I demand of you, all will be well. But if you do not, this will be your graveyard! We can reconcile the two approaches by explaining that the latter description refers to the imposition of the Oral Law upon the people. For that system comprises many more warnings, punishments, enactments, and decrees than does the Written Law. Hence, while the Israelites were eager and delighted to adopt the Written Law as their governing way of life, the Oral Law had to be forced upon them.

8 And the people answered as one – "All that the Lord has spoken we will do." Moshe brought their answer back to the Lord.

9 Then the Lord said to Moshe, "I will come to you in a dense cloud, that the people may hear Me speaking to you. They will then believe you forever." When Moshe reported the words of

---

ABARBANEL

וַיָּשֶׁב מֹשֶׁה אֶת־דִּבְרֵי הָעָם – *Moshe brought their answer back:* The text informs us that on the third day Moshe returned to the mountain after hearing the people's response and understanding their willingness to abide by God's rules. Once he arrived on that holy mountain, Moshe isolated himself and sought to learn how exactly the word of God would be transmitted to the nation of Israel. Thereupon God explained to him: *I will come to you in a dense cloud etc.* (19:9).

VERSE 9

RASHI

וְגַם־בְּךָ יַאֲמִינוּ לְעוֹלָם – *They will then believe you forever:* [Literally, "and they will also believe in you forever." Rashi explains the word "also" – *gam*]. The nation will believe both in you and in the prophets who follow you.

וַיַּגֵּד מֹשֶׁה אֶת־דִּבְרֵי – *Moshe reported the words:* [God first offered to speak directly to the people. To this Moshe said:] I have heard from the people that they would prefer to hear the law from You. There is no comparison between receiving a communication firsthand from the king and hearing the declaration from His messenger. We desire to see our king.

RASHBAM

בְּעַב הֶעָנָן – *In a dense cloud:* God revealed Himself this way so that Moshe would not look upon the Divine Presence.

IBN EZRA

וַיַּגֵּד מֹשֶׁה אֶת־דִּבְרֵי – *Moshe reported the words:* Know that the Egyptians and the Indians both descend from Ham [Noah's son] and each culture draws its practices from the other society. For example, the people of India eschew eating meat, a custom that was once prevalent among the citizenry of Egypt. Those people only abandoned their vegetarianism after they were conquered by the Ishmaelites, who forced their religion upon them. In a second example, Indian philosophers cite many arguments that no person who hears the word of God can survive the encounter. When the Israelites were in Egypt, they were exposed to this doctrine, and hence some of them doubted the veracity of Moshe's prophecy. Hence, when God told Moshe: *I will come to you in a dense cloud, that the people may hear Me speaking to you. They will then believe you forever,* He was responding to an earlier claim by Moshe that some Israelites believed prophecy to be impossible. **בְּדַבְּרִי עִמָּךְ** – *Me speaking to you:* When Israel hears Me relating the Ten Commandments to you, they will forever believe that a human being can survive receiving direct communication from God.

י וַיַּגֵּד מֹשֶׁה אֶת־דִּבְרֵי הָעָם אֶל־יהוה: וַיֹּאמֶר יהוה אֶל־
מֹשֶׁה לֵךְ אֶל־הָעָם וְקִדַּשְׁתָּם הַיּוֹם וּמָחָר וְכִבְּסוּ שִׂמְלֹתָם:
יא וְהָיוּ נְכֹנִים לַיּוֹם הַשְּׁלִישִׁי כִּי ׀ בַּיּוֹם הַשְּׁלִישִׁי יֵרֵד יהוה לְעֵינֵי

SFORNO

וְגַם־בְּךָ יַאֲמִינוּ לְעוֹלָם – *They will then believe you forever:* The Israelites never doubted that prophecy was possible, since they were aware that God had spoken with the patriarchs centuries earlier, and that He was currently communicating directly to Moshe, Aharon, and Miriam. However, the people thought that these prophets received the word of God cloaked in visions and dreams, as God Himself confesses when He states: *If there be a prophet among you, I the LORD make Myself*

known to him in a vision, and speak to him in a dream (Numbers 12:6). However the prophecy of Moshe was different, for it was claimed that he heard the word of God while still in complete control of his faculties. It was that form of delivery that the people found difficult to imagine. But after the nation experienced the revelation of God, they were convinced that a fully conscious human being could hear the voice of God and live.

KELI YAKAR

וַיַּגֵּד מֹשֶׁה אֶת־דִּבְרֵי – *Moshe reported the words:* When the Israelites declaimed: *All that the LORD has spoken we will do* (19:8), they meant that they wanted to hear God Himself deliver his commandments to them. Now, initially, Moshe related to God only the fact of Israel's willingness to observe God's laws, but he did not mention Israel's desire to see their King, thinking that certainly God understood this and would honor their wishes. But when God said to Moshe: *I will come to you in a dense cloud, that the people may hear Me speaking to you. They will then believe you forever,* the leader realized that God still intended to employ him as an intermediary for communicating

with Israel. It was then that *Moshe reported the words of the people to the LORD,* verbatim. God approved Israel's request, saying: If that is what they want, *go to the people and consecrate them today and tomorrow* (19:10). For the nation must sanctify themselves before seeing the face of their holy King. And so at first, God did speak directly to Israel [as related in the Talmud, Makkot 23b], pronouncing the first two Commandments in their hearing. But the nation was terrified of the fire and the lightning and retracted their request, preferring that Moshe receive God's message on their behalf and then pass it along to them [as reported in 20:16].

VERSE 10

RASHI

וְקִדַּשְׁתָּם – *And consecrate them:* [Although the word literally means "to consecrate," here it more generally means to] prepare the people.

Have them make themselves ready today and tomorrow.

IBN EZRA

וְקִדַּשְׁתָּם – *And consecrate them:* This means Israel should cleanse themselves with water.

10 the people to the LORD, the LORD said to Moshe, "Go to the people and consecrate them today and tomorrow; let them
11 wash their clothes and be ready for the third day, for on that third day the LORD will descend on Mount Sinai before all

—————— RABBI AVRAHAM BEN HARAMBAM ——————

וְקִדַּשְׁתָּם – *And consecrate them:* This injunction alludes to the Hebrews' need to develop their inner sanctity, as indicated by the following verse, *Be ready for the third day.* Our verse too clarifies the subsequent text: *Even priests who come near to the LORD must first consecrate themselves* (19:22), a statement which must refer to spiritual preparation, since the priests had undoubtedly already dealt with their external cleansing. To achieve inner sanctity means purifying one's heart and expunging all filthy and polluted thoughts from the mind – of which the verse states: *The LORD knows the thoughts of man, that they are vanity* (Psalms 94:11) – and focusing on the transcendent.

—————— RAMBAN ——————

וְקִדַּשְׁתָּם – *And consecrate them:* The method for Israel to reach a state of sanctity was for them to refrain from contact with their wives [since sexual union makes men and women impure] and to avoid all other sources of impurity. For one who has no contact with impurity is deemed "consecrated."

VERSE 11

—————— RASHI ——————

וְהָיוּ נְכֹנִים – *And be ready:* [The men should separate themselves] from their wives [see 19:15]. **לַיּוֹם הַשְּׁלִישִׁי** – *For the third day:* The third day following the preparation would be the sixth of the month. On the fifth day, Moshe occupied himself with building an altar at the foot of the mountain and erecting the twelve monuments mentioned in Parashat Mishpatim (24:4). Those events occurred now, but the Torah does not insist on presenting events precisely in the sequence that they transpired. **לְעֵינֵי כָל־הָעָם** – *Before all the peoples' eyes:* This verse proves that there were no blind individuals among the Israelites, for God had healed all those with impaired vision.

—————— RASHBAM ——————

יֵרֵד יהוה – *The LORD will descend:* The opening to the previous verse, *The LORD said to Moshe,* must in fact refer to an angel speaking to the prophet. That is why our verse describes God's descent from the mountain in the third person, rather than quoting God as saying: "I will descend before the peoples' eyes."

—————— IBN EZRA ——————

וְהָיוּ נְכֹנִים לַיּוֹם הַשְּׁלִישִׁי – *And be ready for the third day:* Perhaps this instruction meant that the Israelites were not to sleep the night before revelation, since they would hear the voice of God in the morning, just as the High Priest would not sleep at all on the night of Yom Kippur.

יב כָּל־הָעָם עַל־הַר סִינָי: וְהִגְבַּלְתָּ אֶת־הָעָם סָבִיב לֵאמֹר
הִשָּׁמְרוּ לָכֶם עֲלוֹת בָּהָר וּנְגֹעַ בְּקָצֵהוּ כָּל־הַנֹּגֵעַ בָּהָר מוֹת
יג יוּמָת: לֹא־תִגַּע בּוֹ יָד כִּי־סָקוֹל יִסָּקֵל אוֹ־יָרֹה יִיָּרֶה אִם־
בְּהֵמָה אִם־אִישׁ לֹא יִחְיֶה בִּמְשֹׁךְ הַיֹּבֵל הֵמָּה יַעֲלוּ בָהָר:

───────────── RAMBAN ─────────────

לְעֵינֵי כָל־הָעָם – *Before all the peoples' eyes:* The entire nation was to witness God's descent on the mountain. The phenomenon is described later: *To the Israelites the appearance of the Lord's glory on the mountaintop was like* consuming *fire* (24:17). That is, the nation could not actually see God, but a manifestation of His presence, as the verse states: *For no one can see Me and live* (33:20).

───────────── SFORNO ─────────────

וְהָיוּ נְכֹנִים – *And be ready:* It is not just the nation's souls which had to be prepared to receive God's communication; their physical bodies as well needed to be purified for the experience. This was because the revelation the Israelites were about to witness was at a level of prophecy termed "face to face," during which the people would be employing their physical senses.

VERSE 12

───────────── RASHI ─────────────

לֵאמֹר – *Tell them:* [Literally, "saying."] It is the boundary itself which will announce: Take care not to ascend the mountain at this point! You, Moshe, will warn them of the punishment.

───────────── SFORNO ─────────────

כָּל־הַנֹּגֵעַ בָּהָר מוֹת יוּמָת – *Anyone who touches the mountain must be put to death:* The fear here was that the people might *force their way through to look at the Lord, and many will die* (19:21). Were this to happen, the divine celebration would be tainted by the impurity of the corpses. Furthermore, because the relatives of the victims would enter a state of mourning, they would not be able to experience the Divine Presence.

VERSE 13

───────────── RASHI ─────────────

יָרֹה יִיָּרֶה – *Or shot with arrows:* [Rashi understands this term as meaning "or hurled down."] This verse teaches that when a court stones a criminal to death, he is first pushed off the roof of a two-story building. **יִיָּרֶה** – *Shot:* [Differing from the translation here, Rashi holds that this term means] "hurled down to the ground." The verb is the same as that in the verse *He hurled [yara] into the sea* (15:4). **בִּמְשֹׁךְ הַיֹּבֵל** – *When the ram's horn sounds a long blast:* When a long blast is heard from a ram's horn, that will signal that the Divine Presence has departed and that

12 the peoples' eyes. Set a boundary for the people around the mountain; tell them to take care not to ascend to it, not even touch its edge. Anyone who touches the mountain must be put
13 to death. No hand shall touch him: he shall be stoned or shot with arrows; beast or man, he shall not live. When the ram's horn sounds a long blast – only then may they go up on the

——————— RASHI *(cont.)* ———————

the voice of God has stopped speaking. Once I have departed from the mountain, the people will be allowed to ascend it. **הַיֹּבֵל** – *The ram's horn:* A *yovel* is a ram's horn, for in Arabic a ram is referred to as a *yuvela* [see Rosh HaShana 26a]. The sound would be produced from the horn of the ram sacrificed in the episode of the binding of Yitzḥak [in Genesis 22].

——————— RASHBAM ———————

לֹא־תִגַּע בּוֹ יָד – *No hand shall touch him:* When I decreed that whoever touches the mountain shall be put to death, the execution must be carried out from a distance. This way no one else will approach the sinner or the mountain, thereby incurring the death penalty themselves. Hence the culprit was to be shot with arrows or pelted with rocks from a distance.

——————— ABARBANEL ———————

בִּמְשֹׁךְ הַיֹּבֵל – *When the ram's horn sounds a long blast:* Rav Se'adya Gaon writes that this verse implies that it was Moshe's job to blow the shofar upon the departure of the Divine Presence from the site. But I must disagree with this interpretation, since the shofar described in this passage is not an instrument that Moshe would have played, but a sound produced by miraculous means. If Rav Se'adya Gaon's view were true, the text ought to have indicated somehow that Moshe himself would be blowing the shofar, but it does not ever state that he did so. In my opinion, the warning issued here endured as long as the Divine Presence rested on the mountain. Mount Sinai was off limits to all during Moshe's stay on its peak, where he received the first set of tablets and petitioned God not to destroy Israel following the incident of the golden calf. The prohibition to climb the mountain even continued while Moshe carved the second set of tablets, a period which lasted until Yom Kippur. After God forgave Israel for their sin, the shofar was sounded as a sign of acquittal and emancipation. And then, just as the shofar was heard throughout the Israelite camp, the Divine Presence departed from Mount Sinai, and rested in the Tent of Meeting between the cherubim [above the Ark of the Covenant].

——————— GUR ARYEH ———————

הַיֹּבֵל – *The ram's horn:* According to Rashi, the horn used on this occasion came from the ram sacrificed during the binding of Yitzḥak. The significance of this is that God does not use the same sort of instrument that a human being might play. He employs the unique and sacred horn from the animal consecrated to God in Yitzḥak's stead.

יד וַיֵּרֶד מֹשֶׁה מִן־הָהָר אֶל־הָעָם וַיְקַדֵּשׁ אֶת־הָעָם וַיְכַבְּסוּ
טו שִׂמְלֹתָם: וַיֹּאמֶר אֶל־הָעָם הֱיוּ נְכֹנִים לִשְׁלֹשֶׁת יָמִים
טז אַל־תִּגְּשׁוּ אֶל־אִשָּׁה: וַיְהִי בַיּוֹם הַשְּׁלִישִׁי בִּהְיֹת הַבֹּקֶר
וַיְהִי קֹלֹת וּבְרָקִים וְעָנָן כָּבֵד עַל־הָהָר וְקֹל שֹׁפָר חָזָק

VERSE 14

RASHI

מִן־הָהָר אֶל־הָעָם – *From the mountain to the people:* [Although the words "to the people" appear to be superfluous, in fact] they teach something: When Moshe descended from the

mountain, he did not attend to his own business, but went immediately to the people in order to sanctify them.

RAMBAN

וַיֵּרֶד מֹשֶׁה – *So Moshe came down:* We can infer from this verse that Moshe was on the mountain when God said to him: *Go to the*

people and consecrate them (19:10). For Moshe ascended the mountain every time that he wanted to address God.

VERSE 15

RASHI

הֱיוּ נְכֹנִים לִשְׁלֹשֶׁת יָמִים – *Be ready for the third day:* [Literally, "be ready for three days." Simply understood, this means:] "Be ready following three days of preparation," i.e., for the fourth day [in contrast to God's directive in verse 11 to prepare for the "third day"]. Moshe thus added an extra day of his own volition. Such is the opinion of Rabbi Yosei [who in the Talmud argues that revelation took place on the seventh day of the month]. But according to the opinion that the Ten Commandments were pronounced on the sixth day of the month, Moshe did not add an extra day to Israel's preparation. Rather, the phrase in our verse simply means "be ready for the third

day." אַל־תִּגְּשׁוּ אֶל־אִשָּׁה – *Do not draw close to your wives:* Israel must separate from their wives during the three preparatory days, so that after three days the women may immerse and enter a state of purity before receiving the Torah. There was concern that if a couple were intimate during that period, the woman might expel residual semen after having immersed, which would make her impure again. However, if all women were to stay apart from their husbands for three days, any semen in their bodies from beforehand would surely have already putrefied and lost the ability to fertilize – and hence would no longer be impure – by the time of revelation.

IBN EZRA

הֱיוּ נְכֹנִים לִשְׁלֹשֶׁת יָמִים – *Be ready for the third day:* [Literally, "be ready for three days."] Israel was to be ready to receive God on the third day. According to the straightforward meaning of the text, Moshe did not add a third day of preparation to Israel's schedule [see Rashi.]

And I have evidence from the Torah for my position that the phrase *lishloshet yamim* can mean "for the third day." Firstly, during Yosef's confrontation with his brothers, the verse states: *And he put them all together into custody for three days [sheloshet yamim]* (Genesis

14 mountain." So Moshe came down from the mountain to the people; he consecrated them and they cleansed their clothes.
15 "Be ready for the third day," he told them, "and do not draw
16 close to your wives." The third day came; and that morning there was thunder and lightning and a dense cloud on the mountain and the sound of a ram's horn, intensely loud, and

—————————— IBN EZRA *(cont.)* ——————————

42:17), after which the text reports: *Yosef said to them on the third day [bayom hashelishi]* [Genesis 42:18, proving that these forms mean the same thing]. Earlier in the same narrative, Yosef warns the chief baker that *within another three days [sheloshet yamim] shall*

Pharaoh lift up your head from off you (40:19). The baker is killed as predicted: *And it came to pass on the third day [bayom hashelishi], which was Pharaoh's birthday...* [Genesis 40:20, once again showing that the terms are interchangeable].

—————————— ABARBANEL ——————————

הֱיוּ נְכֹנִים לִשְׁלֹשֶׁת יָמִים – *Be ready for the third day:* Moshe had no need to warn Israel to avoid excess eating and drinking during the preparatory period, since there were no Israelites who were drunkards or gluttons. After all, the people's diet consisted solely of cold water and the manna, which they referred to as "the miserable food" (Numbers 21:5). It is also

possible that during the three days of preparation the people did not engage in commerce or unnecessary labor. Instead, they spent their time contemplating the wonders that God was performing on their behalf, and hearing words of wisdom and reproach from Israel's elders and scholars.

VERSE 16

—————————— RASHI ——————————

בִּהְיֹת הַבֹּקֶר – *That morning:* We learn from this phrase that God arrived at the mountain before His audience did. This is never appropriate when a teacher addresses his students – it is most improper for a rabbi to have to sit and wait for his class. Yet we find a similar occurrence described elsewhere: *And*

the hand of the Lᴏʀᴅ was there upon me; and He said to me, Arise, go out into the plain, and I will talk with you there. Then I arose, and went out into the plain: and, behold, the glory of the Lᴏʀᴅ stood there, as the glory which I saw by the river Kevar: and I fell on my face (Ezekiel 3:22–23).

—————————— KELI YAKAR ——————————

וַיְהִי קֹלֹת וּבְרָקִים – *There was thunder and lightning:* Various commentators attempt to explain the nature of these audial and visual displays, with each author suggesting a different homiletical approach based on his understanding. It seems to me that, in a sense, the thunder and lightning presented in an opposite manner to the shofar blast.

For when thunder is heard emanating from the clouds, it rumbles briefly and dissipates. Lightning, of course, is even quicker, flashing momentarily and then vanishing. However, as the Torah attests: *The sound of the ram's horn grew louder and louder* (19:19). The two rates of these phenomena symbolize two different types of individuals who received the

יז מְאֹד וַיֶּחֱרַד כָּל־הָעָם אֲשֶׁר בַּמַּחֲנֶה: וַיּוֹצֵא מֹשֶׁה אֶת־
הָעָם לִקְרַאת הָאֱלֹהִים מִן־הַמַּחֲנֶה וַיִּתְיַצְּבוּ בְּתַחְתִּית
יח הָהָר: וְהַר סִינַי עָשַׁן כֻּלּוֹ מִפְּנֵי אֲשֶׁר יָרַד עָלָיו יהוה בָּאֵשׁ
יט וַיַּעַל עֲשָׁנוֹ כְּעֶשֶׁן הַכִּבְשָׁן וַיֶּחֱרַד כָּל־הָהָר מְאֹד: וַיְהִי קוֹל
הַשֹּׁפָר הוֹלֵךְ וְחָזֵק מְאֹד מֹשֶׁה יְדַבֵּר וְהָאֱלֹהִים יַעֲנֶנּוּ בְקוֹל:

—————————— KELI YAKAR *(cont.)* ——————————

Torah: aged scholars and elderly laypeople. While the first type of person becomes wiser in time, the second group begins to lose their faculties. Similarly, the instrument blowing at this time, which was from Yitzḥak's ram [see Rashi] and was hence associated with that righteous man, sounded with a voice that grew in strength. Like that music, Torah scholars constantly grow in wisdom and vigor. However, the regular thick cloud symbolized

the materialistic lay community, whose sparks shine only fleetingly. Indeed, our Sages explain that the term "shofar" derives from the phrase *shipperu maaseikhem* ["improve your ways"], an idea that corresponds to my point exactly. The shofar was also an allusion to the merit Yitzḥak had earned, credit that continues to grow and reverberate throughout the generations.

VERSE 17

—————————— RASHI ——————————

לִקְרַאת הָאֱלֹהִים – *To meet God:* This phrase informs us that the Divine Presence went out to greet Israel like a groom hurries to receive his bride. This explains Moshe's later declamation: *The Lord came from Sinai* (Deuteronomy 33:2), for that verse does not say that God came to Sinai but from Sinai. **בְּתַחְתִּית הָהָר** – *At the foot of the mountain:* [Alternatively, "under the

mountain."] The straightforward meaning of this phrase is that Israel stood at the bottom of the hill. But the Midrash explains that God uprooted the mountain and held it above the Israelites' head like a barrel [threatening to destroy the people should they refuse to accept His Torah].

—————————— IBN EZRA ——————————

וַיִּתְיַצְּבוּ בְּתַחְתִּית הָהָר – *And they stood at the foot of the mountain:* The people of Israel stood at attention at Mount Sinai much in the same way that their children assembled forty years later to hear Moshe establish the covenant with them [in Deuteronomy 29:9, where the same verb is used]. At the front of the crowd were the firstborn sons, who would minister to God. Behind them stood the tribal leaders, the princes of Israel, followed by the elders and the nation's officers. The men were next,

and they stood in front of the children, who in turn were positioned in front of the women. Bringing up the rear were the foreign converts. Meanwhile, Moshe and Aharon passed beyond the boundary and ascended the mountain near the priests. We know that this was so, even though the Torah does not spell out this description explicitly, since Moshe and Aharon clearly would not have violated God's command, *Go down, and come back together with Aharon* (19:24).

17 all the people in the camp shook. Then Moshe led the people out of the camp to meet God, and they stood at the foot
18 of the mountain. Mount Sinai was enveloped in smoke because the LORD had descended on it in fire. Smoke billowed up from it as if from a furnace, and the mountain shook violently as one.
19 lently as one. As the sound of the ram's horn grew louder and

———————— BEKHOR SHOR ————————

וַיּוֹצֵא מֹשֶׁה אֶת־הָעָם – *Then Moshe led the people out:* Moshe led the people out because they were terrified to come out on their own.

VERSE 18

———————— RASHI ————————

הַכִּבְשָׁן – *A furnace:* A furnace made of lime. Now since the text uses this metaphor, we might have thought that the mountain burned just like a normal, everyday furnace. But a separate verse elaborates: *And you came near and stood under the mountain; and the mountain burned with fire to the heart of heaven* (Deuteronomy 4:11). Why then does our text employ the image of a furnace? To help the reader understand the event by appealing to our experience. We similarly read the verse: *They shall walk after the LORD, who shall roar like* a lion (Hosea 11:10). Is it not God himself who gives the lion the power to roar? And yet, the prophet is content to compare Him to a lion! Rather, Scripture uses imagery of God's own creatures to help us grasp what we essentially cannot know. Again, we find the verse: *And His voice was like the sound of many waters* (Ezekiel 43:2) – did God Himself not provide the waters with their sound? How does the text describe Him in terms of His creations, which are lesser than Him? This too is written to be accessible to our understanding.

———————— RABBEINU BAHYA ————————

וְהַר סִינַי עָשַׁן כֻּלּוֹ – *Mount Sinai was enveloped in smoke:* It was the mountain itself which discharged smoke, not the fire. For the fire that appears before God's glory does not emit smoke.

VERSE 19

———————— RASHI ————————

הוֹלֵךְ וְחָזֵק מְאֹד – *Grew louder and louder:* Normally, as a person continues to blow a horn, the sound becomes weaker and muted as the musician becomes winded. However, in this case, the sound grew increasingly stronger. And why did the tone start off softer and become louder? Because the people would not have been able to cope with such a powerful noise to begin with. **מֹשֶׁה יְדַבֵּר** – *Moshe spoke:* The people heard only the first two commandments directly from God – *I am the LORD your* God who brought you out of the land of Egypt, out of the house of slaves, and Have no other gods than Me (20:2–3). The other statements were first conveyed to Moshe, who then repeated the information to the nation. Meanwhile, God amplified Moshe's voice when he addressed Israel so that everyone could hear him. **יַעֲנֶנּוּ בְקוֹל** – *Answered him aloud:* The phrase means "answered him with a voice" [the letter *bet* prefixed to the word *vekol* means "with" or "by"]. We similarly find the verse *And*

ששי כ וַיֵּרֶד יהוה עַל־הַר סִינַי אֶל־רֹאשׁ הָהָר וַיִּקְרָא יהוה לְמֹשֶׁה

———————————————— **RASHI** *(cont.)* ————————————————

the God that answers by fire [va'esh], let him be God [I Kings 18:24; describing the demonstration

on Mount Carmel], meaning that the God who answers by bringing down the fire.

———————————————— **RASHBAM** ————————————————

מֹשֶׁה יְדַבֵּר – *Moshe spoke:* When Moshe spoke to God his voice was not audible to any of the onlookers. However, God "answered him

aloud," in deafening tones, so as to be heard over the *ram's horn [which] grew louder and louder.*

———————————————— **IBN EZRA** ————————————————

יַעֲנֶנּוּ בְקוֹל – *Answered him aloud:* According to Rav Se'adya Gaon, God periodically sounded the shofar, at which point Moshe would speak in a great voice, and God would subsequently respond with His own "voice" [*kol*], as a later verse states: *Then he heard the voice [kol] speaking to him* [Numbers 7:89; showing

that *kol* can indicate speech, not just a word-less sound]. This is what God meant when He spoke of how *the people may hear Me speaking to you* (Exodus 19:9). However, in my opinion, that phrase refers to the point when God related the Ten Commandments to Moshe.

———————————————— **RAMBAN** ————————————————

יַעֲנֶנּוּ בְקוֹל – *Answered him aloud:* According to the Mekhilta, this verse refers to the actual giving of the Torah, when Moshe pronounced the Ten Commandments to the nation. Rashi accepts this approach as well. And yet, according to the straightforward meaning of this verse, no commandments had yet been uttered at this point. Rather, here, on the third day, the glory of God descended upon the mountain, whereupon *Moshe led the people out of the camp to meet God,* who was appearing to them, *and they stood at the foot of the mountain* (19:17). Moshe then climbed the mountain, stopping just before its summit where the glory of God rested. There he positioned himself in an area set aside for him and from which he spoke to the nation, instructing

them what to do. And as Israel stood there, they heard the voice of God talking to Moshe and commanding him, but they were unable to make out exactly what God was saying. In fact, God was communicating to Moshe the orders we read subsequently: *Go back down – warn the people etc.* (19:21), and *Go down, and come back together with Aharon* (19:24), directions which God imparted before the giving of the Torah and the proclaiming of the Ten Commandments. According to some authors, the sound of the ram's horn growing louder and louder terrified Israel. At that early stage, Moshe would warn the nation to focus their thoughts, for they were about to hear the voice of God, and immediately, *God answered him aloud.*

VERSE 20

———————————————— **RASHI** ————————————————

וַיֵּרֶד יהוה עַל־הַר סִינַי – *And the LORD descended on Mount Sinai:* One might suppose that God actually came down onto the mountain, had

not a different verse stated: *You yourselves have seen that I, from the heavens, have spoken to you* (20:19). How can we reconcile these

20 louder, Moshe spoke and God answered him aloud. And the SHISHI
   LORD descended on Mount Sinai, to the top of the mountain,

———————————— RASHI *(cont.)* ————————————

two descriptions? By saying that God folded the upper and the lower heavens and spread them on the mountain like one would lay out a blanket on a bed. Thereupon the divine throne descended and rested upon these layers of sky.

———————————— IBN EZRA ————————————

וַיִּקְרָא יהוה לְמֹשֶׁה – *And the LORD called to Moshe:* The reason God called Moshe was to enhance the leader's standing among the people. For now they would watch as Moshe climbed to the peak of the mountain where the glory of God rested. The prophet's words would issue from within the fire on the summit there.

———————————— RAMBAN ————————————

וַיֵּרֶד יהוה עַל־הַר סִינַי – *And the LORD descended on Mount Sinai:* If you examine this passage, you will understand that God's great name [the Tetragrammaton, rendered here as "LORD"] descended upon Mount Sinai and dwelled there within the fire. It was from that location that God communicated to Moshe down below, speaking to him while always using exclusively that name [while the surrounding cloud hosted a more imminent aspect of God, expressed by the name *Elohim*], as I have explained in my commentary to verse 3. God cautioned Moshe to *go back down – warn the people not to force their way to look at the LORD* (19:21), meaning that even the nation's nobility would not be permitted to look upon this most sublime manifestation [instead, they only "looked upon God – *Elohim*"; see 24:11]. The entire people heard the voice of "the LORD" emanating from the fire. And even though the verse states: *Then God [Elohim] spoke all these words* (20:1), our Sages teach in the Mekhilta that this term was only used to emphasize God's judgment of transgressors. As our Sages teach elsewhere (Makkot 24a), Israel heard the commandments directly from the Almighty Himself. Note that the scene is later described as follows: *These words the LORD spoke to all your assembly* (Deuteronomy 5:19), straight out of the mountain's fire. We also see the verse, *The LORD talked with you face to face in the mountain out of the midst of the fire* (Deuteronomy 5:4). And all this explains why the first commandment uses this name: *I am the LORD your God* (Exodus 20:2). Now, one might argue that the nation are later quoted as saying to Moshe: *For who is there of all flesh, that has heard the voice of the living God [Elohim] speaking out of the midst of the fire, as we have, and lived?* (Deuteronomy 5:23). But this verse presents no difficulty, since the people do not actually speak of having heard "God" but rather "the voice of God." The people were speaking merely of what they were able to comprehend with their own senses. Hence the nation petitions Moshe [whose faculties were on a much higher level]: *Go you near, and hear all that the LORD our God shall say, and speak to us all that the LORD our God shall speak to you* (Deuteronomy 5:24).

———————————— HIZKUNI ————————————

עַל־הַר סִינַי – *On Mount Sinai:* God intentionally did not wait to give the Torah to the people until after they entered the land of Israel. This was to preclude the nations of the world later arguing that they owe no fealty to God's word since it was not revealed in their own lands.

כא אֶל־רֹאשׁ הָהָר וַיַּעַל מֹשֶׁה: וַיֹּאמֶר יהוה אֶל־מֹשֶׁה רֵד
הָעֵד בָּעָם פֶּן־יֶהֶרְסוּ אֶל־יהוה לִרְאוֹת וְנָפַל מִמֶּנּוּ רָב:
כב וְגַם הַכֹּהֲנִים הַנִּגָּשִׁים אֶל־יהוה יִתְקַדָּשׁוּ פֶּן־יִפְרֹץ בָּהֶם
כג יהוה: וַיֹּאמֶר מֹשֶׁה אֶל־יהוה לֹא־יוּכַל הָעָם לַעֲלֹת אֶל־
הַר סִינָי כִּי־אַתָּה הַעֵדֹתָה בָּנוּ לֵאמֹר הַגְבֵּל אֶת־הָהָר

──────────── HIZKUNI *(cont.)* ────────────

[That is, since the Torah was given in neutral territory, it has a claim on all peoples.] Another reason for this procedure was to avoid internal struggles among the tribes of Israel, who would each vie to host the divine revelation. The name Sin appearing in Scripture [see e.g.,

17:1] is synonymous with Sinai; its name was altered after the Ten Commandments were pronounced there. [The letter *yod,* appended to the word "Sin" to produce "Sinai," has a numerical value of ten.]

VERSE 21

──────────── RASHI ────────────

הָעֵד בָּעָם – *Warn the people:* Caution Israel not to climb up the mountain. **פֶּן־יֶהֶרְסוּ** – *Not to force their way:* [Literally, "lest they destroy."] Rashi explains the sense of the verb:] Lest they impair their position by approaching the mountain through their desire to "look at the Lᴏʀᴅ." **וְנָפַל מִמֶּנּוּ רָב** – *Or many will die:*

Even if only a single person should die due to such an infraction, I deem it to be too many. **פֶּן־יֶהֶרְסוּ** – *Not to force their way:* Scripture uses the term *harisa* in the sense of disassembling component parts of a structure. Here too, the verb connotes that violators will upset the cohesion of the nation.

──────────── IBN EZRA ────────────

פֶּן־יֶהֶרְסוּ – *Not to force their way:* The people are mistaken if they think that they are

honoring Me, when really they are trying to satisfy their own craving to see My glory.

──────────── BEKHOR SHOR ────────────

וְנָפַל מִמֶּנּוּ רָב – *Or many will die:* In a great plague.

──────────── RABBEINU BAḤYA ────────────

וְנָפַל מִמֶּנּוּ רָב – *Or many will die:* Should even a single individual Israelite perish, it will be as if the entire creation of the world has become

undone. This interpretation explains why the verb *venafal* appears in the singular rather than the plural *veyippelu.*

──────────── SFORNO ────────────

הָעֵד בָּעָם – *Warn the people:* When I address them, the Israelites might believe that since they have achieved the power of prophecy and are speaking with God face to face, that

they have reached your level, Moshe. They may therefore attempt to ascend the mountain to the platform set aside for you.

and called Moshe to the mountaintop, and Moshe ascended.

21 The LORD told Moshe, "Go back down – warn the people not to force their way through to look at the LORD, or many will
22 die. Even priests who come near to the LORD must first consecrate themselves, or the LORD will break out against them."
23 Moshe replied to the LORD, "The people cannot climb Mount Sinai. You Yourself warned us to set a boundary around the

---

VERSE 22

RASHI

וְגַם הַכֹּהֲנִים – *Even priests:* This refers to the firstborn sons of Israel, who were initially charged with performing the sacrificial service [before being replaced by the sons of Aharon and the Levites; see Numbers 3:12]. הַנִּגָּשִׁים אֶל־יהוה – *Who come near to the LORD:* Even priests, who generally are permitted to approach God for the sake of offering sacrifices, must not trust in their status and ascend the mountain. יִתְקַדָּשׁוּ – *Must first consecrate themselves:* The priests should prepare themselves to take up their positions. פֶּן־יִפְרֹץ – *Will break out:* The verb means "to breach" – God might kill some of them and create a gap in the nation.

HIZKUNI

וְגַם הַכֹּהֲנִים – *Even priests:* This warning is directed at the seventy elders, who were all firstborn sons. יִתְקַדָּשׁוּ – *Must first consecrate themselves:* This group too must prepare itself and be ready to receive the revelation. They must not assure themselves that because they are already practiced in the service of God and are familiar with His demands, that they need not ready themselves. Another interpretation for this clause: The term "priests" refers to the nation's officers and judges. These men are said to "come near to the LORD" when they teach the law to the nation, as the verse states: *For the judgment is God's* (Deuteronomy 1:17). Here God cautions the judges not to excuse their lack of preparation by saying that they are too busy studying the laws and statutes. The verse cannot be referring to the actual priestly class, since at this early stage those priests had not yet been designated.

RALBAG

וְגַם הַכֹּהֲנִים – *Even priests:* It seems to me that the term "priests" refers to the sons of Aharon, who would be so called in the future. Our verse predicts that the priests will be those *who come near to the LORD* [to perform the sacrificial services]. Aharon's sons thus held the potential to be priests and to *come near to the LORD* even though in practice they had not yet obtained the title, nor the office. [Hence they were ultimately allowed to approach; see 24:9.]

VERSE 23

RASHI

לֹא־יוּכַל הָעָם – *The people cannot:* Moshe assured God that he need not warn the nation again, for they had remained on notice for three days and would not ascend the mountain without permission.

כד וְקִדַּשְׁתּוֹ: וַיֹּאמֶר אֵלָיו יהוה לֶךְ־רֵד וְעָלִיתָ אַתָּה וְאַהֲרֹן
עִמָּךְ וְהַכֹּהֲנִים וְהָעָם אַל־יֶהֶרְסוּ לַעֲלֹת אֶל־יהוה פֶּן־יִפְרָץ־

—————————— RASHBAM ——————————

לֹא־יוּכַל הָעָם – *The people cannot:* According to Rashi, Moshe informed God that the nation had already been warned not to climb the mountain for three days. Hence in our verse, Moshe asks why God cautions the people a second time to avoid approaching it. But Rashi here errs in his understanding of Moshe's response. For even though a warning to behave in a certain way might be issued in advance, at the time that the prohibition actually comes into effect, it is perfectly normal to remind the subjects to take extra precautions. People are thus told: "Remember when you were told that you would have to act in such a way? Well, the hour to comply has arrived." Furthermore, at first glance, the next verse, *The Lord said to him, "Go down, and come back together with Aharon"* (19:24) seems to add no new information at all. In truth, the verse represents an answer that the Holy One, blessed be He, supplies to Moshe in response to a question he posed. For Moshe turned to God and asked as follows. Two days ago, when You told me that Israel was prohibited from climbing the mountain, You said: *Tell them to take care not to ascend to it* (19:12). But now, because You say: *Warn the people not to force their way through to look at the Lord* (19:21), I am trying to understand exactly how much is forbidden to them. Are the Israelites not permitted to even approach the mountain a bit while viewing it from a distance? The Holy One, blessed be He, answered, *Go down, and come back together with Aharon. But do not let the priests or people force their way through to come up to the Lord* (19:24), meaning, that what is forbidden is to ascend the mountain, whereas gazing at the mountain without climbing it is allowed.

—————————— IBN EZRA ——————————

לֹא־יוּכַל הָעָם – *The people cannot:* Rav Se'adya Gaon admits that the purpose of this verse troubled him for many years [since Moshe seems to be merely repeating God's commandment of verse 12]. However, the Gaon subsequently stumbled upon a book describing the court procedures of Persian kings. In this tome he read that a royal messenger is not permitted to report on a mission accomplished until the monarch has commanded him to embark on a new task. Only then may the agent claim to have fulfilled his previous job. [Thus in our case, only after God has issued a new command in verse 21 telling Moshe to caution the nation not to gaze at God, does Moshe have license to report in verse 23 that he has done what he was told in verse 12, namely, warned the nation not to climb Mount Sinai.] In my opinion, this verse reflects Moshe's uncertainty about God's intentions. God had just stated: *Warn the people not to force their way through to look at the Lord* (19:21), it was unclear to Moshe whether he was really meant to tell the people that it was prohibited to stare at God. For he had already told Israel not to pass the boundary in front of the mountain, and he did not understand if he was meant to issue a second warning. In response, *the Lord said to him, "Go down"* (19:24) as I have commanded you. For Israel did have to be warned a second time.

24 mountain and consecrate it." The LORD said to him, "Go down,
and come back together with Aharon. But do not let the priests

VERSE 24

RASHI

רֵד לֶךְ – *Go down:* God instructed Moshe
to return to the people and to warn them
a second time, for it is advisable to caution
a person in advance and then once again
when the warning becomes applicable.
וְעָלִיתָ אַתָּה וְאַהֲרֹן עִמָּךְ – *And come back
together with Aharon:* [Literally, "and you
come back, etc."] Lest Moshe err and think
that Aharon and the priests were to stand
on the mountain together with him, God

emphasized the word "you." Moshe was to
position himself at his own designated spot
on the mountain, Aharon at his specific place,
and the priests at theirs. And so, Moshe penetrated further into the cloud than did Aharon, who in turn proceeded beyond the limit
set for the priests. The rest of the nation was
not permitted to ruin the situation by "forcing
their way through" even a bit "to come up to
the LORD."

IBN EZRA

רֵד לֶךְ – *Go down:* God instructed Moshe and
Aharon to ascend just past the boundary, such
that they would remain in close proximity to
the nation. God anticipated Israel's response

to hearing the Ten Commandments, which
would be: *Speak to us yourself and we will listen*
[20:16; hence the leaders had to be near the
nation to convey the laws to them].

BEKHOR SHOR

רֵד לֶךְ – *Go down:* God instructed Moshe to
go down the mountain to warn the people
to protect themselves, for God had no desire to harm Israel. This is why God warns the

people repeatedly to stay off the mountain.
He wanted to avoid any misfortune that might
occur while giving Israel the Torah.

RABBI AVRAHAM BEN HARAMBAM

וְהַכֹּהֲנִים וְהָעָם אַל־יֶהֶרְסוּ – *But do not let the
priests or people force their way through:* The
question remains how to reconcile God's earlier statement, *Even priests who come near to
the LORD must first consecrate themselves* (19:22),
with the current warning, *But do not let the
priests or people force their way through to come
up.* For the second verse gives the impression
that the priests are on equal footing with the
rest of the nation. Perhaps the explanation

follows the teaching of my grandfather, of
blessed memory, who suggested in the name
of our Sages that the first verse merely defines the priests as a class of people who are
able to approach God on an intellectual level.
This was so even though the priests were not
permitted to come near to God physically.
Unlike the common masses, the priests were
expected to consecrate themselves through
their thoughts and their mental development.

SFORNO

וְעָלִיתָ אַתָּה וְאַהֲרֹן – *And come back together
with Aharon:* The two men were summoned
up the mountain only after God pronounced
the Ten Commandments, and following the

subsequent material in Parashat Mishpatim,
when the verse states: *Ascend to the LORD, you
and Aharon* (24:1).

כ‎ בָּם: וַיֵּרֶד מֹשֶׁה אֶל־הָעָם וַיֹּאמֶר אֲלֵהֶם: וַיְדַבֵּר
ב‎ אֱלֹהִים אֵת כָּל־הַדְּבָרִים הָאֵלֶּה לֵאמֹר: אָנֹכִי
יהוה אֱלֹהֶיךָ אֲשֶׁר הוֹצֵאתִיךָ מֵאֶרֶץ מִצְרַיִם מִבֵּית עֲבָדִים:

VERSE 25

RASHI

וַיֹּאמֶר אֲלֵהֶם – *And told them:* He repeated the warning as instructed.

IBN EZRA

וַיֵּרֶד מֹשֶׁה אֶל־הָעָם – *So Moshe went down to the people:* When Moshe finished passing along God's message to the people, he and Aharon ascended the mountain beyond the border. Immediately, God began to speak.

CHAPTER 20, VERSE 1

RASHI

וַיְדַבֵּר אֱלֹהִים – *Then God spoke:* Throughout Scripture, the term "God" [*Elohim*] means "judge." Sometimes, the Torah discusses actions that merit reward should a person perform them, but which incur no punishment if ignored. Lest one think that the Ten Commandments fall into such a category, straightaway the Torah states: *Then God spoke* – implying that retribution will attend violation of these laws, since God is a judge who punishes. **אֵת כָּל־הַדְּבָרִים הָאֵלֶּה** – *All these words:* The addition of the word "all" [*kol*] teaches that God spoke all Ten Commandments in a single utterance, a feat of which the human mouth is incapable. But if that were so, why does the text proceed to record the separate statements, *I am the Lord your God, Have no other gods etc.* (20:2–14)? After enunciating the entire text simultaneously, God repeated the material sentence by sentence. **וַיְדַבֵּר אֱלֹהִים אֵת כָּל־הַדְּבָרִים הָאֵלֶּה לֵאמֹר** – *Then God spoke all these words:* [The term *lemor* – literally, "to say" – can be understood as a command to the listener to repeat what is being said. Rashi explains:] The word *lemor* teaches that after every positive commandment Israel responded "yes," and "no" after every negative commandment.

IBN EZRA

אֵת כָּל־הַדְּבָרִים הָאֵלֶּה – *All these words:* This text records the Ten Commandments exactly as pronounced by God during revelation, for the passage begins by stating, *Then God spoke all these words* – from the opening statement of *I am the Lord your God* until the final words, *or anything else that is your neighbor's* (20:14). The Ten Commandments are recorded in this passage as a direct citation of God's communication to Israel without any additions or omissions. Only the text we read here was engraved on the stone tablets, contrary to the opinion of Rav Se'adya Gaon, that the statement *Remember the Sabbath to keep it holy* (20:8) appeared on the first tablets, whereas the alternative text *Keep the Sabbath day to sanctify it* (Deuteronomy 5:12) was written on the second tablets. [Hence, in Rav Se'adya Gaon's view, the discrepancy between the language of the Ten Commandments as quoted here and in Deuteronomy.] In my opinion, the version of the Ten Commandments appearing in Parashat Va'ethanan represents Moshe's review of these pronouncements. Note how that text is twice marked by Moshe's interpolation, *As the Lord your God has commanded you* (Deuteronomy 5:14–15).

or people force their way through to come up to the Lᴏʀᴅ,
25 or He will break out against them." So Moshe went down to
20 1 the people and told them.   Then God spoke all these
2 words: "I am the Lᴏʀᴅ your God who brought you

BEKHOR SHOR

וַיְדַבֵּר אֱלֹהִים – *Then God spoke:* When Moshe spoke, he stood between God and Israel. However, when the nation heard the Ten Commandments, they received the communication directly from God. Still, our Sages claim that Israel only heard the first two first commandments – *I am the Lᴏʀᴅ your God* (20:2) and *Have no other gods than Me* (20:3) – from the mouth of the Almighty, while the rest of the text was transmitted to Moshe alone and he repeated them to the people. Indeed, Rabbi Yosef Kara argues that the language of the first two statements appears to reflect the speech of God [appearing as they do in the first person], while the text starting from *Do not speak the name of the Lᴏʀᴅ your God in vain* [20:7, which refers to God in the third person] seems to have been uttered first to an intermediary to then be conveyed to the nation.

GUR ARYEH

אֵת כָּל־הַדְּבָרִים הָאֵלֶּה – *All these words:* According to Rashi, the language of this verse demonstrates how God uttered the entire text of the Ten Commandments in a single pronouncement. God spoke to Israel this way, even though the people were unable to understand such communication, because He wanted to convey to His nation the idea that the entire Torah represents a unified whole and stands as a single composition emanating from God. For the text of the Ten Commandments encompasses the complete scope of the Torah. Just as the Ten Commandments were declared as a single statement, the whole Torah was similarly given as one proclamation. This message answers those who, although accepting the majority of the Torah as the word of God, nevertheless contend that a particular verse was composed by Moshe himself. Our Sages argue that such a person *has despised the word of the Lᴏʀᴅ* (Numbers 15:31), and his approach is tantamount to a complete rejection of the Torah. Indeed, if the entire text of the Torah comprises one statement, then denying the divine authorship of one portion is the same as challenging the legitimacy of the whole.

VERSE 2

RASHI

אֲשֶׁר הוֹצֵאתִיךָ מֵאֶרֶץ מִצְרָיִם – *Who brought you out of the land of Egypt:* My saving you from Egypt is reason enough for you to serve Me. Another interpretation [for God's mention of the exodus here]: At the Sea of Reeds, God revealed Himself to the people as a fierce warrior, whereas here He appeared to them as a compassionate elder [and so this was a reminder that it was the same God speaking]. Now why does God use the term "your God" [*Elohekha*, as if spoken to an individual rather than to a group]? God expressed Himself this way so as to provide Moshe with an argument in Israel's defense later, when the nation creates the golden calf. When Moshe says to God: *Why, O Lᴏʀᴅ, unleash Your anger against Your people* (32:11), he meant: "You did not command all of them: 'You shall have no other

וְלֹא־יִהְיֶה לְךָ אֱלֹהִים אֲחֵרִים עַל־פָּנָי: לֹא־תַעֲשֶׂה לְךָ פֶּסֶל ₃
וְכָל־תְּמוּנָה אֲשֶׁר בַּשָּׁמַיִם מִמַּעַל וַאֲשֶׁר בָּאָרֶץ מִתָּחַת

———— RASHI *(cont.)* ————

gods than Me.' Rather, when You delivered the Ten Commandments, You were speaking to me alone." **מִבֵּית עֲבָדִים** – *Out of the house of slaves:* I removed you from Pharaoh's house, where you toiled as his slaves. You might think that the phrase "house of slaves" indicates that

the Israelites worked as slaves in the homes of other slaves. However, a later verse states: *He redeemed you from the house of slaves, from the grip of Pharaoh, king of Egypt* (Deuteronomy 7:8), which demonstrates that the Hebrews were the king's slaves and not servants' slaves.

———— BEKHOR SHOR ————

אָנֹכִי יהוה אֱלֹהֶיךָ – *I am the* Lord *your God:* In this first commandment, I enjoin you to accept Me as your master and your judge [the title *Elohim* connotes judgment]. God proceeds to explain why Israel should acknowledge His authority in those roles, since He *brought [them] out of the land of Egypt,* and it therefore behooves them more to worship

God than to serve the Egyptians. Had God proffered his creation of them as justifying their service, the nation could have retorted: Did You not form all the nations of the world? He thereby reminded Israel of the special love He demonstrated toward them, and the favorable treatment they received above and beyond what any other nation had experienced.

———— RAMBAN ————

אָנֹכִי יהוה אֱלֹהֶיךָ – *I am the* Lord *your God:* This first precept represents a positive commandment [and not just an introductory statement of fact]. By declaring: *I am the* Lord, God teaches Israel and commands them to know and to believe that the Lord exists in the world, and that He is their God. Included in this credo is that God is the eternal source

of everything in the world; He intentionally and ably willed the universe into reality. And hence the Lord is Israel's God whom they must worship. God here mentions that He effected Israel's emancipation from Egypt, because that act established the fact of His existence and His willingness to act in the world.

———— HIZKUNI ————

אָנֹכִי יהוה אֱלֹהֶיךָ – *I am the* Lord *your God:* [The word *Elohekha* seems to be addressed to an individual, rather than to a group.] Rabbi Levi taught: The Holy One, blessed be He, appeared to Israel like a statue with faces

on multiple sides. Even though a thousand people might view such an image, it always seems that the picture's eyes are looking at each individual.

———— ABARBANEL ————

אָנֹכִי יהוה אֱלֹהֶיךָ – *I am the* Lord *your God:* My son, listen attentively to my words, and examine carefully the nature of this text, and you will see that the passage of the Ten

Commandments is superior to the rest of the Torah in three ways. Firstly, this oration that Israel heard at Mount Sinai was received directly from God, not via the prophet Moshe

3 out of the land of Egypt, out of the house of slaves. Have no
4 other gods than Me. Do not make for yourself any carved image or likeness of any creature in the heavens above or the earth

———————— ABARBANEL *(cont.)* ————————

like the rest of the commandments were. Secondly, these statements were heard by the entirety of the Israelite nation – from the very young to the aged. Every individual Hebrew witnessed the revelation of the Lord, and saw Him speak to them from within the fire. Thirdly, from the lengthy corpus of the Torah, these verses of the Ten Commandments are the only material that God chose

to inscribe Himself onto tablets of stone. All of this shows the great importance of the Ten Commandments. The superior treatment of these directives leads me to conclude that they contain within them the substance of all 613 commandments that God demands of His nation. The ideas contained therein represent the foundations for the entire Torah.

VERSE 3

———————— RASHI ————————

לֹא־יִהְיֶה לְךָ – *Have no:* Why is this phrase used? Since the subsequent verse states: *Do not make for yourself any carved image etc.* (20:4), we might have thought that it is merely the act of creating the idol which is prohibited. How would we know that we may not possess such items that have been fashioned by other people? Therefore the verse states: *Have no other gods than Me.* אֱלֹהִים אֲחֵרִים – *Other gods:* They are not actually "gods"; rather, "others" have simply crafted them and turned them into objects of belief. [Hence the phrase should properly be translated "gods of others."] It is impossible to explain this phrase as actually meaning "other gods" for it would be

disgraceful to equate false deities to God, and to categorize them all as divinities. Another interpretation for this phrase: "gods which are foreign" to their worshippers. For these mistaken people pray to their false gods and are ignored. Their deities thereby give the impression that their followers are strangers [*aherim*] to them, whom they have never met. עַל־פָּנָי – *Than Me:* [Literally, "before Me."] You may never worship other gods, as long as I exist [i.e., ever]. It was necessary to include this detail, lest future Jews argue that only the first generation of Israelites, whom God "brought out of the land of Egypt," (20:2) were required to abide by this rule.

VERSE 4

———————— ḤIZKUNI ————————

פֶּסֶל וְכָל־תְּמוּנָה – *Any carved image or likeness:* Moshe elsewhere explains the reason for this prohibition, stating: *For you saw no manner of form on the day that the Lord spoke to you in Ḥorev out of the midst of the fire* (Deuteronomy 4:15). This statement precludes Israel fashioning idols and claiming that since God hides His countenance from us so that He cannot be seen, we will make images symbolizing Him

before which we will bow. The phrase *vekhol temuna* [literally, "or any likeness"] is prefaced with a seemingly superfluous conjunctive letter *vav* to teaches that no picture whatsoever may be fashioned when its purpose is to be worshipped, even one with no face represented. For example, statues of the god Mercury included no face at all.

ה וַאֲשֶׁר בַּמַּיִם מִתַּחַת לָאָרֶץ: לֹא־תִשְׁתַּחֲוֶה לָהֶם וְלֹא
תָעָבְדֵם כִּי אָנֹכִי יהוה אֱלֹהֶיךָ אֵל קַנָּא פֹּקֵד עֲוֹן אָבֹת
ו עַל־בָּנִים עַל־שִׁלֵּשִׁים וְעַל־רִבֵּעִים לְשֹׂנְאָי: וְעֹשֶׂה חֶסֶד

—————— SFORNO ——————

פֶּסֶל – *Carved image:* It is prohibited to fashion such statues even if they will not be worshipped.

VERSE 5

—————— RASHI ——————

אֵל קַנָּא – *Demand absolute loyalty:* [Literally, "am a jealous God."]: God will act zealously to punish idolaters, and He will act mercifully to forgive those who worship false gods. **לְשֹׂנְאָי** – *For those who hate Me:* This verse should be understood as the Targum renders it: [God will *hold the descendants to account for the sins of the fathers* only] "when the children persist in sinning as their parents did." God

rewards for two thousand generations the kindnesses that people perform. What emerges is that God bestows goodness at a ratio that is five hundred times greater than the amount of punishment He dispenses. For up to two thousand generations of descendants enjoy the benefits of good deeds, whereas only four generations suffer the effects of wickedness.

—————— IBN EZRA ——————

אֵל קַנָּא – *Demand absolute loyalty:* God's attitude here is perfectly reasonable. Given that God created us and sustains us, how could

we possibly give respect to any other deity, who lacks any power to benefit or to harm us?

—————— BEKHOR SHOR ——————

אֵל קַנָּא – *Demand absolute loyalty:* [Literally, "am a jealous God."] The term "jealous" [*kanna*] is the same as that used in the verse: *And the spirit of jealousy come upon him, and he be jealous of his wife* (Numbers 5:14). For God loves Israel so much that He cannot tolerate the nation showing submission to any entity other than Him. This is a great honor and privilege for Israel. **פֹּקֵד עֲוֹן אָבֹת עַל־בָּנִים** – *Hold the descendants to account for the sins of the fathers:* This does not mean that God punishes children for their parents' behavior – for *every man shall be put to death for his own sin* (Deuteronomy 24:16). Rather, it should be

understood as follows: Whenever someone sins, God waits for the person to repent and return to Him. It might occur that the sinner's child develops into a righteous adult and hence will not be punished. And even if the child is wicked as well, God nevertheless delays recompense – perhaps the progeny will repent. Thus God waits for the third and the fourth generations. Only if the great-grandchild maintains the villainous acts of his ancestors, God drives him from the world in punishment for his own sins. For the family has become a clan of established sinners.

—————— RAMBAN ——————

פֹּקֵד עֲוֹן אָבֹת עַל־בָּנִים – *Hold the descendants to account for the sins of the fathers:* This seems

to mean that God indeed punishes children for the bad behavior of their fathers, and

5 beneath or the water beneath the earth. Do not bow down to them or worship them, for I the Lord your God demand absolute loyalty. For those who hate Me, I hold the descendants to account for the sins of the fathers to the third and fourth gen-
6 eration, but to those who love Me and keep My commands –

─────────── RAMBAN *(cont.)* ───────────

drives them from this world. Thus the verse states: *Prepare slaughter for his children for the iniquity of their fathers* (Isaiah 14:21). Furthermore, God punishes the third generation should the sins of the first two generations not be quite sufficient to merit the punishment, as He tells Avraham: *But in the fourth*

generation they shall come back here, for the iniquity of the Amorites is not yet full (Genesis 15:16). At other times, God will call upon the fourth generation to suffer for the acts of the previous three. However, the fifth generation will never be punished for the crimes of their ancestors in the first generation.

─────────── RALBAG ───────────

לֹא־תִשְׁתַּחֲוֶה לָהֶם – *Do not bow down to them:* It is inappropriate to bow down to any foreign god, even when prostrating is not the usual way to serve a particular deity. For the religious expression of bowing is only permitted

when God Himself is the object of devotion. This rule also applies to other acts of worship which are reserved for the service of God: animal sacrifice, the burning of incense, and the pouring of libations.

─────────── GUR ARYEH ───────────

פֹּקֵד עֲוֹן אָבֹת עַל־בָּנִים – *Hold the descendants to account for the sins of the fathers:* According to Rashi, descendants are only punished for the crimes of their fathers when they persist in committing those sins. This interpretation is necessary because another verse promises: *Fathers shall not be put to death for children, neither shall children be put to death for fathers* (Deuteronomy 24:16). Still, given that the same verse continues: *Every man shall be put*

to death for his own sin (Deuteronomy 24:16), how can we even accept that a son's deserved punishment be augmented on account of his father's sins? Know that this is possible, because a child is considered a branch of his father's life, just as the branch of a tree is directly connected to the plant's roots. Hence, when a child continues the nefarious ways of the parent, he is treated as an extension thereof.

VERSE 6

─────────── IBN EZRA ───────────

וְעֹשֶׂה חֶסֶד לַאֲלָפִים – *Act with faithful love for thousands:* Although in our verse God promises reward for many thousands of generations, in a later text, the extent of God's beneficence seems limited to one thousand generations, as the verse states: *Know therefore that the Lord your God, He is God, the faithful God, Who*

keeps covenant and righteousness with those who love Him and keep His commandments to a thousand generations (Deuteronomy 7:9). This however, really presents no difficulty, for what that verse means is: If you observe God's commandments, He will uphold His covenant, which He established with the

─────────── (vertical, right margin) ───────────
CLASSIC COMMENTATORS

לַאֲלָפִים לְאֹהֲבַי וּלְשֹׁמְרֵי מִצְוֹתָי: לֹא תִשָּׂא אֶת־
שֵׁם־יְהֹוָה אֱלֹהֶיךָ לַשָּׁוְא כִּי לֹא יְנַקֶּה יְהֹוָה אֵת אֲשֶׁר־יִשָּׂא
אֶת־שְׁמוֹ לַשָּׁוְא:

────────────── **IBN EZRA** *(cont.)* ──────────────

three patriarchs. In our verse, however, God is making an entirely separate promise. The phrase "for thousands" means "forever," and the verse can therefore be understood in two ways: First, the souls of those who love God are granted eternal life. Second, as a reward for loyalty to God, He will act with eternal kindness toward the children of the righteous adherents who continue their legacy.

──────────────── **RAMBAN** ────────────────

לְאֹהֲבַי וּלְשֹׁמְרֵי מִצְוֹתָי – *To those who love Me and keep My commands:* These are people who are prepared to sacrifice their lives for God. They acknowledge the glorious name of God, His oneness, and His divinity, and deny the reality of every other deity in the world. Such devotees will never worship a foreign god even on pain of death. Such believers are called "those who love God." It is for this reason that Avraham's descendants are referred to as *the seed of Avraham who loved Me* (Isaiah 41:8). For the patriarch was prepared to offer his very life in maintenance of his faith and repudiation of idolatry in Ur Kasdim. According to the Mekhilta, the phrase "those who keep My commands" is an allusion to the elders and prophets of Israel. Rabbi Natan presents a different interpretation, suggesting that our verse praises those people who dwell in the land of Israel and who risk their lives

in the observance of the commandments. Such a Jew might be asked: "Why are you being taken out for execution?" and reply: "Because I circumcised my son." Or he might be questioned: "Why are you being taken out to be burned?" and answer: "It is because I read the Torah." Rabbi Natan teaches us that the current verse describes Jews whose love of God induces them to forfeit their lives to observe the commandments. I will add that simply understood, the text refers specifically to the avoidance of idol worship, since that is a prohibition which we must follow at all times and forever, and for which we must be prepared to die rather than violate. However, Rabbi Natan expands the scope of the verse to include all the Torah's laws, since during times of religious oppression, Jews must choose death over the transgression of any of God's commandments.

──────────────── **ḤIZKUNI** ────────────────

לְאֹהֲבַי – *To those who love Me:* This verse refers to pious individuals [*ḥasidim*]. **וּלְשֹׁמְרֵי מִצְוֹתָי** – *And keep My commands:* This phrase refers to righteous individuals

[*tzadikim*. Generally, the distinction between "righteous" and "pious" individuals is held to be that the former obeys the letter of the law, while the latter goes beyond it].

VERSE 7

──────────────── **RASHI** ────────────────

לַשָּׁוְא – *In vain:* The word means "for no purpose," or "in vain." What constitutes an oath taken in vain? That is when somebody swears

contrary to what everybody knows – for example, if using the name of God a person insists that a stone pillar is really made of gold.

7 I shall act with faithful love for thousands.   Do not speak the name of the Lord your God in vain, for the Lord will not hold guiltless those who speak His name in vain.

———————— RASHBAM ————————

לֹא תִשָּׂא – *Do not speak:* The purpose of all of these commandments is to maintain respect for God. The observance of the Sabbath as well [the fourth commandment] is also intended as a demonstration of loyalty to and recognition of God. Similarly, respecting one's parents [the fifth commandment] is a way of acknowledging God, for honoring parents is comparable to honoring God, as the verse states: *Honor [kabbed] the Lord with your substance* [Proverbs 3:9; the same term appears here in verse 12].

———————— IBN EZRA ————————

לַשָּׁוְא – *In vain:* When a person invokes God's name in making a statement, the intention is: "Just as God is truth, so what I am saying is true." Consequently, if that individual does not honor his word, it is as if he denies the veracity of God. Curiously, in an Egyptian custom that is followed to this day, a person who swears by the name of the king is executed if the oath is violated. Such a scoundrel cannot even save his life by offering to pay a ransom in gold, for he has publicly disparaged the honor of the king. And if such respect is demanded for a human king, how many more thousands of times must one be cautious not to speak carelessly or allow one's tongue to slip into sin by uttering God's name in vain.

———————— RABBI AVRAHAM BEN HARAMBAM ————————

לֹא תִשָּׂא – *Do not speak:* The straightforward meaning of this prohibition is that Jews must never treat God's name lightly, bandy the name about in jest, or at any time say it irreverently. An oath uttered using God's name should be taken seriously, and all the more so should no false or unnecessary oath ever be pronounced.

———————— RAMBAN ————————

אֶת־שֵׁם־יהוה אֱלֹהֶיךָ – *The name of the Lord your God:* The language of this verse, as well as that in the following commandments, gives the impression that Moshe himself is uttering them [since God is referred to in the third person]. However, in the earlier verses it is clear that God is addressing Israel directly, for He says: *I am the Lord who brought you out of the land of Egypt, etc.* (20:2). Based on this shift in style, our Sages claim that the first two commandments were spoken directly by the Almighty to Israel. These statements are after all, the foundation of all belief [see Makkot 24a]. Citing certain other verses however, Ibn Ezra challenges this interpretation, claiming that Israel heard the entire text of the Ten Commandments straight from God. That commentator builds his support from the introductory statement here, *Then God spoke all these words* (20:1), an inclusive declaration that is repeated in Moshe's description, *These words the Lord spoke to all your assembly* (Deuteronomy 5:19). Now allow me to explain the meaning of our Sages' tradition: It was certainly so that the nation heard all of the Ten Commandments, as the straightforward reading of the Torah makes clear. Still, there was a distinction between how the first two messages were communicated and how the rest of the commandments were received. When the Israelites heard the first verses, they understood them perfectly, just as Moshe did. But starting with the third precept, and for

ח זָכוֹר אֶת־יוֹם הַשַּׁבָּת לְקַדְּשׁוֹ: שֵׁשֶׁת יָמִים תַּעֲבֹד וְעָשִׂיתָ

RAMBAN *(cont.)*

the rest of the passage, the communication that Israel heard was indecipherable to them. This was why Moshe needed to step in and interpret God's words to the people until they understood His intent. The reason that God employed this two-tier approach to revelation was so that all the people would have their moments as prophets when they would know with absolute clarity of the existence of God and the prohibition of idolatry. For these two

concepts stand as the most important principles of the entire Torah and its commandments. As for the other commandments, those could be taught to the nation by Moshe after the people heard them uttered in some fashion by God. As a result, when the rest of the Torah's commandments were introduced to the nation directly by Moshe [without first being communicated to Israel by God], Israel believed fully in the prophet's message.

VERSE 8

RASHI

זָכוֹר – *Remember:* God uttered simultaneously the complementary statements *Remember the Sabbath to keep it holy* and *Guard the Sabbath day to keep it holy* (Deuteronomy 5:12). In our verse the term *zakhor* means: Pay attention

to always have the Sabbath on your mind, even during the week. If you perchance come across a choice food in the market – buy it in anticipation of your Sabbath meal.

RASHBAM

זָכוֹר אֶת־יוֹם הַשַּׁבָּת – *Remember the Sabbath:* The term "remember" always refers to some past event. Thus we have the verse *Remember the days of old consider the years of many generations* (Deuteronomy 32:7). Here too, Israel is instructed to remember the six days

of creation, as the text proceeds to elaborate: *For in six days the LORD made heaven and earth* (20:11). The command here is to remember the history of the world's genesis in order to sanctify the day through cessation of labor.

IBN EZRA

זָכוֹר אֶת־יוֹם הַשַּׁבָּת – *Remember the Sabbath:* After the Torah states that the Sabbath must be kept holy, it proceeds to explain how to do this: *Six days you shall work etc.* (20:9). This echoes God who created the world in six days and then rested, thereby making the Sabbath holy, as described in verse 11. The

text there intentionally repeats the language of God "blessing" the day and "making it holy" that described the first Sabbath [in Genesis 2:3]. For God ordained that the souls of those who observe the Sabbath shall merit an enhanced wisdom that is unavailable during the week.

BEKHOR SHOR

זָכוֹר אֶת־יוֹם הַשַּׁבָּת – *Remember the Sabbath:* Remember the Sabbath all the time by counting off the days of the week. In this way you will never err as to which day is the Sabbath.

Now even though currently you need not pay close attention to which day it is, since the phenomenon of the manna announces the arrival of the Sabbath [through the surplus

$^8_9$ Remember the Sabbath to keep it holy. Six days you shall work,

——————————————— BEKHOR SHOR *(cont.)* ———————————————

food appearing on Fridays], when you enter the land of Israel you must count the days

carefully. For at that point the manna will no longer be available to mark time for you.

——————————————— RAMBAN ———————————————

זָכוֹר אֶת־יוֹם הַשַּׁבָּת – *Remember the Sabbath:* Now, after having commanded us to believe in the unique name of God [the first commandment] – testifying to His existence, to His role as Creator of the universe, and to His omniscience and omnipotence – having insisted that we focus all of our faith and honor toward Him alone [the second commandment], and having demanded that we treat mention of His name with respect [the third], God arrives at the fourth commandment: to establish an eternal sign and remembrance of God's creation of the world. This is why our Sages declare that the Sabbath is equal in importance to all of the Torah's other commandments combined [see Ḥullin 5a]. For

those who keep the Sabbath testify to the fundamental principles of Jewish faith – creation of the world, providence, and prophecy. Furthermore, Rabbi Yitzḥak is quoted in the Mekhilta as saying that Jews should refrain from naming the days of the week in the way that gentiles do, but should always label their days in reference to the Sabbath. For in all other cultures, people name the days and thereby assign significance to each weekday. The Christians, for example, name the days according to the celestial bodies. However, Israel only considers each day of the week in relation to the Sabbath – calling the first day *Eḥad BeShabbat* ["the first day the Sabbath"], etc.

——————————————— RABBEINU BAḤYA ———————————————

זָכוֹר אֶת־יוֹם הַשַּׁבָּת – *Remember the Sabbath:* The physical world operates through alternating states of light and darkness, day and night. In this way, people are not compelled to engage in work at all hours, but are allowed periods of rest from their toil. Hence the verse states: *Man goes forth to his work and to his labor until the evening* (Psalms 104:23), whereas the night is set aside for sleep and rejuvenation. In a similar vein, God instituted

the Sabbath to protect people from living lives of unceasing labor. The Sabbath provides individuals with one day of rest per week when they are relieved from the hardship of exertion and industry. Now the reason that the Sabbath falls every seven days, and not every fifth or sixth day, is that seven days is a unit of time intermediate between a day and a month. Furthermore, many commandments are based on the number seven.

——————————————— SFORNO ———————————————

לְקַדְּשׁוֹ – *To keep it holy:* In other words, in anticipation of the Sabbath, the individual should arrange and complete all of his affairs

during the week, such that his mind is not troubled by financial issues when the Sabbath arrives.

VERSE 9

——————————————— RASHI ———————————————

וְעָשִׂיתָ כָּל־מְלַאכְתֶּךָ – *And carry out all your labors:* When the Sabbath begins, imagine that

you really have finished all of your labors [thus driving them from your thoughts].

כָּל־מְלַאכְתֶּךָ: וְיוֹם הַשְּׁבִיעִי שַׁבָּת לַיהוָה אֱלֹהֶיךָ לֹא־
תַעֲשֶׂה כָל־מְלָאכָה אַתָּה ׀ וּבִנְךָ וּבִתֶּךָ עַבְדְּךָ וַאֲמָתְךָ
וּבְהֶמְתֶּךָ וְגֵרְךָ אֲשֶׁר בִּשְׁעָרֶיךָ: כִּי שֵׁשֶׁת־יָמִים עָשָׂה
יהוָה אֶת־הַשָּׁמַיִם וְאֶת־הָאָרֶץ אֶת־הַיָּם וְאֶת־כָּל־
אֲשֶׁר־בָּם וַיָּנַח בַּיּוֹם הַשְּׁבִיעִי עַל־כֵּן בֵּרַךְ יהוָה אֶת־יוֹם

יא

י

—————— RABBI AVRAHAM BEN HARAMBAM ——————

שֵׁשֶׁת יָמִים תַּעֲבֹד – *Six days you shall work:* This verse grants Israel permission to work for six days; it does not demand that they do. And while the Sages read this statement as a

command, that is but a homily intended to encourage human productivity, as King David argues: *For you shall eat the labor of your hands: happy shall you be* (Psalms 128:2).

—————— HIZKUNI ——————

וְעָשִׂיתָ כָּל־מְלַאכְתֶּךָ – *And carry out all your labors:* Much of your labor [for completing all of it is impossible]. The sense of this statement is similar to the verse *or this time I will*

set all of My plagues upon you [9:14; there too, the hailstorm was certainly not literally "all" the plagues].

VERSE 10

—————— RASHI ——————

אַתָּה וּבִנְךָ וּבִתֶּךָ – *Neither you, nor your son or daughter:* Prevent your young ones from performing labors on the Sabbath. But is it not possible that the text refers to adult children? No, since the verse has already warned them how to behave on the holy day [that is, the opening word "you" is directed at all

adults]. Rather, the text proceeds to caution parents – they must also guide their youngsters to avoid forbidden actions. Hence the Talmud teaches (Shabbat 121a): If a minor attempts to extinguish a candle on the Sabbath, he must be stopped, since adults must ensure that their children "rest" on the Sabbath too.

—————— SFORNO ——————

שַׁבָּת לַיהוָה אֱלֹהֶיךָ – *A Sabbath to the Lord your God:* The day should be devoted entirely to God through the study and teaching of Torah

and the observance and performance of commandments. One should also enjoy the day, and thus honor God.

VERSE 11

—————— RASHI ——————

וַיָּנַח בַּיּוֹם הַשְּׁבִיעִי – *And He rested on the seventh day:* God wrote this about Himself to give the impression that He rests. He did that to construct an *a fortiori* argument on our behalf. [If God, who neither requires nor takes any respite, nevertheless is said to rest, then certainly] people who strive and toil

to exhaustion should rest on the Sabbath. בֵּרַךְ... וַיְקַדְּשֵׁהוּ – *Blessed...and made it holy:* God blessed the Sabbath by providing Israel with manna beforehand to prepare for it. And He made it holy by withholding manna on the Sabbath itself.

10 and carry out all your labors, but the seventh is a Sabbath to the
LORD your God. On it, do no work – neither you, nor your son
or daughter, your male or female servant, your livestock, or the
11 migrant within your gates. For in six days the LORD made heav-
en and earth, the sea, and all that they contain, and He rested
on the seventh day. And so the LORD blessed the Sabbath day

—————————— RASHBAM ——————————

בֵּרַךְ – *Blessed:* As I have written in my commentary to the book of Genesis, when God
created the Sabbath, He blessed the day. For
by the time the Sabbath was made, God had
provided humanity with all of the resources
necessary to sustain life, which means that the
Sabbath was the most blessed of all things.
This is why God made the day holy by demanding that we rest thereon. Our changed
behavior stands as a testament to God's fashioning of all the world's needs and the subsequent cessation of His labor.

—————————— BEKHOR SHOR ——————————

כִּי שֵׁשֶׁת־יָמִים – *For in six days:* By observing
the Sabbath, adherents to the Torah testify as
to their belief in God's creation of the world.
This is why *the LORD blessed the Sabbath day
and made it holy.* Now in the later repetition
of the Ten Commandments, the verse that
commands the Sabbath reads: *And remember
that you were a servant in the land of Egypt,
and that the LORD your God brought you out
from there with a mighty hand and a stretched
out arm* (Deuteronomy 5:15). Thus, when you
rest on the Sabbath day, you should remember the difficult toil of your Egyptian slavery,
when you were never granted any respite. But
now that you have the Sabbath, your behavior
on that day should remind you that you are
free people thanks to the compassion that
the God showed your ancestors. Meanwhile,
here in the Torah's first account of the Ten
Commandments, the Torah states: *Remember the Sabbath* (20:8), since it asks us to recall
God's creation of the world. For it makes sense
to use language of remembrance with regard
to past events, as in the verse *Remember not
the former things, neither consider the things
of old* (Isaiah 43:18). On the other hand, when
the Ten Commandments are repeated, the
discussion revolves around the emancipation from Egypt, which was a relatively recent
episode. It was therefore inappropriate to ask
Israel to "remember" but instead to "guard"
(Deuteronomy 5:12). And so, when the Sages
composed the Sabbath *Kiddush,* they used
the verb "remember" twice, declaring that
the Sabbath should be kept as a memorial
to both creation and the exodus [since for
later generations, both events took place in
the distant past].

—————————— RALBAG ——————————

וַיָּנַח בַּיּוֹם הַשְּׁבִיעִי – *And He rested on the seventh day:* This verse means that on the seventh
day God ceased the miraculous creation He
had performed during the previous six days.
Nevertheless, the world continued to exist
and was sustained by the laws of nature God
had put in place. This is why our Sages argue
that the term "and He rested" is in fact a transi-
tive verb, meaning: "He let His world be."

יב הַשַּׁבָּת וַיְקַדְּשֵׁהוּ: כַּבֵּד אֶת־אָבִיךָ וְאֶת־אִמֶּךָ
לְמַעַן יַאֲרִכוּן יָמֶיךָ עַל הָאֲדָמָה אֲשֶׁר־יהוה אֱלֹהֶיךָ
יג נֹתֵן לָךְ: לֹא תִרְצָח לֹא תִגְנֹב לֹא
תִנְאָף

VERSE 12

——————————————— RASHI ———————————————

לְמַעַן יַאֲרִכוּן יָמֶיךָ – *Then you will live long:* If you honor your parents, your days will be lengthened; but if you disrespect them, your days will be shortened. Many statements in the Torah are meant to imply their converse – sometimes a positive promise of reward implies a negative threat of punishment, or vice versa.

——————————————— BEKHOR SHOR ———————————————

כַּבֵּד אֶת־אָבִיךָ וְאֶת־אִמֶּךָ – *Honor your father and mother:* Even though I have commanded you to dedicate all of your respect and worship to Me, you must nevertheless *Honor your father and mother.* Never forget all the good your parents have done by bringing you into the world and supporting you to adulthood. Your father and mother constantly care for you, while all their toil is solely for your benefit. If you respect your parents and repay them even part of the debt you owe them, I know that you will transfer that sense of gratitude to Me and appreciate all of the beneficence I have granted you. For I have brought you into this life, and I will shepherd you into the next.

——————————————— ABARBANEL ———————————————

כַּבֵּד אֶת־אָבִיךָ וְאֶת־אִמֶּךָ – *Honor your father and mother:* God has commanded us to honor our parents to impress upon us the importance of the traditions they impart to us. It is incumbent upon us to believe the principles of faith they teach us and to trust in their veracity, as the verse states: *Remember the days of old, consider the years of many generations: ask your father, and he will recount it to you; your elders, and they will tell* (Deuteronomy 32:7). Iyov, too, is told: *For inquire, I pray you, of the former age, and attend assiduously to what* their fathers have sought out (Job 8:8). Because the lessons of our faith are transmitted by our parents, the overarching system of religious belief is dependent on our regard for them. Therefore this commandment is grouped with the previous four on the first tablet, since all five issues attempt to ensure proper attitudes toward God. Contrary to what we might expect, the demand to respect one's parents did not appear on the second tablet with the last five rules, which all govern interpersonal relationships.

VERSE 13

——————————————— RASHI ———————————————

לֹא תִנְאָף – *Do not commit adultery:* The term "adultery" specifically denotes sex with a woman who is married to another man. We know this to be so because the verse that defines the couple's punishment states: *And the man who commits adultery with another man's wife, who commits adultery with his neighbor's wife, the adulterer and the adulteress*

12 and made it holy.   Honor your father and mother.
Then you will live long in the land that the LORD your God is
13 giving you.   Do not murder.   Do not
commit adultery.   Do not steal.   Do not

—————————————— RASHI *(cont.)* ——————————————

shall surely be put to death (Leviticus 20:10). And a later verse reads: *Rather like a wife who commits adultery, who takes strangers instead of her husband* (Ezekiel 16:32). **לֹא תִגְנֹב** – *Do not steal:* This is a warning against kidnapping and selling human beings, whereas a separate statement, *You shall not steal* (Leviticus 19:11), prohibits stealing property. How do we know that it is not the reverse: the current verse forbidding theft, and the second proscribing kidnapping? We invoke the exegetical principle of learning a thing from its context. The text in question is juxtaposed with the prohibitions of murder and adultery, which are capital offenses. Hence, the commandment *Do not steal* must also refer to a crime that warrants capital punishment [the penalty for kidnapping and selling people – see Exodus 21:16].

————————————————— IBN EZRA —————————————————

לֹא תִרְצָח – *Do not murder:* Do not murder a person, either with your hands or through your speech. That is, *do not bear false witness against your neighbor* to trick the court into murdering him. Furthermore, do not utter gossip about another person that could end up getting him killed, and do not give somebody bad advice that might lead to his death. Conversely, when you become privy to information that could save a person's life, you are a murderer if you keep that knowledge to yourself and do not speak up.

————————————————— BEKHOR SHOR —————————————————

לֹא תִנְאָף – *Do not commit adultery:* Because the Torah forbids murdering people, it seems to be concerned about reducing the size of the population. This might imply that we should take every opportunity to expand the number of human beings in the community, and that a man should be encouraged to procreate with any woman he finds, even if she is married to somebody else or is his own relative. It is to counter this argument that the Torah commands: *Do not commit adultery.*

————————————————— RAMBAN —————————————————

לֹא תִרְצָח לֹא תִנְאָף לֹא תִגְנֹב – *Do not murder. Do not commit adultery. Do not steal:* With these commandments, God makes the following declaration: Behold! I have commanded you to acknowledge in mind and in action that I have created everything. I have instructed you to honor your parents, who took part in your formation. And now I am warning you not to destroy the products of My handiwork by shedding the blood of those human beings I have made to honor Me. Nor shall you commit adultery, because that would undermine the principle of honoring one's parents by causing children to deny the truth and accept falsehood. If you lie with another man's wife, your children will believe her husband to be their father and will respect him instead of you. This is analogous to idolatry, when one worships a piece of wood as their deity, rejecting the true God in heaven who fashioned us from nothing.

יד תַעֲנֶה בְרֵעֲךָ עֵד שָׁקֶר:
לֹא
לֹא־
תַחְמֹד בֵּית רֵעֶךָ
תַחְמֹד אֵשֶׁת רֵעֶךָ וְעַבְדְּוֹ וַאֲמָתוֹ וְשׁוֹרוֹ וַחֲמֹרוֹ וְכֹל אֲשֶׁר
לְרֵעֶךָ:
שביעי טו וְכָל־הָעָם רֹאִים אֶת־הַקּוֹלֹת וְאֶת־הַלַּפִּידִם וְאֵת קוֹל הַשֹּׁפָר

——————————— AKEDAT YITZHAK ———————————

עֵד שָׁקֶר – *False witness:* Here the Torah teaches us to use our voices in productive ways, employing our speech for the betterment of society. If an individual has knowledge that can benefit another, he should testify on that person's behalf. On the other hand, one must avoid all forms of false testimony. Included in this commandment is the prohibition of revealing another person's secrets or private information, or spreading gossip against other people. This warning governing speech appears fourth on the second tablet, devoted to interpersonal relations, because it ranks fourth behind the ultimate crime of murder, which sits first on this list. In the same way, discussion of God's creation of the world [a central aspect of Sabbath remembrance] occupies the fourth level following the opening precept *I am the Lord your God* (20:2) on the first tablet, which comprises spiritual issues.

——————————— SFORNO ———————————

לֹא תִנְאָף – *Do not commit adultery:* This refers primarily to sex with a married woman, which is the most common type of proscribed sexual act. Still, the prohibition includes all cases of forbidden sexual relations [including, e.g., incest].

VERSE 14

——————————— IBN EZRA ———————————

לֹא תַחְמֹד – *Do not crave:* This commandment has confounded many people, who argue that it is impossible for a person not to covet in his heart a beautiful thing that he sees and longs to own. Allow me to describe a parable for you which will explain the matter. Consider a simple yet sound-minded farm boy who catches a glimpse of a gorgeous princess. Such a man will not dream about sleeping with the woman, since he knows in his heart that such a union is out of the question. Similarly, a normal man does not desire to lie with his mother, attractive though she may be, since he has been conditioned from childhood to understand that that woman is forbidden to him. In the same manner, every intelligent person must train himself to acknowledge that it is not his brains nor his wisdom that will aid him in acquiring wealth or a lovely wife, but that he will receive only what God allots to him. Thus the verse states: *For there is a man whose labor is with wisdom, and with knowledge, and with skill; yet he must leave it for a portion to a man who has not labored in it* (Ecclesiastes 2:21). And so do our Sages argue: Children, life, and food are not dependent on merit, but on the constellations (Mo'ed Katan 28a). If one keeps this attitude in mind, he will neither covet nor crave. And since a man knows that God has ruled his neighbor's wife to be strictly off-limits, that woman will become more distant in his eyes than a princess

₁₄ bear false witness against your neighbor. Do not crave your neighbor's house. Do not crave your neighbor's wife, his male or female servant, his ox, his donkey, or anything else that is your neighbor's."

₁₅ Every one of the people witnessed the thunder and lightning shevi'i

———————————————————— IBN EZRA *(cont.)* ————————————————————

is to a peasant. If one takes this approach to heart, he will be satisfied with his lot and will waste no energy dreaming of acquiring that which belongs to somebody else. For once we are convinced that God has no intention of letting us have those things we covet, we understand that no plan to obtain them through force, schemes or cunning will ever succeed. Then we will trust in our Creator to sustain us and to provide for us what He deems correct.

———————————————————— RABBI AVRAHAM BEN HARAMBAM ————————————————————

לֹא תַחְמֹד – *Do not crave:* The mind struggles to understand why God included these commandments in His revelation to the nation of Israel, selecting just these from within the large corpus of Torah law. There are two basic approaches to the question. The first is that only divine wisdom can comprehend the secrets behind God's choices. The second hypothesizes that the Ten Commandments represent the fundamental principles behind all 613 commandments.

———————————————————— RABBEINU BAHYA ————————————————————

לֹא תַחְמֹד – *Do not crave:* This, of course, is an emotion-based commandment, and its basic premise is that a person should harbor no hope of getting hold of a neighbor's possessions – whether land or movable property. One must not even think about such things, since the danger exists that coveting another's property might lead to murder. Witness how Aḥav longed to possess the vineyard belonging to Navot, a desire that led to his death [see I Kings 21].

VERSE 15

———————————————————— RASHI ————————————————————

וְכָל־הָעָם רֹאִים – *Every one of the people witnessed:* [Literally, "saw."] This description teaches that no one was blind among the Israelites. Furthermore, we know that no one was mute among the people, since the verse states: *And the people answered as one – "All that the Lord has spoken we will do"* (19:8). Finally, nobody suffered an inability to hear, as the verse states: *They replied, "All that the Lord has spoken we shall do and we shall heed"* (24:7). **רֹאִים אֶת־הַקּוֹלֹת** – *Witnessed the thunder:* The Israelites actually saw sounds during their experience, something which is otherwise impossible. **אֶת־הַקּוֹלֹת** – *The thunder:* [Literally, "sounds" or "voices."] They saw the sounds emanating from the mouth of God. **וַיַּעַמְדוּ מֵרָחֹק** – *And they stood at a distance:* The entire nation leapt backward a distance of twelve miles, the entire length of the Israelite camp. But the ministering angels descended and guided them back to their places, as the verse states: *Kings [malkhei] of armies flee [yiddodun], they flee* [Psalms 68:13; the midrash Rashi cites reads *malkhei* as *malakhei* – "angels," and *yidodun* as *yedaddun* – "lead them back"].

וְאֶת־הָהָר עָשֵׁן וַיַּרְא הָעָם וַיָּנֻעוּ וַיַּעַמְדוּ מֵרָחֹק: וַיֹּאמְרוּ טו
אֶל־מֹשֶׁה דַּבֵּר־אַתָּה עִמָּנוּ וְנִשְׁמָעָה וְאַל־יְדַבֵּר עִמָּנוּ
אֱלֹהִים פֶּן־נָמוּת: וַיֹּאמֶר מֹשֶׁה אֶל־הָעָם אַל־תִּירָאוּ כִּי יו
לְבַעֲבוּר נַסּוֹת אֶתְכֶם בָּא הָאֱלֹהִים וּבַעֲבוּר תִּהְיֶה יִרְאָתוֹ

──────────────────── RASHBAM ────────────────────

רֹאִים אֶת־הַקּוֹלֹת – *Witnessed the thunder:* [Literally, "saw the thunder."] The nation saw hail and the stones falling, as an earlier verse states: *Pray to the* Lord. *Enough of God's thunder*

and hail [9:28; that is, God's thunder might have had physical manifestations the people could see].

──────────────────── RAMBAN ────────────────────

וְכָל־הָעָם רֹאִים אֶת־הַקּוֹלֹת – *Every one of the people witnessed the thunder:* According to some commentators, this passage occurred after the giving of the Torah. As evidence, they cite Moshe's description of the event: *And it came to pass, when you heard the voice out of the midst of the darkness…that you came near to me, all the heads of your tribes, and your elders; and you said, Behold, the* Lord *our God has shown us His glory and His greatness, and we have heard His voice out of the midst of the fire…. If we hear the voice of the* Lord *our God any more, then we shall die* (Deuteronomy 5:20-22). However, I am of a different opinion regarding the sequence of events appearing in this and the previous chapter. It seems that first, in the *morning there was thunder and lightning and a dense cloud on the mountain and the sound of a ram's horn* (19:16) even before the Divine Presence had descended upon the mountain. These sights and sounds caused the Israelites throughout their camp to tremble, as the verse states: *All the people in the camp shook* (19:16). But Moshe emboldened his charges and directed them out of the camp to receive God: *Then Moshe led the people out of the camp to meet God, and they stood at the foot of the mountain* (19:17). And as the nation stood there at the bottom of the mountain, anticipating God's

approach, *the* Lord *descended on it in fire* (19:18), and *the mountain burned with fire to the heart of heaven, with darkness, clouds, and thick darkness* (Deuteronomy 4:11). The hill itself shook and pitched, as the verse describes: *And the mountain shook violently* (Exodus 19:18), as mountains do during an earthquake. *As the sound of the ram's horn grew louder and louder* (19:19), the people saw what was happening and moved backward away from the boundary that had been set up to prevent them from approaching the mountain. It was at that point that the people begged Moshe to stop God from speaking to them, for they feared for their lives. The vision that appeared to them caused them distress and sapped them of all strength. The Israelites believed that if they heard the voice of God they would all be killed. Nevertheless, Moshe assured them saying: *Do not be afraid, God has come to lift you up* (20:17). This allayed the nation's fears and *the people remained at a distance* where they stood. For despite Moshe's guarantees of their safety, they did not wish to come near the boundary at all. Moshe on the other hand, *approached the thick darkness where God was* (20:18) but did not enter the cloud. It was then that God pronounced the Ten Commandments. Afterward, the tribal heads and the nation's elders came to Moshe and said: *If*

and the sound of the ram's horn and the smoke-covered mountain; they saw and they shook – and they stood at a distance,
16 and said to Moshe, "Speak to us yourself and we will listen,
17 but let not God say any more to us, or we will die." "Do not be afraid," said Moshe to the people, "God has come to lift you up,

——————————————— RAMBAN *(cont.)* ———————————————

we hear the voice of the LORD our God any more, then we shall die (Deuteronomy 5:22). God agreed to Israel's request and said: *I have heard*

the voice of the words of this people, which they have spoken to you: they have well said all that they have spoken (Deuteronomy 5:25).

VERSE 16

——————————————————— RASHBAM ———————————————————

וַיֹּאמְרוּ אֶל־מֹשֶׁה – *And they said to Moshe:* After Israel heard the Ten Commandments, they protested to Moshe. **דַּבֵּר־אַתָּה עִמָּנוּ** – *Speak to us yourself:* Had the nation not asked Moshe

to act as a conduit for God's law, it is likely that God would have spoken all the rest of the commandments directly to the people.

——————————————————— IBN EZRA ———————————————————

וַיֹּאמְרוּ אֶל־מֹשֶׁה – *And they said to Moshe:* It was the priests and the tribal heads who approached Moshe, for they were close to him. This complaint was lodged after the Ten Commandments were uttered, for the men were

terrified that further exposure to the voice of God would kill them. In response to the request, Moshe comforted them, saying: *Do not be afraid* (20:17).

——————————————— RABBI AVRAHAM BEN HARAMBAM ———————————————

דַּבֵּר־אַתָּה עִמָּנוּ – *Speak to us yourself:* The people felt confident asking Moshe to receive God's message on their behalf because they fully trusted in his mission. This was as God had predicted when He said: *The people may hear Me speaking to you. They will then believe you forever* (19:9). **וְאַל־יְדַבֵּר עִמָּנוּ אֱלֹהִים** – *But let not God say any more to us:* The people were aware that the commandments they had just

heard did not comprise all of the Torah's laws, but they did not know that the last commandment they heard regarding coveting was actually the final direct communication they would receive from God. **פֶּן־נָמוּת** – *Or we will die:* Following the experience of revelation, the people's strength was exhausted, and they felt unable to endure further the sound of God's voice.

VERSE 17

——————————————————— RASHI ———————————————————

לְבַעֲבוּר נַסּוֹת אֶתְכֶם – *To lift you up:* Your reputation will grow among the nations, for God will make you great as the world learns that He has revealed Himself to you in all His glory. **נַסּוֹת** – *To lift up:* The verb *lenassot* means to raise or to exalt, as in the verses *Lift up a*

standard [nes] for the people (Isaiah 62:10); *Behold, I will lift up My hand to the nations, and set up My standard [nisi] to the peoples* (Isaiah 49:22); and *As a banner [kanes] on a hill* (Isaiah 30:17). A banner or standard stands tall and erect. **וּבַעֲבוּר תִּהְיֶה יִרְאָתוֹ** – *So that the*

יח עַל־פְּנֵיכֶם לְבִלְתִּי תֶחֱטָאוּ: וַיַּעֲמֹד הָעָם מֵרָחֹק וּמֹשֶׁה נִגַּשׁ

מפטיר אֶל־הָעֲרָפֶל אֲשֶׁר־שָׁם הָאֱלֹהִים: וַיֹּאמֶר יהוה יט

אֶל־מֹשֶׁה כֹּה תֹאמַר אֶל־בְּנֵי יִשְׂרָאֵל אַתֶּם רְאִיתֶם כִּי מִן־

כ הַשָּׁמַיִם דִּבַּרְתִּי עִמָּכֶם: לֹא תַעֲשׂוּן אִתִּי אֱלֹהֵי כֶסֶף וֵאלֹהֵי

RASHI *(cont.)*

awe of Him will be: Once you have seen God as fearsome and threatening, you will understand that He is unique in all the world. You will therefore continue to fear His presence even afterward.

RASHBAM

נַסּוֹת אֶתְכֶם – *Lift you up:* [Differing from the translation here, Rashbam holds that the phrase means] "rebuke you."

RAMBAN

נַסּוֹת אֶתְכֶם – *Lift you up:* [Differing from the translation here, Ramban holds that the phrase means] "habituate you" to have faith in Him. For since God revealed His Divine Presence to you, belief in Him has entered your hearts and you will cleave to Him. Now such trust will never depart from your souls. Furthermore, it is God's wish that you remain "in

awe of Him always," when you recognize that He alone is God in the heavens and the earth. This will instill great reverence of God in you. Alternatively, Moshe might be arguing that is the sight of the great fire on the mountain which should terrify Israel into submission. In other words, their fear of being burned will prevent them from sinning.

SFORNO

נַסּוֹת אֶתְכֶם – *Lift you up:* [Differing from the translation here, Sforno holds that the word *nassot* means "habituate."] In this context, the sense is] to get the people accustomed to the phenomenon of prophecy. Their experience was similar to that of Eliyahu, who received God's word when fully conscious, as the verse states: *And when Eliyahu heard it, he wrapped*

his face in his mantle, and went out, and stood in the entrance of the cave (I Kings 19:13). Nevertheless, the communication that the people received might not have been transmitted as clearly as it always was to Moshe, about whom the Torah states: *And there arose not a prophet since in Israel like Moshe, whom the Lord knew face to face* (Deuteronomy 34:10).

VERSE **18**

RASHI

נִגַּשׁ אֶל־הָעֲרָפֶל – *Approached the thick darkness:* Moshe passed through three barriers to reach the presence of God: darkness [*ḥoshekh*], cloud [*anan*], and thick darkness [*arafel*]. A later verse lists these: *The mountain burned with fire to the heart of heaven, with*

darkness, clouds, and thick darkness (Deuteronomy 4:11). The term *arafel* connotes a thick cloud, as the verse states: *Then the Lord said to Moshe, "I will come to you in a dense cloud"* (19:9).

so that the awe of Him will be with you always, keeping you
18 from sin." But the people remained at a distance while Moshe
19 approached the thick darkness where God was.   Then   MAFTIR
the LORD said to Moshe, "This is what you shall tell the Israelites: You yourselves have seen that I, from the heavens, have
20 spoken to you. Have no others alongside Me; make yourselves

---

IBN EZRA

וַיַּעֲמֹד הָעָם מֵרָחֹק – *But the people remained at a distance:* This is the second time the Torah mentions that the people stood at a distance from the mountain [the first time being verse 15], in order to contrast the opposite movement of Moshe. For while the nation remained apart from God, *Moshe approached the thick darkness.*

VERSE 19

RASHI

כֹּה תֹאמַר – *This is what you shall tell:* Use these words exactly. אַתֶּם רְאִיתֶם – *You yourselves have seen:* What a person hears described by others cannot compare to what he sees with his own eyes. For one who receives only a secondhand report, one is unsure whether to believe it or not. כִּי מִן־הַשָּׁמַיִם דִּבַּרְתִּי – *I, from the heavens, have spoken:* Our verse claims that God addressed Israel from the heavens, while a previous verse states: *And the LORD descended on Mount Sinai, to the top of the mountain* (19:20). How can these descriptions be reconciled? By a third verse, which states: *Out of heaven He made you hear His voice, that He might instruct you: and upon earth He showed you His great fire; and you did hear His words out of the midst of the fire* (Deuteronomy 4:36). This shows that while God's glory remained in the heavens, His fire and His might descended to earth. Another possible resolution: God folded the heavens and spread them on top of the mountain, as the verse states: *He bowed the heavens also, and came down* (II Samuel 22:10).

RABBEINU BAHYA

אַתֶּם רְאִיתֶם – *You yourselves have seen:* The entire nation of Israel had witnessed the signs and the wonders that God had performed on their behalf. They first saw the ten plagues that God visited upon the Egyptians, and now they experienced the giving of the Torah. This is why God emphasizes that *you yourselves have seen* My acts from the start to the finish. Similarly, in the initial passage concerning the covenant with Israel, God first states: *You yourselves have seen what I did to the Egyptians* (19:4). God now declares: *You yourselves have seen that I, from the heavens, have spoken to you.* While He communicated to the people, His glory rested upon Mount Sinai, but the voice emerged from the heavens.

VERSE 20

RASHI

לֹא תַעֲשׂוּן אִתִּי – *Have no others alongside Me:* Do not create images of My celestial servants who labor for Me in the heavens. אֱלֹהֵי כָסֶף – *Silver gods:* This is a warning against fashioning the Tabernacle's cherubim, which will stand "alongside Me" [adorning the

CLASSIC COMMENTATORS

כא זָהָב לֹא תַעֲשׂוּ לָכֶם: מִזְבַּח אֲדָמָה תַּעֲשֶׂה־לִּי וְזָבַחְתָּ עָלָיו

———————— RASHI *(cont.)* ————————

cover of the Ark of the Covenant], out of silver [rather than the prescribed gold]. If you
do deviate from My instructions and make
them out of silver, I will consider them to be
idolatrous. **וֵאלֹהֵי זָהָב** – *Golden gods:* This is
a warning against adding more cherubim to
the two that I mandate. If you make four, for
example, I will consider them to be gods of

gold. **לֹא תַעֲשׂוּ לָכֶם** – *Make yourselves no:* Do
not permit yourselves to place cherubim in
your synagogues or in your study halls, seeing those of the Tabernacle as a model and a
precedent. This is the sense of the prohibition
Make yourselves no silver gods, no golden gods
[that is, within your own precincts].

———————— RASHBAM ————————

אֱלֹהֵי כֶסֶף וֵאלֹהֵי זָהָב – *Silver gods, golden gods:*
It is forbidden even to fashion statues to represent the true God, for there are those who believe that there is some substance to the idols
themselves. Now it is true that God ordered

Israel to make statues of cherubim to adorn
the Ark of the Covenant, but these were only
intended to represent God's celestial throne.
They were in no way meant to be worshipped.

———————— IBN EZRA ————————

לֹא תַעֲשׂוּן אִתִּי – *Have no others alongside Me:*
Consider that I dwell in heaven and I spoke to
you without any recourse to intermediaries
[hence, why would you need to deal with other gods?], as the verse states: *The Lord talked
with you face to face* (Deuteronomy 5:4). Now
do not be troubled by our verse's repetition of

the phrase *lo taasu* [meaning "do not make"],
for the Torah is merely employing a figure of
speech. We find a similar repetition in verse 14,
where the warning *lo taḥmod* ["do not crave"]
is written twice. There is no additional significance to the second mention.

———————— RABBI AVRAHAM BEN HARAMBAM ————————

לֹא תַעֲשׂוּ לָכֶם – *Make yourselves no:* According to Rav Se'adya Gaon, the initial phrase
in this verse – *lo taasun itti* [literally, "do not
fashion alongside Me"] – is a warning against
adopting supplementary gods in addition to
the Lord. Israel is forbidden to believe in any

deity other than God. The subsequent phrase
lo taasu lakhem [literally, "do not fashion for
you"] more generally prohibits the creation
of images and pictures. The verse does not
repeat itself, but rather addresses different
false beliefs and practices.

———————— RALBAG ————————

לֹא תַעֲשׂוּן אִתִּי – *Have no others alongside Me:*
The first phrase in the verse, *lo taasun itti* [liter-
ally, "do not fashion alongside Me"], means: Do
not fashion gods of gold or gods of silver to
be set up in the Temple. This is followed by a
second prohibition: *lo taasu lakhem* [literally,
"do not fashion for you"], meaning: Neither

are you permitted to place such idols in your
homes or indeed in any place. This interpretation is supported by the ensuing verse, which
states: *Make for Me an altar of earth* (20:21). In
other words, while you are forbidden to create
any sorts of statues for veneration within My
house, you are to construct an object which

21 no silver gods, no golden gods. Make for Me an altar of earth and on that sacrifice your burnt offerings and peace offerings,

—————————————— RALBAG *(cont.)* ——————————————

can in no way be construed as a deity. This is the altar, which features no images that might be mistaken for gods. It is there that you shall worship Me.

VERSE 21

—————————————— RASHI ——————————————

מִזְבַּח אֲדָמָה – *An altar of earth:* [Although the Tabernacle's altar was made out of acacia wood covered in bronze, and not out of earth, this verse commands only that] the altar that you construct shall be attached to the earth. That is, do not build it on pillars or positioned on a stone foundation. Another interpretation: The hollow space within the bronze altar was filled with earth whenever Israel reached a new camp site. תַּעֲשֶׂה־לִי – *Make for Me:* From the start of its construction, the altar should be dedicated to

Me. בְּכָל־הַמָּקוֹם אֲשֶׁר אַזְכִּיר אֶת־שְׁמִי – *Wherever I cause My name to be invoked:* In every location where I grant you permission to utter My ineffable name, that is where *I will come to you and I will bless you* by manifesting My Divine Presence. Thus we learn that Israel was only permitted to pronounce the tetragrammaton at the site where the Divine Presence appears. And that location is the Temple. Only there were the priests allowed to utter this name when they raised their hands to bless the nation.

—————————————— RASHBAM ——————————————

מִזְבַּח אֲדָמָה תַּעֲשֶׂה־לִי – *Make for Me an altar of earth:* The nations of the world used to set up sacred trees upon their altars as a form of idolatry. Therefore, when God instructed Israel in the proper form of service, He said: When you build an altar, make sure to construct it out of earth, which is not usually adorned with pictures or statues but is smoothed flat. And should you determine to make the altar out of stones [see verse 22], these must be positioned whole, since when masons chisel stone with iron they tend to carve pictures and images into the surface.

—————————————— IBN EZRA ——————————————

מִזְבַּח אֲדָמָה תַּעֲשֶׂה־לִי – *Make for Me an altar of earth:* Some commentators suggest that because there is a tendency to carve images into stones, that material may not be used in construction of the altar unless preserved uncut [see verse 22]. Perhaps these authors can explain to us why the Tabernacle was replete with images of cherubim and why two golden cherubim were positioned atop the cover of the Ark of the Covenant. Other writers argue that our verse [mandating an altar of earth] is

merely prohibiting construction of the altar in an elevated place, but surely the language of the verse does not mean that. The fact that the following sentence states: *If you make Me an altar of stones* proves that the term "earth" in the previous verse is meant to be taken literally. Now our Sages explain that this commandment dictates that the bronze altar [of the Tabernacle, described in 27:1–8] was to be filled with earth. The Sages spoke the truth, and this is what the Israelites actually did. But

אֶת־עֹלֹתֶ֙יךָ֙ וְאֶת־שְׁלָמֶ֔יךָ אֶת־צֹֽאנְךָ֖ וְאֶת־בְּקָרֶ֑ךָ בְּכָל־
הַמָּקוֹם֙ אֲשֶׁ֣ר אַזְכִּ֣יר אֶת־שְׁמִ֔י אָב֥וֹא אֵלֶ֖יךָ וּבֵרַכְתִּֽיךָ׃
כב וְאִם־מִזְבַּ֤ח אֲבָנִים֙ תַּֽעֲשֶׂה־לִּ֔י לֹֽא־תִבְנֶ֥ה אֶתְהֶ֖ן גָּזִ֑ית כִּ֧י

———————— IBN EZRA *(cont.)* ————————

the straightforward meaning of the verse does not relate to the bronze altar, since the earth that was used then was incidental and not critical to its structure.

———————— RABBI AVRAHAM BEN HARAMBAM ————————

מִזְבַּח אֲדָמָה תַּעֲשֶׂה־לִּי – *Make for Me an altar of earth:* My father's father, of blessed memory, taught that this verse is an allusion to the altars situated at Shilo, Nov, and Givon, as well as hinting at the Temple. Rav Se'adya Gaon explains why the verse states: *I will cause My name to be invoked,* rather than: You will cause My name to be invoked. According to him, this teaches that it will not be the people of Israel who choose the site of the Temple and the place for God's sacrifices, but God Himself.

Thus King David stated: *For the Lord has chosen Zion: He has desired it for His habitation* (Psalms 132:13). In my opinion, the sense of God's command is as follows: When you worship Me and invoke My name, I will remember it and come to you, even when no sacrifices have been offered. What this means is that sacrifices do not represent the sole way to recognize God; rather they serve as a catalyst to the true worship of God, which is that of the heart.

———————— SFORNO ————————

מִזְבַּח אֲדָמָה תַּעֲשֶׂה־לִּי – *Make for Me an altar of earth:* You do not need to build Me temples of silver, gold and precious jewels in order to draw Me close to you. A simple altar of earth will achieve that.

VERSE 22

———————— RASHI ————————

וַתְּחַלְלֶהָ – *You profane it:* We learn from here that placing an iron tool upon the altar profanes it. Why is this so? Because the purpose of the altar is to extend people's lives [sins sacrifices can atone for sin], whereas the nature of iron [weapons] is to shorten a person's life. Hence these two things are incompatible, and it is inappropriate for the latter to be placed upon the former. Furthermore, since the altar stands as a mediator to create peace between Israel and their Father in Heaven, it cannot tolerate the presence of an item designed to

cut down and destroy. We can learn a valuable lesson from this prohibition: Here we have an altar of stones, which lack the power of sight, hearing, and speech, and yet because this inanimate object is tasked with bringing God and Israel closer together, the Torah warns us not to wield a sword upon it. Consider then a counselor who mends a rift between a husband and wife, or resolves a feud between families, or bridges a gap between neighbors – such an intermediary must surely be protected from any kind of suffering.

your sheep and your cattle. Wherever I cause My name to be
22 invoked, I will come to you and I will bless you. If you make
Me an altar of stones, do not build it of hewn stone, for in

──────────────────── BEKHOR SHOR ────────────────────

וַתְּחַלְלֶהָ – *You profane it:* Subsequently, if you use these hewn stones to construct an altar, the structure will be profane. You will have violated the sanctity of the altar, since I have no interest in objects of destruction.

──────────────────── RAMBAN ────────────────────

לֹא־תִבְנֶה אֶתְהֶן גָּזִית – *Do not build it of hewn stones:* The reason behind this commandment has been spelled out by our Sages: The Torah seeks to elevate the sanctity of the altar. For an item of violence that shortens human life cannot be used to construct an object of peace that lengthens life [by atoning for humanity's sins]. Rabbi Avraham Ibn Ezra offers a different approach: Were stones to be hewn to build the altar, that would result in some pieces being discarded and ending up in the garbage, while other sections would be fashioned into the altar of God. Or some of the chipped-off stone might be later used to make altars in the service of foreign gods. For idolaters might believe that using remnants of the altar for this alien worship would bring them success. Meanwhile, the Rambam has written in *The Guide of the Perplexed* (3:45) that our verse represents a precaution against imitating idolaters, since their practice was to build altars out of hewn stones. But in my opinion, the reason for this prohibition is that iron is the element used to fashion a sword [*ḥerev*] and this weapon is used to destroy [*maḥariv*] the world. Now Esav, whom God hates, is heir to the sword, as the verse states: *By your sword shall you live* (Genesis 27:40), and the sword creates his power in the heavens and on the earth. For the sword succeeds due to the power of Mars and the constellations of bloodshed, and it is through them that Esav's strength is manifested. Hence no sword may be associated with the house of God.

VERSE 23

──────────────────── RASHI ────────────────────

וְלֹא־תַעֲלֶה בְמַעֲלֹת – *Do not ascend with steps:* When you construct the ramp that leads up to the altar, do not put steps – *eschelons* in Old French – on it. Rather, the surface should be a smooth incline. אֲשֶׁר לֹא־תִגָּלֶה עֶרְוָתְךָ – *For your nakedness must not be exposed on it:* If ascending the altar meant climbing stairs, the priests who performed the service would have to take wide steps. And even though walking in this fashion would not really expose the individual, since the priests wore trousers, as the verse states, *Make them linen trousers to cover their nakedness, reaching from waist to thigh* (28:42), nevertheless, taking wide paces [to stretch to the stairs] is similar to exposing oneself, which would be disrespectful to the altar's stones. This teaches us a lesson about how to act toward human beings. If the Torah is concerned with behaving modestly toward stones, which sense no feeling of shame, and yet warns us not to treat them discourteously, then certainly one must always consider the sensitivities of a fellow person created in the image of God.

כג חַרְבְּךָ הֵנַפְתָּ עָלֶיהָ וַתְּחַלְלֶהָ: וְלֹא־תַעֲלֶה בְמַעֲלֹת עַל־
מִזְבְּחִי אֲשֶׁר לֹא־תִגָּלֶה עֶרְוָתְךָ עָלָיו:

——————— RAMBAN ———————

וְלֹא־תַעֲלֶה בְמַעֲלֹת עַל־מִזְבְּחִי – *Do not ascend to My altar with steps:* Since the Torah begins to detail the necessary requirements for the altar here, it completes the description, not reserving this final detail for the elaborate discussion of the topic in the book of Leviticus. This supports the position of the Sages [that the discussion here refers to the altar in the Tabernacle], though no such evidence is necessary. The reason steps are outlawed by the Torah is that awe of the altar and its glory serve to enhance the honor of God. Know that each of God's commandments is based on many reasons, since each law benefits the individual on both a physical and a spiritual level.

——————— ABARBANEL ———————

וְלֹא־תַעֲלֶה – *Do not ascend:* It seems to me that this verse cannot simply represent an instruction to the priests to ascend to the altar using a ramp. For why would the Torah at this point single out such a narrow detail from the many particulars related to the laws of the altar, the priests, and their vestments? Furthermore, the command in this verse seems

23 wielding a sword upon it, you profane it. Do not ascend to My altar with steps, for your nakedness must not be exposed on it.

——————————— ABARBANEL *(cont.)* ———————————

to apply to all of Israel and not to the priests alone. Rather, the true meaning of this passage is as follows: First, God commands Israel to build *an altar of earth* (20:21), adding that should the people wish to use stones in the altar's construction, they must not be hewn nor subjected to any sort of carving. But then God warns the people that in addition to avoiding dressed stones, they are not to use any exalted [*me'uleh*] materials like gold and silver, which of course are even more beautiful than uncut stones. [According to this interpretation, the verse would be better translated: "Do not adorn my altar with exalted substances."] For the altar of the burnt offering [*ola*] signifies a state of nature, which is why it was formed with hollow planks, and soil from the ground, or stones taken straight from the earth. Hence the Israelites were not to employ substances that they considered precious. Note that God had previously forbade the fashioning of gods of silver and gold [in 20:20]. He now declares that if Israel uses those same metals in building the altar, they will betray their attraction to foreign gods, thereby "exposing their nakedness."

18TH CENTURY

RABBI ḤAYYIM IBN ATTAR – *OR HAḤAYYIM*,
1696, MOROCCO – 1743, ISRAEL

19TH CENTURY

RABBI YAAKOV TZVI MECKLENBURG –
HAKETAV VEHAKABBALA,
1785 – 1865, GERMANY

SHADAL, 1800 – 1865, ITALY

RABBI SAMSON RAPHAEL HIRSCH,
1808 – 1888, GERMANY

MALBIM, 1809 – 1879, UKRAINE

RABBI NAFTALI TZVI YEHUDA BERLIN –
HAAMEK DAVAR, 1816, BELARUS – 1893, POLAND

RABBI YEHUDA ARYEH LEIB ALTER –
SEFAT EMET, 1847 – 1905, POLAND

20TH CENTURY

RABBI MEIR SIMḤA OF DVINSK – *MESHEKH
ḤOKHMA*, 1843, LITHUANIA – 1926, LATVIA

RABBI JOSEPH B. SOLOVEITCHIK,
1903, LITHUANIA – 1993, USA

NEHAMA LEIBOWITZ,
1905, LATVIA – 1997, ISRAEL

פרשת יתרו
PARASHAT YITRO

CONFRONTING
MODERNITY

יח ‫א‬ וַיִּשְׁמַ֞ע יִתְר֣וֹ כֹהֵ֤ן מִדְיָן֙ חֹתֵ֣ן מֹשֶׁ֔ה אֵת֩ כָּל־אֲשֶׁ֨ר עָשָׂ֤ה ‫יד‬
אֱלֹהִים֙ לְמֹשֶׁ֔ה וּלְיִשְׂרָאֵ֖ל עַמּ֑וֹ כִּֽי־הוֹצִ֧יא יהוה אֶת־יִשְׂרָאֵ֖ל
‫ב‬ מִמִּצְרָֽיִם: וַיִּקַּ֗ח יִתְרוֹ֙ חֹתֵ֣ן מֹשֶׁ֔ה אֶת־צִפֹּרָ֖ה אֵ֣שֶׁת מֹשֶׁ֑ה
‫ג‬ אַחַ֖ר שִׁלּוּחֶֽיהָ: וְאֵ֖ת שְׁנֵ֣י בָנֶ֑יהָ אֲשֶׁ֨ר שֵׁ֤ם הָֽאֶחָד֙ גֵּֽרְשֹׁ֔ם

CHAPTER 18, VERSE 1

OR HAHAYYIM

יִתְר֣וֹ כֹהֵ֣ן מִדְיָן חֹתֵ֣ן מֹשֶׁה – *Moshe's father-in-law Yitro, priest of Midyan:* It is possible that although Yitro had earned the respectable title of "Priest of Midyan," he disdained that honorific and preferred to be known as Moshe's father-in-law. [In verse 2 only the latter appellation appears in the Hebrew, though it is left untranslated in this edition.] **אֵת כָּל־אֲשֶׁר עָשָׂה אֱלֹהִים** – *All that God had done:* In order to praise Yitro, the text mentions his desire to learn all the details of the

miracles Israel had experienced, demonstrating how much he loved the people. Consider that when one person greatly dislikes another, it pains him to hear tales of the other's success and good fortune, and he will certainly not be interested in the particulars of those accomplishments. But one who loves another bears an insatiable appetite for information about the friend. Thus God recorded in His book how much Yitro loved Israel.

SHADAL

יִתְר֣וֹ כֹהֵ֣ן מִדְיָן – *Yitro, priest of Midyan:* The Ramban writes that the name Hovav [used in reference to this character in Numbers 10:29] was a new appellation given to Yitro after he embraced the Israelite faith. It is quite common for converts to Judaism to adopt new names, a practice supported by the verse *He calls His servants by another name* (Isaiah 65:15). Now it does seem likely that Israel began at some point to refer to Yitro as Hovav, a name that might derive from the Hebrew word for adoration [*havivut*], or some other long forgotten root. However, I must take issue with the Ramban and other commentators who argue that Yitro converted to the new religion. For if that were so, how could he have then responded to Moshe's request that he

accompany the nation to the land Israel by stating: *I will not go; but I will depart to my own land, and to my kindred* (Numbers 10:30)? With this declaration, Yitro expresses a wish to sever his current connections with Israel. Furthermore, we find in a subsequent generation an individual named Hever the Kenite [who according to Judges 4:11 was a descendant of Hovav] who, although living in the land of Israel, was friendly with [the Canaanite king] Yavin, an enemy of the Hebrews. There is no way that Sisera [Yavin's general] would have sought refuge from Israel's army with Hever's wife Yael [in Judges 4:17], if the Kenites had been a family of righteous converts immersed in Israelite society for some time.

MALBIM

יִתְר֣וֹ כֹהֵ֣ן מִדְיָן – *Yitro, priest of Midyan:* As the priest of Midyan who served the nation's gods, Yitro until this point had believed – like all

ancient peoples – that there existed a panoply of deities in the universe. According to this theology, each tutelary spirit ruled over a particular

18 1 Moshe's father-in-law Yitro, priest of Midyan, heard about all that God had done for Moshe and for His people Israel
2 when the LORD brought Israel out of Egypt. Yitro had received
3 Moshe's wife Tzipora after he had sent her home, together

——————— MALBIM *(cont.)* ———————

country and was responsible for a specific element of the natural world. Still, Yitro thought that there was one supreme being above all, a "god to the gods" in the words of our Sages. When Yitro learned about the miracles that Israel had enjoyed in the recent months, he naturally attributed each phenomenon to the intervention of the god of that realm. Thus, from Yitro's perspective, the descent of the manna was the handiwork of the god of bread; the

god of water caused water to flow out of the rock; and the victory over Amalek was won with the aid of the god of war. However, when he learned of Israel's emancipation from slavery, which was achieved with a mighty hand and an outstretched arm, and during which the gods of Egypt were judged, Yitro understood that it was the LORD alone who was responsible for the entire exodus. He thus understood that this was the God who had worked all these wonders.

VERSE 2

——————— RABBI SAMSON RAPHAEL HIRSCH ———————

אַחַר שִׁלּוּחֶיהָ – *After he had sent her home:* Presumably the weight of Moshe's responsibilities had led him to send his wife and sons back home to Midyan. This would have allowed Moshe to devote all his time and energy to

fulfilling his mission as leader. This separation caused the couple no strife, and their marriage remained healthy. The Torah hints at the harmony of the family by referring to Yitro as "Moshe's father-in-law" and to Tzipora as "Moshe's wife."

——————— MALBIM ———————

וַיִּקַּח – *Had received:* Even though Moshe had sent his wife away, no offense was taken, for it was understood that Moshe was not rejecting her. Hence the verse refers to her as

Moshe's wife Tzipora [even] after he had sent her home. For Moshe had only temporarily separated from Tzipora while God liberated the Israelites.

——————— HAAMEK DAVAR ———————

אַחַר שִׁלּוּחֶיהָ – *After he had sent her home:* Before the Torah was given, it was understood that when a man banished his wife, the couple was divorced and the woman was free to marry another man. But here the Torah emphasizes that such was not the case with

Tzipora, who remained "Moshe's wife" despite being sent back to her father's home. For even while she was separated from Moshe, Tzipora never stopped thinking about him or considering him her husband.

VERSE 3

——————— OR HAHAYYIM ———————

שֵׁם הָאֶחָד גֵּרְשֹׁם – *One was named Gershom:* Even though the Torah already provided the reason for this name in Parashat Shemot (2:22), it repeats it here to identify this son as the

same one born to Moshe in Midyan. We are not to think that the earlier boy died and that a new son was born and was named after his brother.

CONFRONTING MODERNITY

ד כִּי אָמַר גֵּר הָיִיתִי בְּאֶרֶץ נָכְרִיָּה: וְשֵׁם הָאֶחָד אֱלִיעֶזֶר כִּי־
ה אֱלֹהֵי אָבִי בְּעֶזְרִי וַיַּצִּלֵנִי מֵחֶרֶב פַּרְעֹה: וַיָּבֹא יִתְרוֹ חֹתֵן
מֹשֶׁה וּבָנָיו וְאִשְׁתּוֹ אֶל־מֹשֶׁה אֶל־הַמִּדְבָּר אֲשֶׁר־הוּא חֹנֶה
שָׁם הַר הָאֱלֹהִים: וַיֹּאמֶר אֶל־מֹשֶׁה אֲנִי חֹתֶנְךָ יִתְרוֹ בָּא
ז אֵלֶיךָ וְאִשְׁתְּךָ וּשְׁנֵי בָנֶיהָ עִמָּהּ: וַיֵּצֵא מֹשֶׁה לִקְרַאת חֹתְנוֹ

──────────── MALBIM ────────────

שֵׁם הָאֶחָד גֵּרְשֹׁם – *One was named Gershom:* The details of Moshe's life are recorded in the names of his sons, which is a true sign that he loved them. When Moshe named his eldest boy Gershom, saying: *I have been a stranger [ger] in a foreign land,* what he meant was that as a baby, he had been hidden from Pharaoh, and that he was a stranger in Egypt like the rest of the Israelites. What's more, when his son was born, Moshe was living in Midyan, which was altogether a foreign land. And it is always much harder to be a stranger outside of one's homeland than to remain in the place of one's birth.

──────────── MESHEKH ḤOKHMA ────────────

גֵּר הָיִיתִי בְּאֶרֶץ נָכְרִיָּה – *I have been a stranger in a foreign land:* The Torah mentions the names of Moshe's sons in order to praise him, showing the depth of the love he felt for his people. After all, Moshe had grown up in Pharaoh's home and wed the daughter of Midyan's priest. He lived largely apart from the community, while the Hebrews were mired in mud and clay. Still, when Gershom was born, Moshe in Midyan considered himself *a stranger in a foreign land,* since he thought of the land of Egypt, where his compatriots were, as his homeland. The pain he felt at being separated from his people was so acute that the name he gave his child reflected that difficulty. At the time, Moshe still gave little thought to how God had saved him from Pharaoh's sword.

VERSE 4

──────────── RABBI SAMSON RAPHAEL HIRSCH ────────────

וְשֵׁם הָאֶחָד אֱלִיעֶזֶר – *And the other, Eliezer:* The purpose of stating here the names of Moshe's sons and their meanings is to show how from the start Moshe was honest with his father-in-law, revealing his past and describing his relationship to his enslaved brethren. For Moshe's history is encapsulated in the names he gave his sons. His second son Eliezer was born shortly after Moshe's return to Egypt.

──────────── MALBIM ────────────

וְשֵׁם הָאֶחָד אֱלִיעֶזֶר – *And the other, Eliezer:* [Literally, "and one was named Eliezer."] It would have been simpler for the text to have stated "and the other" [rather than "and one"]. By expressing itself this way, the Torah indicates that each son was individually responsible for a different facet of Moshe's fortune. For when Eliezer was born, a new constellation took position to protect Moshe, allowing him to stand before kings and ministers. Eliezer was therefore not considered second to Gershom, but significant in his own right.

with her two sons. One was named Gershom, for Moshe had
4 said, "I have been a stranger in a foreign land," and the other,
Eliezer, for he had said, "My father's God has helped me, sav-
5 ing me from Pharaoh's sword." And now Moshe's father-in-law
Yitro came to Moshe in the desert, bringing his sons and his
6 wife, to where he was encamped by the mountain of God. Yitro
sent word to Moshe, "I am coming to you – your father-in-law
7 Yitro – together with your wife and both of your sons." Moshe
went out to greet his father-in-law and bowed down and kissed

VERSE 5

OR HAHAYYIM

אֲשֶׁר־הוּא חֹנֶה שָׁם – *To where he was encamp-*
ed: The verse explains how Yitro was able to
locate Moshe within the vast wilderness of
the desert. For Moshe had earlier related to
his father-in-law the location where God had
appeared to him in the burning bush. On that
occasion God had told him: *Having brought*
the people out of Egypt, you come to serve God
upon this mountain (3:12). Hence Moshe was
able to tell Yitro upon which mountain the
Torah would be given.

RABBI SAMSON RAPHAEL HIRSCH

הַר הָאֱלֹהִים – *The mountain of God:* According
to the Ramban, Mount Ḥorev stands closer to
Midyan than to Egypt. This explains the earlier
verse, *Moshe was tending the flock of his father-*
in-law Yitro…and came to Ḥorev, the mountain
of God (3:1). This meant that Yitro had to pass
by the mountain of God on his way to Refidim
[where Israel was most recently located]. Yitro
also likely suspected that Moshe would be lo-
cated by the mountain since he had explained
to him the true purpose of Israel's journey
through the wilderness, which had of course
been revealed to Moshe before he left Midyan
for Egypt [see 3:12]. Thus Yitro first traveled to
Ḥorev, and from there he dispatched a message to Moshe.

MALBIM

וּבָנֶיו וְאִשְׁתּוֹ – *His sons and his wife:* The sons are mentioned first since they held greater importance in Moshe's eyes.

VERSE 6

HAAMEK DAVAR

וְאִשְׁתְּךָ וּשְׁנֵי בָנֶיהָ – *With your wife and both of*
her sons: Yitro mentioned Tzipora first since
Moshe had more of an obligation to honor
his wife than his sons.

VERSE 7

OR HAHAYYIM

וַיֵּצֵא מֹשֶׁה לִקְרַאת חֹתְנוֹ – *Moshe went out*
to greet his father-in-law: [Although Moshe
was in fact greeting his whole family, the text
mentions only Yitro since] the honor due to
his father-in-law alone was great enough
by itself to warrant his departure from the

CONFRONTING MODERNITY

וַיִּשְׁתַּחוּ֙ וַיִּשַּׁק־ל֔וֹ וַיִּשְׁאֲל֥וּ אִישׁ־לְרֵעֵ֖הוּ לְשָׁל֑וֹם וַיָּבֹ֖אוּ
הָאֹֽהֱלָה: וַיְסַפֵּ֤ר מֹשֶׁה֙ לְחֹ֣תְנ֔וֹ אֵת֩ כָּל־אֲשֶׁ֨ר עָשָׂ֤ה יהוה֙ ח
לְפַרְעֹ֣ה וּלְמִצְרַ֔יִם עַ֖ל אוֹדֹ֣ת יִשְׂרָאֵ֑ל אֵ֤ת כָּל־הַתְּלָאָה֙ אֲשֶׁ֣ר
מְצָאָ֣תַם בַּדֶּ֔רֶךְ וַיַּצִּלֵ֖ם יהוה: וַיִּ֣חַדְּ יִתְר֔וֹ עַ֥ל כָּל־הַטּוֹבָ֖ה ט
אֲשֶׁר־עָשָׂ֥ה יהוה לְיִשְׂרָאֵ֑ל אֲשֶׁ֥ר הִצִּיל֖וֹ מִיַּ֥ד מִצְרָֽיִם:

——————————— OR HAHAYYIM *(cont.)* ———————————

Israelite camp. Or the verse might be specifying that Moshe went out directly to the tent where Yitro was staying and neglected to visit his wife and sons. The language of the verse supports the Sages' interpretation

of the subsequent clause [ambiguous in the Hebrew] that it was Moshe who bowed and kissed Yitro rather than vice versa, since it emphasizes how he went out to honor the man.

——————————— RABBI SAMSON RAPHAEL HIRSCH ———————————

וַיֵּצֵא מֹשֶׁה לִקְרַאת חֹתְנוֹ – *Moshe went out to greet his father-in-law:* Even though Moshe was now the leader of a great host and an

emissary of God, he still maintained his courteous behavior in dealing with other people.

VERSE 8
——————————— OR HAHAYYIM ———————————

וַיְסַפֵּר מֹשֶׁה לְחֹתְנוֹ – *And Moshe told his father-in-law:* Since the opening verse of this chapter states that *Yitro heard about all that God had done for Moshe and for His people Israel* (18:1), why did Moshe need to repeat to his father-in-law *all that the* Lord *had done to Pharaoh and the Egyptians for Israel's sake?* It is possible that there were details that had not yet reached Yitro's ears that Moshe filled in by reviewing the tale of the exodus. Secondly, although Yitro may have already learned about the miracles that God had performed on the nation's behalf, these stories may have seemed too wondrous and exaggerated for him to believe,

which is why Moshe now had to assure him that the rumors were all true. Alternatively, perhaps Yitro was skeptical that the Egyptian hold over the Israelites had truly been severed, since he was well aware of the power of that empire. Hence Moshe related to Yitro a detail that only the Israelites knew, namely the destruction of Egypt's guardian angel. According to our Sages, this slain protector was what Israel saw lying dead on the beach of the Sea of Reeds. When he heard this, Yitro understood that Israel had broken completely free of the Egyptian bondage.

——————————— MALBIM ———————————

וַיְסַפֵּר מֹשֶׁה לְחֹתְנוֹ – *And Moshe told his father-in-law:* This verse stands in contrast to the earlier statement of Yitro's belief in *all*

that God had done for Moshe and for His people Israel (18:1), a formula suggesting that Moshe was the primary recipient of God's favor. But

him. Each asked after the other's welfare, and they went inside
8 the tent. And Moshe told his father-in-law all that the LORD
had done to Pharaoh and the Egyptians for Israel's sake, all the
hardship they had encountered along the way, and how the
9 LORD had rescued them. Yitro delighted in all the good that
the LORD had done for Israel, in His liberating them from the

─────────────── MALBIM *(cont.)* ───────────────

now *Moshe told his father-in-law all that the
LORD had done to Pharaoh and the Egyptians
for Israel's sake,* emphasizing that everything
had been done on Israel's behalf, and not
for him. Thus the Sages quote God as telling
Moshe: "Any greatness that you have achieved
has been for the purpose of serving Israel"
[see Berakhot 32a]. Moshe corrected another
misconception of Yitro, as we see from the
shift in language between these two verses.
The opening statement reveals Yitro's impression that multiple higher powers were
responsible for Israel's salvation. [The word
"God" – *Elohim* – is technically plural] To
address this error, Moshe informs him that in
fact Israel experienced what *the LORD had done
to Pharaoh,* emphasizing that it was "the LORD"
alone who executed the emancipation, and
that there is none like Him. Thirdly, Yitro had
at first focused solely on the positive nature
of the exodus, seeing the liberation as representing *all that God had done for Moshe and
for His people Israel.* He did not at all focus on
the plagues that had smitten Egypt, believing
that the punishments had been issued by a
force of evil. Here too Moshe was intent on
pointing out that the torments were what *the
LORD had done to Pharaoh and the Egyptians.*
That dimension of the ordeal was performed
by God as well, and it should also be viewed
as a positive good since the suffering was administered *for Israel's sake.*

VERSE 9

─────────────── MALBIM ───────────────

וַיִּחַדְּ יִתְרוֹ עַל כָּל־הַטּוֹבָה – *Yitro delighted in
all the good:* Yitro was also pleased to hear
of the suffering that the Egyptians had endured, since he recognized that from their
misery good had sprouted for Israel. Our verse
thus confirms that Moshe's father-in-law now
acknowledged the unity of God, and believed
that there was just one deity governing the
universe, rather than competing forces of
good and evil [where the latter would have
been responsible for punishing the Egyp-
tians].

─────────────── HAAMEK DAVAR ───────────────

עַל כָּל־הַטּוֹבָה – *In all the good:* Yitro rejoiced
upon hearing of all the honor and greatness
God bestowed upon Israel when the need
arose, specifically the protective clouds [of
divine glory], the manna, and the [miraculous]
well of water. אֲשֶׁר הִצִּילוֹ מִיַּד מִצְרָיִם – *In His
liberating them from the Egyptians:* This was the
most significant development, for the emancipation of Israel was eternal, and therefore
outweighed all of the other wonders [which
had been fleeting].

יֹ וַיֹּ֣אמֶר֮ יִתְרוֹ֒ בָּר֣וּךְ יְהֹוָ֔ה אֲשֶׁ֨ר הִצִּ֥יל אֶתְכֶ֛ם מִיַּ֥ד מִצְרַ֖יִם
וּמִיַּ֣ד פַּרְעֹ֑ה אֲשֶׁ֤ר הִצִּיל֙ אֶת־הָעָ֔ם מִתַּ֖חַת יַד־מִצְרָֽיִם׃
יֹֽא עַתָּ֣ה יָדַ֔עְתִּי כִּֽי־גָד֥וֹל יְהֹוָ֖ה מִכָּל־הָאֱלֹהִ֑ים כִּ֣י בַדָּבָ֔ר אֲשֶׁ֥ר
יֹֽב זָד֖וּ עֲלֵיהֶֽם׃ וַיִּקַּ֞ח יִתְר֣וֹ חֹתֵ֣ן מֹשֶׁ֗ה עֹלָ֥ה וּזְבָחִ֖ים לֵֽאלֹהִ֑ים
וַיָּבֹ֨א אַהֲרֹ֜ן וְכֹ֣ל ׀ זִקְנֵ֣י יִשְׂרָאֵ֗ל לֶֽאֱכָל־לֶ֛חֶם עִם־חֹתֵ֥ן מֹשֶׁ֖ה

VERSE 10

MALBIM

וַיֹּאמֶר יִתְרוֹ בָּרוּךְ יְהוה – *And Yitro said, "Blessed be the* Lord*"*: I have already explained that the verse from Psalms which states: *Blessed be the name of the* Lord *from this time forth and for evermore* (Psalms 113:2) addresses the beliefs held by the nations of the world. The gentile peoples may accept that there is a first cause [a creator] whom they refer to as the "God of gods," but they believe that He is only to be praised and not blessed. For a blessing represents the abundance that emanates from God,

and these peoples do not acknowledge that God influences the world by bestowing upon it the largesse of His providence. For according to this approach, after God created the world, He delegated the running of it to the stars in the heavens. Therefore God Himself only deserves our praise – for having made the earth in the first place – but not our blessing. In our *parasha*, we see Yitro rejecting the position of the gentiles, admitting that God is blessed when he declares: *Blessed be the* Lord.

VERSE 11

SHADAL

מִכָּל־הָאֱלֹהִים – *Than all gods:* The Egyptians had dominated the Israelites, abusing them unrestrainedly until their lives were suffused with bitterness and all means of suffering. The oppressors' creative torments extended to drowning the Hebrew babies in the river and withholding the basic provisions they required to fulfill their miserable quota of slave labor. It was clear that no salvation of Israel would emerge via any natural avenue. Only God Himself could be up to the task of extricating

His people from the mire. Indeed, if the Israelites had not been so weak and demoralized, the Egyptians would surely have limited the cruelty they perpetrated against them, for fear of a violent rebellion by the slaves. But the God of Israel, who bears sufficient strength to rescue a poor and weak nation from the powerful and mighty superpower that was Egypt, defied that nation's gods, who were no match for Him. Thus did God demonstrate that He *is greater than all gods.*

MALBIM

אֲשֶׁר זָדוּ עֲלֵיהֶם – *What they schemed against others:* By paying the Egyptians back measure for measure, God demonstrated His greatness. For only a being who dominates all of the powers in the world could execute such justice. A force which excels in only one

particular sphere would be unable to inflict punishment such as Egypt suffered. For example, an agent who controls the lightning can unleash its fire, while a master of the seas can wield its waters. But the Egyptian plagues encompassed all elements of the natural world,

10 Egyptians – and said, "Blessed be the LORD who has rescued
you from Egypt and Pharaoh and liberated the people from
11 the Egyptians' hands. Now I know that the LORD is greater
than all gods – for He brought upon them what they schemed
12 against others." Then Yitro brought a burnt offering and sacrifices to God. And Aharon and all the elders of Israel came

——————————— MALBIM *(cont.)* ———————————

illustrating that however the oppressors attempted to torment the Hebrews, God was
capable of responding in kind. He therefore
inflicted torments the Egyptians deserved

and which matched the abuse they had devised. Hence Yitro deduced that only a God
who *is greater than all gods* would be capable
of such feats.

VERSE 12

——————————— OR HAḤAYYIM ———————————

עֹלָה וּזְבָחִים – *A burnt offering and sacrifices:*
Yitro presented many peace offerings to be
sacrificed, and this was a signal that he meant
to host the Israelite leadership in the attendant feast. It was evident from his actions
that he intended that these important personages participate in his display of gratitude,
although the verse does not explicitly mention his calling upon Aharon and the elders

of Israel to dine with him. That is, when these
people saw that Yitro had brought a great
many sacrifices, they understood that the
man could surely not consume all of the meat
by himself, and feared it would go to waste.
They therefore honored Moshe's father-in-
law at their own initiative and did not stand
on the ceremony of being formally invited
to join him.

——————————— RABBI SAMSON RAPHAEL HIRSCH ———————————

עֹלָה וּזְבָחִים – *A burnt offering and sacrifices:*
The term "sacrifices" [*zevaḥim*] denotes peace
offerings, which are mostly eaten by the do-
nors after select parts are burned on the altar.
This combination proves that physical enjoyment in this world can itself constitute service of God, for when a person brings a peace

offering, it is as if he is dining at the divine
table. The Talmud refers to this phenomenon
as "being granted food from the table of the
Almighty" [see Yevamot 87a], for the meal
which follows the sacrifice takes place in the
presence of God.

——————————— MALBIM ———————————

וַיִּקַּח יִתְרוֹ – *Then Yitro brought:* Yitro brought
a burnt offering following his conversion.
For when a gentile joins in the covenant of
Israel, he must be circumcised, immerse in
a ritual bath, and offer a sacrifice. Now this
interpretation follows the approach which
holds that Yitro's arrival came after the Torah was given, in which case the sacrifices

were offered on the Tabernacle's altar. However, some authors contend that Yitro visited
Moshe before the Torah was given to Israel [as
the ordering of the Torah text suggests]. If so,
the father-in-law offered his sacrifices on the
altar Moshe had built and named "The LORD is
My Banner" (17:15). This altar was constructed
at Ḥorev, where Moshe was encamped.

יג לִפְנֵי הָאֱלֹהִים: וַיְהִי מִמָּחֳרָת וַיֵּשֶׁב מֹשֶׁה לִשְׁפֹּט אֶת־הָעָם שני

יד וַיַּעֲמֹד הָעָם עַל־מֹשֶׁה מִן־הַבֹּקֶר עַד־הָעָרֶב: וַיַּרְא חֹתֵן

מֹשֶׁה אֵת כָּל־אֲשֶׁר־הוּא עֹשֶׂה לָעָם וַיֹּאמֶר מָה־הַדָּבָר

הַזֶּה אֲשֶׁר אַתָּה עֹשֶׂה לָעָם מַדּוּעַ אַתָּה יוֹשֵׁב לְבַדֶּךָ וְכָל־

טו הָעָם נִצָּב עָלֶיךָ מִן־בֹּקֶר עַד־עָרֶב: וַיֹּאמֶר מֹשֶׁה לְחֹתְנוֹ

VERSE 13

RABBI SAMSON RAPHAEL HIRSCH

לִשְׁפֹּט אֶת־הָעָם – *To serve the people as judge:* Moshe subsequently explains to his father-in-law that *the people come to me to inquire [lidrosh] of God* (18:15), which means that the populace sought God's teaching and assistance. The concept of inquiry *[derisha]* comprises all the ways in which we relate to God in our lives, through all of our experiences and trials. If we are to have the LORD as our God, we must consequently seek Him and strive to determine His will. Thus when the prophet says: *For, thus says the LORD to the house of Israel,* *Seek me [dirshuni] and you shall live* (Amos 5:4), he expresses the most comprehensive request that God demands of man. Indeed, it is our hope that by seeking the teaching and salvation of God we will in the end find God Himself. When we consider God in the context of even the most trivial aspects of our lives, our whole existence becomes suffused with the divine. This is what God means when He states: *They shall make Me a sanctuary and I will dwell in their midst* (25:8).

HAAMEK DAVAR

וַיְהִי מִמָּחֳרָת – *The next day:* This incident occurred on the day after Yitro offered his sacrifices, when he achieved the heightened spiritual awareness he had sought [by way of the offerings]. The issue that he raised with Moshe regarding his judgments was informed by the Divine Spirit. According to the Mekhilta, this verse refers to the day after Yom Kippur. However, the *Tur HaArokh* argues that a scribal error has crept into that text, and that the conversation took place "on the day after the atonement *[kappara]*," meaning the day after the sacrifices were brought.

VERSE 14

MALBIM

מַדּוּעַ אַתָּה יוֹשֵׁב לְבַדֶּךָ – *Why do you sit alone:* Moshe had not appointed judges to assist him because the Torah had not yet been given to Israel. This meant that God had not established civil laws for administering the nation. For the people had only been instructed in a scant few rules at Mara [see 15:25] and given the general commandment to act justly toward the oppressed. Had Moshe set up a court system wherein the judges would determine rulings based solely on their own intuition, the litigants likely would have rejected their verdicts. People found liable would have subsequently appealed their cases to Moshe. Now Yitro believed that Moshe too was determining trials solely according to his own

13 to break bread with Moshe's father-in-law before God. The SHENI
next day Moshe sat to serve the people as judge. From morn-
14 ing to evening the people stood before him. When Moshe's father-in-law saw everything Moshe did for the people, he asked,
"What is this that you do for the people? Why do you sit alone
while all the people stand over you from morning to evening?"
15 "The people come to me to inquire of God," Moshe replied.

———————— MALBIM *(cont.)* ————————

reasoning and intellect, and did not think that he was governing by the laws of God. This is what he meant when he asked Moshe: *What is this that you do for the people?* That is, the task you are performing alone could easily be handled by others just as capable as you. Now when he Yitro noted that *all the people stand [nitzav] over you from morning to evening,* his choice of verb was intentional, since there is a difference between the terms *nitzav* and *omed* [both of which mean "stand"]. For while *amida* simply represents the opposite of sitting, *hatzava* connotes support or strength. So for example, ministers of the king who serve him food and are responsible for guarding him are said to be "*nitzavim* over him," whereas servants who merely cater to the king can be said

to be "*omedim* over him." Most of the nation, such as those who came to Moshe with quarrels or questions, fit into the latter category which is why the verse states: *From morning to evening the people stood [vayaamod] before him* (18:13). The people stood there of their own volition to hear Moshe's teachings. Yitro however, perceived the scene differently, asking why *all the people stand [nitzav] over you from morning to evening.* In his opinion, the people's posture reflected an imposing attitude toward Moshe. For every individual wanted to force his case on the leader, to have it resolved, and to go home. Yitro thus viewed the people standing there not as an accommodating and patient public, but as a pushy and unruly mass.

———————— HAAMEK DAVAR ————————

מַדּוּעַ אַתָּה יוֹשֵׁב לְבַדֶּךָ – *Why do you sit alone:* Yitro posed two questions to his son-in-law. Firstly, when he asked: *Why do you sit alone while all the people stand over you?* he did not mean to ask why Moshe alone sat, while the people were forced to stand. For could seats then have been provided for all the masses of people who sought their leader's advice?

Rather, what Yitro meant was: Why do you not seat one or two other capable men next to you to assist you in this work? Secondly, Yitro wanted to know: Why do *all the people stand over you,* when it is clear that only a minority of them have issues that require your abilities to resolve?

VERSE 15

———————— OR HAHAYYIM ————————

כִּי־יָבֹא אֵלַי הָעָם לִדְרֹשׁ אֱלֹהִים – *The people come to me to inquire of God:* Moshe's response to Yitro really doesn't answer his father-in-law's question at all, for the man could clearly

see that the people were lining up regularly to inquire of God. Yitro was challenging Moshe about the wisdom of the procedure, which was sure to exhaust the nation. He was not

יט כִּי־יָבֹא אֵלַי הָעָם לִדְרֹשׁ אֱלֹהִים: כִּי־יִהְיֶה לָהֶם דָּבָר
בָּא אֵלַי וְשָׁפַטְתִּי בֵּין אִישׁ וּבֵין רֵעֵהוּ וְהוֹדַעְתִּי אֶת־חֻקֵּי

——————————— OR HAHAYYIM *(cont.)* ———————————

asking about the subject of the discussions between Moshe and the people, but was rather distressed that Moshe sat alone with no assistance from other judges. Now had Moshe failed to understand Yitro's question, he should have asked him what he meant; it was inappropriate for him to merely repeat the basis for Yitro's question. But in fact, Moshe understood his father-in-law's query slightly differently. He thought that when Yitro said: *What is this that you do* (18:14), he believed that Moshe was compelling the people to come only to him rather than seeking aid from others. The fact that Moshe refused to appoint other judges meant that the people would become exhausted and frustrated at having only one address for their grievances. All that was required was for Moshe to relinquish some of his authority and to find other wise men who could help to lighten his load. It was in answer to this accusation that Moshe explained that it had not been his policy to serve as the nation's lone adjudicator, but what could he do? *The people come to me to inquire of God* and are unwilling to trust anyone else with

their disputes. And as for Yitro's question as to why the people should insist on the current system despite the hassle it created, Moshe explained that he was inherently the most qualified individual to treat Israel's problems. Focusing on the language of the verse, our Sages interpreted Moshe's statement as admitting that he employed divine assistance in judging Israel. The verse states: *When they have a dispute, they come [ba] to me and I judge* (18:16). Curiously, the verb *ba* here appears in the singular, suggesting that something besides the people was coming to Moshe. According to the Sages, it was the dispute or issue itself which made itself clear to Moshe through the agency of divine inspiration. In that way, Moshe was able to judge correctly every time, a power that no other magistrate could boast. Accordingly, there would be no advantage to appointing judges to ease Moshe's case load, since their dockets would remain empty. Furthermore, explains Moshe, *I make God's laws and teachings known* (18:16), a feat of which only he was capable since it was he who received communications from God.

VERSE **16**

——————————— SHADAL ———————————

אֶת־חֻקֵּי הָאֱלֹהִים וְאֶת־תּוֹרֹתָיו – *God's laws and teachings:* The term "laws" [*hukkim*] here does not refer to the eternal commandments that comprise the central part of Israel's law, since that would imply that Yitro arrived at the camp following the giving of the Torah. Rather, Moshe is referring to temporary instructions he had received from God for administering the nation's affairs. When Moshe eventually delivered God's law to the nation, he did so in a public forum, and not to

individuals one by one who appeared before him. And when he thus addressed the people as a whole, he did not need to sit before them for the entire day as is described here. Now it is true that the word *hok* generally does not denote a judgment on a private matter, but a general statute that is permanently applicable to the entire community. Still, here the term signifies specific rulings that Moshe issued based on general laws that God had revealed to him.

16 "When they have a dispute, they come to me and I judge between one neighbor and another, and I make God's laws and

———————————— MALBIM ————————————

כִּי־יִהְיֶה לָהֶם דָּבָר בָּא אֵלַי – *When they have a dispute, they come to me:* Moshe here alluded to the tendency of righteous people, when they have a disagreement between them, to view their quarrel as a matter of religious significance, as a question of the permissibility of some act. For example, when it is unclear whether a certain financial move constitutes theft, it is sufficient to send one of the two individuals to seek the legal resolution to the difficulty. This is why Moshe uses the singular form of the verb: *When they have a dispute, they come* [literally, "he comes"] *to me,* meaning that only one of the two would appear before him with the question. In a case where one citizen has caused damaged to another's property, the responsible party would consult with Moshe regarding how much he must pay the other according to Torah law. [Because both disputants agree to the facts of the case and are merely uncertain as to the law, and they each trust the other's good intentions, a single representative can seek a ruling.] Still, on occasion, both parties would come together when they disagreed

as to the facts of the situation, which is when Moshe would *judge between one neighbor and another.* There was a third sort of business which Moshe was responsible for, and that was to teach the public *God's laws and teachings,* that is, the practical commandments, most of which are "laws" [*ḥukkim*] a term that usually refers to seemingly arbitrary decrees. The "teachings" [*torot*] that Moshe transmitted to the Israelites were principles of faith, such as the existence and nature of providence, prophecy, reward and punishment, and the development of the proper ethical character. In this verse, Moshe also responds to Yitro's complaint that the people were being made to stand while he sat and talked to them. Whenever Moshe would *judge between one neighbor and another,* his decisions were informed not by his own reasoning, but by God's laws. He therefore used these opportunities to make this material known to the people. Eager to learn, understand, and obey the word of God, the people crowded around their leader, creating a forum that was standing room only.

———————————— HAAMEK DAVAR ————————————

אֶת־חֻקֵּי הָאֱלֹהִים וְאֶת־תּוֹרֹתָיו – *God's laws and teachings:* Moshe explained to Yitro that it was necessary for him to teach Israel God's laws and that he could not rely on his human intuitions when judging them. The "laws" [*ḥukkim* – the term connotes decrees whose rationales are inaccessible to us] are not like the charitable acts of visiting the sick and burying the dead, which represent decent behavior and are also commandments from God. Those practices are not stated explicitly

in the Torah text, but are subsumed within the general injunction to *love your neighbor as yourself* (Leviticus 19:18), and the details of their application are therefore left to the subjective reasoning of the generation's scholars. Moshe took the position that although some cases that were brought before him could indeed be adjudicated by others, it was his knowledge of God's will regarding the *ḥukkim* that demanded he hear all the people's cases.

הָאֱלֹהִים וְאֶת־תּוֹרֹתָיו: וַיֹּאמֶר חֹתֵן מֹשֶׁה אֵלָיו לֹא־טוֹב ‏יז
הַדָּבָר אֲשֶׁר אַתָּה עֹשֶׂה: נָבֹל תִּבֹּל גַּם־אַתָּה גַּם־הָעָם הַזֶּה ‏יח
אֲשֶׁר עִמָּךְ כִּי־כָבֵד מִמְּךָ הַדָּבָר לֹא־תוּכַל עֲשֹׂהוּ לְבַדֶּךָ:
עַתָּה שְׁמַע בְּקֹלִי אִיעָצְךָ וִיהִי אֱלֹהִים עִמָּךְ הֱיֵה אַתָּה לָעָם ‏יט
מוּל הָאֱלֹהִים וְהֵבֵאתָ אַתָּה אֶת־הַדְּבָרִים אֶל־הָאֱלֹהִים:
וְהִזְהַרְתָּה אֶתְהֶם אֶת־הַחֻקִּים וְאֶת־הַתּוֹרֹת וְהוֹדַעְתָּ לָהֶם ‏כ

VERSE 17

MALBIM

לֹא־טוֹב הַדָּבָר אֲשֶׁר אַתָּה עֹשֶׂה – *What you are doing is not good:* The system you are practicing is bad for you because it will exhaust you, and it is bad for the nation since they too will become fed up. You will become worn out because *it is too heavy a burden for you* (18:18), and the

workload will sap you of your strength. You will end up like a man weakened after carrying a heavy object for too long a time. Meanwhile, the people will become frustrated because *you cannot carry it alone* (18:18), and most will despair of ever having their cases heard.

HAAMEK DAVAR

הַדָּבָר אֲשֶׁר אַתָּה עֹשֶׂה – *What you are doing:* Yitro disapproved of Moshe serving as an intermediary for *the people [who] come to inquire of God* (18:15) and making *God's laws and*

teachings known (18:16), since he could never perform these services adequately unaided. Yitro then proceeded to explain how to properly teach the nation.

VERSE 18

OR HAHAYYIM

נָבֹל תִּבֹּל – *You will be worn away:* There are two ways to interpret the word *tibbol.* The first is as indicating the reduction of one's strength, leading to fatigue relative to one's previous condition. When tiredness like this affects a person, he nevertheless remains capable of fulfilling his obligations, even though it might require a bit more effort to do so. However, the term can also refer to utter exhaustion that leads to total incapacitation. Hence Yitro warned Moshe that should he maintain his

current practice of judging the people all day, every day, he would become so worn out that he would be unable to function. This is what the father-in-law meant when he said: *You cannot carry it alone* – even if you put in the extra effort, you will have no strength left to continue such work. Perhaps the doubling of the verb in this verse [*navol tibbol*] refers to both Moshe and the people, implying that both parties would be unable to endure.

VERSE 19

SHADAL

וִיהִי אֱלֹהִים עִמָּךְ – *And may God be with you:* May God help you. This was said in an affectionate way, as if to say: May God have mercy

on you [and not negatively, as in: God help you!].

17 teachings known." Moshe's father-in-law said to him, "What
18 you are doing is not good. You will be worn away, and this
people along with you. It is too heavy a burden for you. You
19 cannot carry it alone. Now listen to me, let me advise you; and
may God be with you. You speak for the people before God,
20 and bring their concerns to Him. And you must acquaint them
with His precepts and laws, and make known to them the

———————————— HAAMEK DAVAR ————————————

הֱיֵה אַתָּה לָעָם מוּל הָאֱלֹהִים – *You speak for the people before God:* There are two types of intermediaries between man and God, just like there are two different avenues for a citizen wishing to communicate with a human king. Firstly, a king might appoint an advisor to represent him, somebody who is familiar with his opinions and who can speak on his behalf. Alternatively, the people might meet with a diplomat who has the king's confidence and can relate their grievances to him. The difference between these two types of intermediaries is this: The minister whom the king delegates to address the people has no real affinity to them; he is merely fulfilling the duty set to him by his sovereign. Such a person presents the beliefs of the king without interceding with him on the people's behalf. But the second type of official is the people's confidant and counselor. As such, he will seek the king's assistance to benefit them. These two arrangements also exist for those wishing to address to God. For not everyone is capable of eloquent speech before the King of Kings,

and fewer are worthy of receiving God's word through prophecy. Hence the citizens of Israel have only two options: The first is to speak with a prophet whom God has appointed to serve as His voice on earth. Such a person is empowered to express God's opinion even on personal matters. For example, we find that Sha'ul visited Shmuel to ask for assistance in locating his father's lost donkeys [see I Samuel 9]. Likewise, the prophet Eliyahu rebuked King Ahazyahu for not seeking God's advice regarding his illness [see II Kings 1]. The second alternative is the common practice of visiting the scholars of the generation and petitioning them to pray to God on one's behalf, even though these holy men are not prophets. So our Sages state [see Bava Batra 116a]: If someone has a sick family member, he should visit a sage who will pray for him. Now Yitro advised Moshe to not merely act as a prophet who relates the divine will to the people, but to also extend himself to speak to God on the Israelites' behalf, and to transmit their requests back to Him.

VERSE 20

———————————— RABBI SAMSON RAPHAEL HIRSCH ————————————

וְאֶת־הַמַּעֲשֶׂה אֲשֶׁר יַעֲשׂוּן – *And the way they must act:* Yitro advised Moshe to teach his charges the proper way to interact with one another. For when it comes to civil matters, it is easy for disputants to view their case objectively and to accept that a just resolution must be cut and dried. And yet, we sometimes overlook

the fact that although one party may be acquitted according to letter of the law and not liable to make any payment, he still ought to alter his behavior and improve upon it. This he should do for the sake of developing his own good standing and personal ethics. Thus Yitro here refers to training the Israelites to extend

כא אֶת־הַדֶּ֙רֶךְ֙ יֵ֣לְכוּ בָ֔הּ וְאֶת־הַֽמַּעֲשֶׂ֖ה אֲשֶׁ֣ר יַעֲשֽׂוּן: וְאַתָּ֣ה
תֶחֱזֶ֣ה מִכָּל־הָ֠עָ֠ם אַנְשֵׁי־חַ֜יִל יִרְאֵ֤י אֱלֹהִים֙ אַנְשֵׁ֣י אֱמֶ֔ת
שֹׂ֖נְאֵ֣י בָ֑צַע וְשַׂמְתָּ֣ עֲלֵהֶ֗ם שָׂרֵ֤י אֲלָפִים֙ שָׂרֵ֣י מֵא֔וֹת שָׂרֵ֥י
כב חֲמִשִּׁ֖ים וְשָׂרֵ֥י עֲשָׂרֹֽת: וְשָׁפְט֤וּ אֶת־הָעָם֙ בְּכָל־עֵ֔ת וְהָיָ֞ה
כָּל־הַדָּבָ֤ר הַגָּדֹל֙ יָבִ֣יאוּ אֵלֶ֔יךָ וְכָל־הַדָּבָ֥ר הַקָּטֹ֖ן יִשְׁפְּטוּ־
כג הֵ֑ם וְהָקֵל֙ מֵֽעָלֶ֔יךָ וְנָשְׂא֖וּ אִתָּֽךְ: אִם־אֶת־הַדָּבָ֤ר הַזֶּה֙ תַּעֲשֶׂ֔ה

─────── RABBI SAMSON RAPHAEL HIRSCH *(cont.)* ───────

themselves beyond the letter of the law and occasionally forfeit their rights for the benefit of others. In this way the attributes of righteousness and grace are introduced to the realm of law and justice. Now it would be inappropriate for a judge to require that the beneficiary of his verdict act altruistically and not insist upon his rights; still, those people who wish to act correctly must demand such behavior of themselves. It is this message of compassion that Yitro urged Moshe to inculcate in the Israelites. Furthermore, if we accept that this incident took place before the giving of the Torah, it suggests that this idea of suppressing what one deserves in favor of kindness toward others represents a basic human duty.

VERSE 21

─────── OR HAḤAYYIM ───────

וְאַתָּה תֶחֱזֶה – *You, as well, must seek out:* Yitro here emphasized that it was Moshe who must select the judges, and not the people. Under such an arrangement, Moshe would still be viewed as the chief justice, with the magistrates as his representatives. Moshe would then receive some merit for the service the other judges performed for the nation.... Now permit me to explore the question of why the Torah attributed the institution of establishing judges to Yitro. It seems that the man was given credit for this development as a reward for having humbled himself before Moshe, God's servant, although he was his father-in-law. Notwithstanding, surely God could have repaid Yitro in a manner that did not suggest a lack of wisdom on the part of His own nation. For the story makes it seem

that until the arrival of the priest of Midyan in the Israelite camp, it had not occurred to anyone to set up a system of courts. Perhaps the message that God was trying to convey to that generation, and to all future eras of Jewish people, was that indeed Israel does not hold a monopoly on wisdom. There are many wise personalities among the gentiles, a fact which we see quite clearly from the advice Yitro supplies Moshe, and the attributes that he lists of who would make capable judges. The Israelites must understand that God did not choose them as His favored nation because of their exceptional intellect relative to the gentiles, for we are no wiser than they are. Yitro's perception is evidence of this. Rather, God's selection of Israel is a sign of His supreme grace and His love for the patriarchs.

─────── HAAMEK DAVAR ───────

מִכָּל־הָעָם – *Among the people:* Note that Yitro does not suggest that Moshe seek candidates

from within "Israel," but from the "people" [connoting the common masses]. This implies

21 path they are to walk and the way they must act. You, as well, must seek out among the people, capable men – God-fearing, trustworthy men, who despise corruption; and appoint them over the people as leaders of thousands, hundreds, fifties, and 22 tens. Have them serve as daily judges for the people; let them bring the major cases to you, but judge the minor ones themselves. In this way they will lighten your load, and bear it to-23 gether with you. If you do this, and God so commands, then

——————————— HAAMEK DAVAR *(cont.)* ———————————

that Yitro understood, through divine inspiration, that even if there are no suitable Torah scholars available, it is worthwhile to appoint judges from among the laymen, as the Talmud describes the judges of Syrian courts [who ruled according to common sense; see Sanhedrin 23a].

VERSE 22

——————————— MALBIM ———————————

וְשָׁפְטוּ אֶת־הָעָם בְּכָל־עֵת – *Have them serve as daily judges:* Once there was a plethora of judges, the entire people could be judged. Furthermore, trials could take place at any time and there would be no long delays of legal proceedings. And as for Moshe's concern that his appointed assistants will be unfamiliar with God's laws, these men would still be able to refer to Moshe on difficult matters, while they could handle the less taxing issues on their own. And since most court cases address trivial issues, Moshe's workload would be lightened substantially. What's more, the presence of additional judges would also aid the leader with the more complicated cases. For these men would be present at those hearings too, and would be able to hear the claims, accept the witnesses' testimonies and question them, and be available to pronounce sentencing.

VERSE 23

——————————— SHADAL ———————————

וְגַם כָּל־הָעָם הַזֶּה עַל־מְקֹמוֹ יָבֹא בְשָׁלוֹם – *And all these people will be able to go home in peace:* If Moshe followed Yitro's advice, the entire nation would not be required to visit the leader for their cases to be heard, but would be able to appear before local magistrates. This meant that disputants would go to the court that is closest to them, and the confusion of all the people descending on one spot would be alleviated. Hence going to judgment would be a peaceful affair.

——————————— RABBI SAMSON RAPHAEL HIRSCH ———————————

עַל־מְקֹמוֹ יָבֹא בְשָׁלוֹם – *Will be able to go home in peace:* [Literally, "will arrive at its place in peace."] It seems that the verse does not mean that the quarreling parties will arrive home peacefully, but that each individual will reach the point of contentment and the position that he deserves. Is that not the true responsibility of a judge — to ensure that every person who comes before him ends up in his proper place?

CONFRONTING MODERNITY

כד וַיִּשְׁמַע מֹשֶׁה לְקוֹל חֹתְנוֹ וַיַּעַשׂ כָּל אֲשֶׁר אָמָר: שלישי
וַיִּצַוְּךָ אֱלֹהִים וְיָכָלְתָּ עֲמֹד וְגַם כָּל הָעָם הַזֶּה עַל מְקֹמוֹ יָבֹא
בְשָׁלוֹם:

כה וַיִּבְחַר מֹשֶׁה אַנְשֵׁי חַיִל מִכָּל יִשְׂרָאֵל וַיִּתֵּן אֹתָם רָאשִׁים
עַל הָעָם שָׂרֵי אֲלָפִים שָׂרֵי מֵאוֹת שָׂרֵי חֲמִשִּׁים וְשָׂרֵי

VERSE 24

──────────────── RABBI SAMSON RAPHAEL HIRSCH ────────────────

וַיִּשְׁמַע מֹשֶׁה לְקוֹל חֹתְנוֹ – *Moshe listened to his father-in-law:* The method by which Israel's first national institution was established is most instructive for us, not least because it was created just prior to the giving of the Torah described in the next chapter. What this episode describes is nothing less than the leadership deficiencies of Moshe the lawgiver. Here is a man who had such poor organizational skills that his father-in-law had to teach him the most basic idea for managing the populace under his care. Moshe worked himself to exhaustion hearing the people's quarrels and questions rather than making the logical adjustment of hiring additional judges for his own sake and for the people's benefit. A man like this, who required Yitro's advice on such an obvious matter, surely could not have possessed the intellect necessary to invent the Torah's laws and statutes all on his own. It was only because Moshe was a loyal servant of God and could be trusted to repeat God's teachings to the nation that he was best suited for the job he held.

──────────────── MALBIM ────────────────

וַיִּשְׁמַע מֹשֶׁה לְקוֹל חֹתְנוֹ – *Moshe listened to his father-in-law:* According to the recapitulation of this episode told in the book of Deuteronomy, Moshe only chose his judges in the second year after the exodus, as the nation was traveling from the Sinai Desert to the land of Israel [after the Torah was given at Sinai]. Now according to the approach which argues that Yitro arrived at the nation's encampment before the revelation took place, which is what the order of the text here indicates, how do we understand this statement that *Moshe listened to his father-in-law?* [That is, how could the Torah claim that Moshe heeded Yitro's advice, when he apparently implemented the plan only a year later?] Remember that I have already explained the difference between the two constructions *lishmoa bekol* and *lishmoa lekol* [both mean "listen to"; the latter is used in this verse]. When the Torah uses the phrase *lishmoa bekol,* it implies that the listener has accepted the speaker's message, whereas *lishmoa lekol* means only that the addressee has heard what the other person has to say and is considering the matter. Hence our verse takes the trouble to say that Moshe *did all that [Yitro] said.* If the verse had stated, *vayishma bekol* such a clause would have been unnecessary, since it would have been clear that Moshe had adopted his father-in-law's advice. However, since the text states *vayishma lekol,* the reader remains uncertain whether or not Moshe was convinced that Yitro's plan was correct. Hence our verse tells us that when the advice was delivered, Moshe began to consider its merits and deficiencies, but that he was not able to act right away to establish a court system. This was because God had not yet communicated the civil laws listed in Parashat Mishpatim, and Moshe was hesitant to empower judges

you will endure, and all these people will be able to go home in
24 peace." Moshe listened to his father-in-law and did all that he   SHELISHI
25 said. Moshe chose capable men from all Israel and made them
chiefs over the people, leaders of thousands, hundreds, fifties,

——————————— MALBIM *(cont.)* ———————————

to rule cases based only on their reasoning
and common sense. Hence Moshe waited to

enact Yitro's plan until after he had taught the
people God's decrees.

——————————— HAAMEK DAVAR ———————————

וַיַּעַשׂ כֹּל אֲשֶׁר אָמָר – *And did all that he said:* Moshe accepted Yitro's advice to start praying to
God on behalf of individual Israelites.

VERSE 25

——————————— MALBIM ———————————

וַיִּבְחַר מֹשֶׁה אַנְשֵׁי־חַיִל – *Moshe chose capable
men:* When Moshe recounts this episode in
the book of Deuteronomy, he said to the
people: *Take wise men, and understanding,
and known among your tribes, and I will make
them rulers over you* (Deuteronomy 1:13). [This
verse seems at odds with ours, claiming that
the people selected the judges, rather than
Moshe]. But there is no contradiction between
the two versions of the judicial appointments.
Although the people were able to nominate
men who were wise and knowledgeable ruling out the fools and imbeciles, only Moshe
possessed the divine inspiration necessary to
discover which prospects were God-fearing
men who despised corruption. This explains
Yitro's choice of verbs when he advises: *You,
as well, must seek out* [*teḥezeh,* a verb with
connotations of prophecy] *among the people,*

capable men (18:21). And so, after the Israelites
presented Moshe with their candidates, who
were all intelligent and learned individuals, the
leader used his powers of perception to narrow the group down to those men who also
held the qualities that only he could divine.
When Moshe later recalled: *I took the chiefs
of your tribes, wise men, and known, and made
them heads over you* (Deuteronomy 1:15), what
he meant was that he selected from among
the wise men whom the people brought to
him. And when the Torah here reports that
Moshe chose capable men from all Israel, this
refers, as I have already written, to men who
were characterized by all three critical attributes [mentioned in verse 21]. Hence the most
important selection was indeed performed by
Moshe, as Yitro had suggested.

——————————— HAAMEK DAVAR ———————————

אַנְשֵׁי־חַיִל מִכָּל־יִשְׂרָאֵל – *Capable men from all
Israel:* Moshe was well aware that the nation of
Israel contained many venerable scholars who
could be trusted to rule according to Torah
law. This is why he narrowed down his search
to focus on those learned men. With this
group, Moshe did not need to check the candidates to see whether they were *God-fearing,
trustworthy men, who despise corruption* [18:21;

hence these qualities are absent from Moshe's
criteria in this verse]. For any Torah scholar
who served as Moshe's student would have
already refined his character until he was righteous, honest and forthright. Nevertheless,
Moshe still had to ascertain which of these
men were "capable" by examining their tem-
perament and their ability to exercise authority over the community.

כו עֲשָׂרֹת: וְשָׁפְטוּ אֶת־הָעָם בְּכָל־עֵת אֶת־הַדָּבָר הַקָּשֶׁה

כז יְבִיאוּן אֶל־מֹשֶׁה וְכָל־הַדָּבָר הַקָּטֹן יִשְׁפּוּטוּ הֵם: וַיְשַׁלַּח

מֹשֶׁה אֶת־חֹתְנוֹ וַיֵּלֶךְ לוֹ אֶל־אַרְצוֹ:

יט א בַּחֹדֶשׁ הַשְּׁלִישִׁי לְצֵאת בְּנֵי־יִשְׂרָאֵל מֵאֶרֶץ מִצְרָיִם בַּיּוֹם רביעי

VERSE 26

——————— **HAAMEK DAVAR** ———————

אֶת־הַדָּבָר הַקָּשֶׁה – *Any major case:* [Literally, "a difficult case."] Since the chosen judges were all men versed in the laws of the Torah and were committed to applying them to their judgments, it really made no difference if the cases that they heard were "large" or "small" [*gadol* or *katon*, the terms Yitro used in verse 22], since the ruling regarding a financial dispute is the same regardless of the size of the monetary stakes. However, when the judges were faced with a "difficult" [*kasheh*] question, whose interpretation according to Torah law was not obvious, that was when they appealed to their teacher Moshe for assistance. Note that although the text states that these judges brought the difficult matters to Moshe, the verse does not explicitly state he had to deal with "every" [*kol* – also appearing in verse 22] such case. This is because even when the lower courts were unable to determine how to rule in a given situation, they did not immediately run to Moshe to interpret the law for them, but first asked the appellate court above them for their understanding. And even in the event that a problem proved too difficult for the second tier of judges, and Moshe's help was necessarily sought, the leader did not take over the case completely. The entire substance of the case – the arguments and the defense – was not repeated for Moshe's sake but was presented to him in précis. Furthermore, Moshe did not declare a verdict to the litigants, but rather explained his reasoning and conclusions to the judges who had approached him. After the complex issue had been simplified, the inferior judges once again took control of the decision. This is why the verse states: *They decided every minor matter themselves* [here the word "every" – *kol* – does appear]. Yitro, on the other hand, had suggested that when any difficult question presented itself, the less capable judges should go immediately to Moshe who would hear the case from its beginning, and effectively become the presiding judge in that situation.

——————— **RABBI JOSEPH B. SOLOVEITCHIK** ———————

אֶת־הַדָּבָר הַקָּשֶׁה – *Any major case:* [Literally, "a difficult case."] The *Ḥatam Sofer* points out that when Yitro proposed to Moshe that he lighten the burden of his magistracy, he said: *Have them serve as daily judges for the people; let them bring the major cases to you, but judge the minor ones themselves* (18:22). But when Moshe accepts Yitro's advice here, and later when he repeats the story [in Deuteronomy 1:17], he changes the phraseology of the proposal: instead of the "major" cases, he instead speaks of the "difficult" ones. This, says the *Ḥatam Sofer*, characterizes the difference between Yitro's attitude to law and that of Moshe. Yitro believed that when there was a dispute between two people in a minor case involving a small sum, there was no need to bother Moshe with it. Yitro felt it was sufficient that the leaders over tens deal with it. Moshe should sit in judgment only when great sums

26 and tens. They judged the people every day. Any major case
they brought to Moshe, but they decided every minor matter
27 themselves. Then Moshe parted from his father-in-law, and the
latter went forth, back to his own land.

19 1 On the first day of the third month after the Israelites had left   REVI'I

——————————— RABBI JOSEPH B. SOLOVEITCHIK *(cont.)* ———————————

were involved. This is the attitude of a gentile who says: *Let them bring the major cases to you.* And to this day, in fact, gentiles have small claims courts for dealing with cases involving minor sums. But in Moshe's view, it was not the sum under contention which determined the importance of a case, but rather the problem of law which was at issue. If the law

was direct and clear, even if the case involved millions of dollars, then lower courts should adjudicate the matter. But if it was a difficult case, complex, then *bring it to me, and I will hear it* (Deuteronomy 1:17), even if it involved one penny. The amount of money at stake played no part in determining the complexity of the case.

VERSE 27

——————————— MALBIM ———————————

וַיְשַׁלַּח מֹשֶׁה אֶת־חֹתְנוֹ – *Then Moshe parted from his father-in-law:* According to the approach which states that Yitro visited Israel before the giving of the Torah, he ended up staying with the nation for a full year. For it was only later, when Moshe was preparing to lead the people to the land of Israel, that he eventually said to Yitro: *We are journeying to the place of which the LORD said, I will give it you: come you*

with us, and we will do you good: for the LORD has spoken good concerning Israel (Numbers 10:29). It was then that Moshe implemented his father-in-law's advice and appointed judges to assist him in governing the nation. Yitro, however, declined Moshe's request and preferred to return to Midyan. That later episode is summarized here with the words: *Then Moshe parted from his father-in-law.*

CHAPTER 19, VERSE 1

——————————— OR HAHAYYIM ———————————

בַּחֹדֶשׁ הַשְּׁלִישִׁי – *On the first day of the third month:* Why did God wait until the third month to give Israel His Torah? After all, when one loves another, he does his utmost to expedite their union. And should you argue that it took that long for Israel to travel from Egypt to Mount Sinai, the difficulty remains unresolved, for we know that when Avraham's servant Eliezer journeyed to Aram Naharayim to find a wife for Yitzhak [in Genesis 24], the earth contracted for him [allowing him to arrive faster; see Sanhedrin 95a]. If God was prepared to help Eliezer make such a leap on

behalf of Yitzhak, He certainly should have compressed both the earth and the sky for the sake of the exalted marriage between Israel and the Torah. But in fact, the delay that the Torah describes does not betray any lack of affection of the Holy One, blessed be He, for His people. Rather, it indicates that a preparatory period was required before revelation could take place. Because Israel had endured centuries of exile in the impure land of Egypt and had become polluted by that environment, they were required to wait a full seven weeks for the Torah, during which they were

ב הַזֶּ֖ה בָּ֣אוּ מִדְבַּ֣ר סִינָ֑י: וַיִּסְע֣וּ מֵרְפִידִ֗ים וַיָּבֹ֙אוּ֙ מִדְבַּ֣ר סִינַ֔י

─────────── OR HAHAYYIM *(cont.)* ───────────

to purify themselves. This is why our verse refers back to Israel's exodus from Egypt. The text is not merely establishing the emancipation as a date relative to the current event, but explaining that because the nation had recently emerged from that society of decay, it had to wait until the third month to be fit to receive the Torah.

─────────── RABBI SAMSON RAPHAEL HIRSCH ───────────

בָּ֣אוּ מִדְבַּ֣ר סִינָ֑י – *They came to the Sinai Desert:* Prior to Israel's arrival at the Sinai Desert, whenever they came to a new area of the wilderness they would examine the location to consider whether or not it was an appropriate site for encampment. However, the people understood that Mount Sinai represented the ultimate purpose of their travels. It was from this point, so they were told, that they were fated to accept the burden of divine service. Now these people were so fully the sons of Avraham, so deserving of the title "Israel," and so influenced by the events they had experienced, that when Mount Sinai came into view, all physical considerations that had concerned them earlier disappeared, and they set up camp as "Israel" [referred to in the singular in the next verse to indicate unity of purpose]. This eagerness on the part of the nation supports the understanding that all of Israel's outbursts and discontent that we have read about had nothing to do with a lack of faith or trust in God, but rested only in the doubts they felt toward the leadership of Moshe and Aharon.

─────────── HAAMEK DAVAR ───────────

בַּחֹ֖דֶשׁ הַשְּׁלִישִׁ֑י – *On the first day of the third month:* The early commentators have already explained the meaning behind the Torah's shift in style when describing this leg of the journey. [Other descriptions use a simple formula like that found in verse 2 here, without such a dramatic introductory sentence.] The traditional explanation for this deviation is that from the very start of the nation's travels, their primary destination, the very purpose of the exodus, was Mount Sinai and the acceptance of the Torah. Thus, the opening of this chapter announces that Israel had reached the site that represented the goal of the entire journey. And yet, we still must explain why the Torah uses the extra phrase "on that day" [*bayom hazeh*, in the middle of the verse; the phrase is untranslated in this edition]. This language [which has the effect of setting off the first clause of the verse and emphasizing it] stresses the significance of the third month, as the Talmud states: A certain Galilean scholar lectured: Blessed be the Merciful One, who delivered a tripartite Torah [the Torah, the Prophets, and the Writings] to a tripartite people [Priests, Levites, Israelites], through a third-born [Moshe, who was the third child in his family], on the third day [of preparation] in the third month (Shabbat 88a). The Torah was given deliberately in the third month, and our verse clarifies that the arrival at the site of revelation took place on the first of that month.

─────────── MESHEKH HOKHMA ───────────

בַּחֹ֖דֶשׁ הַשְּׁלִישִׁ֑י – *On the first day of the third month:* If one searches the length and breadth of the Torah, he will not find another passage that starts as ours does, specifying a month without an introductory conjunctive letter *vav*. [In the biblical narrative, such conjunctions

2 Egypt they came to the Sinai Desert. Setting out from Refidim
they had arrived at the Sinai Desert, encamping in the wilderness, and there Israel camped, facing the mountain,

——————— MESHEKH ḤOKHMA *(cont.)* ———————

commonly serve to connect new stories to
those that precede them.] Here however, the
text starts in a way reminiscent of the book
of Genesis [which begins: *When God began*

creating the heavens and the earth, with no
introductory "and"], since like the creation of
the world, the giving of the Torah represented
a brand new start.

VERSE 2

——————— OR HAḤAYYIM ———————

וַיִּסְעוּ מֵרְפִידִים – *Setting out from Refidim:* The
Torah precedes its description of revelation by
reporting three methods of preparation for
that event, the three areas in which God insisted that the Israelites improve themselves
before he bestowed His treasure upon them.
The first requirement was fortitude and dili-
gence, for the Torah is incompatible with la-
ziness. Know that sloth is like a weed which
grows among plants and causes them to lose
their dominance. And so, when the Torah
states: *Setting out from Refidim they had arrived
at the Sinai Desert,* it is not interested merely
in reporting the point of Israel's departure.
Rather, the message of the verse is that Israel
arrived at the Sinai Desert in a state of weakness [*rifyon*, evoking the name Refidim]. Note
how our Sages comment on the verse *Then, at
Refidim, Amalek came and attacked Israel* (17:8):

"The place was so called because at that time
Israel slackened [*rippu*] in their performance of
God's commandments" (Sanhedrin 106a). Now
the second criterion for receiving the Torah
was an attitude of humility and modesty, as
the Sages argue: "One will only retain his Torah
study when he allows himself to be treated
like a wilderness upon which all people walk"
(Eruvin 54a). The Torah alludes to this point
when it states: *Encamping in the wilderness,*
that is, the people became meek and submis-
sive like the desert floor. The third process necessary for revelation was for the formation of
a community of scholars, united in common
purpose and mentality. Therefore the verse
states: *And there Israel camped [vayiḥan],* using
the singular form of the verb, implying that the
nation acted as a single individual. It was only
then that they were ready to receive the Torah.

——————— MESHEKH ḤOKHMA ———————

וַיִּסְעוּ מֵרְפִידִים – *Setting out from Refidim:* After
their miraculous salvation at the Sea of Reeds,
the Israelites put their trust in Moshe completely [as the verse states: *And they believed in
the LORD and in Moshe his servant,* 14:31]. However, following Yehoshua's defeat of Amalek
at Refidim [in chapter 17], the nation turned
its hopeful eyes to him, while their enthusi-
asm for Moshe cooled. This accorded with the
tradition that the descendants of Esav [which
included Amalek] were destined to fall at the

hands of Raḥel's offspring [of which Yehoshua,
of the tribe of Efrayim, was one; see Bava Batra
123b]. And so God told Moshe: *I will come to
you in a dense cloud, that the people may hear
Me speaking to you. They will then believe you
forever* (19:9). Moshe required a new revelation in view of the people to restore their faith
in him. With that wondrous display, Israel's
impression of their leader would be permanently raised to the level it had been at the
Sea of Reeds.

ג וַיַּחֲנוּ בַּמִּדְבָּר וַיְחַן־שָׁם יִשְׂרָאֵל נֶגֶד הָהָר: וּמֹשֶׁה עָלָה
אֶל־הָאֱלֹהִים וַיִּקְרָא אֵלָיו יהוה מִן־הָהָר לֵאמֹר כֹּה
ד תֹאמַר לְבֵית יַעֲקֹב וְתַגֵּיד לִבְנֵי יִשְׂרָאֵל: אַתֶּם רְאִיתֶם
אֲשֶׁר עָשִׂיתִי לְמִצְרָיִם וָאֶשָּׂא אֶתְכֶם עַל־כַּנְפֵי נְשָׁרִים

VERSE 3

OR HAHAYYIM

וּמֹשֶׁה עָלָה אֶל־הָאֱלֹהִים – *Moshe went up to God:* When God first appeared to Moshe at the burning bush, He foretold what would happen after the exodus, saying: *Proof that I have sent you will come when, having brought the people out of Egypt, you come to serve God upon this mountain* (3:12). He thus informed Moshe that He would give Israel the Torah on that very site. Therefore, when the nation arrived at Mount Sinai, Moshe demonstrated his loyalty by immediately going up to God, even before he was called for. Had Moshe waited for God to summon him to the mountaintop, it would have suggested negligence on Moshe's part and a lack of interest in communing with God. Instead, the leader quickly began his approach to God as soon as the nation arrived at the mountain. Had God not told Moshe earlier that the nation would *come to serve God upon this mountain,* he would have remained on the ground and awaited further instructions.

SHADAL

לְבֵית יַעֲקֹב... לִבְנֵי יִשְׂרָאֵל – *To the house of Yaakov...the people of Israel:* This is the Torah's poetic device of repeating the same idea using different words. Since this oration introduced the Torah as a whole to the Israelites, God used pleasant language to appeal to the hearts of the nation.

MALBIM

וּמֹשֶׁה עָלָה אֶל־הָאֱלֹהִים – *Moshe went up to God:* Now that the time was ripe for revelation, and the nation had arrived at the appointed spot, the Torah begins to describe the role that Moshe would play as intermediary between God and Israel on this momentous occasion. Moshe initiated his interaction with God, not waiting for a call to ascend the mountain. Rabbi Avraham Ibn Ezra is troubled that Moshe is said to have gone up first and was called only afterward, but really the sequence of events poses no difficulty. For I have already explained elsewhere that the verb *kara* ["he called"] has a slightly different meaning when it is followed by the preposition *el,* compared to when it is only accompanied by the letter *lamed.* For in the latter case, it connotes that the speaker is summoning the listener, while the preposition *el* indicates that the person being spoken to is already standing before the caller, who is asking merely for the addressee to pay attention. Hence, in our case, it was after Moshe had appeared before God on the mountain, that the latter invited him to attend to His speech. Furthermore, all other prophets received their communications in a vague sort of way. Instead of ascending to God, they remained passive while He came down to speak with them. This was because unlike Moshe, God's other messengers never fully shed their material and physical dimensions.

3 while Moshe went up to God. And the LORD called to him from the mountain: "This is what you shall say to the house
4 of Yaakov, what you shall tell the people of Israel: You yourselves have seen what I did to the Egyptians: how I lifted you

———————— MALBIM *(cont.)* ————————

Moshe however, transcended his body and hence could rise up from the earth to commune with the Almighty, as alluded to in the phrase *Moshe went up to God.*

———————— RABBI JOSEPH B. SOLOVEITCHIK ————————

לְבֵית יַעֲקֹב... לִבְנֵי יִשְׂרָאֵל – *To the house of Yaakov...the people of Israel:* We have two traditions, two communities, two chains of transmission – the tradition community of the fathers and that of the mothers. "*This is what you shall say to the house of Yaakov* – refers to the women; *what you shall tell the people of Israel* – the men" (Rashi). *Heed, my son, your father's instruction, and do not forsake your mother's teaching* (Proverbs 1:8). What is the distinction between "your father's instruction" and "your mother's teaching"? One learns much from one's father: how to read a text – the Bible or the Talmud, how to comprehend, how to analyze, how to conceptualize, how to classify, how to infer, how to apply. Father's tradition is an intellectual-moral one. That is why it is identified with "instruction" [*musar*], which is the biblical term for discipline. What is "your mother's teaching [*tora*]"?

What Torah does the mother pass on? Permit me to draw upon my own experiences. I used to watch my mother arranging the house in honor of a holiday. I used to see her recite prayers; I used to watch her recite the *sidra* every Friday night, and I still remember the nostalgic tune. I learned from her very much. Most of all I learned that Judaism expresses itself not only in formal compliance with the law, but also in a living experience. She taught me that there is a flavor, a scent, and warmth to mitzvot. I learned from her the most important thing in life – to feel the presence of the Almighty and the gentle pressure of His hand resting upon my frail shoulders. Without her teachings, which quite often were transmitted to me in silence, I would have grown up a soulless being, dry and insensitive.

VERSE 4

———————— OR HAḤAYYIM ————————

אַתֶּם רְאִיתֶם אֲשֶׁר עָשִׂיתִי לְמִצְרָיִם – *You yourselves have seen what I did to the Egyptians:* With this statement, God intended to elicit two simultaneous emotions from the Israelites: love and fear of God. On the one hand, in the verse's opening clause, God reminds Israel of *what I did to the Egyptians,* referring to the vengeful torments that He visited upon them, compelling them to submit to His will. Remember, God tells His nation, how many

plagues I directed at the recalcitrant oppressors who refused to heed My command to release Israel from bondage. That should serve as a warning sign to all people who consider defying the will of God, who remains prepared to punish sinful individuals with torments just like those Israel witnessed in Egypt. Therefore, let the people take what they have seen as a lesson for their own future, to fear God and His punishments. For Israel too will suffer the

ה וְאָבֶא אֶתְכֶם אֵלָי: וְעַתָּה אִם־שָׁמוֹעַ תִּשְׁמְעוּ֙ בְּקֹלִי
וּשְׁמַרְתֶּם אֶת־בְּרִיתִי וִהְיִיתֶם לִי סְגֻלָּה מִכָּל־הָעַמִּים כִּי־

———————— OR HAHAYYIM *(cont.)* ————————

wrath of God should they elect to ignore His Torah and His laws. But the reference to Egypt is also meant to evoke reverence of God, quite apart from the pain He is capable of unleashing against them. Recalling the astonishing feats of the exodus was meant to show Israel God's feelings of affection for them, since He performed all of His marvels on their behalf. In order to rescue the nation from slavery, God upset the natural order of the world and smashed an entire state. Once the Israelites recognized this, they would surely understand the tremendous righteousness God exercised for their sake, and that in turn would stir their own feelings of adulation for Him. The previous verse alludes to these two complementary emotions of fear and love when it employs both the term "say" *tomar* [a verb considered to have mild connotations], indicating that fear of God is insufficient for a relationship with Him and that there must be love as well, and the word "tell" *vetaggeid* [viewed as a harsher synonym], showing that love of God cannot by itself cultivate the proper attitude of submission to Him – there must be reverence as well.

———————— RABBI SAMSON RAPHAEL HIRSCH ————————

אַתֶּם רְאִיתֶם – *You yourselves have seen:* The foundation of the nation's faith in God should not rest purely on blind faith, because such trust can always be challenged by doubt. Rather, the basis for Israel's solid belief in God is their own sensed experience of His existence.

———————— HAAMEK DAVAR ————————

אַתֶּם רְאִיתֶם – *You yourselves have seen:* The purpose of this introduction is similar to the conditions that a husband lays out prior to his marriage. Alongside the list of responsibilities incumbent on the wife in their household, the man promises to provide food, lodging, and other needs for the woman, committing to care for and protect her. The relationship between God and Israel is similar, which is why the blessing at a wedding ceremony includes the language "He who sanctifies His nation Israel with betrothal and the wedding canopy." The Talmud [in Yoma 54a] compares Israel in the wilderness to a bride and subsequently to a wife. And a later verse employs this metaphor clearly when it states: *Thus says the Lord; I remember in your favor, the devotion of your youth, your love as a bride, when you did go after Me in the wilderness, in a land that was not sown* (Jeremiah 2:2). Hence God outlines the expectations that He has of Israel as an expression of their union, and what He in turn intends to do for them.

VERSE 5

———————— OR HAHAYYIM ————————

וִהְיִיתֶם לִי סְגֻלָּה מִכָּל־הָעַמִּים – *You will be My treasure among all the peoples:* What God meant to convey by referring to Israel as His treasure was to say that the Israelites would be alone among all of the earth's peoples who worship Him directly. Even though the

5 up on eagles' wings and brought you to Me. Now, if you faithfully heed My voice and keep My covenant, you will be My
treasure among all the peoples, although the whole earth is

———————————— OR HAHAYYIM (cont.) ————————————

nations might not worship God per se, any
service that they perform is ultimately for
God's benefit, considering that it is His subor-
dinates that are the objects of their devotion.
For example, should a community honor and
revere the sun, or the moon, or the stars, since
those entities are of course subservient to God
anyway, those people are in essence serving
God's servants.

———————————— RABBI SAMSON RAPHAEL HIRSCH ————————————

וִהְיִיתֶם לִי סְגֻלָּה מִכָּל־הָעַמִּים – *You will be
My treasure among all the peoples:* The term
"treasure" [*segula*] connotes a possession
that a single individual owns and to which
no other person has any rights at all. When
the word is used to characterize the relationship between Israel and God, it signifies that
we have been acquired by Him exclusively
and completely. Our entire being and all our
needs rest on God and on God alone. It is He
who provides for us, and there is no other
power or being in the universe who can direct our lives or our actions to any degree.
כִּי־לִי כָּל־הָאָרֶץ – *Although the whole earth is
mine:* The nature of the relationship that I am
now forging with you is not exceptional or
singular, but represents the ideal type of association that should be striven for between
Me and the entire world. For truly, every nation and all of humanity are destined to be
Mine, and I will educate all people toward that
purpose.

———————————— MALBIM ————————————

וִהְיִיתֶם לִי סְגֻלָּה מִכָּל־הָעַמִּים – *You will be My
treasure among all the peoples:* Being God's
treasure is not the same thing as being a "holy
nation" (19:6). For when something is considered a treasure, it is because the owner places great importance and value on it, due its
beauty and its inherent worth. The possession
is guarded in a royal or national treasury. Now
God referred to Israel as His treasure, even
though they had not yet begun to worship
Him, nor grown into a "holy nation." On the
other hand, once Israel elevates, separates,
and thereby sanctifies itself, it can merit being
called "holy" due to its actions.

———————————— HAAMEK DAVAR ————————————

סְגֻלָּה מִכָּל־הָעַמִּים – *Treasure among all the
peoples:* Should a gentile wish to worship
God and to thereby distance himself from
the impurity of the gentiles, he may convert to Judaism and adopt our people as his
own and our Torah as his law. This is what
God means when He refers to Israel as a
"treasure," just as a treasure chest is a recep-
tacle that contains things put in from outside.
כִּי־לִי כָּל־הָאָרֶץ – *Although the whole earth is
mine:* Scattered throughout the nations of
the world are individuals who are worthy of
transforming their lives by accepting upon
themselves the service of God. Before the Torah was given, all people worshipped God in
manners of their own devising. However, from
this point onward, the only legitimate way
to serve God would be to join the treasured
status of Israel.

טו לִי כָּל־הָאָרֶץ: וְאַתֶּם תִּהְיוּ־לִי מַמְלֶכֶת כֹּהֲנִים וְגוֹי קָדוֹשׁ י

───────────── MESHEKH ḤOKHMA ─────────────

וִהְיִיתֶם לִי סְגֻלָּה מִכָּל־הָעַמִּים – *You will be My treasure among all the peoples:* Certainly Israel holds a special status at a time when the earth's other nations are blinded by their false beliefs and refuse to acknowledge the oneness of the Creator. However, even in a future era when God is universally recognized, Israel will still enjoy the status of God's treasured nation. For even when *the whole earth is [God's],* Israel will stand out as exceptional. At this point, the nation of Israel is humiliated and persecuted among the gentiles; but if they are one day triumphant in this world, then all of humanity will surely declare that God is one and His name is one. They will abandon their statues and their idols and will act unanimously to discover the truth. We therefore recite with hope in our prayers: "Everything alive will gratefully acknowledge You, Sela! and praise Your name sincerely, O God." When will such a time arise? When "God is our salvation and help" [the continuation of the same prayer in the *Amida*]. That is, when the servants of the true God are no longer degraded, the nations of the world will be led to acknowledge their God. Our verse reflects the prediction that when Israel comes into its own right as God's treasured people, this itself will induce other nations to accept Him, such that the whole earth will be His.

VERSE 6

───────────── OR HAḤAYYIM ─────────────

מַמְלֶכֶת כֹּהֲנִים – *Kingdom of priests:* Perhaps we can suggest that in this statement, God is not referring to the nation at all, but to Moshe and Aharon. In the previous verses, God addressed Israel saying that they would be His *treasure among all the peoples,* and Moshe might have gotten the impression that his charges would now be no different from him in God's eyes. God therefore reassured His messengers, telling Moshe and Aharon specifically: *A kingdom of priests and a holy nation you shall be to Me.* For Aharon would found a dynasty of priests, while Moshe and his family [the tribe of Levi] would be holy and distinct from the rest of Israel.

───────────── SHADAL ─────────────

מַמְלֶכֶת כֹּהֲנִים וְגוֹי קָדוֹשׁ – *A kingdom of priests and a holy nation:* All nations of the world believed that the members of their own priestly classes were close to and beloved by their gods, and that in turn these deities granted the requests and desires of the holy men. God here acknowledged this idea but expanded it by promising that the entire nation can develop a strong bond with Him. God guaranteed that He would be attentive to Israel's calls whenever they turned to Him, and that he would preside over every area of their lives. Thus the entire community could be characterized as priests and holy individuals. Needless to say, this offer stands only as long as the nation observes the Torah's commandments.

───────────── RABBI SAMSON RAPHAEL HIRSCH ─────────────

מַמְלֶכֶת כֹּהֲנִים – *Kingdom of priests:* With this statement, God declared that each and every individual Israelite is considered a "priest" when he accepts God's absolute rule over his

6 Mine. A kingdom of priests and a holy nation you shall be to Me. These are the words you must speak to the Israelites."

───────── RABBI SAMSON RAPHAEL HIRSCH *(cont.)* ─────────

life. When a person takes the will of God into account before acting in any way, when he is committed to publicizing the name of God around the world, when he serves as a model and an example for realizing the mission of God for humanity, he is elevated to the status of a priest of God. **וְגוֹי קָדוֹשׁ** – *And a holy nation:* Just as individually you will appear as priests, so too as a collective your community will emanate an aura of sanctity. You will be one nation, unique among the peoples of the world. For your national goal will not be your own national glorification but your ambition to make the law of divine ethics the universal code of human behavior. This is the meaning of sanctity.

───────────── MALBIM ─────────────

מַמְלֶכֶת כֹּהֲנִים – *Kingdom of priests:* This command is directed at Israel's leadership: Since you are the nation's elite and its elders, I command you to make yourselves *a kingdom of priests and a holy nation,* for it is the priests who are the select few chosen for divine service. A tree cannot be composed entirely of fruit, necessarily requiring roots, a trunk, bark, and branches, which are all subordinate to and protect the plant's fruit, and similarly a body cannot consist only of a heart and a brain, but needs the skeletal and circulatory systems, the arms and the legs to support and carry the heart and the brain where the soul of a person dwells. So too we find that among the general population of a nation most of the people are like the trunk and the leaves of a tree, or the flesh and blood of a body. These masses of individuals support the holy people devoted to God, the treasured few representing the fruit or the heart of the entity. Nevertheless, God also promises the common folk that they will be dear to Him if they observe His Torah.

───────────── HAAMEK DAVAR ─────────────

מַמְלֶכֶת כֹּהֲנִים – *Kingdom of priests:* This declaration is a command over and beyond Israel's obligation to observe the Torah. For without honoring that commitment, the nation does not even deserve the title "Israel." But additionally, the people are instructed to make themselves "a kingdom of priests," meaning that in their interpersonal relations, they must act righteously and properly like noblemen do. It is hard to define exactly what it means to "act righteously and properly," and the definition of genteel behavior and manners differs according to the time and the place. Because of this, the injunction to lead honorable lives is not included within the condition God already stipulated [in the previous verse, *If you faithfully heed My voice…you will be My treasure*]. That is, developing a virtuous character cannot form a specific law within the Torah's system, nor be critical to the definition of Judaism, even though it represents God's will. **וְגוֹי קָדוֹשׁ** – *And a holy nation:* Holiness defines the interactions between man and God [as opposed to interpersonal relations], and people sanctify themselves by abstaining even from those indulgences that are technically permitted.

חמישי

ז אֵלֶּה הַדְּבָרִים אֲשֶׁר תְּדַבֵּר אֶל־בְּנֵי יִשְׂרָאֵל: וַיָּבֹא מֹשֶׁה
וַיִּקְרָא לְזִקְנֵי הָעָם וַיָּשֶׂם לִפְנֵיהֶם אֵת כָּל־הַדְּבָרִים הָאֵלֶּה
ח אֲשֶׁר צִוָּהוּ יְהוָה: וַיַּעֲנוּ כָל־הָעָם יַחְדָּו וַיֹּאמְרוּ כֹּל אֲשֶׁר־
דִּבֶּר יְהוָה נַעֲשֶׂה וַיָּשֶׁב מֹשֶׁה אֶת־דִּבְרֵי הָעָם אֶל־יְהוָה:

VERSE 7

OR HAHAYYIM

לְזִקְנֵי הָעָם – *The elders of the people:* Instead of addressing the entire nation of Israel [as verse 3 seems to demand] Moshe wisely communicated God's message only to the people's representatives. For Moshe was desperately afraid that some mishap might upset the entire enterprise of revelation and thereby undermine the foundation of the world. Now at this point, the earth already shook in trepidation at the possibility that Israel would refuse to accept God's Torah, and hence Moshe devised a plan to decrease the chances that this would happen. He did not, at first, approach the people as a whole, but instead summoned their elders to persuade them to agree to receive the commandments. Still, the entire nation stood by and listened while Moshe spoke to the leaders, even though his words were directed to this select group alone. Moshe's idea was that only the delegates should respond to God's demands and not the people, for Moshe feared that the common folk might shout out some inappropriate reaction. But Moshe felt confident that the elders would answer positively to God's proposal to make them His holy nation, and their example would persuade their followers to fall into line. But the Israelites, sons of the living God, understood the wisdom of Moshe's plan and saw how nervous he was that they would refuse to accept the Torah. They therefore removed any suspicion Moshe might have had and did not even allow the elders to respond before speaking up themselves in unison as the verse states: *All that the Lord has spoken we will do* willingly and voluntarily (19:8). This remarkable verse demonstrates the unanimity that Israel felt in agreeing wholeheartedly to submit to the will of God. For six hundred thousand individuals shouted in a single voice that they were prepared to accept the Torah. The entire nation spoke in a single chorus, each person uttering word for word what the group was saying, timed precisely with everybody else. How fortunate is the world that it contains such a nation!

SHADAL

וַיָּשֶׂם לִפְנֵיהֶם – *And set before them:* Moshe relayed God's message to Israel and gave them a chance to weigh whether they wanted to accept or refuse His offer. For initially, the matter of the Torah was not presented to the nation as a command or edict. Instead, the nation willingly agreed to enter into a covenant with God, as the next verse states: *And the people answered as one – "All that the Lord has spoken we will do"* (19:8).

RABBI SAMSON RAPHAEL HIRSCH

וַיָּשֶׂם לִפְנֵיהֶם – *And set before them:* The language here implies that Moshe did more than merely repeat God's words to the elders. He took pains to explain and clarify the content of the divine message. This is why the nation was able to respond: *All that the Lord has spoken we will*

7 So Moshe came and summoned the elders of the people, ḤAMISHI
and set before them all that the LORD had commanded him.
8 And the people answered as one – "All that the LORD has
spoken we will do." Moshe brought their answer back to the

——————————— RABBI SAMSON RAPHAEL HIRSCH *(cont.)* ———————————

will do (19:8), for indeed everything had been laid out for them for their consideration before agreeing to become God's treasured people.

Israel now comprehended all the details of what it meant to be *a kingdom of priests and a holy nation* (19:6).

VERSE 8

——————————————— OR HAḤAYYIM ———————————————

וַיָּשֶׁב מֹשֶׁה אֶת־דִּבְרֵי הָעָם – *Moshe brought their answer back:* This verse does not mean that Moshe reported to God only Israel's willingness to do what He had demanded of them.

Rather, Moshe brought Him a description of the nation's unanimous and simultaneous response, as I have described.

——————————————— MALBIM ———————————————

וַיַּעֲנוּ כָל־הָעָם יַחְדָּו – *And the people answered as one:* The people of Israel were unwilling to accept the division of their society into classes, but wanted a system such as that which will reign in the future, when all people will stand on equal footing, as the verse states: *And the glory of the LORD shall be revealed, and all flesh shall see it together: for the mouth of the LORD has spoken it* (Isaiah 40:5). Even at this early stage of their national history, Israel wanted each of their members to be thus included within the *kingdom of priests and a holy nation* (19:6), and that equality should reign within the community. This is why the verse

emphasizes that *the people answered as one*. Furthermore, the people's response intimates that they did not wish for Moshe and Aharon to serve as intermediaries between God and themselves, and they were certainly opposed to the elders acting in that capacity. The Israelites all wanted to attain the level of prophecy required to receive the Torah directly from God rather than through Moshe. As our Sages argue, Israel wanted to see their king for themselves. And this was exactly Koraḥ's error when he declared: *All the congregation are holy, every one of them* (Numbers 16:3).

——————————————— SEFAT EMET ———————————————

כֹּל אֲשֶׁר־דִּבֶּר יהוה נַעֲשֶׂה – *All that the LORD has spoken we will do:* Says the psalmist: *Bless the LORD, you angels of His, you mighty ones who perform His bidding, hearkening to the voice of His word* (Psalms 103:20). This verse praises Israel for having put their willingness to "perform" the commandments even before hearing them [see 24:7 – *We shall do and we shall heed*]. For although we may rest assured that God would only obligate us to do things

that are within our capability, what Israel was in fact acquiescing to was deeper: learning God's message through the performance of commandments themselves. For every action carries within it the power of the word of God, and this is what the phrase "perform His bidding" signifies [in the psalm mentioned above. Literally the phrase can be translated "making His word," implying that obedience is itself a creative act that imparts understanding

ס וַיֹּאמֶר יְהוָה אֶל־מֹשֶׁה הִנֵּה אָנֹכִי בָּא אֵלֶיךָ בְּעַב הֶעָנָן
בַּעֲבוּר יִשְׁמַע הָעָם בְּדַבְּרִי עִמָּךְ וְגַם־בְּךָ יַאֲמִינוּ לְעוֹלָם
י וַיַּגֵּד מֹשֶׁה אֶת־דִּבְרֵי הָעָם אֶל־יְהוָה: וַיֹּאמֶר יְהוָה אֶל־
מֹשֶׁה לֵךְ אֶל־הָעָם וְקִדַּשְׁתָּם הַיּוֹם וּמָחָר וְכִבְּסוּ שִׂמְלֹתָם:

———————————— SEFAT EMET *(cont.)* ————————————

of the divine word]. And so, when Israel fulfills the will of God, they merit the ability to hear His "voice," which signifies something more profound than speech, as the Zohar teaches. The "voice" is to be found deep within [and is thus pure and unified], while "speech" [which is outwardly directed] ramifies into various expressions. Through their behavior and their acceptance of the reign of God, the people

of Israel were granted the honor of hearing the "voice" [*kol*] of God [during the revelation; see 19:19]. This idea explains the Sages' claim that "remember the Sabbath" (20:8) and "guard the Sabbath" (Deuteronomy 5:12) were uttered simultaneously. [That is, these two phrases are different articulations of the same ineffable, higher idea, embodied in the "voice" Israel heard at Sinai.]

———————————— MESHEKH HOKHMA ————————————

וַיַּעֲנוּ כָל־הָעָם יַחְדָּו – And the people answered as one: Among the Torah's commandments, some may only be performed by the priests, some by the Levites, and still others just by the High Priest. The king of Israel has some obligations that are limited to him, as does the Sanhedrin. If an individual has a house, he must attend to those rules that are incumbent upon a homeowner, whereas farmers are governed by agricultural statutes. Thus it is only the community of Israel as a whole which is responsible for observing the entire corpus of Torah law. And because all members of the nation are accountable for each other [see Shevuot 39a], we all receive credit for the fulfillment of others' commandments. Still, each

individual should also take care to study the laws that he is not obligated in, for the merit of such commandments nevertheless accrues to him. At the very least, one should support those scholars who are devoted to the study of such statutes. Furthermore, when Israel later declared: *All that the Lord has spoken we shall do and we shall heed* (24:7), they agreed not only to observe the laws that were applicable to them, but to study and understand all the particulars of the Torah. Here, however, the people merely proclaimed: *All that the Lord has spoken we will do*, because they were speaking as a community, and only as a whole could they all cover the entire range of the commandments.

VERSE 9

———————————— OR HAHAYYIM ————————————

וְגַם־בְּךָ יַאֲמִינוּ לְעוֹלָם – They will then believe you forever: Until this point, Israel had believed in Moshe in the sense that he was a servant of God, who favored him by answering his prayers. However, the people still had difficulty accepting the idea that God spoke directly

to Moshe. This was because an ancient philosophy held that it was impossible for a human being to survive a communication from the Almighty, an idea which scholars among the nations supported with a range of arguments and proofs. Of course, this did not necessarily

9 LORD. Then the LORD said to Moshe, "I will come to you in a dense cloud, that the people may hear Me speaking to you. They will then believe you forever." When Moshe reported 10 the words of the people to the LORD, the LORD said to Moshe, "Go to the people and consecrate them today and tomorrow;

—————————— OR HAHAYYIM *(cont.)* ——————————

mean that God did not hear or respond to human speech, or that He lacked feelings of love toward specific people or was willing to honor their requests. Hence, when the Torah stated earlier that Israel *believed in the* LORD *and in Moshe His servant* (14:31), it meant that the nation accepted that Moshe was the loyal subject of God, and that God was happy to attend to Moshe's prayers and to grant what he requested – not that God spoke to Israel's leader. And therefore, in our verse, God says that because *the people may hear*

Me speaking to you, they will then believe you forever. That experience would prove undeniably that God does speak to human beings, and that they are able to live through the encounter. Furthermore, the arrangement God employed here, whereby Moshe acted as an intermediary for the people, would establish the institution of prophecy that would stand for generations, long after Moshe was gone. That phenomenon would clearly uproot the erroneous belief from human thought that God does not speak with people.

—————————— SHADAL ——————————

בַּעֲבוּר יִשְׁמַע הָעָם בְּדַבְּרִי עִמָּךְ – *That the people may hear Me speaking to you:* At this point, God merely hinted to Moshe regarding the revelation at Mount Sinai, but He did not fully clarify what was about to happen. Note that God does not say here that the people will hear Him speaking to them, which is what He ought to have said if this verse referred to the recitation of the Ten Commandments, as Rabbi Avraham Ibn Ezra and the Rambam believe. Rather, what He states is: *That the people may hear Me speaking to you,* referring to God's communication to Moshe, which took place prior to the giving of the Torah, as the verse describes: *Moshe spoke and God answered him aloud* (19:19). Such is the interpretation of this verse according to Rav Se'adya Gaon and others. In answer

to this, Moshe related the people's response [demonstrating their faith], arguing that there was therefore no need for such a scheme, for Moshe was not yet aware of the divine plan to proclaim the Torah before the entire nation. Then *the* LORD *said to Moshe, "Go to the people and consecrate them... for on that third day the* LORD *will descend on Mount Sinai before all the peoples' eyes"* (19:10–11). God thus hinted to Moshe that His arrival in a thick cloud had a purpose beyond what was stated earlier, to solidify the people's faith in Moshe. Rather, the Holy One, blessed be He, wished to bestow upon the Israelites a great and honorable gift, an experience that would require two days of sanctification, namely that they were about to hear the Torah recited from God Himself.

VERSE 10

—————————— HAKETAV VEHAKABBALA ——————————

וְקִדַּשְׁתָּם הַיּוֹם וּמָחָר – *Consecrate them today and tomorrow:* The general instruction to Israel to sanctify themselves meant that the people

should use the upcoming two days to prepare themselves for revelation. All the Israelites were to strive to suppress the cravings and

יא וְהָיוּ נְכֹנִים לַיּוֹם הַשְּׁלִישִׁי כִּי ׀ בַּיּוֹם הַשְּׁלִשִׁי יֵרֵד יהוה לְעֵינֵי
יב כָל־הָעָם עַל־הַר סִינָי: וְהִגְבַּלְתָּ אֶת־הָעָם סָבִיב לֵאמֹר
הִשָּׁמְרוּ לָכֶם עֲלוֹת בָּהָר וּנְגֹעַ בְּקָצֵהוּ כָּל־הַנֹּגֵעַ בָּהָר מוֹת

—————————— **HAKETAV VEHAKABBALA** *(cont.)* ——————————

desires that normally dominated their souls. They were to rise above their usual concerns and standard pursuits. For that sort of

separation and elevation constitutes the entire foundation of the Torah.

—————————— **RABBI SAMSON RAPHAEL HIRSCH** ——————————

לֵךְ אֶל־הָעָם וְקִדַּשְׁתָּם – *Go to the people and consecrate them:* At this moment an event was occurring which was to be commemorated for generations: God was about to stand opposite the nation of Israel and allow His words to emanate directly into the ears of the people. God's speech would not originate amongst the people themselves, and thus the Torah

of the Jews is the only law code in history that was not created by the nation meant to adopt it. Judaism is the only religion that was not invented by human beings to shape the spiritual contours of their lives. It is exactly this objectivity of the Torah that sets our culture firmly apart from other all other legal and belief communities around the world.

—————————— **MALBIM** ——————————

לֵךְ אֶל־הָעָם וְקִדַּשְׁתָּם – *Go to the people and consecrate them:* God agreed with the nation's request to use the Ten Commandments as an experiment to speak with Him face to face, without recourse to Moshe as an intermediary. God would thereby test the people to see if they could endure the experience. If they passed the trial, they would receive the entire Torah directly from Him. In preparation for the ordeal, the Israelites had to be sanctified and purified to the very highest degree. Therefore,

Moshe was told to instruct his charges to order their thoughts and to perfect their character in addition to cleansing their bodies. Although the only particular explicitly stated is a direction to let the people *wash their clothes,* that is in fact an allusion to immersion of the body, which is the clothing of the soul. Thus when the verse states: *Go to the people and consecrate them,* God refers to the inner sanctification of beliefs and behavior.

VERSE 11

—————————— **HAKETAV VEHAKABBALA** ——————————

יֵרֵד – *Will descend:* Whenever the Torah uses the verb "descend" in reference to God, it

means that God is revealing His presence so that people will become aware of Him.

—————————— **HAAMEK DAVAR** ——————————

וְהָיוּ נְכֹנִים לַיּוֹם הַשְּׁלִישִׁי – *And be ready for the third day:* According to my approach, wherein the command to Israel to consecrate themselves [stated in verse 10] meant that the men should separate from their wives,

the instruction to *be ready for the third day* must represent a different demand on the people. I believe Israel was being told to prepare to witness – to see and to hear – great wonders. They were warned to prevent them

11 let them wash their clothes and be ready for the third day, for
on that third day the LORD will descend on Mount Sinai be-
12 fore all the peoples' eyes. Set a boundary for the people around
the mountain; tell them to take care not to ascend to it, not
even touch its edge. Anyone who touches the mountain must

———————————— HAAMEK DAVAR *(cont.)* ————————————

from being shocked when they suddenly experienced the sights and sounds of revelation.
Furthermore, the Israelites were told to mentally ready themselves through meditation,
each according to his ability. There was no
fixed method or measure to this anticipation
of meeting the divine, as we see when Moshe
too was told at one point to ready himself before accepting the second set of tablets. There
God told him: *Be ready in the morning. Climb
Mount Sinai in the morning and present yourself*

to Me there on the mountaintop (34:2). Now we
know that there was no one better prepared
to receive prophecy from God than Moshe,
who had separated from his wife some time
before. Rather, these extra preparations were
necessary because at that time God sought to
expose Moshe to an additional wonder that
he had not yet seen. Similarly, we must all
establish our own foundations before encoun-
tering any manifestation of God.

VERSE 12

———————————— OR HAHAYYIM ————————————

וְהִגְבַּלְתָּ אֶת־הָעָם – *Set a boundary for the
people:* It seems that the prohibition not to
climb Mount Sinai only became operative
on the third day [when the Torah was given.
In contrast, the separation of husbands and
wives took effect at the start of the first day].
Nevertheless, the decree was issued at this
point so that Israel would be accustomed to
viewing the hill with a measure of reverence,

and so they would start distancing themselves
from the site even during the three days of
preparation. It would be inaccurate to claim
that anyone who touched the mountain during that preparatory period was liable to be
executed, for it is unreasonable to suggest
that the place was sanctified before the descent of God's presence there.

———————————— HAKETAV VEHAKABBALA ————————————

וְהִגְבַּלְתָּ אֶת־הָעָם סָבִיב – *Set a boundary for the
people around:* [The words "the mountain" in
the translation here are not in the original Hebrew, giving the impression that the boundary
might have been around the Israelite camp.]
This clause should not be interpreted literally
as "Set a boundary around the people," since
it makes no sense to ring a border around the
people themselves. Consider the families who

stood at the back of the camp, farthest away
from the mountain – they ought not be under any constraints of movement, and no limitations were to be set around their end of the
compound. Furthermore, there was never any
problem for the Israelites to leave the site by
the sides of the camp. The verse means that a
restriction was placed on the people because
a boundary was set around the mountain.

———————————— MALBIM ————————————

וְהִגְבַּלְתָּ אֶת־הָעָם סָבִיב – *Set a boundary for
the people around:* Although this decree most

straightforwardly refers to a physical restraint
on the people's movement, the statement also

יג יוּמָת: לֹא־תִגַּע בּוֹ יָד כִּי־סָקוֹל יִסָּקֵל אוֹ־יָרֹה יִיָּרֶה אִם־
בְּהֵמָה אִם־אִישׁ לֹא יִחְיֶה בִּמְשֹׁךְ הַיֹּבֵל הֵמָּה יַעֲלוּ בָהָר:
יד וַיֵּרֶד מֹשֶׁה מִן־הָהָר אֶל־הָעָם וַיְקַדֵּשׁ אֶת־הָעָם וַיְכַבְּסוּ

────────────── MALBIM *(cont.)* ──────────────

contains a more profound meaning. God also warned Israel not to attempt to seek to deep an understanding of his nature, or to explore areas of thought beyond their comprehension. The human mind is bound by limitations which must not be transcended, as we read regarding the four scholars who entered the orchard [see Ḥagiga 14a]. One of these men attempted to "climb the mountain" to glimpse [the Divine Presence] and was stricken and died, being unable to endure the power of the great light, just as anyone who tries to look directly at the sun will be blinded by its strength. Alternatively, when one tries to grasp knowledge that is above his purview, he will be damaged mentally or will abandon the Torah altogether [the fates of two of the other men in the tale]. This is the metaphorical meaning of the precaution *Anyone who touches the mountain must be put to death* (19:12).

────────────── HAAMEK DAVAR ──────────────

וְהִגְבַּלְתָּ אֶת־הָעָם סָבִיב – *Set a boundary for the people around:* [The words "the mountain" in the translation here are not in the original Hebrew.] Note that the text here does not make reference to the mountain, as it does subsequently: *Set a boundary around the mountain and consecrate it* (19:23). This is because the current instruction is directed at the people, describing how they should arrange themselves around the site. Aharon was to stand at the head of the camp, with the priests in order of importance behind him. That party was to be followed by the elders and ministers. Next in line would be the common men, and the nation's women and children.

VERSE **13**

────────────── MALBIM ──────────────

לֹא־תִגַּע בּוֹ יָד – *No hand shall touch him:* There would be no need for a human hand to execute any violator of this rule, for the mountain, which was trembling on that day, would be prepared to spew boulders at people who approached it, thereby stoning them to death. Alternatively, the transgressor would be "shot," meaning that the mountain would shoot the trespasser off it, catapulting him into the valley. [The words "with arrows" in the translation here do not appear in the Hebrew.] Still, our Sages understand this verse as a directive to the court to stone the sinner to death, since this verse is invoked as a proof text for the laws governing that form of capital punishment. And even though we could try to twist our interpretation of how the mountain itself was supposed to execute the criminal and show parallels between the hill's actions and the court's, we really ought to abandon our own reading for the straightforward exegesis of the Sages.

────────────── MESHEKH ḤOKHMA ──────────────

בִּמְשֹׁךְ הַיֹּבֵל – *When the ram's horn sounds a long blast:* Immediately after God warned Israel not to ascend the mountain while His presence was at the site, He described the

13 be put to death. No hand shall touch him: he shall be stoned
or shot with arrows; beast or man, he shall not live. When
the ram's horn sounds a long blast – only then may they go
14 up on the mountain." So Moshe came down from the mountain to the people; he consecrated them and they cleansed

——————————— MESHEKH ḤOKHMA *(cont.)* ———————————

signal for that decree's end. God did this to
teach us proper etiquette, to not end a discussion with a negative message. For without the
statement regarding the prohibition's repeal,
the verse would have finished with the words
Beast or man, he shall not live. Now according to our Sages, of blessed memory, the entire point of our religion is to root out of our
hearts the false beliefs of idolatry. Hence it was
demonstrated to the Israelites that throughout their experience at Mount Sinai, they saw
no visual representation of God whatsoever.
I have explained this at length in my commentary to chapter 12, where I elaborate that
no creature in this world truly possesses holiness, since sanctity is the sole domain of the
Creator. The people of Israel were therefore
taught that God's revelation on Mount Sinai
was not due to any sort of holiness of the peak
itself. That was the purport of the statement
*When the ram's horn sounds a long blast – only
then may they go up on the mountain.* In fact, at
that point even wild beasts and cattle would

be invited to graze on the hill. For the site was
special only as long as the Divine Presence
rested there. So taught Rabbi Yosei: It is never
a location that lends honor to a person, rather
it is the place itself that is honored by the presence of a distinguished individual [see Taanit
21a]. Now this wonderful idea finds application in the following case as well: The Torah
considers the Temple to be a holy site, a place
whose sanctity is eternal. And yet, in order
to impress upon us that it is not the structure itself that has any sort of worth, the law
permits any impure individual to touch the
back of the building, even those who have
previously come into contact with a corpse
[which imparts the most severe impurity]. This
law teaches that our reverence is due only to
the One whose presence dwells within the
Temple; its inner space is only sacred because
of Him. And so the interior of the Temple contains the stone tablets and the altar of glory
[whereas the exterior walls of the Temple hold
no significance].

VERSE **14**

——————————— HAAMEK DAVAR ———————————

וַיְּכַבְּסוּ שִׂמְלֹתָם – *And they cleansed their
clothes:* The people busied themselves with
washing their clothes, but the text does not
report that Moshe established the boundary God charged him with marking, for that
would not be necessary until the third day,
when God would descend. Nevertheless, the
married couples did separate from each other
immediately. The text is careful to point out
that Moshe consecrated the people, rather
than that they did so themselves. This meant

that beyond avoiding all physical contact with
women, Moshe exhorted the men to clear
their minds of any sexual thoughts. It was the
Midrash Rabba which first suggested this idea,
stating that the prophet Elisha was labeled as
"holy" because his Shunamite hostess [see II
Kings 4] never discovered a drop of semen on
his bedclothes. Moshe therefore engaged in
fiery rhetoric to convince the men to purify
themselves and elevate their minds.

טו שִׂמְלֹתָ֑ם: וַיֹּ֙אמֶר֙ אֶל־הָעָ֔ם הֱי֥וּ נְכֹנִ֖ים לִשְׁלֹ֥שֶׁת יָמִ֑ים
טז אַֽל־תִּגְּשׁ֖וּ אֶל־אִשָּֽׁה: וַיְהִי֩ בַיּ֨וֹם הַשְּׁלִישִׁ֜י בִּֽהְיֹ֣ת הַבֹּ֗קֶר
וַיְהִי֩ קֹלֹ֨ת וּבְרָקִ֜ים וְעָנָ֤ן כָּבֵד֙ עַל־הָהָ֔ר וְקֹ֥ל שֹׁפָ֖ר חָזָ֣ק
יז מְאֹ֑ד וַיֶּֽחֱרַ֥ד כָּל־הָעָ֖ם אֲשֶׁ֥ר בַּֽמַּחֲנֶֽה: וַיּוֹצֵ֨א מֹשֶׁ֧ה אֶת־
הָעָ֛ם לִקְרַ֥את הָֽאֱלֹהִ֖ים מִן־הַֽמַּחֲנֶ֑ה וַיִּֽתְיַצְּב֖וּ בְּתַחְתִּ֥ית

VERSE 15

MALBIM

אַֽל־תִּגְּשׁ֖וּ אֶל־אִשָּֽׁה – *Do not draw close to your wives:* Allow me to explain the distinction between the two Hebrew synonyms for "draw close": *karav* and *niggash.* The former verb is used when the two parties are equals and it is a simple matter to approach one another. The latter, on the other hand, connotes a situation where one person must overcome some difficulty in order to draw close to the other. This explains why *keriva* is always used when a man is united with a woman, for the two people must be equally cautious not to engage in illicit sexual relations, and hence they are on equal footing. Thus we find the verse *None of you shall approach [lo tikrevu]*

to any that is near of kin to him, to uncover her nakedness: I am the LORD (Leviticus 18:6). However, in the current case, it was the situation of the women specifically which formed the obstacle to cohabitation. For in the event that a couple did have sexual intercourse [a circumstance that makes both the man and woman impure following contact with semen] the man could simply immerse in a ritual bath and become pure immediately. The woman, however, needed be concerned that she might still expel the semen at any time during the next three days and would then be impure at the moment of revelation. This is why the Torah employs the verb *tiggeshu.*

VERSE 16

RABBI SAMSON RAPHAEL HIRSCH

וַיֶּֽחֱרַ֥ד כָּל־הָעָ֖ם אֲשֶׁ֥ר בַּֽמַּחֲנֶֽה – *And all the people in the camp shook:* What the nation witnessed was the entire natural world trembling at the approach of God's glory, while the people alone were able to stand unmoving to receive the presence of the Master of the Universe. Israel was slowly learning that when a human being enters the service of God in full consciousness

and awareness, he rises to an exalted level unmatched anywhere in the world. At that moment, his relationship with the divine is an intimate and a direct one that requires no intermediary. And while the heavens and the earth, indeed the entire planet and everything on it, quake around him, that individual can stand erect and ready to meet His God.

MALBIM

וַיְהִי֩ קֹלֹ֨ת וּבְרָקִ֜ים וְעָנָ֤ן כָּבֵד֙ עַל־הָהָ֔ר – *There was thunder and lightning and a dense cloud on the mountain:* Even before God's arrival upon the mountain, the three mighty but light elements of nature trembled in anticipation of

the divine. These are water, wind, and fire. For the wind produces the thunder, the fire creates the lightning, and the water forms the basis for the dense cloud and the accompanying rain (as our Sages state, rain fell

15 their clothes. "Be ready for the third day," he told them, "and
16 do not draw close to your wives." The third day came; and
that morning there was thunder and lightning and a dense
cloud on the mountain and the sound of a ram's horn, intense-
17 ly loud, and all the people in the camp shook. Then Moshe
led the people out of the camp to meet God, and they stood

──────────── MALBIM *(cont.)* ────────────

at that moment as well). Nevertheless, none of these phenomena were manifested in a natural way but were rather miraculous. In the usual course of events, clouds appear before lightning is seen, and the lightning flashes before thunder is heard. On this occasion, however, the thunder came first; the nation then saw lightning flash across the sky, even though no cloud had yet formed; and finally the cloud took shape in the sky, followed by an unnatural sounding of the ram's horn. This last sound was miraculous since no actual horn was employed. While all of this was happening, the elements of the Israelites' bodies corresponding to those three weightless facets of nature were also stirred. However, because the element of earth had not been activated – the ground had not risen nor had

it moved – the representative earthy part of the people remained still. Grounded. The Israelites did not shed the heaviness of their bodies to rise on the spiritual wings to greet their God. As a result, the nation merely trembled where they stood in the camp but did not move from there. Just as when the breath that blows the ram's horn passes through a narrow and constricted space, the sound reverberates, so too God's holy spirit, breathed into the nation, was slowed by the physical earthy matter obstructing it, which caused the Israelites to tremble. For the nation had not been prepared to hear the voice of the LORD without trembling – indeed, this was the condition for Israel receiving the Torah: the people stood in the camp and shook, but did not move from their places.

VERSE 17

──────────── OR HAHAYYIM ────────────

וַיּוֹצֵא מֹשֶׁה אֶת־הָעָם – *Then Moshe led the people out:* Perhaps the people required Moshe's assistance in leaving the camp because they trembled in fear of the mountain.

But Moshe led the nation out and positioned them at the foot of the Mount Sinai so that they would receive the Torah while standing on their feet.

──────────── MALBIM ────────────

וַיּוֹצֵא מֹשֶׁה אֶת־הָעָם – *Then Moshe led the people out:* Because of their condition, Moshe had to lead the people out of the camp against their will, using his strength, his speech, and his merit. At that point, the nation was able to meet God directly, since the Divine Presence had already begun its descent from the heavens to the earth. In fact, it would have

been more appropriate for the Israelites to have preceded God's arrival at the site and waited there for Him. The people's weakness illustrated that they were not yet worthy of becoming a kingdom of priests and a holy nation simply by dint of their own preparations on earth. They still required God himself to stir their souls when He began to emerge. Now

יח הָהָר: וְהַר סִינַי עָשַׁן כֻּלּוֹ מִפְּנֵי אֲשֶׁר יָרַד עָלָיו יהוה בָּאֵשׁ
יט וַיַּעַל עֲשָׁנוֹ כְּעֶשֶׁן הַכִּבְשָׁן וַיֶּחֱרַד כָּל־הָהָר מְאֹד: וַיְהִי קוֹל
הַשֹּׁפָר הוֹלֵךְ וְחָזֵק מְאֹד מֹשֶׁה יְדַבֵּר וְהָאֱלֹהִים יַעֲנֶנּוּ בְקוֹל:

───────── MALBIM (cont.) ─────────

through his strength, Moshe was able to bring the people out *and they stood [vayityatzevu] at the foot of the mountain.* The usage of the verb *nitzav* is intentional here, for there is a difference between that term and the word *amad* [both mean "stand"]. For the former term connotes a situation where great effort is required

to remain in place. This means that although the people were gathered around the mountain, they did not stay there comfortably and fearlessly, but were agitated and afraid. They needed strength to remain at the mountain and not run away.

───────── HAAMEK DAVAR ─────────

לִקְרַאת הָאֱלֹהִים – *To meet God:* [The word order in the Hebrew yields: "Then Moshe led the people to meet God out of the camp."] The verse would read better if it stated: "Then Moshe led the people out of the camp to meet God" [as the translation here has rendered it]. What the word order teaches is that although God was already present within the Israelite camp, His presence there was

not revealed explicitly. And at this point, the manifestation of God left the camp, so to speak, and moved to the mountain. Moshe followed suit by directing his charges out of the compound to commune with God, who had already departed. [Hence the sense of the verse is: Then Moshe led the people to meet God, who had already gone out of the camp.]

VERSE 18

───────── OR HAḤAYYIM ─────────

וְהַר סִינַי עָשַׁן כֻּלּוֹ – *Mount Sinai was enveloped in smoke:* At that time, the fire engulfed the mountain and burned up its rocks. This is similar to the process of fashioning an oven, where stones are fired to create lime. That is what happened to the stones on the

mountain – the fire that raged turned them into lime. Hence the verse reports that *the mountain shook violently as one,* for when the heat of a fire overcomes rock it makes a terrible cracking sound.

───────── MALBIM ─────────

וְהַר סִינַי עָשַׁן כֻּלּוֹ – *Mount Sinai was enveloped in smoke:* What the Torah describes here is the awakening of the mountain on two fronts. Firstly, the hill *was enveloped in smoke because the Lord had descended on it in fire.* The smoke covered the surface of the mountain due to the presence of the consuming fire, for all fire produces smoke. The entirety of the mountain was wreathed in smoke because the presence

of God engulfed the whole site. Secondly, smoke actually emerged from the interior of the mountain, which is what the verse means when it states: *Smoke billowed up from it as if from a furnace.* For the smoke of a furnace is created when flames are trapped by the lime covering the oven. Similarly, here, smoke escaped from the depths of the mountain's ash, causing the entire edifice to tremble and

18 at the foot of the mountain. Mount Sinai was enveloped in smoke because the LORD had descended on it in fire. Smoke billowed up from it as if from a furnace, and the mountain
19 shook violently as one. As the sound of the ram's horn grew louder and louder, Moshe spoke and God answered him aloud.

———————————— MALBIM *(cont.)* ————————————

quake. This was a supernatural event, since usually earthquakes are caused by vapors and smoke held within the belly of the earth with no avenue of release, leading the ground to shake and shift. However, when smoke and gas are able to escape their confines and emerge from the earth, the land will no longer tremble. Nevertheless, on this occasion, even though the smoke billowed into the sky, the mountain still tremored and quaked. This hinted to the people that because they had not prepared adequately to meet God, they would not be able to receive the Torah by way of His

grace, or awe, but rather through the terror at the prospect of punishment. For it is through fire and the shaking of mountains that God executes judgment. This is what our Sages, of blessed memory, meant when they stated that God held Mount Sinai above Israel's heads like an inverted barrel [see Shabbat 88a]. The nation only accepted God's commandments because they were afraid of His revenge. Without that fear, Israel would not have agreed to accept the written or the oral Torah. It was the fire, the noise, and the fear of suffering that persuaded them.

VERSE 19

———————————— OR HAHAYYIM ————————————

מֹשֶׁה יְדַבֵּר וְהָאֱלֹהִים יַעֲנֶנּוּ בְקוֹל – *Moshe spoke and God answered him aloud:* The text does not specify what it was exactly that Moshe said to God. It is possible that the man recited words of song and praise, as would be fitting as Moshe prepared to meet the arrival of the Almighty upon the mountain. *And God answered him aloud* by sounding the ram's horn, signaling to Moshe His approval of the agent's speech. Alternatively, the verse might

be suggesting that God verbally responded to Moshe at that moment. He *answered him aloud* so that *the people would hear [God] speaking to [him]* (19:9). This exchange would prove to the people the existence of prophecy. Finally, this verse illustrates the tremendous heights that Moshe had reached. For it is far more impressive for man to speak and elicit an answer from God, than vice versa.

———————————— MALBIM ————————————

מֹשֶׁה יְדַבֵּר וְהָאֱלֹהִים יַעֲנֶנּוּ בְקוֹל – *Moshe spoke and God answered him aloud:* It was at this point that God informed Moshe that He intended to speak to the people, to tell them that He was the one communicating with Moshe, whom He had appointed as His emissary to deliver the Torah. Once the nation heard that, they would be convinced of Moshe's agency and prophecy. For the people had to understand

that Moshe was the only person entrusted by God to bring His Torah to the world. Thus God stated: *I will come to you in a dense cloud, that the people may hear Me speaking to you. They will then believe you forever* (19:9). This meant that Israel would hear the speech that Moshe was directing at God and would similarly hear God's response and agreement with Moshe, as expressed in verse 23. The nation would

כ וַיֵּ֨רֶד יְהוָ֧ה עַל־הַ֛ר סִינַ֖י אֶל־רֹ֣אשׁ הָהָ֑ר וַיִּקְרָ֨א יְהוָ֧ה לְמֹשֶׁ֛ה ששי
כא אֶל־רֹ֥אשׁ הָהָ֖ר וַיַּ֥עַל מֹשֶֽׁה: וַיֹּ֤אמֶר יְהוָה֙ אֶל־מֹשֶׁ֔ה רֵ֖ד
הָעֵ֣ד בָּעָ֑ם פֶּן־יֶהֶרְס֤וּ אֶל־יְהוָה֙ לִרְא֔וֹת וְנָפַ֥ל מִמֶּ֖נּוּ רָֽב:

MALBIM *(cont.)*
---

recognize Moshe as God's emissary and as teacher of His Torah, including its oral interpretation. The significance of God's response "aloud" [alternatively, "with a voice"] was this: Even though Moshe's prophecy was received throughout as clear, unmediated comprehension, where no sound or image was necessary, still when it came time to give the Torah God created a voice and a sound to convey

His communication. God saw that Israel's trembling indicated that they were not truly ready to receive the Torah directly, without the mediation of Moshe as His agent. And knowing Israel would state quite clearly: *Speak to us yourself and we will listen, but let not God say any more to us, or we will die* (20:16), He prepared Moshe to be His messenger in this area.

HAAMEK DAVAR

הֹולֵךְ וְחָזֵק מְאֹד – *Grew louder and louder:* The sound that Israel heard was unusual in that it did not start off loud and grow softer, as normally happens when a musician tires. Rather, on this occasion the call of the ram's horn grew constantly in intensity. This was to teach God's nation the wonder of the Oral Law, which similarly grows in strength as time goes by. Now the powerful sound of the horn was actually produced by the smoke, a feature of the episode that also bears symbolism. For the smoke illustrates the darkness of human suffering, which causes people to feel shrouded in fog. And yet, Israel was assured here that through all of their future ordeals of exile, the voice of their traditions would become more powerful.

If the history of the Jewish nation had been spent living peacefully in the land of Israel, the depth and scope of the Oral Law would not have developed to the degree that it did. We see this clearly during the First Temple period. It was only when King Yoshiyahu [see II Kings 22–23] glimpsed the possibility of exile that he strove to improve Torah observance across the land by instructing the Levites to expand the Oral Law (see my commentary to Exodus 13:16.) Indeed, we see that during the length of Israel's exile, it is the torments that the Jews endure that cause the study and interpretation of Torah to grow more elaborate. And this in turn ensures that the Jewish people will never disappear. (Harḥev Davar)

VERSE 20

MALBIM

אֶל־רֹאשׁ הָהָר – *To the top of the mountain:* Initially, God spread His presence over the entire mountain, as the verse states: *Mount Sinai was enveloped in smoke because the LORD had descended on it* (19:18). What this meant was that the divine manifestation was close to the Israelites, who were standing at the foot

of the mountain. However, when God saw the people's lack of preparation rendered them unable to tolerate the divine fire and speech from such close proximity, God withdrew completely from the mountain. He then descended a second time just to the mountain peak, which was at a fair distance from Israel's

20 And the LORD descended on Mount Sinai, to the top of the SHISHI
mountain, and called Moshe to the mountaintop, and Moshe
21 ascended. The LORD told Moshe, "Go back down – warn the
people not to force their way through to look at the LORD, or

─────────────── MALBIM *(cont.)* ───────────────

camp. God subsequently *called Moshe to the mountaintop,* summoning him to climb the mountain where He planned to speak to him,

as promised in the statement *I will come to you in a dense cloud, that the people may hear Me speaking to you* (19:9).

─────────────── HAAMEK DAVAR ───────────────

וַיִּקְרָא יהוה לְמֹשֶׁה – *The LORD called Moshe:* [Literally, "called to Moshe"] Note that the verse employs just the letter *lamed* as a short form of the word *el* ["to"]. This is in contrast to verse 3. which uses the longer form *elav* in connection with God's call to Moshe. This

is because in the previous case, when God called Moshe, the latter was already in place, and God addressed him out of courtesy. Here however, Moshe was summoned to ascend to the top of the mountain. All calls to a person to physically approach use this form.

VERSE 21
─────────────── OR HAHAYYIM ───────────────

פֶּן־יֶהֶרְסוּ – *Not to force their way through:* [The word *yehersu* can also mean "destroy."] Said God to Moshe: I do not want the people to think that it is worth climbing the mountain and being condemned to certain death for a glimpse at Me. They should not rely on the verse *Because Your steadfast love is better than life, my lips shall praise You* (Psalms 63:4), which suggests that through their physical deaths, they might be granted spiritual life. This is

what the verse means when it uses the phrase *pen yehersu* – lest they seek to destroy themselves in order to see God. The consequence of such an approach will be that *many will die* [alternatively: "some will fall greatly"]. This means not only that the individuals will not survive the encounter with God, but that they will experience a fall after that fall [losing even their share in the afterlife].

─────────────── MALBIM ───────────────

הָעֵד בָּעָם – *Warn the people:* Even though God had already instructed Moshe to mark a boundary around the mountain to prevent Israel from climbing it [in verse 12], there are three reasons why the warning was now repeated. Firstly, recall that the nation had asked that God speak to them directly rather than through Moshe. God honored this request and pronounced the Ten Commandments aloud to the nation. At that time, even Moshe was barred from standing on the mountain, and he positioned himself below among

the Israelites. But now that God summoned Moshe to ascend Mount Sinai [in verse 20], the people believed that they, like their leader, were permitted to join him there, since they considered themselves to be on the same spiritual level as Moshe. Hence God had Moshe explain to Israel that although he was able to cross the boundary around the mountain, they were still prohibited from doing so. And there was a second reason to caution Israel again: By this point, the light of the Divine Presence had been lifted from the entire

כב וְגַם הַכֹּהֲנִים הַנִּגָּשִׁים אֶל־יהוה יִתְקַדָּשׁוּ פֶּן־יִפְרֹץ בָּהֶם
כג יהוה: וַיֹּאמֶר מֹשֶׁה אֶל־יהוה לֹא־יוּכַל הָעָם לַעֲלֹת אֶל־
הַר סִינָי כִּי־אַתָּה הַעֵדֹתָה בָּנוּ לֵאמֹר הַגְבֵּל אֶת־הָהָר
כד וְקִדַּשְׁתּוֹ: וַיֹּאמֶר אֵלָיו יהוה לֶךְ־רֵד וְעָלִיתָ אַתָּה וְאַהֲרֹן

─────── MALBIM *(cont.)* ───────

mountain and was limited to its peak, which rose at some distance from the Israelite camp. Because the principal mass of the mountain separated the people from the manifestation of God, the Israelites thought that it would be alright for them to climb just the foot of the hill, where there was no obvious presence of God. Hence the nation was assured that such an effort would be futile, since anyway they would be unable to *look at the LORD* from so far. The third understanding for our verse is highlighted by Targum Yonatan's translation, which renders the warning as: "Lest they focus before God to see." The sense of this is that even if the people did not physically cross the boundary around the mountain, they were still to respect the more internal threshold of perception, eschewing the idea that they had seen an image of God. For Israel had not fully divested itself of the idea that they could behold God, and they were liable to give Him some form in their minds. This would severely damage the true beliefs and cause many Israelites to err. This in turn would impair Moshe's stature, for the leader only held his position of greatness for the sake of teaching the nation. Therefore, when the verse states: *Many will die* [alternatively translated: "a great one will fall"], it can be understood as warning of the diminishment of that great man.

VERSE 22

─────── OR HAHAYYIM ───────

וְגַם הַכֹּהֲנִים – *Even priests:* It was understood that the priests – either the firstborn sons or the descendants of Aharon – would hold an exalted status and greater access to the sacred place of divine worship. Nevertheless, here they were told that their privileges did not extend to climbing the mountain. The priests were instructed to "consecrate themselves," that is, to recognize that their sanctity did not allow them to cross the boundary established for the entire nation. In fact, the priests were effectively told that their sanctity was of no consequence at that moment.

─────── HAAMEK DAVAR ───────

וְגַם הַכֹּהֲנִים – *Even priests:* The priests were invited to stand closest to the mountain during revelation, but they too were commanded to prepare themselves mentally for the experience. **פֶּן־יִפְרֹץ בָּהֶם** – *Will break out against them:* The danger existed that the intensity of the Divine Presence might injure the priests should they not prepare themselves. For the glaring light of God might end up burning them, as I have written above. On the other hand, because the rest of the Israelite nation were less receptive to the perception and understanding of God, there was less fear that their lack of readiness might cause them damage.

22 many will die. Even priests who come near to the LORD must
first consecrate themselves, or the LORD will break out against
23 them." Moshe replied to the LORD, "The people cannot climb
Mount Sinai. You Yourself warned us to set a boundary around
24 the mountain and consecrate it." The LORD said to him, "Go
down, and come back together with Aharon. But do not let

VERSE 23

OR HAHAYYIM

לֹא־יוּכַל הָעָם לַעֲלֹת אֶל־הַר סִינָי – *The people cannot climb Mount Sinai:* It seems to me that at first the entire nation was warned not to touch or climb the mountain, and no distinction was made among the various classes among the people. However, God subsequently instructed Moshe to consecrate the priests, and hinted to him that these men were being given a special place on the mountain where they could view the revelation. At that point there existed the fear that Israel might apply one of the traditional exegetical principles to God's statement as follows: One such rule states that when a detail that is originally included in a category is singled out in order to teach something, that lesson applies to the entire category and not just to the highlighted detail. Now here, Aharon and the priests were included in God's overall prohibition not to approach the mountain, and yet the priests were eventually singled out and allowed to climb part way up the hill. Employing the axiom stated above, the people reasoned that the exception did not relate solely to the priests, but to the whole category, meaning that the entire nation was now permitted to climb a short way up the mountain, or at the very least to the area beneath where the priests stood. And even though the Torah had not yet been given to Israel, and it seems unlikely that they would have known the principles that are employed in its interpretation, it is possible that somewhere among the hundreds of thousands of Israelites, some clever individual might have intuited this law of logic.

HAAMEK DAVAR

לֹא־יוּכַל הָעָם לַעֲלֹת אֶל־הַר סִינָי – *The people cannot climb Mount Sinai:* The principal warning issued in verse 21 had been against actually ascending the mountain, not simply crossing the boundary, as the language of that verse makes clear: *Not to force their way through to look at the LORD.* Moshe here argued that such a transgression would be impossible, for *You Yourself warned us to set a boundary around the mountain* so that no one could climb it.

VERSE 24

HAKETAV VEHAKABBALA

לֵד־רֵד – *Go down:* Said God to Moshe: Now that I am about to pronounce the first two commandments to Israel, go down from the mountain and join the people at its foot. Still, the moment will arrive when you will *come back together with Aharon,* for I know that after I utter the those initial commandments, the nation will beg you: *Speak to us yourself and we will listen, but let not God say any more to us, or we will die* (20:16). And so you will ascend the mountain to receive the last eight commandments, which you will then convey to the Israelites. Thus does the verse later report: *Moshe approached the thick darkness where God was* (20:18).

עִמָּךְ וְהַכֹּהֲנִים וְהָעָם אַל־יֶהֶרְסוּ לַעֲלֹת אֶל־יהוה פֶּן־יִפְרָץ־
בָּם: כֹּא וַיֵּרֶד מֹשֶׁה אֶל־הָעָם וַיֹּאמֶר אֲלֵהֶם: וַיְדַבֵּר

--------------------------------- SHADAL ---------------------------------

לֵרֶד **– Go down:** It seems to me that Moshe was reluctant to descend the mountain, and would have preferred to stay there rather than return and warn the people. God would not agree to that, but told Moshe that after He gave Israel the Torah, he could climb back up the mountain with Aharon. Thus a later verse states: Then He said to Moshe, "Ascend to the LORD, you and Aharon" (24:1). But Moshe cannot have been on the mountain while God was delivering the Torah to Israel, but stood rather as an Israelite among the nation. Support for this comes from the people's demand Speak to us yourself and we will listen, but let not God say any more to us, or we will die (20:16). [That is, the people were able to speak directly to Moshe because he was there with them.]

--------------------------------- MALBIM ---------------------------------

וַיֹּאמֶר אֵלָיו יהוה לֵךְ־רֵד **– The LORD said to him, "Go down":** At this point, God agreed with Moshe that there was no need to issue an additional warning to the nation. He thereby fulfilled the promise that He made back in verse 9, when He said: The people may hear Me speaking to you. They will then believe you forever, which was a prediction that the people would witness Him accepting the prophet's position [increasing his standing in their eyes]. Nevertheless, God instructed Moshe to go back down and stand at the foot of the mountain while He pronounced the Ten Commandments to Israel, in order to ensure that no one would dare to climb the mountain during revelation. The command God gave to Moshe to climb the hill again later would be fulfilled following the declaration of the Ten Commandments, when the verse states: Then He said to Moshe, "Ascend to the LORD, you and Aharon, Nadav and Avihu, and seventy of Israel's elders and bow down from afar" (24:1). At that point it would be critical to remind the rest of the nation that they had not achieved the level of their leaders, lest they attempt to force their way through to look at the LORD (19:21). Still, this last limitation had not yet been finally decided; had Israel not petitioned Moshe saying: Speak to us yourself and we will listen (20:16), and had they been able to tolerate the overwhelming sound of the ram's horn, the entire nation would have been allowed to ascend the mountain. Indeed, this is the meaning of the verse: When the ram's horn sounds a long blast – only then may they go up on the mountain (19:13). Hence, God's statement to Moshe was conditional: If you go down, and come back together with Aharon only, and the nation does not receive the entire Torah from Me directly, then the nation and the priests should not force their way through to look at the LORD (19:21). Rather, all the people were to stand in their designated positions, not approach the mountain, nor climb it along with Moshe.

VERSE 25

--------------------------------- MALBIM ---------------------------------

וַיֵּרֶד מֹשֶׁה **– So Moshe went down:** Moshe did exactly as the God had commanded him, namely standing at the bottom of the mountain as God delivered the Ten Commandments

the priests or people force their way through to come up to the
25 LORD, or He will break out against them." So Moshe went down
20 1 to the people and told them.   Then God spoke all these

———————— MALBIM *(cont.)* ————————

to the nation. **וַיֹּאמֶר אֲלֵהֶם** – *And told them:*
[Literally, "and said to them"; it is unclear what

he said. Malbim explains:] Moshe related to
the people what God had spoken to him.

CHAPTER 20, VERSE 1

———————— OR HAḤAYYIM ————————

אֵת כָּל־הַדְּבָרִים הָאֵלֶּה לֵאמֹר – *All these words:*
When God first pronounced the full text of
the Ten Commandments in one utterance, as
I have explained, the people were unable to
accommodate the full strength of the statements, and were only able to discern the first
two precepts. At that point all of the Israelites'
souls departed, as the verse states, *my soul
failed when he spoke* (Song of Songs 5:6), and
they were unable to understand any more of
God's communication. Meanwhile the subsequent commandments were carved into
the hillside with flames of fire manifesting
the voice of God, and stood visible on Mount
Sinai until the people's souls returned to them
with the dew of resurrection. Thereupon these
commandments were transformed into sound
to be heard by each individual Israelite. You
will therefore find that the first two commandments are recorded in the text precisely as
pronounced by God, in the first person: *I am
the LORD your God who brought you out of the
land of Egypt,* and *Have no other gods than Me*
(20:2–3), for God Himself was speaking to the
Israelites in all His glory. However, from that
point through the remainder of the passage,

the voice of God was communicated through
His celestial messenger. This explains why the
following statements refer to God in the third
person: *But the seventh is a Sabbath to the LORD
your God* (20:10), *For in six days the LORD made
heaven and earth. . . . And so the LORD blessed
the Sabbath day and made it holy* (20:11). The
voice that addressed Israel on God's behalf
could not have said: "But the seventh is a Sabbath to me," or: "For in six days I made heaven
and earth, and I rested on the seventh day."
For the entity that spoke these words was
merely God's angelic emissary. Understand
this idea well and appreciate it. Now even
though our Sages claim that Israel heard
this material from Moshe [and not through
the independent voices themselves], what
they may have meant was that Moshe possessed the strength to hear the entire text
of the Ten Commandments, and his soul did
not expire after the first two statements like
everyone else's. And then, when the voices
that remained to repeat the remainder of the
passage to Israel issued forth to continue the
communication, they were accompanied by
the voice of Moshe speaking to the nation.

———————— HAKETAV VEHAKABBALA ————————

אֵת כָּל־הַדְּבָרִים הָאֵלֶּה לֵאמֹר – *All these words:*
Why did the Sages feel the need to inform us
that God initially spoke the entire text of the
Ten Commandments in a single utterance, only
to then declare each precept separately and

distinctly, as cited by Rashi quoting the Mekhilta? Firstly, this idea seems to me to reflect the
point that there is a value to the whole as well
as significance to the particulars. Secondly,
from the perspective of the laws' author [God],

ג אֱלֹהִים אֵת כָּל־הַדְּבָרִים הָאֵלֶּה לֵאמֹר: אָנֹכִי
יהוה אֱלֹהֶיךָ אֲשֶׁר הוֹצֵאתִיךָ מֵאֶרֶץ מִצְרַיִם מִבֵּית
ד עֲבָדִים: לֹא־יִהְיֶה לְךָ אֱלֹהִים אֲחֵרִים עַל־פָּנָי: לֹא־תַעֲשֶׂה

——————————— HAKETAV VEHAKABBALA *(cont.)* ———————————

who represents the ultimate cosmic oneness, the whole Torah really does stand as a single commandment. It is only from the recipients' viewpoint that the corpus comprises a range of statutes. Therefore the Torah was presented as a single unit, but also as a collection of different decrees. And because God wished to demonstrate that the Ten Commandments contained a general message, He began by pronouncing them all together. And so when Israel first heard the sound of the combined text of all the precepts, they accepted it and understood it as a complex communication from the mouth of God. (This is contrary to Ramban's presentation of this idea.) Israel surely must have derived something from the experience, since what point would there have been for the nation to be exposed to a jumbled sound that meant nothing to them? For the revelation that the Lord orchestrated here was strictly for the benefit of His people, as the verse states: *Gather Me the people*

together, and I will make them hear My words, that they may learn to fear Me all the days that they shall live upon the earth (Deuteronomy 4:10). If the Israelites had understood nothing from God's initial speech to them, how could He justify saying that He would make them hear His words so that they might fear Him – how would the nation possibly learn to fear God under such circumstances? Moshe also later states: *And the Lord spoke to you out of the midst of the fire…. And He declared to you His covenant* (Deuteronomy 4:12) – would God deliver a speech and a statement to the nation in a manner that was indecipherable to them? After presenting the people with a general message of the Ten Commandments, God elaborated each one specifically. It was then that the nation heard only the first two statements from God directly; the latter eight were first transmitted to Moshe, who then conveyed them to the people.

VERSE 2

——————————— OR HAḤAYYIM ———————————

אֲשֶׁר הוֹצֵאתִיךָ מֵאֶרֶץ מִצְרַיִם – *Who brought you out of the land of Egypt Egypt:* Why does the verse state both that God took Israel *out of the land of Egypt*, and *out of the house of slaves* – is this not redundant? By expressing the exodus in two ways, God intends to

emphasize the severity of the nation's circumstances. For not only had the Israelites been imprisoned in Egypt, an inescapable land suffused by impurity, but they had been slaves there – the lowest level of society. And yet God brought them out.

——————————— RABBI SAMSON RAPHAEL HIRSCH ———————————

אָנֹכִי יהוה אֱלֹהֶיךָ – *I am the Lord your God:* The fundamental truth that defines the Jewish experience is not the belief in God's existence, nor even that God is the only deity in

the universe. It is rather that the Lord – who is the one and the only real divine being – is *my* God. He created and fashioned me, sustains me now, and continues to guide me and

2 words: "I am the LORD your God who brought
3 you out of the land of Egypt, out of the house of slaves. Have
4 no other gods than Me. Do not make for yourself any carved

———————————— RABBI SAMSON RAPHAEL HIRSCH *(cont.)* ————————————

direct my life. My faith is not that I am incidentally connected to God through a causal chain with tens of thousands links going back to the creation of the world thousands of generations ago [i.e., that God has not been involved with the world since creation]. Instead, it is my guiding principle that every breath I take is a direct gift and consequence of God's power and grace. As such it is incumbent upon me to devote every waking moment of my life and every future plan solely to His service. Again, the critical point is not my knowledge that there is a God in the world, but that I have a personal relationship with Him, that my fate rests in His hands, and that my actions are guided by His will. Thus there can be only one response to God's declaration that *I am the LORD your God*: Indeed! You are my God! The immediate evidence for this fact of providence is Israel's emancipation from Egypt, an event that we witnessed with our very eyes. Now there are two dimensions to this history: When the text states that God *brought you out of the land of Egypt,* it portrays Him as director of our national fate. But beyond that, the succeeding statement that He removed us from *the house of slaves* implies that God thereby acquired us as His own servants. And that means that every action of ours must be dedicated to serving Him.

———————————— SEFAT EMET ————————————

אָנֹכִי יהוה אֱלֹהֶיךָ – *I am the LORD your God:* The Midrash states that when God pronounced the first of the Ten Commandments, saying: *I am the LORD your God,* all of humanity trembled. For every individual believed that God was addressing him or her and identifying Himself as the God of all people. However, once they heard the continuation of the verse, *Who brought you out of the land of Egypt,* they understood that God was speaking exclusively to the nation of Israel. Of course, it is true that when God stated: *I am the LORD your God,* He did have the entire world in mind, but concomitantly He gave Israel the unique task of persuading the other nations to accept the reign of God over themselves. For every person in the world must reach the understanding that God rules over the universe. It is to this special responsibility of Israel that the verse refers when it states: *A kingdom of priests and a holy nation you shall be to Me* (19:6). For even though it is an undeniable truth that God is the ruler of the world, it is His will that Israel spread this message to our fellow human beings, who will then crown Him as their monarch as well.

VERSE 3

———————————— NEHAMA LEIBOWITZ ————————————

לֹא־יִהְיֶה לְךָ אֱלֹהִים אֲחֵרִים עַל־פָּנָי – *Have no other gods than Me:* The true understanding of the prohibition of idolatry comes with the understanding that taking any means to an end – even the most noble and worthy end – and making that means into the ultimate goal of our lives, transgresses the command of *Have no other gods than Me.* This concept applies to nonmaterial things as well. Even ideas and values that are produced by our spirit and our souls and which we believe to be true and necessary are subject to this

לְךָ פֶסֶל וְכָל־תְּמוּנָה אֲשֶׁר בַּשָּׁמַיִם מִמַּעַל וַאֲשֶׁר בָּאָרֶץ
מִתַּחַת וַאֲשֶׁר בַּמַּיִם מִתַּחַת לָאָרֶץ: לֹא־תִשְׁתַּחֲוֶה לָהֶם
וְלֹא תָעָבְדֵם כִּי אָנֹכִי יהוה אֱלֹהֶיךָ אֵל קַנָּא פֹּקֵד עֲוֹן אָבֹת
עַל־בָּנִים עַל־שִׁלֵּשִׁים וְעַל־רִבֵּעִים לְשֹׂנְאָי: וְעֹשֶׂה חֶסֶד

<hr>
NEHAMA LEIBOWITZ (cont.)
<hr>

precaution when we are tempted to devote the core of our beings to them. We risk turning concepts such as nationalism and the homeland into religions themselves when they cease to be methods and tools in the service of the Creator and become purposes in their own right. When that happens, all our physical and mental energies become subject to these virtues, whose demands are unlimited and absolute. Such worship is the greatest manifestation of idolatry and the most dangerous.

VERSE 4
<hr>
OR HAHAYYIM
<hr>

לֹא־תַעֲשֶׂה לְךָ פֶסֶל וְכָל־תְּמוּנָה – *Do not make for yourself any carved image or likeness:* It seems that this verse cautions against a sort of idolatry different from that expressed in the previous verse, *Have no other gods than Me.* This commandment is directed at an individual who argues as follows: Indeed, I do believe wholeheartedly that the LORD is the true God in the universe, and I fully accept that there is no other god than Him. However, I also feel that because of God's unfathomable greatness and the vast gulf that separates Him from me, I am incapable of grasping His nature. How can I possibly hope to speak to the Master of the Universe and present my puny requests to Him? Surely it is inappropriate, even rude, for such a lowly creature as I to appear before such an exalted king, especially since I have so many minor and objectively insignificant needs. Upon thinking such thoughts, the individual will be tempted by his evil inclination to avoid addressing God directly, and to turn instead to one of His celestial ministers who serve Him in the heavens [i.e., the sun, the moon, and the stars]. These entities, so he believes, will be able to assist him themselves, and furthermore will intercede on his behalf with the great King, who grants them His attention. Now in order to curry favor with these intermediaries, the individual will honor them, bless them, and bow before them in all manner of homage. Because he hopes that this minister of God will take on his personal burdens as his own, the human only feels it right to attend to this patron's needs [through acts of worship]. Of course, this thinking represents a grave error that has ensnared many idolaters who surely know, on an intellectual level, that the entities they are serving are not gods. Still, these people are mostly interested in establishing a relationship with an intermediary that can stand between God and themselves. The Torah refers to this sort of behavior as the construction of a "carved image" [*pesel*, evoking the word *pesolet*, meaning "waste"], for the votary knows in his heart that the object of his devotion has no divine powers, but rather is an insignificant nothing compared to the Creator of the world who fashioned it.

image or likeness of any creature in the heavens above or the
5 earth beneath or the water beneath the earth. Do not bow down
to them or worship them, for I the LORD your God demand absolute loyalty. For those who hate Me, I hold the descendants
to account for the sins of the fathers to the third and fourth gen-
6 eration, but to those who love Me and keep My commands –

VERSE 5

OR HAḤAYYIM

פֹּקֵד עֲוֹן אָבֹת עַל־בָּנִים – *I hold the descendants to account for the sins of the fathers:* The fact that God does not immediately punish the sins of the wicked is astonishing. After all, to the community at large it appears that evil people continue in their nefarious ways with impunity, and that their nasty behavior even raises them to the heights of success. And yet, when we consider the period of four generations which God sets as the limit of His patience, we realize that justice is ultimately done. As the verse states: *Until I entered the sanctuary of God; then*

I understood their end (Psalms 73:17), that is, at the end of the allotted time, the full weight of God's punishment will descend upon the family for the transgressions that have been perpetrated. I must also point out that while suffering for sin extends through the fourth generation, God's wrath is limited to that. God does not visit pain upon the fifth generation for the disobedience of their distant ances- tor. Conversely, when God bestows rewards to those who honor His will, such beneficence is stretched over thousands of generations.

MALBIM

אֵל קַנָּא – *Demand absolute loyalty:* [Literally, "am a jealous God."] Note that there is a dif- ference between the terms "jealous" [*kana*] and "vengeful" [*nokem*]. A person motivated by jealousy attempts to rectify a dishonor he has suffered, but one seeks vengeance only when he has suffered actual and direct harm. Now when God reacts to the sin of idolatry, He behaves like a man whose wife has been disloyal to him. In fact, it is quite common

to find idolatry portrayed with the metaphor of adultery. For when people betray God by worshipping a foreign god, they impugn His honor, as the verse states: *They provoked Him to jealousy with strange gods* (Deuteronomy 32:16). In such a circumstance, the language of vengeance would be inappropriate, since no real harm has taken place. However, God does demand vengeance when a physical wrong such as theft or murder has been committed.

VERSE 6

OR HAḤAYYIM

וְעֹשֶׂה חֶסֶד לַאֲלָפִים – *I shall act with faith- ful love for thousands:* When the Holy One, blessed be He, rewards those who do His bidding, He does not bestow all of His good- ness at once, but chooses a method of distri- bution that will endure for generations. Thus He grants each subsequent stage of the fam- ily the graciousness that they require. In this

way God ensures protection and salvation for thousands of generations. Thus our Sages ar- gued: Imagine if the Holy One, blessed be He, had conferred upon our patriarchs all of the reward they deserved in this world – how would their descendants survive and be sus- tained throughout their centuries of exile?

לַאֲלָפִים לְאֹהֲבַי וּלְשֹׁמְרֵי מִצְוֹתָי: לֹא תִשָּׂא אֶת־
שֵׁם־יהוה אֱלֹהֶיךָ לַשָּׁוְא כִּי לֹא יְנַקֶּה יהוה אֵת אֲשֶׁר־יִשָּׂא
אֶת־שְׁמוֹ לַשָּׁוְא:
זָכוֹר אֶת־יוֹם הַשַּׁבָּת לְקַדְּשׁוֹ: שֵׁשֶׁת יָמִים תַּעֲבֹד וְעָשִׂיתָ

——— HAAMEK DAVAR ———

לְאֹהֲבַי – To those who love Me: According to our Sages, the phrase "those who love Me" refers to Jews who are prepared to forfeit their lives in order to observe the commandments. The Sages rejected the straightforward interpretation of this verse as referring to those people who simply fulfill His will, since that understanding would parallel with the preceding text. When verse 5 states: For those who hate Me, I hold the descendants to account for the sins of the fathers to the third and fourth generation, it must be describing individuals who worship idols and thereby reject the entire Torah. Therefore, in our verse as well, God praises those who act righteously toward their Creator in an exceptional, unnatural manner. In response, God is prepared to treat such martyrs in kind, with a reward that goes beyond the natural order of things. For while all those who obey God can hope to be rewarded for their fealty, individuals who make the ultimate sacrifice to demonstrate their loyalty will be treated to an unusual level of providence. This is what the text means by "faithful love."

——— MESHEKH ḤOKHMA ———

לְאֹהֲבַי – To those who love Me: The Mekhilta teaches us that the words "those who love Me" are a reference to the patriarch Avraham, while it is the prophets and the elders of Israel who are said to "keep My commandments." What this means is that because Avraham was himself a descendant of Noaḥ [that is, he was technically a gentile, not having been born into the covenant], he was not actually commanded to sanctify the name of God, as the Talmud argues [see Sanhedrin 74b]. Nevertheless, since the man truly loved God, he fulfilled the commandments even without being ordered to do so. On the other hand, when the prophets and elders observe the Torah's law, they are responding to the decrees of God, and hence are referred to as those who "keep My commandments."

VERSE 7

——— SHADAL ———

לֹא תִשָּׂא – Do not speak: [Literally, "do not carry."] This text warns the Torah's adherents not to carry the name of God unnecessarily on their lips. We find a similar expression in the verse Nor will I take up [essa] their names upon my lips (Psalms 16:4)…. The Talmud discusses the case of an individual who swears that a column of wood is in fact wood as an example of an unnecessary oath. In my opinion, the prohibition of uttering such a true but useless statement is not what is truly forbidden here, but is a preventive measure put in place by the Sages. For even such a pointless oath displays a lack of respect for the divine, and when a person becomes accustomed to uttering unwarranted oaths, he will eventually have no trouble swearing falsely. Our Sages therefore included in this verse's prohibition merely saying God's name gratuitously, an act which certainly dishonors the Almighty. Indeed, the most straightforward

₇ I shall act with faithful love for thousands.   Do not speak the name of the LORD your God in vain, for the LORD will not hold guiltless those who speak His name in vain.

⁸₉ Remember the Sabbath to keep it holy. Six days you shall work,

———————————————— SHADAL *(cont.)* ————————————————

meaning of the verse forbids mere mention of the name of God for no purpose. Now because Onkelos wished to avoid rendering the word *shav* ["in vain," which appears twice in the verse] the same way in both instances, he translated the first usage as *lemaggana* ["in vain"], and the second usage as *leshikra* ["falsely"]. The translator thereby expanded the prohibition to include swearing unnecessarily, while limiting the major punishment threatened by this

verse ["will not hold guiltless"] to occasions of false oaths. לֹא יְנַקֶּה – *Will not hold guiltless:* A person who swears falsely does not fear being found out, for he thinks that people will believe his statement, and lies are not often discovered. Hence God declares that even though one may escape unpunished from a human court, He guarantees that He *will not hold guiltless* the sinner who uses His name to perpetuate a lie.

———————————————— RABBI SAMSON RAPHAEL HIRSCH ————————————————

לֹא תִשָּׂא – *Do not speak:* It is clear that when we express ourselves with an oath, we acknowledge both facets of our recognition of God. Firstly, we admit that God has complete control over our actions – including the speech of our mouths; and secondly, we confess that God is the master of our destiny.

Swearing in the name of God is a declaration that we intend to stake our divinely controlled fates on the truth of our claims and the faultlessness of our actions. A false oath, therefore, is a denial of the true involvement of God in our lives. There is nothing more dishonorable than that.

VERSE 8

———————————————— OR HAHAYYIM ————————————————

לְקַדְּשׁוֹ – *To keep it holy:* With this term, the Torah instructs us to prepare throughout the week for the upcoming Sabbath. Hence our Sages advise us to prepare for the Sabbath starting on the first day of the week [see Beitza 16a]. Elsewhere, the Sages teach that on the first Friday in history, soon after man was created, he sinned and was found guilty. But the Sabbath day appeared before God in defense of man and said: Master of the Universe! No person was ever killed on the other days of the week, why should I be the first to suffer

the indignity of having man executed during my watch? Thus was man saved from capital punishment thanks to the Sabbath. And when humanity saw the power that the Sabbath held, they composed the song, *A psalm, A poem for the Sabbath day* (Psalms 92:1). This is what God meant when He commanded: *Remember the Sabbath day* – do not forget the Sabbath which saved humanity and allowed all future descendants of the first man and woman to be born.

———————————————— RABBI SAMSON RAPHAEL HIRSCH ————————————————

זָכוֹר אֶת־יוֹם הַשַּׁבָּת – *Remember the Sabbath:* With this commandment, God recalls

the distant past when He first established a memorial to His act of creation, soon after

כָּל־מְלַאכְתֶּךָ: וְיוֹם הַשְּׁבִיעִי שַׁבָּת לַיהוָה אֱלֹהֶיךָ לֹא־
תַעֲשֶׂה כָל־מְלָאכָה אַתָּה ׀ וּבִנְךָ וּבִתֶּךָ עַבְדְּךָ וַאֲמָתְךָ

—————— RABBI SAMSON RAPHAEL HIRSCH *(cont.)* ——————

God made the first man and tasked him with guardianship of the earth as His envoy. The Sabbath day testified to the recognition of this reality. But when man began to forget that relationship, civilization deteriorated until humanity was in a sorry state. It was at that point that the nation of Israel was chosen to publicize the word of God to humanity and lead society back to the path God intends for all of us. Therefore, in our text, the Sabbath is

not presented as a new institution. Rather, the Torah makes reference to the Sabbath with the assumption that the reader is familiar with the holy day. For the Sabbath had existed and endured since the days of the first human beings. From this point on, the nation was to behave differently than mankind had throughout the previous generations that had neglected the Sabbath.

—————————— MALBIM ——————————

זָכוֹר אֶת־יוֹם הַשַּׁבָּת – *Remember the Sabbath:* In the current passage, God explains the commandment of the Sabbath by reminding Israel that He created the world, and that the seventh day stands as a memorial to that history. However, in the retelling of the Ten Commandments [in Deuteronomy 5], God associates the Sabbath with Israel's emancipation from Egypt. There are two reasons for this shift. Firstly, it is impossible to accept the veracity of the exodus and its attendant wonders without believing that the world had a Creator. For those who believe that the world has always existed will find it difficult to explain how God could make alterations to the way it runs, performing the wonders described in this book. The second reason is as follows: Consider that at the time the Ten Commandments were first presented, the Israelites were meant to be immortal, as the verse states: *The tablets were the work of God, and*

the writing was God's writing, engraved [*ḥarut*] on the tablets (32:16), a term which our Sages explain should be understood as if written *ḥerut* [meaning "freedom"]. They meant by this that upon receiving the original tablets, Israel was freed from the grip of the angel of death. It was due to this remarkable shift that a remembrance of the creation of the world had to be imposed. For once the reign of the angel of death had ended, and people lived forever, humanity might have started believing that the world too had always existed. Hence the first version of the precepts included the Sabbath as a reminder that there was a beginning to the universe. On the other hand, the explanation for the holy day appearing in Deuteronomy was written after the sin [of the golden calf], at which point this need had dissipated. For by then, people were no longer immortal and continued to die as they always had.

—————— RABBI JOSEPH B. SOLOVEITCHIK ——————

זָכוֹר אֶת־יוֹם הַשַּׁבָּת – *Remember the Sabbath:* The commandment to remember the Sabbath begins in effect on the first day of the week. All week long, a person anticipates the Sabbath

and yearns for it. The philosophical idea that lies behind this law is the Jewish longing for sanctity [*kedusha*]. The Jew finds himself daily in a mundane world, and he constantly

10 and carry out all your labors, but the seventh is a Sabbath to the
LORD your God. On it, do no work – neither you, nor your son
or daughter, your male or female servant, your livestock, or the

—————————— RABBI JOSEPH B. SOLOVEITCHIK *(cont.)* ——————————

yearns for sanctity. Similarly, the requirement of extending the Sabbath a few minutes before and after expresses our eagerness to embrace it and our reluctance to part with it. This emotional relationship to the Sabbath is also reflected in the use of spices during the recitation of *Havdala*. The early commentaries explain their function in pragmatic terms: the departure of our added spirit [*neshama yetera*, said to inhere in our bodies for the duration of the Sabbath] creates a sensation of weakness, even faintness, in each Jew. The spices act as a stimulant to revive the Jew.

VERSE 9

—————————— RABBI SAMSON RAPHAEL HIRSCH ——————————

שֵׁשֶׁת יָמִים תַּעֲבֹד – *Six days you shall work:* The idea here is not for Israel to spend the week laboring for its own glorification and proving that human beings are masters of their world. Rather, this work should be viewed as divine service, as efforts to build the kingdom of God. We ought to consider ourselves as emissaries of God, dispatched to earth to perform His duties for the sake of His world. This is the meaning of the verse *And the LORD God took the man, and put him into the garden of Eden to till it and to keep it* (Genesis 2:15). It is the human obligation to improve our world by taking its unformed materials and fashioning them into purposeful objects. Humanity thereby assists in advancing God's intentions for the universe.

——————————————— HAAMEK DAVAR ———————————————

שֵׁשֶׁת יָמִים תַּעֲבֹד – *Six days you shall work:* The term "labor" [*avoda*] refers to work that people perform to make a living, like cultivating a plot of land or laboring for an employer. Furthermore, everyone is a slave [*eved*] to his or her own needs, as our Sages write in explanation of the verse *And man became a living soul* (Genesis 2:7). The term *avoda* also appears in the Torah's prohibition of labor on festivals, which it refers to as "laborious work" [*melekhet avoda*] (Leviticus 23:7). That is, work that is directed toward making a living is forbidden on a holiday, whereas activities required to immediately sustain oneself [i.e., for cooking] are permitted. וְעָשִׂיתָ כָּל־מְלַאכְתֶּךָ – *And carry out all your labors:* Even necessary activities for your enjoyment, such as baking, cooking and the like. [That is, even such labors are forbidden on the Sabbath, unlike on festivals.]

VERSE 10

——————————————— OR HAHAYYIM ———————————————

שַׁבָּת לַיהוה אֱלֹהֶיךָ – *A Sabbath to the LORD your God:* When Jews observe the Sabbath day in honor of God, they testify to His existence and acknowledge that He is their master. Hence our Sages argue that the worth of the Sabbath is equal to all of the Torah's other commandments added up together. Perhaps this idea is alluded to in the very word *shabbat* [with a numerical value of 702], as follows: Moshe the prophet taught the nation of Israel 611 [out of 613] commandments, whereas God pronounced the first two – *I am the LORD your*

אַ וּבְהֶמְתֶּךָ וְגֵרְךָ אֲשֶׁר בִּשְׁעָרֶיךָ: כִּי שֵׁשֶׁת־יָמִים עָשָׂה
יהוה אֶת־הַשָּׁמַיִם וְאֶת־הָאָרֶץ אֶת־הַיָּם וְאֶת־כָּל־אֲשֶׁר־
בָּם וַיָּנַח בַּיּוֹם הַשְּׁבִיעִי עַל־כֵּן בֵּרַךְ יהוה אֶת־יוֹם הַשַּׁבָּת

──────── OR HAHAYYIM *(cont.)* ────────

God (20:2) and *Have no other gods than Me* (20:3) — to the people directly [see Makkot 24a]. Now these two commandments are themselves a microcosm of all the Torah's laws, the first representing the scope of positive commandments, while the second stands for all the prohibitions. Furthermore, our Sages have already explained that God established the positive commandments for the sake of His attribute of Compassion, since it is performance of these rules that yields reward for their adherents. And this dimension of mercy

is symbolized by the Tetragrammaton *yod-heh-vav-heh* [with a numerical value of 26]. But God issued the negative commandments in association with His attribute of Justice, linked to the name *Adonai* [with a value of 65]. Hence the two introductory precepts, which are general statements for the rest of the Torah, can be viewed as having a joint numerical value of 91. If one adds 91 to the other 611 commandments that Moshe introduced to the nation, the sum of 702 is reached, which is the value of the word *shabbat*.

──────── SHADAL ────────

לֹא־תַעֲשֶׂה כָל־מְלָאכָה — *On it, do no work:* This prohibition is certainly directed at both men and women [despite the masculine form in the Hebrew]. It must be so because the verse mandates that both sons and daughters are subject to this law, as are male and female servants. This proves that men and women alike are commanded to honor the Sabbath day, with women expected to observe its restrictions out of their own free will. For if the verse described a situation where a wife was subject to her husband's authority like a

maidservant, it would have ordered the man of the family to instruct his wife to abstain from labor just like he must direct his children and household help. Indeed, throughout the Torah the commandments are generally expressed in the masculine form even when they apply to both men and women. Still, our Sages exempted women from commandments whose performance is restricted to a particular time, which suggests that by their times the status of women had changed and men had imposed a stricter regimen on them.

──────── RABBI SAMSON RAPHAEL HIRSCH ────────

לֹא־תַעֲשֶׂה כָל־מְלָאכָה — *On it, do no work:* By refraining from work on the Sabbath, the Jew demonstrates that all of his labor during the week is devoted to the service of God. When Sabbath arrives, the individual sheds the veneer of glory he has covered himself with and positions himself in the proper place of humility beneath the throne of God.... There is no hint whatsoever in the Torah that the

commandment of abstaining from work on the Sabbath is only the means to some higher end. [The author is criticizing Jews who justified violating the Sabbath in order to ostensibly enhance its atmosphere — for example, playing an organ in synagogue.] Throughout the Torah, he who abstains from work is said to observe the Sabbath, while anyone who performs work is said to desecrate the holy day.

11 migrant within your gates. For in six days the LORD made heaven and earth, the sea, and all that they contain, and He rested on the seventh day. And so the LORD blessed the Sabbath day

────────────── RABBI SAMSON RAPHAEL HIRSCH *(cont.)* ──────────────

Even who does not attend the synagogue at all on Sabbath to pray with the community or to hear the rabbi's sermon has not violated the day. Rather, observance of the day means not performing work.

────────────── HAAMEK DAVAR ──────────────

שַׁבָּת לַיהוה אֱלֹהֶיךָ – *A Sabbath to the LORD your God:* This verse emphasizes that the LORD is your God in order to remind you that He cares for you and provides your needs. Since it is God's will that Jews should not pursue their livelihoods through forbidden labor on the Sabbath day, we should honor that demand [while recognizing that God will sustain us nonetheless].

VERSE 11

────────────── SHADAL ──────────────

וַיָּנַח בַּיּוֹם הַשְּׁבִיעִי – *And He rested on the seventh day:* It seems to me that there is a difference between the cessation of work that an Israelite undertakes on the Sabbath and the rest that he affords his servants and beasts of burden. For when a master allows his employee a respite from his toil, he does so out of compassion and mercy for another being. When a free person avoids labor on Sabbath, he undoubtedly also benefits on a physical level from the rest; but that by itself does not seem to justify the institution of the Sabbath for these people, who have the liberty to take time off whenever they need. Rather, the purpose of the Sabbath is that entire community should rest at the same time on the same day, thereby allowing families the opportunity to come together to eat and drink and converse, and cultivating feelings of neighborly love and appreciation. Additionally, when the congregation of Israel is all resting from work, the people are able to gather in the house of God, where they can hear Torah lessons from their sages. Note that the Torah intentionally employs the active verb "rested" [*vayanaḥ*] in this verse instead of the more passive sounding "ceased" [*vayishbot*, which appears in the creation story in Genesis 2:2]. This reminds Israel that their Sabbath would be deficient if it were only defined only by the absence of labor. No, the purpose of the Sabbath is for the people to rest actively by engaging in behavior that is pleasurable to them. Necessarily, this will add a social element to the day as people gather in groups to celebrate. God furthermore explained that the goal of observing the day is to remind the world of its creation. People who keep the Sabbath recognize that the one God fashioned the heavens and the earth and that there is no other deity besides Him. Because of God's great love for this commandment, because of the great social benefits that the day bestows, because of the critical memories that it invokes, and finally because of its exclusivity to the Israelite nation, God determined to refer to this day as a "sign" of the bond between God and His people [see 31:13].

CONFRONTING MODERNITY

יב וַיְקַדְּשֵׁהוּ: כַּבֵּד אֶת־אָבִיךָ וְאֶת־אִמֶּךָ
לְמַעַן יַאֲרִכוּן יָמֶיךָ עַל הָאֲדָמָה אֲשֶׁר־יהוה אֱלֹהֶיךָ
יג נֹתֵן לָךְ: לֹא תִרְצָח לֹא תִגְנֹב לֹא־
תִּנְאָף

——————— RABBI SAMSON RAPHAEL HIRSCH ———————

בֵּרַךְ... וַיְקַדְּשֵׁהוּ – *Blessed...and made it holy:* By making the Sabbath holy, God blessed it. At the same time, humanity's cessation from labor on the Sabbath, which is a function of the day's holiness, is not a limitation or a restriction but a blessing. Indeed, any blessing which mankind can hope to achieve, any development of society or of any individual person, depends on maintaining the sanctity of the Sabbath. And that is because the Sabbath is a testament to the reign of God in the world and His dominance over earth's inhabitants whom He created. It is on this day that human beings voluntarily descend from their perch of eminence and offer themselves and all that they own to the service of God, with total submission and humility.

VERSE 12

——————— RABBI SAMSON RAPHAEL HIRSCH ———————

כַּבֵּד אֶת־אָבִיךָ וְאֶת־אִמֶּךָ – *Honor your father and mother:* The exodus from Egypt and the giving of the Torah are the two foundational events of Jewish history. These two great deeds that God performed for the Jewish people are what moved us to accept Him as our ruler and director over all facets of our lives. Now these two events are facts of history and we recognize that they took place on specific dates. However, the only reason we acknowledge the truths of these narratives is because of the power of our traditions. And traditions are only worth anything because children willingly trust that their parents have transmitted to them accurate information. Hence the entire body of Jewish law and practice rests on the obedience that children must display to their parents, the conveyors of their history, faith, and religion.

——————— MALBIM ———————

כַּבֵּד אֶת־אָבִיךָ וְאֶת־אִמֶּךָ – *Honor your father and mother:* I have already explained in my commentary to the book of Leviticus that the commandment to honor one's mother and father and the obligation to observe the Sabbath are intimately connected. For God fashioned human beings when He created the world during history's first six days, and had He not at that point desisted from further labor He would have continued to make more people in the same way [by constructing them from the earth]. This in turn would have made parenthood superfluous, as God Himself would craft each individual person. However, because God rested on the seventh day, He allowed the world to continue through the mechanism of reproduction, wherein parents give birth to children. In this way human parents effectively partner with God in the formation of a child, with the parents creating the physical body of the offspring and God supplying the infant's soul by breathing life into him. And this is why our passage juxtaposes the precept of remembering the Sabbath to the commandment to

12 and made it holy.   Honor your father and mother.
Then you will live long in the land that the LORD your God is
13 giving you.   Do not murder.   Do not
commit adultery.   Do not steal.   Do not

———————— MALBIM *(cont.)* ————————

honor one's father and mother. We find another pairing of these two ideas in the verse *You shall fear every man his mother, and his father, and keep My sabbaths: I am the LORD your God* (Leviticus 19:3), which implies that in a sense, honoring one's parents is tantamount to respecting God. Now when we revere our parents for having provided us with physical existence, we are rewarded with longevity in the physical world [as this verse states: *Then you will live long*]. But the second version of the Ten Commandments goes even further in describing the benefits of fulfilling this commandment, promising: *Honor your father and your mother, as the LORD your*

God has commanded you; that your days may be prolonged, and that it may go well with you, in the land which the LORD your God gives you* (Deuteronomy 5:16). The added detail "that it may go well with you" constitutes a response to those who believe that the cruelties of life on earth outweigh its joys. These are individuals who are fed up with their lives and disgusted with their lots, cursing their parents for having brought them into the world in the first place and subjecting them to nothing but misery. God therefore promises that when a person respects his father and mother, his life will in fact go well for him.

VERSE 13

———————— RABBI SAMSON RAPHAEL HIRSCH ————————

לֹא תִרְצָח – *Do not murder:* The first five of the Ten Commandments decree that Israel recognize and acknowledge God as master and ruler over our fates and our actions. The first statement, *I am the LORD your God* (20:2), phrases this principle as a positive commandment, while the second, *Have no other gods than Me* (20:3), makes it a prohibition as well. The precept *Do not speak the name of the LORD your God in vain* (20:7) establishes this fact as the basis for our individual and communal lives. *Remember the Sabbath to keep it holy* (20:8) establishes a weekly memorial to this belief, while *Honor your father and mother* (20:12) is meant to ensure the idea's transmission from one generation to the next through home life and practice. At this point, the Torah embarks on the next set of five precepts, whose fulfillment demonstrates the application of this

religious ideal within the practical running of society. For example, if God is the true and only author of our lives and destinies, if it is He who governs all of our actions, then surely He is similarly responsible for the fate of each one of our friends and neighbors. This means that God is cognizant of any injustice that one Jew may perpetrate against another. For the will of God sustains every other person with just as much providence as it affords me. It is God who grants all my compatriots life and bestows upon them the same rights that I enjoy. This means that my neighbor's life is holy and everything that he owns is sacred to God: his life, his wife, his freedom, his wealth, his honor, and all of his property receive divine attention and therefore possess sanctity. As a result, we are forbidden to take another's life, to rob a man of his wife, to steal

יד תַעֲנֶה בְרֵעֲךָ עֵד שָׁקֶר׃ לֹא
תַחְמֹד בֵּית רֵעֶךָ לֹא־
תַחְמֹד אֵשֶׁת רֵעֶךָ וְעַבְדֹּו וַאֲמָתוֹ וְשׁוֹרוֹ וַחֲמֹרוֹ וְכֹל אֲשֶׁר
לְרֵעֶךָ׃
טו וְכָל־הָעָם רֹאִים אֶת־הַקּוֹלֹת וְאֶת־הַלַּפִּידִם וְאֵת קוֹל הַשֹּׁפָר שביעי

——————— RABBI SAMSON RAPHAEL HIRSCH *(cont.)* ———————

his freedom [the rabbinic interpretation for the prohibition *Do not steal* refers to kidnapping and enslavement], to impugn his honor or his happiness by testifying falsely against him, or to covet anything that he possesses or calls his own.

VERSE 14

——————— RABBI SAMSON RAPHAEL HIRSCH ———————

לֹא תַחְמֹד – *Do not crave:* The Mekhilta explains the difference between "craving" [*ḥemda*] and "desire" [*taava*. The parallel text of the Ten Commandments in Deuteronomy 5:18 includes both verbs in this precept]. According to the Sages, "desire" is merely an inner longing to possess something, whereas "craving" involves actively scheming to procure the object, as later verses state: *The carvings of their gods shall you burn with fire: you shall not crave the silver or gold that is on them, or take it to you* (Deuteronomy 7:25); and *No one will crave your land when you go up, three times a year, to appear before the LORD your God* (Exodus 34:24). In the latter case the Torah is obviously not assuring Israel that the surrounding nations will not dream of owning their land, but that nobody will take advantage of the Israelites' absence to cross their borders and grab their farms…. In general, I must emphasize that the Ten Commandments hold no greater sanctity or importance than any other commandments in the Torah, nor does their message incorporate all the ideas presented by the other laws. In fact, as a preface to His pronouncement of these declarations,

God declared that these precepts were only an introduction to the full substance of the Torah, a preparation for the future legislation that He would reveal to Israel: *I will come to you in a dense cloud, that the people may hear Me speaking to you. They will then believe you forever* (19:9). That verse clearly explains that the purpose of the experience at Mount Sinai was to ready Israel for receiving the rest of the commandments, which God would convey to them through His emissary Moshe. By hearing the voice of God directly, there would be left no doubt in the people's minds that *these words the LORD spoke to all your assembly* (Deuteronomy 5:19), for they saw the manifestation of God with their own eyes. Following that episode, the nation would be willing to accept as divinely authored any additional laws that their leader and teacher put before them. They would therefore consent to fulfill the Torah wholeheartedly and faithfully. Nevertheless, the Ten Commandments do stand out as the fundamental tenets of our religion, and as category headings for all the Torah's other decrees and commandments.

14 bear false witness against your neighbor.   Do not
crave your neighbor's house.   Do not
crave your neighbor's wife, his male or female servant, his ox,
his donkey, or anything else that is your neighbor's."

15 Every one of the people witnessed the thunder and lightning   SHEVI'I
and the sound of the ram's horn and the smoke-covered mountain; they saw and they shook – and they stood at a distance,

VERSE 15

──────────────── SHADAL ────────────────

וַיַּעַמְדוּ מֵרָחֹק – *And they stood at a distance:*
This verse does not describe a backward
movement taken by the Israelites following
revelation. Indeed, as my student Rabbi David
Ḥazak argues, these words refer to Israel's reaction upon going out to greet God [in 19:17].

It was then that the people experienced the
thunder and lightning (19:16) and jumped back,
remaining at a distance from the mountain.
They were not even willing to approach as far
as the boundary permitted them, out of fear
for what was happening before their eyes.

──────────────── HAAMEK DAVAR ────────────────

רֹאִים אֶת־הַקּוֹלֹת וְאֶת־הַלַּפִּידִם – *Witnessed the
thunder and the lightning:* According to Rashi,
the Israelites saw the thunder that emanated
from the mouth of God. What this means is
that the thundering mentioned in this verse
was not the usual celestial rumblings that accompany lightning during a storm. Rather,
this term describes the sound of the Ten
Commandments being pronounced by God
in His power and majesty. Simultaneous with
the declaration of these laws were sparks of
fire and lightning in the form of letters. These
spelled out each commandment for the people to behold. And although regular thunder
and lightning were not occurring at that point,
the sound of the ram's horn continued to reverberate as it had before God descended on
Mount Sinai [in 19:19]. Thus during our Rosh
HaShana prayers we remember how that
unique call of the horn accompanied the giving of the Torah – we do not recall the thunder that clapped prior to the speech of God.
Nevertheless, the ram's horn only sounded to
emphasize the depth of God's message, as
the verse states: *As the sound of the ram's horn*

*grew louder and louder, Moshe spoke and God
answered him aloud* (19:19). That is, the sound
taught Israel that every precept that they
heard from God held layers of explanation
beyond the straightforward meaning of what
the people understood. These deeper levels
would later be explicated by Moshe when he
spoke with the nation. וַיַּרְא הָעָם – *They saw:*
The verse appears to repeat itself, having first
stated that *Every one of the people witnessed,*
and now again saying that *they saw.* In fact,
the initial phrase means that Israel were privileged to witness a holy and exalted sight that
not even angels get to see. Subsequently, the
text comments that *they saw and they shook,*
which means that the nation saw [i.e., com-
prehended] that they were in fact too feeble
to endure the experience. The description
here is akin to an individual who finds himself carrying a burden that is too heavy for
him. It is nearly impossible for the person to
stand still, but easier to move around with the
weight. Similarly were the Israelites encum-
bered by the gravity of God's sanctity, leading
them to tremble and shift where they stood.

טז וְאֶת־הָהָר עָשֵׁן וַיַּרְא הָעָם וַיָּנֻעוּ וַיַּעַמְדוּ מֵרָחֹק: וַיֹּאמְרוּ
אֶל־מֹשֶׁה דַּבֵּר־אַתָּה עִמָּנוּ וְנִשְׁמָעָה וְאַל־יְדַבֵּר עִמָּנוּ
יז אֱלֹהִים פֶּן־נָמוּת: וַיֹּאמֶר מֹשֶׁה אֶל־הָעָם אַל־תִּירָאוּ כִּי
לְבַעֲבוּר נַסּוֹת אֶתְכֶם בָּא הָאֱלֹהִים וּבַעֲבוּר תִּהְיֶה יִרְאָתוֹ
יח עַל־פְּנֵיכֶם לְבִלְתִּי תֶחֱטָאוּ: וַיַּעֲמֹד הָעָם מֵרָחֹק וּמֹשֶׁה נִגַּשׁ
יט אֶל־הָעֲרָפֶל אֲשֶׁר־שָׁם הָאֱלֹהִים: ‹וַיֹּאמֶר יהוה‹   מפטיר

VERSE 16

———————— RABBI SAMSON RAPHAEL HIRSCH ————————

וְאַל־יְדַבֵּר עִמָּנוּ אֱלֹהִים – *But let not God say any more to us:* With this protestation, the Israelites confirmed that indeed God had spoken to them as one person speaks to another. The whole purpose of the experience had been to impress this remarkable fact on the people. For the revelation of Mount Sinai established for all time the reality that God communicates with human beings. This had the effect of convincing humanity how twisted was the ancient belief that divine revelation was nothing more than divine inspiration, and that God did not speak directly to Moshe so much as through the prophet's own heart. Such a perspective reduces the concept of prophecy into non-prophecy. Indeed, the existence and actuality of God addressing man is affirmed throughout the Torah, with every passage that begins with the common formula "then the Lord said to Moshe."

———————— HAAMEK DAVAR ————————

פֶּן־נָמוּת – *Or we will die:* The people feared that if they were not cautious and did not prepare themselves properly for any subsequent meeting with God, they would die. In fact, this had almost happened to Moshe, who had not been ready for a previous encounter with God [in 4:24]. But now the nation was concerned that in the future, they would not be granted the time or instructions to adequately prepare themselves to receive God as they had before the revelation at Sinai. For Israel believed that it was God's intention to speak the entirety of the Written Law to the people directly, while transmitting only its oral interpretation to Moshe, who would then pass it along to the people. Therefore, the Israelites requested that Moshe himself convey to them the remainder of the Written Law, and not God.

VERSE 17

———————— OR HAHAYYIM ————————

לְבַעֲבוּר נַסּוֹת אֶתְכֶם – *To lift you up:* [Alternatively, "to test you."] The initial revelation examined Israel's ability to endure exposure to the divine, so that the people would not be able to later complain that God should have spoken directly to all of them. For behold, He had done just that, and the people demonstrated their inability to cope with the power of God's manifestation.

———————— MALBIM ————————

אַל־תִּירָאוּ – *Do not be afraid:* Moshe explained to his charges that God had been aware that the people were not prepared to see Him face to face, yet He still came and recited the Ten

16 and said to Moshe, "Speak to us yourself and we will listen,
17 but let not God say any more to us, or we will die." "Do not be
afraid," said Moshe to the people, "God has come to lift you up,
so that the awe of Him will be with you always, keeping you
18 from sin." But the people remained at a distance while Moshe
19 approached the thick darkness where God was.   Then MAFTIR

———————————————— MALBIM *(cont.)* ————————————————

Commandments directly to them. For that was a test to see if they were able to hear God's speech emanating directly from Him. Now I have already written, in my commentary to the story of the *Akeda* [in Genesis 22], that a test is sometimes administered for the sake of its subject, while on other occasions the true purpose of the challenge is its effect on the observers. Here, even though God knew the extent of the

Israelites' capabilities, the people had to learn about themselves by going through the experience, as did those watching the incident [i.e., future readers of the Torah]. After all, the nation had requested that God bestow His Torah upon them without recourse to any emissary. And hence, God had to show them that this was ill-advised, for they were not ready for prophecy of such intensity.

VERSE 18

———————————————— HAKETAV VEHAKABBALA ————————————————

הָעֲרָפֶל – *The thick darkness:* Whenever the term *arafel* appears in Scripture, the commentators interpret it as the phenomenon described in the verse *Clouds and thick darkness surround Him* (Psalms 97:2). What this implies is the fact that the divine glory is obscure and hidden even from the ministering angels, as another verse states: *And He made darkness pavilions round about Him, the heavy mass of waters, and thick clouds of the skies* (II Samuel 22:12). Actually, the exact meaning of the term *arafel* is a bright and pure light, such that all darkness [*ofel*] has been completely drained [*arui*] from it, leaving a tremendous radiance. For just like the darkness envelops objects within it and hides them from sight, similarly

a powerful luminosity emanating from God conceals Him who is behind it, preventing onlookers from seeing through. Support for this interpretation of *arafel* as meaning light comes from the verse *The light dwells with Him* (Daniel 2:22). Furthermore, we recite in prayers: "You did make them hear your voice from heaven, revealing Yourself to them in pure light [*arpilei tohar*]." [The statement appears in the *Musaf* service on Rosh HaShana; the appearance of the word "pure" seems to imply that *arafel* in this context has a bright and shining appearance.] Now Moshe did not actually enter the *arafel* but merely approached it, like a person who advances toward the gate of the palace but does not enter it to see the king.

VERSE 19

———————————————— RABBI SAMSON RAPHAEL HIRSCH ————————————————

אַתֶּם רְאִיתֶם – *You yourselves have seen:* The people of Israel had seen firsthand that God had addressed each and every one of them personally, with no intermediary whatsoever.

That proved to the world that no agent is required for man to receive divine communication, nor for God to come close to His creations. This point is critical, for it establishes

אֶל־מֹשֶׁה כֹּה תֹאמַר אֶל־בְּנֵי יִשְׂרָאֵל אַתֶּם רְאִיתֶם כִּי מִן־
הַשָּׁמַיִם דִּבַּרְתִּי עִמָּכֶם: לֹא תַעֲשׂוּן אִתִּי אֱלֹהֵי כֶסֶף וֵאלֹהֵי כ
זָהָב לֹא תַעֲשׂוּ לָכֶם: מִזְבַּח אֲדָמָה תַּעֲשֶׂה־לִּי וְזָבַחְתָּ עָלָיו כא
אֶת־עֹלֹתֶיךָ וְאֶת־שְׁלָמֶיךָ אֶת־צֹאנְךָ וְאֶת־בְּקָרֶךָ בְּכָל־

──────── RABBI SAMSON RAPHAEL HIRSCH *(cont.)* ────────

as folly human beings' tendency to fashion some sort of symbol alongside God, even if to merely create some representation for them to look at. Should God ever wish to reveal His glory and special closeness to us, He will do it through His blessing and by dwelling in our midst. We never see God through some image or picture of Him, but discover Him through His works and the effects of His glory in our lives.

──────── HAAMEK DAVAR ────────

דִּבַּרְתִּי עִמָּכֶם – *I have spoken to you:* In this I have acted contrary to how people expect deities to behave, for I do not consider it beneath My dignity to speak to the humble masses. Whereas other nations believe that divine beings only address the most elite members of society, behold *I have spoken to you* directly to demonstrate that you require no intermediary to receive My word. And clearly this works in the opposite direction as well – the Holy One, blessed be He, hears Israel's prayers straight from their mouths. And in response to our petitions, He extends His providence to us directly and through no agent.

VERSE 20

──────── RABBI SAMSON RAPHAEL HIRSCH ────────

לֹא תַעֲשׂוּן אִתִּי – *Have no others alongside Me:* Do not fashion any symbol or representation of Me whatsoever. Whatever image you do create to portray the supernatural to your eyes in any way will always be just a god of silver, a golden statue, or a physical idol. Human beings feel the need to give figure and shape to their gods – but you must not do such a thing.

──────── HAAMEK DAVAR ────────

אֱלֹהֵי כֶסֶף וֵאלֹהֵי זָהָב – *No silver gods, no golden gods:* [Why does the Torah specifically mention these two materials?] We can explain that the God established two celestial bodies in the heavens: the sun is the greater being, with power over the treasures of gold, while the moon, which is closer to earth, rules over the treasures of silver. Therefore, since the sun and the moon are represented on earth by gold and silver, it might have occurred to us to fashion these metals into objects of worship – not out of belief that they wield any independent power, but with the intention of making them intermediaries between us and God. To preclude such a plan, God reminds us: *You yourselves have seen that I, from the heavens, have spoken to you* (20:19), informing Israel that there is no need for any intermediary in their relationship with God – neither to carry our prayers to Him, nor to convey His providence to us. For God is always aware of and involved in our lives.

the Lord said to Moshe, "This is what you shall tell the Israelites: You yourselves have seen that I, from the heavens, have
20 spoken to you. Have no others alongside Me; make yourselves
21 no silver gods, no golden gods. Make for Me an altar of earth
and on that sacrifice your burnt offerings and peace offerings,

VERSE 21

———————————————— RABBI SAMSON RAPHAEL HIRSCH ————————————————

מִזְבַּח אֲדָמָה תַּעֲשֶׂה־לִּי – *Make for Me an altar
of earth:* While I do not permit you to create
representations of things that are with Me in
My domain [see the previous verse], I do command you to remodel the objects that exist in
your realm. For while you are not allowed to
lower anything in the heavens, such as the sun
and the moon, toward you, you are required
to elevate toward Me that which is on the
earth. And when you appear before Me, do

not present images in the way that you imagine they exist with Me in the heavens. Rather,
build structures in the way that I command
you to work those materials that are near at
hand. As such, turn to the earth, not the heavens, and use the soil of the land to rise up to
God. The altar that you construct in My honor
must therefore be made out of earth that has
been given a higher purpose.

———————————————————————— HAAMEK DAVAR ————————————————————————

בְּכָל־הַמָּקוֹם אֲשֶׁר אַזְכִּיר אֶת־שְׁמִי – *Wherever I
cause My name to be invoked:* It seems to me
that this entire passage is an interpretation and
elaboration of the first commandment, *I am the
Lord your God* (20:2). First God lays out the fact
of His providence over the nation in the first
place. He then develops the idea by adding:
Who brought you out of the land of Egypt (20:2),
informing us that He removed Israel from an
impure land where sanctity was impossible.
And so here God wishes to outline the differ-
ences between the land of Egypt and the holy
land of Israel. For there were no earthen altars
in Egypt − even when Israel was commanded
to offer the Passover sacrifice, the ritual ex-
cluded a feature that would be present in all
future celebrations of the holiday, namely the

casting of blood against the altar. Rather, at
that first Passover festival, Israel made do with
the side posts and lintels of their doorways.
There could be no altar of earth in Egypt because the land was a polluted place. Our verse
highlights an additional distinction between
future divine service and that which occurred
in Egypt by referring to *your burnt offerings and
peace offerings.* The only sacrifice the Israelites
ever brought while they were still in the land
of their bondage was the Passover offering,
which had no ability to atone for their sins,
unlike the sacrifices mentioned in our verse. In
the coming generations however, Israel would
bring burnt offerings and peace offerings, sacrifices that call down blessings upon the do-
nors − every individual according to his need.

———————————————————————— MESHEKH HOKHMA ————————————————————————

אֶת־צֹאנְךָ וְאֶת־בְּקָרֶךָ – *Your sheep and your
cattle:* Should the verse not have read "from
your sheep" and "from your cattle"? In fact, the
verse teaches that during the nation's sojourn

in the desert, the people were forbidden to
eat any meat other than the permitted parts
of sacrifices [see Leviticus 17:3−4]. Whenever
they wished to eat meat, they needed to bring

הַמָּקוֹם אֲשֶׁר אַזְכִּיר אֶת־שְׁמִי אָבוֹא אֵלֶיךָ וּבֵרַכְתִּיךָ:
כב וְאִם־מִזְבַּח אֲבָנִים תַּעֲשֶׂה־לִּי לֹא־תִבְנֶה אֶתְהֶן גָּזִית כִּי
כג חַרְבְּךָ הֵנַפְתָּ עָלֶיהָ וַתְּחַלְלֶהָ: וְלֹא־תַעֲלֶה בְמַעֲלֹת עַל־
מִזְבְּחִי אֲשֶׁר לֹא־תִגָּלֶה עֶרְוָתְךָ עָלָיו:

⸺ MESHEKH ḤOKHMA *(cont.)* ⸺

their sheep and their cattle as burnt offerings and peace offerings. [The word "from" would therefore be inappropriate, since sacrifices accounted for all animals that the Israelites might wish to eat.]

VERSE 22

⸺ SHADAL ⸺

כִּי חַרְבְּךָ הֵנַפְתָּ עָלֶיהָ וַתְּחַלְלֶהָ – *For in wielding a sword upon it, you profane it:* The prohibition of using iron to construct the altar is here linked to that material's use in the fashioning of swords, but the actual reason for the ban on iron is otherwise. God's real concern is that should iron be used to cut the stones, the craftsmen will end up carving images in the altar's building blocks. If God had made that point explicitly, the people would have dismissed the warning, arguing that they would not be tempted to create pictures on the stones even if they did use iron implements to cut them.

⸺ RABBI SAMSON RAPHAEL HIRSCH ⸺

וְאִם־מִזְבַּח אֲבָנִים תַּעֲשֶׂה־לִּי – *If you make Me an altar of stones:* At the end of your travels through the wilderness, when the time arrives for you to settle the land and begin permanent habitation in your state, you will exchange the portable altar for a solid structure of stone. When that happens, every stone that you position in the new altar will call you to consecrate your lives and direct the aims of your nation to the service of God. No iron tool may touch the stones that form this structure, for a stone that is cut with an iron utensil is

your sheep and your cattle. Wherever I cause My name to be
22 invoked, I will come to you and I will bless you. If you make
Me an altar of stones, do not build it of hewn stone, for in
23 wielding a sword upon it, you profane it. Do not ascend to
My altar with steps, for your nakedness must not be exposed
on it.

──────────── **RABBI SAMSON RAPHAEL HIRSCH** *(cont.)* ────────────

automatically profaned. The meaning of the altar, which signifies human growth and development, cannot be associated with the destruction of human life. And hence a sword, which represents force and violence, cannot be employed in the sanctification of that structure. On the contrary, the altar should be built with righteousness and humaneness, for

it is these principles that emanate from the Temple. Indeed, situated next to the altar in the Temple was the Chamber of Hewed Stone, the eternal citadel of the Torah's justice [where the Sanhedrin would meet]. For it is the law that symbolizes righteousness for the Jewish people, not the sword or the clenched fist.

──────────── **RABBI JOSEPH B. SOLOVEITCHIK** ────────────

לֹא־תִבְנֶה אֶתְהֶן גָּזִית – *Do not build it of hewn stone:* The altar itself cannot be hewn, but must contain imperfections that reflect those

of the sinner whose sin offerings are sacrificed upon it.

VERSE 23

──────────── **HAAMEK DAVAR** ────────────

וְלֹא־תַעֲלֶה בְמַעֲלֹת עַל־מִזְבְּחִי – *Do not ascend to My altar with steps:* With this detail as well, the Torah contrasts future service of God with Israel's practice [of the Passover sacrifice] in Egypt. For if the family doorway's lintel was too

high to reach, they were permitted to climb steps to reach it and spread the animal's blood there. However, once the nation arrived in the land of Israel, the holiness of the altar would preclude them from climbing steps to its top.

פרשת יתרו
PARASHAT YITRO

THE **BIBLICAL**
IMAGINATION

RABBI SHAI FINKELSTEIN

RECEIVING THE TORAH AND OUR HUMANITY

The chapters of the book of Exodus that report the revelation at Mount Sinai and the giving of the Torah fired the imaginations of the Sages, inspiring them to write more detailed accounts of the exchange that took place when Moshe climbed into the heavens. One of these aggadic descriptions appears in the Talmud (Shabbat 88b–89a), and it is worth quoting at length:

> Rabbi Yehoshua ben Levi taught: When Moshe ascended on High to receive the Torah, the ministering angels said before the Holy One, blessed be He: Master of the Universe, what is one born of a woman doing here among us? God said to them: He came to receive the Torah. But the angels scoffed: Why, the Torah is a hidden treasure that was concealed by you nine hundred and seventy-four generations before the world was even created, and You wish to give it to flesh and blood? "What is man that You are mindful of him, and the son of man that You think of him?" (Psalms 8:5). Rather, "LORD our Master, how glorious is Your name in all the earth that Your majesty is placed above the heavens" (Psalms 8:2). [That is, the rightful place of God's majesty, the Torah, is in the heavens.] The Holy One, blessed be He, said to Moshe: Provide them with an answer as to why the Torah should be given to the people of Israel. Moshe said before Him: Master of the Universe, I am afraid lest they burn me with the breath of their mouths. But God assured him: Grasp My throne of glory for strength and protection, and provide them with an answer. As the verse states: "He causes him to grasp the front of the throne, and spreads His cloud over it" (Job 26:9), while Rabbi Naḥum explained: This text teaches that God spread the radiance of His presence and His cloud over Moshe. Said Moshe before God: Master of the Universe, the Torah that You are giving me, what is written in it? God said to him, the Torah states: "I am the LORD your God Who brought you out of the land of Egypt, out of the house of slaves" (Exodus 20:2). Said Moshe to the angels: Tell me, did you descend to Egypt? Were you ever enslaved to Pharaoh? Why should the Torah be yours? Again Moshe asked: What else is written in the book? God said to him: The Torah states, "Have no other gods than Me" (20:3). Said Moshe to his interlocutors: Do you dwell among the nations who worship idols that you require this special warning? Again Moshe asked: What else is written in Your Torah? God said to him: "Remember the Sabbath to keep it holy" (20:8). Moshe asked the angels: Do you perform

labor that you require rest and rejuvenation? Again Moshe asked God: And what else is written in it? God said to him: "Do not speak the name of the LORD your God in vain" (20:7). And so, Moshe asked the angels: Do you conduct business with one another that may lead you to swear falsely? Again Moshe asked God: And what else is written in this book? God said to him: "Honor your father and your mother" (20:12). Moshe challenged the angels: Do you have a father or a mother that would render the commandment to honor them at all relevant to you? And finally Moshe asked: What else does the Torah contain? God answered him: "Do not murder, do not commit adultery, do not steal" (20:13). Moshe again turned to the angels and asked: Is there jealousy among you, or is there an evil inclination within you that would render these commandments necessary? Immediately the angels agreed with the Holy One, blessed be He, that He had made the right decision to give the Torah to the people of Israel, as the closing verse of the aforementioned psalm states: "LORD our Master, how glorious is Your name in all the earth" (Psalms 8:10), omitting the final phrase "that Your majesty is placed above the heavens." Immediately, each and every angel became an admirer of Moshe and passed something to him, as the verse states: "You ascended on high, you took a captive, you took gifts on account of man, and even among the rebellious also that the LORD God might dwell there" (Psalms 68:19), meaning that as reward for having been granted the title "man," by the angels, he received gifts from them.

This surprising talmudic passage raises several difficult questions. How could the angels have objected so strongly as to challenge God's intentions? Is it not the entire nature and function of these beings to fulfill His will? Furthermore, why does Moshe choose the strategy he does to best the angels in their debate? How do these simple arguments so thoroughly convince the angels that he should be allowed to leave the heavens with the Torah under his arm? Additionally, why, at the close of the story, is Moshe rewarded for simply being a "man"? And finally, how are we to understand the significance of God's throne of glory earlier in the passage? How does grasping it provide Moshe with the strength to withstand celestial scrutiny?

According to the angels' initial assessment, the Torah should not have been given to human beings, who are rife with weaknesses, passions, and failures. The fallible nature of humanity flashed like a warning light, cautioning that people do not deserve the Torah. For by bestowing such a gift upon the likes of humans, by giving them an expression of the will, communications, and expectations of God, the danger appeared that they would use the Torah's wisdom for nefarious purposes, impugning God's honor.

Now since we possess free will, we enjoy the ability to disobey the commands of God should we choose that path. In doing so, we not only ignore what is written in the Torah, but we sin brazenly by flouting the will of God. This behavior can only be viewed as a desecration of the divine name. In our story, the angels are reluctant to accept a situation where human beings are granted the power to mock the Creator's designs. It is thus precisely their loyalty to God that drives them to challenge His plan to bestow the Torah upon flesh and blood. How can human beings, molded from physical matter, ever conform fully to spiritual values and use them to shape their lives?

Notably, Moshe does not dispute the angels' central claim. On the contrary, the prophet agrees with their argument, but deftly uses their concern against them. For Moshe understood that God's aim in giving the Torah, indeed the very purpose of the Law itself, is to heighten humanity's spirituality and strengthen its connection to God while still constrained by physical limitations. Moshe knew the risk inherent in instructing creatures with free will to act in a certain way. But at the same time God, Moshe, and indeed the Torah itself were hopeful that people can be persuaded to use those teachings in productive and positive ways to guide their paths through life. The chance that Israel will pick this option, even if not perfectly, is worth the danger that accompanies it. For when we voluntarily accept the lifestyle that God has suggested we live, God is honored and consecrated far more than if we had never been commanded in the first place.

When an individual chooses to fulfill the will of the Creator by following instructions that are not always in concert with that person's own desires, he or she demonstrates a deep connection to the Master of the Universe. The renunciation of our own preferences in order to observe the commandments demonstrates submission to God. And this explains why Moshe builds his arguments with examples of human behavior that are influenced by emotions of jealousy, the pursuit of honor, and other passions that drive human hearts – it is specifically those areas of life which require the guidance of the Torah and its commandments.

The struggle between human beings and their desires is as old as creation, and the struggle to reconcile the forces of intellectual will and emotional impulse reflect the twin domains of earth and heaven. Finding a successful balance between these two realms within our hearts can result in a stronger association, a bridge between humanity and God. For realizing one's spiritual potential means affirming God's will that His most majestic earthly creation should choose to seek its Father in heaven. Indeed, this seeking of God represents mankind's very purpose and goal on this earth. The character of the world we inhabit and the nature of the society that we bequeath to coming generations depends

on striving to perfect this formula in our relationship with God on a personal, national, and global level.

We often find ourselves trapped in situations that tempt us to act inappropriately. The physical qualities within us can be attracted downward to the basest level that the earth itself represents. Still, even if we are pulled toward sin, we still understand that with some effort, we can imitate the nature and attributes of God. We too can create and fashion worlds through our thought and imagination and by striving to mimic the examples set by God. We thus constantly juggle our inclination to submit to the divine will and our desire to satisfy our own passions. At times we climb the Tower of Babel, declaring our own self-importance and dominance of the landscape; at other times we wallow in self-deprecation, admitting that we are nothing but dust and ashes. We constantly face a double challenge: our first task is the effort to define ourselves – how should we live our lives and what is the correct interplay between the physical needs of the human animal and the spiritual calling of the celestial soul? The second, which can only be addressed once we have adequately confronted the first, is to develop our relationship with God.

Now let us consider the experience of revelation at Mount Sinai. That episode served to create an unbreakable bond between heaven and earth in the way we have just described. For as Moshe climbed the mountain to receive the Torah in the heavens, God came down in the opposite direction, allowing His Divine Presence to dwell among the people. Here are Rashi's comments on 19:20, describing the meeting between God and Israel:

> One might suppose that God actually came down onto the mountain, had not a different verse stated: "You yourselves have seen that I, from the heavens, have spoken to you" (20:19). How can we reconcile these two descriptions? By saying that God folded the upper and the lower heavens and spread them on the mountain like one would lay out a blanket on a bed. Thereupon the divine throne descended and rested upon these layers of sky.

At that moment, God addressed the nation in a direct and intimate fashion, embracing them with the faith in their fortitude and good sense to choose the correct path. What emerges is the truth that only human beings wield the ability to reveal God's existence in this world through fulfilling the commandments; no such power exists within the sphere of the angels. This is the deeper meaning behind Moshe's line of argumentation.

God presented Moshe with the Torah to deliver to the nation of Israel as a reward for being called "man." This symbolizes how the message inherent in the Ten Commandments and the giving of the Torah addresses not only to the Jew-

ish people; it is a universal calling. All human beings have the ability to author their own fates; humanity can and must develop. The Jewish credo is thus that mankind as a whole need not choose between living a spiritual existence and existing in the physical world. Our challenge is to learn how to combine and reconcile these two areas of human nature.

The method of finding this balance is not always clear; the equilibrium is occasionally upset. And yet the goal remains fixed – the joining of heaven and earth. And so, God instructs Moshe: "Grasp My throne of glory," for the divine seat represents God's attachment to the world He created. The strength and endurance of this throne depends on human beings, who hold the choice of fulfilling God's commandments. If we choose wisely, we can serve as a model for all of civilization, and every nation on earth will join together as links in the chain that binds heaven to earth.

"THOSE WHO RELISH IT MERIT LIFE"[1]

One of the Torah's most well-known commandments is that of the Sabbath. The instruction to observe this holy day appears within the Ten Commandments in our *parasha*, as well as in the parallel text in the book of Deuteronomy. There are in fact some twenty occasions where the Torah discusses the topic of the Sabbath throughout its five books. This ubiquity attests to the importance of the commandment and the centrality of the Sabbath to the observant lifestyle of the Jewish family. But beyond this relatively narrow perspective, I would like to claim that the law of the Sabbath contributes significantly to our quality of life in a more all-encompassing manner.

The commandment of the Sabbath represents not a single law, but an abundance of details such as the thirty-nine principal forbidden labors (*melakhot*). These archetypes are further broken down into corollary actions, which are also avoided on the Sabbath, and to these the Sages added various precautionary measures to help Israel behave correctly. The Sabbath also comprises another dimension, identified in our *parasha*: "Remember the Sabbath to keep it holy" (20:8). What exactly does it mean to remember the Sabbath? Precisely how does one fulfill that commandment? According to the Sages, the verse forms the basis for the practice of reciting *Kiddush* on the Sabbath eve. But there is a deeper implication to this injunction, one with special import for our modern generation.

In his comments to verse 20:8, the *Or HaḤayyim* (Rabbi Ḥayyim Ibn Attar, eighteenth century) explains the instruction to remember the Sabbath as follows:

> The Sages teach that on the first Friday in history, soon after man was created, he sinned and was found guilty. But the Sabbath day appeared before God in defense of man and said: Master of the Universe! No person was ever killed on the other days of the week, why should I be the first to suffer the indignity of having man executed during my watch? Thus was man saved from capital punishment thanks to the Sabbath. And when humanity saw the power that the Sabbath held, they composed the song, "A psalm, A poem for the Sabbath day" (Psalms 92:1). This is what God meant when He commanded: "Remember the Sabbath day" – do not forget the Sabbath which saved humanity and allowed all future descendants of the first man and woman to be born. Respect the Sabbath and sanctify it because it sustains and

---

sanctifies every individual Israelite. In a similar vein, we find that should a person be saved from danger on a particular day, the anniversary of his rescue continues to hold special significance for him every year thereafter. How much more so ought we to honor the Sabbath, for in that case it was the day itself which brought about our salvation.

The *Or HaHayyim* uses the midrash to explain the process of God forgiving humanity in an exchange that took place on the first Sabbath of all time. In it, God granted the first man and woman the opportunity to begin a new chapter in their short lives, and essentially renewed human existence thanks to the intervention of the Sabbath. Hence, when we descendants of that first couple remember the Sabbath, we reflect on the power of the day to bestow salvation upon us, to afford us forgiveness, to allow our lives to rejuvenate.

Inherent in the Sabbath is a power of renewal that finds expression not only in the physical rest that the day affords; the Sabbath operates on a spiritual plane as well. This time is meant to be spent thinking about the meaning of our lives, a consideration that is all the more essential in the face of modernity and its unrelenting rat race. When we remember the Sabbath, we infuse our physically focused lives with deeper substance and higher significance.

In his commentary to the book of Exodus, Rabbi Samson Raphael Hirsch (nineteenth century) presents a different perspective on the command to remember the Sabbath day. In this author's opinion, the text under consideration reflects a national responsibility that Israel holds toward the rest of the world. Writes Rabbi Hirsch:

With this commandment, God recalls the distant past when He first established a memorial to His act of creation, soon after God made the first man and tasked him with guardianship of the earth as His envoy. The Sabbath day testified to the recognition of this reality. But when man began to forget that relationship, civilization deteriorated until humanity was in a sorry state. It was at that point that the nation of Israel was chosen to publicize the word of God to humanity and lead society back to the path God intends for all of us. Therefore, in our text, the Sabbath is not presented as a new institution. Rather, the Torah makes reference the Sabbath with the assumption that the reader is familiar with the holy day. For the Sabbath had existed and endured since the days of the first human beings. From this point on, the nation was to behave differently than mankind had throughout the previous generations that had neglected the Sabbath.[2]

---

2.   Rabbi Samson Raphael Hirsch on Exodus 20:8.

According to Rabbi Hirsch's interpretation, the Sabbath was originally devised as a commandment incumbent upon all of humanity, only becoming a Jewish custom at the point when the rest of the nations neglected its commemoration. Rightfully, all people would be required to guard the Sabbath and observe it. However, the neglect of the Sabbath of creation caused mankind to degenerate to the point where spirituality was essentially absent from our tumultuous lives, which became fixated on acquisition and "the bottom line." The Jewish people were selected not exactly to "remember" but to "remind" both itself and the rest of humanity of the concept of the Sabbath with its message of freedom and renewal.

Rabbi Joseph B. Soloveitchik (twentieth century), for his part, claims that remembering the Sabbath represents a yearning for holiness on the part of every Jew. The days of the week are counted in honor of the Sabbath, and extra time is added to the beginning and end of the day to symbolize our longing for the sanctity of closeness to the Almighty. The special flourishing of our souls which is said to occur on this day is a result of this cleaving to the sacred.[3]

On the other hand, Rabbi Ovadya Sforno (sixteenth century) provides an altogether different take on what it means to remember the Sabbath day. In Sforno's opinion, the Jewish people must constantly recall the Sabbath during all of their dealings throughout the week. In this way, the commandment to remember the Sabbath is similar to the order to remember Amalek (see Deuteronomy 25:17), or to observe the month of Aviv (when Passover is celebrated, as stated in Deuteronomy 16:1). Furthermore, when our verse demands that the day be remembered "to keep it holy," it means that if someone keeps the Sabbath in mind while going about his or her routine weekday business, making sure to take care of all loose ends before the Sabbath, such a person will able to be oblivious of secular matters once the sacred day arrives.

If we take Sforno's understanding to heart, it emerges that Sabbath observance is not merely a one-day affair. Rather, attention to the Sabbath is required throughout all seven days of the week. When going about one's daily toil, the individual should recognize that any success he or she achieves is thanks to God's assistance; the laborer in the field is not working alone. By remembering that the Sabbath is slated to arrive in another three days, or in another two days, the worker invests even the weekdays with sanctity. This allows the individual to transcend the daily grind once the Sabbath begins and focus on holiness and spirituality.

---

3. See *Chumash Mesoras Harav*, ed. Dr. Arnold Lustiger (New York: OU Press and Ohr Publishing, 2017), commentary on Exodus 20:8.

One of the main difficulties facing our generation is the challenge of unplugging from our busy lives of production, achievement, and action. We worry that if we tune out, or turn off, we might miss some exciting or important experience. This "fear of missing out" – now well known by the acronym "FOMO" –is a phobia that grips much of contemporary youth. People who suffer from this anxiety feel the need to be constantly appraised the activities of their close and distant friends, to be immersed in the events that swirl around the general culture and society. This obsession leads to a compulsion to unceasingly check social media and fusion to one's smartphone.

We should heed Sforno's advice. He showed us that the Sabbath naturally grants inner peace to those who observe it, because it aids us in setting the correct priorities in life. For when we live our days in the awareness that the Sabbath is coming, we understand the depth of meaning to our existence. One need not work to exhaustion, nor engage in frivolous pursuits; instead, the Jew should acknowledge the importance of his or her family, a message that is stated right here in the Torah's description of the Sabbath: "Six days you shall work, and carry out all your labors, but the seventh is a Sabbath to the LORD your God. On it, do no work – neither you, nor your son or daughter, your male or female servant, your livestock, or the migrant within your gates" (20:9–10).

The commandment of the Sabbath thus carries a special significance for our own period of Jewish history. This is true of the higher ideals of the Sabbath that we have discussed here, represented by the phrase "Remember the Sabbath" in our *parasha*. But it is of course no less true of the more technical prohibitions of labor on the day, which directly force us to slow down and gain perspective. These regulations are traditionally symbolized by the alternative form of the phrase, "Guard the Sabbath," appearing in the version of the Ten Commandments in Deuteronomy (5:12). Together, these two pillars of the Sabbath directly address one of the greatest ills plaguing our generation. It therefore behooves us to consider both dimensions of the holy day and to unite the two approaches in the spirit of the rabbinic claim that "'Remember' and 'guard' were uttered as one."

HUMANITY'S SOCIAL OBLIGATION
AS A GLIMPSE TOWARD THE DIVINE

Parashat Yitro describes one of the most famous events within the entire Tanakh – the giving of the Torah and God's declaration of the Ten Commandments. Perhaps the least well-understood of these laws is the last: "Do not crave [*lo taḥmod*] your neighbor's house. Do not crave your neighbor's wife, his male or female servant, his ox, his donkey, or anything else that is your neighbor's" (20:14). The parallel text in Parashat Va'etḥanan contains a slightly different version of this command: "Do not crave [*lo taḥmod*] your neighbor's wife. Do not set your desire [*lo titaveh*] on your neighbor's house, or field, or male or female servant, or ox, or donkey, or anything that belongs to your neighbor" (Deuteronomy 5:18). The demand set forth in these passages is unusual: it is uncommon (although not unheard of) for the Torah to ask its adherents to control their emotions and their thoughts. One might very well ask how God could command such a thing. But before we address this more dramatic question, this essay will start by tackling the following more specific issues:

1. What is the difference between the terms *lo taḥmod* and *lo titaveh*, which appear to be synonymous?
2. What is the purpose of this prohibition?
3. The Mekhilta of Rabbi Shimon bar Yoḥai on the commandment in our *parasha* answers the first question as follows:

This account of the Ten Commandments uses only the verb *taḥmod* whereas a later telling uses the additional verb *titaveh* (Deuteronomy 5:18). This teaches that there are two distinct prohibitions: craving and desiring. One violates the command "*lo titaveh*" by merely thinking: Oh, if I only I possessed ..., whereas one violates "*lo taḥmod*" when he hatches a concrete plan to wrest the object from its owner.

The Mekhilta defines *taava* as the emotion of wanting what belongs to somebody else, while identifying *ḥemda* as formulating a scheme to get that item for oneself. This distinction begins to help us understand the text, and allows us to turn to the question of the commandment's purpose. To reach a fuller understanding of the matter, let us to examine the works of the various commentators.

In his *Mishneh Torah* (*Hilkhot Gezela Vaaveda* 1:11), the Rambam writes as follows:

Note that indulging one's desires [*taava*] leads to scheming [*ḥimud*], which in turn leads to theft. For should the owner of the object of one's desire refuse to sell it, even when his neighbor offers an exorbitant sum for it, or has his friends cajole the owner on his behalf, the obsessed individual will eventually end up stealing the item. Hence the prophet states: "They lust for others' fields and seize them, eye others' homes and assume them as theirs" (Micah 2:2). Furthermore, if the owner detects the robbery and stands up to defend his property or otherwise prevent the theft of his goods, it is possible that the covetous man will resort to murder in order to satisfy his craving. The classic illustration of this is the story of Aḥav and Navot [as told in I Kings 21].

According to the Rambam, the commandment "Do not crave" is not an independent issue, but rather a precautionary measure to prevent people from transgressing more serious prohibitions. For the Torah knows the inclination of human beings – the violation of a sin makes the next indiscretion easier and more attractive. Notwithstanding, there is at least one talmudic passage (see Bava Batra 3a) that would seem to indicate that looking covetously at one's neighbor's property is itself a form of damages. This could indicate a view counter to the Rambam's – one which views the commandment not as ancillary but important in and of itself.

Our next step takes us to Philo's commentary on the Ten Commandments, where he writes as follows:

Whenever an individual is stricken with the curse of desire, his entire soul is consumed with efforts to procure what he covets…. The object appears in his imagination but remains just outside of his reach; he chases what his heart wants, but he can never catch it.

Philo understands that because covetousness dwells in the mind, it can lead people to destroy themselves in pursuit of fanciful dreams. Hence the Torah warns against such harmful thoughts as a form of self-protection.

The three commentaries we have examined present three different understandings of the commandment "Do not crave." One suggests that the prohibition be seen as a precautionary measure to prevent man's degeneration into baser sins; another that it can be viewed as a positive sin in its own right; and the last frames it as an effort to stem the darker sides of our own characters, cultivating inner purity.

Now let us turn to the difficulty stated at the onset: How can the Torah command its adherents not to feel certain emotions? This quandary is confronted

explicitly by Rabbi Avraham Ibn Ezra (twelfth century), who explains that this commandment is in essence an injunction to condition ourselves to be satisfied with what we have – every person must work to appreciate and respect the integrity of his fellow's property. Here is what that exegete writes in his comments on 20:14:

> This commandment has confounded many people, who argue that it is impossible for a person not to covet in his heart a beautiful thing that he sees and longs to own. Allow me to describe a parable for you which will explain the matter. Consider a simple yet sound-minded farm boy who catches a glimpse of a gorgeous princess. Such a man will not dream about sleeping with the woman, since he knows in his heart that such a union is out of the question. Similarly, a normal man does not desire to lie with his mother, attractive though she may be, since he has been conditioned from childhood to understand that that woman is forbidden to him. In the same manner, every intelligent person must train himself to acknowledge that it is not his brains nor his wisdom that will aid him in acquiring wealth or a lovely wife, but that he will receive only what God allots to him. Thus the verse states: "For there is a man whose labor is with wisdom, and with knowledge, and with skill; yet he must leave it for a portion to a man who has not labored in it" (Ecclesiastes 2:21). And so do our Sages argue: Children, life, and food are not dependent on merit, but on the constellations (Moed Katan 28a). If one keeps this attitude in mind, he will neither covet nor crave. And since a man knows that God has ruled his neighbor's wife to be strictly off-limits, that woman will become more distant in his eyes than a princess is to a peasant. If one takes this approach to heart, he will be satisfied with his lot and will waste no energy dreaming of acquiring that which belongs to somebody else. For once we are convinced that God has no intention of letting us have those things we covet, we understand that no plan to obtain them through force, schemes or cunning will ever succeed. Then we will trust in our Creator to sustain us and to provide for us what He deems correct.

Rabbi Samson Raphael Hirsch (nineteenth century) expands on this concept in his comments on the same verse. To him, our inner lives, while important in their own right, are also crucial gateways to the Jewish people's public, social, even national existence, thus serving an important function within the body of the Ten Commandments as a whole. Writes that author:

> It is specifically with this final commandment that God affixes His stamp to the social elements of the Ten Commandments. After all, even human

lawmakers would normally institute such banal prohibitions as "Do not murder" and "Do not commit adultery." However, it is only God who can command His followers not to crave, because only He can read the minds of men. Everything is laid out before the eyes of God – the actions that take place on His earth, the thoughts that cloud the brains of mankind, and the feelings that stir human emotions....

Now if we consider the sequence in which the Torah presents its fundamental principles, we find that this order itself illuminates the holistic nature of the entire Torah taken together. The first section of these precepts [the first five laws, which govern man's relationship to God] begins with the statement "I am the LORD your God" (20:2) and ends with the directive "Honor your father and mother" (20:12). The second set starts with "Do not murder" (20:13) and ends with "Do not crave" (20:14). At the outset, God demands that we recognize Him intellectually by accepting certain truths: that God is the Master of history, and that there are no other deities. However, intellectual awareness of God is insufficient. Such recognition must be expressed in our speech – hence Jews are ordered to refrain from speaking the name of God in vain [in 20:7]; in our activities – when we must cease our labors on the Sabbath [20:8–10]; and through our family relationships – as the Torah orders us to honor our parents [in 20:12]. We then shift to the law code regulating interpersonal relationships, which begins by limiting our behavior and our speech: "Do not murder. Do not commit adultery. Do not steal. Do not bear false witness against your neighbor" (20:13). And yet, it is not enough for us to govern our actions and control our words; in the very next verse the Torah demands that we master our hearts and minds as well, when it decrees: "Do not crave your neighbor's house etc." (20:14). This larger structure of the Ten Commandments reveals the following truth: No faith system is worth anything if it does not reach its adherents' speech and actions, family life and societal dealings. It is only through our regular activity and social intercourse that we can prove whether or not we are truly the servants of God. And the converse is also true: a social system of interpersonal relations that is designed with an eye solely to external niceties while paying no attention to inner faith, conscience, and purity of spirit – things which only God can divine – is similarly destined to crumble when faced with any challenge. Every good deed and noble act must have its roots in the human heart; every sincere thought must lead to action, as the individual keeps his eyes simultaneously focused on God and trained on fulfilling His will. This is the spirit that animates the entire foundation of God's Torah and which unites the two halves of the

Ten Commandments, the "religious" or "ritual" side and the "social" laws featured in the second half. Together these ten concepts form an indivisible whole.

Thus the prohibition "Do not crave" represents a foundation stone for building the Jewish community. Our religion urges us to learn to control our emotions as a basis for managing our actions. The laws we have been discussing do not merely relate to the nebulous musings of the mind, but serve to govern the social lifestyle of our people. Proper thoughts are necessary to ensure that Israel as a whole is guided by justice, righteousness, and compassion.

This final commandment, which rounds out the Ten Commandments, thus acts as a parallel statement to the opening declaration "I am the LORD your God." While that first verse demands that we recognize the Almighty on an intellectual plane, so does the prohibition on coveting our neighbors' property demand our recognition of God in the practical sphere, internalizing His expectations in our opinions, thoughts, interpersonal encounters.

For commentaries and the Biblical Imagination
turn to the left side of this volume.

For the complete Rashi and haftara
turn to the right side of this volume.